ETHNICITY AND ETHNIC RELATIONS IN CANADA: A Book of Readings

Edited by

Jay E. Goldstein
Rita M. Bienvenue

Department of Sociology
University of Manitoba

Butterworths

Toronto

CANADA: BUTTERWORTH & CO. (CANADA) LTD.
                   TORONTO: 2265 Midland Avenue, Scarborough,
                   M1P 4S1

UNITED KINGDOM: BUTTERWORTH & CO. (Publishers) LTD.
                   LONDON: 88 KINGSWAY, WC2B 6AB

AUSTRALIA: BUTTERWORTH PTY. LTD.
                   SYDNEY: 586 Pacific Highway, Chatswood,
                             NSW 2067
                   MELBOURNE: 343 Little Collins Street, 3000
                   BRISBANE: 240 Queen Street, 4000

NEW ZEALAND   BUTTERWORTHS OF NEW ZEALAND LTD.
                   WELLINGTON: 77-85 Custom House Quay, 1

SOUTH AFRICA: BUTTERWORTH & CO. (SOUTH AFRICA)
                   (PTY.) LTD.
                   DURBAN: 152/154 Gale Street

Canadian Cataloguing in Publication Data

Main entry under title:

Ethnicity and ethnic relations in Canada

ISBN 0-409-83433-5

1. Canada — Population — Ethnic Groups.* 2. Canada — Race relations.
I. Goldstein, Jay E., 1945- II. Bienvenue, Rita M., 1931-

FC104.E85   301.45'1'0971   C79-094647-5
F1035.A1E85

Table of Contents

Introduction

Social scientists generally recognize that most, if not all, nation states are pluralistic in the sense that they contain a multiplicity of ethnic groups. A cursory look at the contemporary world reveals that such differing countries as Switzerland, Malaysia, Brazil, South Africa, and Canada can all be described as multi-ethnic societies. At any given time in history, human populations can and have been identified in terms of differences in culture, language, race, or religion. The journalistic and scientific literature is replete with examples of demographic studies giving detailed accounts of national, regional and local populations. Ethnic categories vary in size and in geographic concentration, and these demographic variables constitute an important base from which intergroup relations eventually emerge.

The significance of ethnic diversity and intergroup relations is readily apparent. Almost daily we hear of issues and conflicts between Whites and Blacks in South Africa, between Christians and Moslems in Lebanon. From radio, television, newspapers, and magazines we learn of the political concerns of the Scots and the Welsh in the United Kingdom and of the Bretons and the Corsicans in France. From the USSR, we hear reports regarding discrimination against Jews and the assimilation of Ukrainians. Within our own borders we are constantly reminded of the relative powerlessness of our own Native Peoples and their resentment regarding the denigration of their culture and language.

Sociological interest in the field of ethnic relations dates back to the origins of the discipline where considerable thought was given to the nature of race and the importance of stratification. Since then the body of literature has grown steadily as national and international studies have systematically focused on the varying dimensions of intergroup contacts. From a seemingly haphazard series of events, efforts have been made to identify and order recurring patterns of intergroup relations. These writings vary in perspective, and in method, but from an accumulation of theory and research we are gaining an increasing understanding of the meaning of ethnicity and the importance of ethnic relations.

The selections in this book have been organized around several of the basic concepts and processes which have guided research and theory on ethnic relations in Canada. The readings in Part I address fundamental issues in the study of ethnic relations: clarifying the meaning of the concepts of ethnicity and ethnic group; measuring ethnic identification; developing a typology of patterns of ethnic relations; and, formulating theoretical propositions that can explain such patterns. In Part II the selections focus upon factors that reinforce or weaken the cultural differences among ethnic groups. The readings in this part pertain to the process of ethnic assimilation as it affects Native Peoples, French-Canadians, and immigrant groups.

The existence of ethnic stratification or a hierarchy of ethnic groups in Canada has been denoted by the concept of a "vertical mosaic." The readings in Part III deal with the existence of inequalities in regard to access of positions of economic power, cultural rights, prestige, and occupational attainment and social mobility.

Social psychological aspects of ethnic relations are dealt with in Part IV. Here are found analyses of the relationship between ethnic prejudice and stereotyping, techniques of impression management in situations with a potential for interethnic conflict, and the attitudes of Canadians toward ethnic groups and a multicultural policy.

In a multi-ethnic society such as Canada, conflicts may arise between ethnic groups or about policies concerning ethnic relations. The readings in Part V examine contemporary issues and conflicts involving self-determination for native peoples, nationalism in Quebec, an apparent rise in hostile attitudes toward non-white ethnic groups, and the pursuit of a policy of multiculturalism.

Ethnicity and Ethnic Relations

The first section of this book contains articles specifically focussing on the nature of ethnicity and ethnic relations. Isajiw, for instance, reviews the contemporary literature in terms of two sociological perspectives (the objective and subjective) and their implications for the definition of ethnic groups. The objective approach to social reality assumes that groups exist as distinct social units — independent of the feelings and beliefs of participants. Accordingly, sociologists who utilize this approach have defined ethnic groups in terms of such distinguishing characteristics as language and customs. On the other hand, the subjective approach to social reality assumes that groups exist in the minds of individuals. This leads to a definition of ethnic groups based on individuals' sense of identification with others who share, or perhaps once shared, common cultural characteristics. What is needed, Isajiw suggests, is a syntheses of these two approaches in order to arrive at a definition that would be appropriate to the North American scene. Accordingly, Isajiw presents a definition of ethnic groups that takes into account several objective characteristics that distinguish one population from another while incorporating criteria which pertain to a subjective sense of belonging to a specific cultural or linguistic unit.

Stymeist examines the subjective nature of ethnic identification in a study focussing upon a multi-ethnic town in northern Ontario. Here, the objective dimensions of ethnic diversity could be established in terms of statistical categories but the subjective nature of ethnic identification proved to be of considerable complexity. The subjective definitions of ethnic groups that existed in the minds of non-native members of the community formed an elaborate and fairly flexible system of categorizations and subcategorizations. Stymeist noted that, from one interactional setting to another, an individual's identity could shift from one category to another. While ethnicity did provide a basis for the temporary formation of groups, ethnicity was no longer a central feature of the social organization of the town nor was it a central feature in the identity of individuals.

The next selection focusses on the identification of recurring patterns of intergroup relations. Hunt and Walker present three ideal type patterns that are meant to serve as useful tools in the analysis of multi-ethnic societies. These are patterns of integration, segregation, and cultural pluralism. The authors describe the features of the basic social structures that are associated with each type and examples are given of societies in which they are approximated. According to Hunt and Walker's discussion, Canada tends toward the pattern of cultural pluralism.

The final selection is an attempt by Lieberson to develop a theory that would account for types of initial contacts and their implications for subsequent patterns of intergroup relations. Two basic types of initial encounters are identified: those in which a migrant group is superordinate to an indigenous group and those in which an indigenous group is superordinate to a migrant group. Possible patterns of intergroup relations are discussed in terms of variations in conflict, adjustments to other groups, assimilation and nationalism. As Lieberson notes, his theory is a "rudimentry" one intended to identify broad similarities and differences in recurring patterns of intergroup relations. As knowledge about ethnic relations increases, the incorporation of additional independent variables into theories will permit more precise predictions about the initial outcomes of ethnic contacts and the long-term patterns of intergroup relations.

Ethnic Groups: Persistence and Change

The study of multi-ethnic societies involves an examination of processes which reinforce or weaken the cultural distinctions which exist between groups. In the first article Berger describes the culture of the Dene and Inuit peoples as they have been portrayed during the Mackenzie Valley Pipeline Inquiry. The observations of social scientists and the comments of Native People serve as a basis for a discussion of values relating to the meaning of land, and the importance of traditional social and political organization. From this report it becomes apparent that while contacts with the institutions of the larger society have resulted in the modification of traditional values, these values still differ considerably from those of Euro-Canadians and this fact has strongly influenced the negative response of Native People to the pipeline proposal.

The second article focusses upon the effects of industrialization on the Acadian community in Nova Scotia. Tremblay suggests that while industrialization has not occurred within the community itself, the industrial way of life has had a major impact on the cultural and structural features of Acadian society. Technical and occupational changes, for instance, have lead to the development of a class system and the breakdown of the extended family. Patterns of out-migration and the adoption of new values have not only altered the nature of community organization but have had an important impact on group ideology. These and other interrelated changes are leading to increasing degrees of cultural and linguistic assimilation. Tremblay suggests that a number of economic and institutional changes within the community itself would need to be initiated if Acadians are to avoid complete assimilation into the surrounding environment.

Reitz reports on a study designed to examine the importance of language retention as a determinant of ethnic community participation. The study focusses on urban Canadians of German, Italian, Polish, and Ukrainian origins, and measures the association between language knowledge and participation in the ethnic community. The findings indicate that language retention and participation in the community both decline with successive generations of Canadian-born. With other variables held constant, language retention emerges as an important prerequisite to community participation. Hence, the proposition that language serves to unify members into a cohesive community is largely supported. Given relatively high rates of linguistic assimilation, Reitz also suggests that ethnic participation will diminish over time unless other factors emerge to promote group solidarity.

Ujimoto compares the Japanese community in Vancouver before and after the Second World War and highlights some of the major changes which have taken place. The prewar Japanese community was a large and cohesive one in which members were able to maintain their language, customs and social organizations. In contrast, the postwar community became a less integrated ethnic collectivity with lower degrees of institutional completeness. Ujimoto discusses several factors that explain these changes including the effects of the wartime evacuation, and the social and geographical mobility of second and third generation Canadians. Emphasis is also given to postwar immigrants whose technical and linguistic skills enabled them to develop relationships outside the Japanese community. These and other related factors have, essentially, resulted in a decreasing emphasis on ethnic identity and a concomitant decrease in community cohesion.

The last article in this section describes the efforts of Chassidic Jews in

Montreal to counter pressures toward assimilation. Shaffir characterizes religious communities such as the Chassidic Jews and Hutterites as intentional communities — that is communities which are organized to promote identities and actively resist assimilation. These communities stand in contrast to other ethnic groups which are not specifically designed to retain identities. Groups such as the Japanese and the Acadians, for instance, must rely on individual and family efforts to passively resist assimilation. Shaffir describes the techniques utilized by the Chassidic community to minimize the impact of secular education. The group recognizes the potential problems which secular education poses, and evidence suggests that members have successfully adopted a number of measures to counter its influence.

Ethnic Inequalities

The study of ethnic stratification involves the examination of patterned inequalities between ethnic groups. Inequality in access to the power structure of the Canadian economy is the subject of the first selection. Here Clement examines the ethnic composition of the corporate elite, i.e., those persons who occupy the upper-most positions in large corporations. Clement indicates that Anglo-Canadians have dominated and continue to dominate the corporate elite. French-Canadians continue to be under-represented, while Canadians of other ethnic origins (termed the "third ethnics") have almost no representation in positions of power in the Canadian economy. Clement describes the historical factors that have contributed to the domination of the corporate elite by Anglo-Canadians, and the different avenues for mobility that exist for Anglo-Canadians, French-Canadians, and the "third" ethnics.

The next selection focusses upon the nature and extent of inequalities between English- and French-speaking Canadians. Morris and Lanphier orient their discussion of inequalities around the concepts of individual, collective, and cultural rights. Individual rights would entail equal treatment of English- and French-speaking Canadians who have equal qualifications and abilities. Collective rights would be designed to ensure that English- and French-speaking Canadians are proportionately represented in positions in government, education, business, and other institutions even though they may differ in their qualifications. Cultural rights would accord equal status to each culture, with equal representation of English-speaking and French-speaking Canadians in any bilingual organizations. After reviewing evidence regarding English-French differences in economic status, political power, and language status, Morris and Lanphier conclude that the culture of French-Canadians enjoys lower prestige than that of English-Canadians, and this places French-speaking Canadians at a disadvantage in seeking political and economic power. In addition, while English-speaking Canadians appear willing to accord individual rights to French-Canadians, they are unwilling to grant French-Canadians the collective and cultural rights that are being sought by French-Canadians themselves. This is a matter of particular relevance to the developing debate over special constitutional status or sovereignty association for Quebec.

The next article addresses the issue of inequalities in the prestige of ethnic groups. Pineo describes the results of a national survey that investigated the social standing of over thirty ethnic and related groups. Among English-speaking Canadians there exists an ethnic prestige hierarchy in which English-Canadians enjoy an "elite" status, followed by the French and other northern and western European ethnic groups, then eastern and southern Europeans, and finally non-Causcasian ethnic groups. Among French-Canadians, however, both the English and French groups enjoy equal social standing and are at the top of the ethnic prestige hierarchy. The findings reveal major differences between English- and French-speaking Canadians in perceptions of ethnic prestige, and are consistent with Morris and Lanphier's assertion that among English-Canadians, French-Canadian culture has less prestige than does English-Canadian culture. Pineo notes that knowledge and consensus about ethnic prestige are lower than they are for occupational prestige. This may indicate that ethnic prestige is a less important element in Canadian social structure than is occupational prestige.

The significance of ethnicity in regard to occupational stratification is the focus of the last selection in this section. Darroch examines John Porter's hypothesis that ethnicity is a fundamental determinant of occupational attainment and social mobility in Canada. His analysis indicates that while the rank ordering of major ethnic groups in terms of occupational status has remained constant over time, the actual differences between them systematically have declined. While Darroch challenges the conventional wisdom that ethnicity is a major source of inequality in occupational status and social mobility, he agrees with Clement's conclusions regarding the significance of ethnicity in the recruitment of individuals to positions of power.

Ethnic Attitudes

One aspect of ethnic relations which has received attention from social scientists is that of individual attitudes and behavior toward ethnic groups. Two of the major concepts in the social psychology of ethnic relations are ethnic stereotypes and ethnic prejudice. Ethnic stereotypes may be defined as socially shared beliefs about ethnic groups based upon folk knowledge (i.e., knowledge derived from observations made in the course of everyday life). Ethnic prejudice denotes negative affect and negative beliefs toward a particular ethnic group. In the first paper in this section, Mackie examines long held assumptions about ethnic stereotypes and the relationship between stereotypes and ethnic prejudice. One assumption is that ethnic stereotypes are basically inaccurate (i.e., they are essentially fallacious beliefs). The second assumption is that stereotyping and prejudice are strongly interrelated. Neither of these assumptions was confirmed by Mackie's research.

Her study suggests that the accuracy of ethnic stereotypes is variable and that persons can hold ethnic stereotypes without having negative feelings toward the group itself.

Niels Braroe analyzes the social psychological mechanisms that help to prevent overt conflict between Indians and Whites in a Prairie community. Braroe indicates that Whites and Indians in Jasper are involved in a caste-like system of ethnic relations in which Indians are clearly subordinate to Whites. In situations characterized by large inequalities between ethnic groups, the potential for intergroup opposition is high, when (as Braroe indicates is the case in Jasper) the subordinate group begins to identify with the values of the dominant group, but is prohibited from acting in terms of these values. Braroe describes how in their self-presentations, Indians and Whites have worked out a form of accommodation that allows day-to-day interaction to proceed in a non-conflictual fashion while maintaining the superordinate-subordinate relationships between these ethnic groups.

The attitudes of Canadians toward immigrants, ethnic groups, and a multiculturalism policy are the subject of a national survey, the results of which are summarized in the selection by Berry, Kalin, and Taylor. In this comprehensive study, the structure of attitudes and the relationship between individual attitudes and several psychological variables and demographic variables are examined. After reviewing their findings the authors conclude that three conditions must be met in order for intergroup tolerance to prevail: individuals must have a clear sense of group membership, a positive (but not highly ethnocentric) appreciation of their own group, and a sense of cultural and economic security. In the absence of any of these conditions, intolerance of other groups may result. This conclusion suggests that the reduction of ethnic prejudice involves creating a social climate in which individuals do not view others as threatening their individual or collective well being.

Ethnic Conflict

The final set of readings deals with issues and conflicts in Canadian ethnic relations. These include the land rights of Native People, the secessionist movement in Quebec, the apparent increase in racial prejudice, and the policy of multi-culturalism announced by the federal government in 1971.

The issue of Indian land rights dates back to the early contacts between European settlers and Indians. In the 1970's, Indian (and Inuit) claims to lands they traditionally have occupied have become highly visible examples of inter-ethnic conflict in Canada. Writing as Indian Claims Commissioner, Lloyd Barber provides an overview of the history of land claims settlements and the bases for long-standing controversies over land rights. His review makes it apparent that there has been considerable variation from one region of the nation to another in terms of recognizing and settling the claims of Indians to their lands. Where Indian lands were surrendered through treaties, grievances have arisen about the fulfillment of treaty provisions. Where no settlement of land claims occured, Indian organizations have been seeking formal recognition of their aboriginal rights. From Barber's perspective, an equitable settlement of Indian claims is required not only to correct past injustices, but also to permit Native Peoples to determine their own future in Canadian society.

The election of the Parti Québécois in October, 1976 marked a new phase in the debate regarding the place of Quebec in Canadian confederation. For the first time, Quebecers had elected a government that explicitly supported the objective of independence for Quebec. Sometime in late 1979 or early 1980, citizens of that province will be voting in a referendum to determine whether their provincial government should enter into negotiations with Ottawa about sovereignty association. Public opinion surveys held in early 1979 revealed that a majority of Quebecers would vote to give the Parti Québécois government a mandate to enter into such negotiations.

The selection by Bernard describes the bases for nationalist sentiments in Quebec and the view of the costs and benefits of confederation held by Quebecers. Bernard indicates that there is strong support for greater autonomy for Quebec, even among persons who arc not in favour of independence itself. The response of Canadians outside the province to this desire for greater autonomy within confederation will determine whether support for an independent Quebec waxes and wanes in the years ahead.

The adoption of an immigration policy based upon achieved characteristics (such as education, occupational skills, and knowledge of the official languages) rather than ascribed characteristics (such as nationality or race), along with a high rate of natural increase among native Indians and Inuit has lead to an increase in the size of the non-white population in Canada. Along with this increase has come a rise in the intensity of the negative attitudes toward racially defined ethnic groups such as Blacks and East Indians. The article by Clairmont and Wien describes the historical development and contemporary nature of race relations in Canada and highlights both similarities and differences between race relations in the United States and Canada. Clairmont and Wien indicate that race relations in Canada pose questions regarding social policies and how these could be formulated to create a harmonious multiracial society. In addition, they contend that sociological theories need to be developed in order to explain the persistence of group loyalties based upon physical types when ascriptive characteristics are supposed to decline in significance in modern societies.

In the final selection, John Porter presents a critical analysis of the principle of multiculturalism. From Porter's perspective, the continued emphasis upon ethnic origins and upon the maintenance of distinctive ways of life among ethnic groups is an anachronism in a "post-industrial" society such as Canada. He indicates that historically and territorially, Canada is a bicultural or biethnic society (i.e., a society composed of the English and French ethnic groups). Porter is neither opposed to a bicultural society, nor is he opposed to a policy of multiculturalism which involves the perpetuation of knowledge about the historical cultures of Canada's ethnic groups. It is a policy of multicultralism designed to promote the persistence of ethnic communities that Porter finds problematic. His concern about the latter version of multiculturalism is that it will reduce the rate of assimilation of non-British, non-French groups and thus possibly perpetuate ethnic stratification. Such an outcome would interfere with the goal of individual equality, a goal whose attainment Porter considers to be important.

*   *   *

It is hoped that the selections included in this book will inform the reader and also stimulate further examination of the literature on ethnic relations in Canada and other societies. The bibliographical references in these selections can serve as starting points for additional readings.

I.

Ethnicity and Ethnic Relations

Chapter 1

Definitions of Ethnicity*

Wsevolod W. Isajiw

Very few researchers of ethnic relations ever define the meaning of ethnicity. To find out how often social scientists use explicit definitions of ethnicity in their empirical research, 65 sociological and anthropological studies dealing with one or another aspect of ethnicity were examined. Only 13 of these included some definition of ethnicity; 52 had no explicit definition at all.**

The authors who give no definition of ethnicity never give any reasons for not including it. Indeed there may be good reasons for not explicitly stating any definition of ethnicity. There is always the danger that any definition may be either too narrow and therefore inapplicable to the ethnic groups under study, or else too general and hence devoid of substantive meaning. For example, Raoul Naroll's definition of ethnic unit as people who are domestic speakers of a common distinct language and who belong either

---

*Reprinted from *Ethnicity* 1:1 (1970) by permission of the author and the publisher.

**The studies were taken from: *American Journal of Sociology*, 1946-1971, 13 studies; *American Sociological Review*, 1949-1969, 11 studies; *Social Forces*, 1945-1968, 10; *Social Problems*, 1953-1969, 7; *Phylon*, 1948-1969, 5; *Human Organization*, 1959-1961, 3; *American Anthropologist*, 1955-1967, 3; *Sociometry*, 1962, 2; *Sociological Inquiry*, 1965-1966, 2; Other (*Canadian Review of Sociology and Anthropology, Canadian Journal of Economics and Political Science, Sociological Quarterly, Sociological Review, Pacific Sociological Review, Human Relations, Man, Journal of Marriage and the Family, Explorations in Enterpreneurial History*), 1956-1968, 9 studies.

to the same state, or the same contact group, i.e., at least two nuclear families in relative territorial continguity (Naroll, 1964), may be a useful definition for anthropological research of "tribal" societies, but it would be difficult to apply it fruitfully to ethnic groups in North America.

An alternative can be to define ethnicity in a relatively loose sense, as, for example, any group of people who identify themselves or are in any way identified as Italians, Germans, Indians, Ukrainians, etc. It seems that the studies of various ethnic groups which do not explicitly define ethnicity, implicitly assume some such definition. Indeed, if the purpose of the study is to describe the group, to give a historical account of any event in the life of the group, or to enumerate or even statistically correlate any distribution of features in the group, such definition may be sufficient. But any attempt to go beyond description, any attempt at explanation or meaningful comparison requires not only an explicit definition of ethnicity, but a definition which is denotative rather than merely connotative, since the latter alone tells us little about the nature of a group as an ethnic group.

To give an example, a study done in 1959 by B. C. Rosen has examined differences in motivation, values and aspirations of six ethnic and racial groups in order to explain their dissimilar social mobility rates (Rosen, 1959). The study has shown that these groups differed in their orientation toward achievement. Achievement motivation and achievement aspirations were more characteristic of Greeks, Jews and white Protestants than of Italians, French-Canadians and Negroes. At the same time, Greeks, Jews, and white Protestants showed a higher rate of upward social mobility than did Italians, French-Canadians and Negroes. Differences in orientations towards achievement are, hence, offered as explanation of the differences in mobility rates.

Yet, from the point of view of logic of science, the study remains essentially descriptive rather than explanatory. It correlates value orientations with mobility aspirations and with actual occupational distribution, but although the value orientation variable looks as a plausible explanatory variable, there is no logical reason to consider it as such because there is no logical justification why it, rather than any other variable, should have been chosen as the independent variable. One could just as plausibly reverse the chain of explanation and argue that it is differential occupational distribution which accounts for differential mobility aspirations and for differential value orientations. The only way in which a logical justification can be made for choosing one rather than another set of variables as explanatory variables is when an *a priori* decision, albeit tentative, is made as to which are the most salient attributes of the phenomenon under study, in this case, the phenomenon of ethnicity. What is necessary, therefore, is an explicit definition of ethnicity which itself would provide a connection to a more general theory. Seemingly, Rosen's study implicitly assumes that there is some inherent connection between ethnicity and value orientations but we don't know why there should be any.

The point which I am trying to make with this example is that there are many, indeed too many, studies which pretend to give us explanations of various phenomena connected with ethnicity yet in effect give us at best description of various correlates of ethnicity simply because they fail to make the link between the empirically observed phenomena and any theory which may provide the explanatory import. The link, of course, would be a logically sufficient definition of ethnicity.

Abstract and Specific Definitions

In addition to the 65 studies, 27 definitions of ethnicity, taken from more theoretically oriented works, were examined. What follows is based on analysis of these definitions. Any definition is to an extent arbitrary. Most significantly, variations among definitions depend on the level of generalization, the methodological approach used, and the types of variables included.

The level of generalization can be either abstract or specific. It is one thing to ask what ethnicity is, in general, regardless of place, but it is a different matter to ask what ethnicity means in North America, in Europe, among tribal societies, or among the second generation immigrants. Most of the 27 definitions examined dealt with ethnic groups in North America.

Thus Theodorson and Theodorson in their *Modern Dictionary of Sociology* (Theordorson, 1969) define ethnic group as "a group with a common cultural tradition and a sense of identity which exists as a subgroup of a larger society. The members of an ethnic group differ with regard to certain cultural characteristics from the other members of their society."

Similar definition is offered by the *International Encyclopedia of the Social Sciences*. Milton Gordon in his definition of ethnic group, makes a specific reference to America (Gordon, 1964). He states:

> When I use the term 'ethnic group', then, to refer to a type of group contained within the national boundaries of America, I shall mean by it any group which is defined or set off by race, religion, or national origin, or some combination of these categories. . . . All of these categories have a common social-psychological referent, in that all of them serve to create, through historical circumstances, a sense of peoplehood for groups within the United States, and this common referent of peoplehood is recognized in the American public's usage of these three terms, frequently in interchangeable fashion.

The European usage of the concept reflects, of course, the European experiences of ethnicity. Definitions referring to ethnic groups in Europe, never conceive them as subgroups of a larger society. They are usually seen as either coterminous with society conceived as a state or in some way close to being coterminous. If not explicit, there is usually an implicit reference to actual or potential political group determination. Referring to J. T. Delos' work, E. K. Francis states that "an ethnic group, if we understand Delos rightly, would almost be identical with a nation which has not yet become fully conscious of itself" (Francis, 1947). Hence the term ethnic group itself is not used very often in European sociological literature. Instead, the preferred terms are "nation" or "nationality". Both of these terms can apply also to situations in which an ethnic group may have no independent political boundaries, but which has developed its self-consciousness to the point where independent political boundaries are a logical next step. In any case, unlike in the North American experience, reference to political and often territorial boundaries is central. Similarly, to apply either to situations such as the Balkans or to immigrants, the phrase "national minorities" is often used. The term still retains the implicit political dimension, but avoids any assumptions which the notion of subsociety might carry.

Culture plays an important role in definitions referring to European ethnic groups. But the notion of culture is specific. Culture is defined more in normative rather than descriptive terms. It is the so called "high culture," i.e., it is seen not so much as a product of simple common living, but as a product of self-awareness. It is heritage rather than simply ethnic culture. As E. K. Francis has put it, "every ethnic group has a distinctive culture, but a common culture pattern does not necessarily constitute an ethnic group" (Francis, 1947). We should say it does not constitute a nation or nationality.

Descriptive definition of culture, however, is characteristic of anthropological attempts to define ethnicity. For anthropologists the focus is on discrete groups — tribal societies as culture bearing units. In his famous attempt to develop a definition of the ethnic unit, R. Naroll defines a tribe as "that group of people whose shared, learned way of life constitutes a 'culture' rather than a mere 'subculture' " (Naroll, 1964). Naroll has analysed ten various definitions of tribe and tribal communities and came up with six criteria by which an ethnic unit can be defined. They are: (1) distribution of particular traits being studied, (2) territorial contiguity, (3) political organization, (4) language, (5) ecological adjustment, (6) local community structure. This conception of ethnic unit is to some extent alien to the European conception of a nation, but as was already pointed out, is hardly applicable to the North American experience. For all the similarities with the European case, this definition remains specific to tribal societies.

A question arises whether a specific definition could be given of ethnic groups in Canada as distinguished from ethnic groups in the United States and vice versa? One answer to this has been in terms of cultural assimilation, that is, United States has been seen as a society which assimilates immigrants much faster than Canada by readily "melting" the immigrants' cultures, whereas Canada has been considered as a society allowing the retention of cultural variety. The problem with this formulation, however, is that it is not clear whether the differences concern two different types of cultural processes or only the degree of assimilation. The latter would not warrant two different definitions of ethnicity.

Nonetheless, the differences between ethnic groups in Canada and the United States may not be a matter of culture. The boundaries of ethnic groups may not be determined by culture. Anthropologist Fredrik Barth in his attempt to define ethnicity has pointed out that ethnic group boundaries are a matter of membership and only socially relevant factors are diagnostic for membership, not the overt "objective" differences which are generated by other factors (Barth, 1969, pp. 14-15). Hence, "the critical focus of investigation from this point of view becomes the ethnic *boundary* that defines the group, not the cultural stuff that it encloses." Accordingly,

> the cultural features that signal the boundary may change, and the cultural characteristics of the members may likewise be transformed, indeed even the organizational form of the group may change — yet the fact of continuing dichotomization between members and outsiders allows us to specify the nature of continuity, and investigate the changing cultural form and content. (Barth, 1970, p. 14)

Barth's definition is especially applicable to ethnic groups which are in the process of change. Barth goes on to say that although ethnic categories take cultural differences into account, we should assume no simple one-to-one relationship between ethnic units and cultural similarities and differences. The reason is that "the features that are taken into account are not the sum of 'objective' differences, but only those which the actors themselves regard as significant."

Subjective and Objective Definitions

This type of definition differs from all the others mentioned previously, not only because it can focus better on ethnic groups in the process of change, but more significantly, because it implies a methodological approach distinct and different from that implicit in the other definitions. The two approaches can be called objective and subjective. They are distinct approaches inasmuch as they are not reduceable to one another. They reflect the two general theoretical trends in contemporary social science, the structural and the phenomenological methodologies. Of the 27 definitions examined, 10 used the subjective approach either by itself or in some combination with the objective approach. In contrast to the objective approach by which ethnic groups are assumed to be existing as it were "out there" as real phenomena, the subjective approach defines ethnicity as a process by which individuals either identify themselves as being different from others or belonging to a different group or are identified as different by others, or both identify themselves and are identified as different by others. The psychological identification as being different is on account of the various attributes of one's background, cultural, religious, racial, etc., or on account of one's being a member of groups with different backgrounds.

Thus, according to Lloyd Warner the term ethnic refers to "any individual who considers himself, or is considered to be a member of a group with a foreign culture and who participates in the activities of the group" (Warner and Srole, 1945, p. 28). According to Shibutani and Kwan, "an ethnic group consists of people who conceive of themselves as being of a kind. They are united by emotional bonds and concerned with the preservation of their type" (Shibutani and Kwan, 1965, p. 40).

The *International Encyclopedia of the Social Sciences gives* a definition which in a peculiar way combines both the subjective and the objective approach, although the emphasis rests on the subjective approach. According to the *Encyclopedia,* "an ethnic group is a distinct category of the population in a larger society whose culture is usually different from its own. The members of such a group are, or feel themselves, or are thought to be, bound together by common ties of race or nationality or culture" (IESS, Vol. 5, p. 167).

The subjective approach has the advantage over the objective approach that by focussing on the psychological identity it makes it much easier for the definition to embrace the second or the third ethnic generation than would a definition emphasizing the observed sharing of culture or other attributes. Nathan Glazer and Daniel Moynihan describing what an ethnic group is state:

> Concretely, persons think of themselves as members of that group, with that name; they are thought of by others as members of that group, with that name; and most significantly, they are linked to other members of the group by new attributes that the original immigrants would never have recognized as identifying their group, but which nevertheless serve to mark them off, by more than simply name and association in the third generation and even beyond. (Glazer and Moynihan, 1963, p. vi)

But the most interesting of all subjective definitions of ethnicity is that of Max Weber. Max Weber consistently excludes any reference to objective criteria. He states (Weber, 1968, Vol. 1, p. 389):

> We shall call "ethnic groups" those human groups that entertain a subjective belief in their common descent because of similarities of physical type or of customs or both, or because of memories of colonization and emigration; this belief must be important for the propagation of group formation; conversely it does not matter whether or not an objective blood relationship exists. Ethnic membership (Gemeinsamkeit) differs from the kinship group precisely by being a presumed identity, not a group with concrete social action, like the latter. In our sense ethnic membership does not constitute a group; it only facilitates group formation of any kind, particularly in the political sphere. On the other hand, it is primarily the political community, no matter how artificially organized, that inspires the belief in common ethnicity. This belief tends to persist even after the disintegration of the political community, unless drastic differences in the custom, physical type, or, above all, language exist among its members.

Ethnicity for Max Weber is a matter of belief. We can say that inasmuch as it is a matter of propagation of group formation, it is a matter of ideology. Max Weber's definition reflects most directly the European ethnic experience. Significantly, however, Max Weber takes an explicit position on the basic issue behind the question of the subjective as against the objective definitions of ethnicity. The issue is, are ethnic groups real social groups or are they only categories of classification? If they are only categories then one has to accept Weber's argument that any social organization existing within an ethnic group is due not to the factor of culture, but to the political factor. Most of the other subjective definitions, however, do not appear to assume that only the political community inspires the belief in common ethnicity. The usual assumption is that the psychological ethnic identification can be made on the basis of several attributes, such as cultural differences, race, language, religion, etc. Hence there is no reason to assume why organization of common activity should not develop on the basis of any of these attributes or a combination of them. Nevertheless, the implications of Max Weber's argument go deeper. We will return to his definition later. It will suffice to point out here that most of the definitions examined in this study do not assume that ethnicity as ethnicity, is only a category, rather, that it refers to actual concrete groups.

Inclusion of Attributes

Among the 27 definitions examined, 12 more or less distinct attributes of ethnic groups can be singled out. In the order of the number of times that each attribute was stated they are:

Attributes	No. of times stated
1. Common national or geographic origin or common ancestors	12
2. Same culture or customs	11
3. Religion	10
4. Race or physical characteristics	9
5. Language	6
6. Consciousness of kind: "we feeling," sense of peoplehood, loyalty	4
7. *Gemeinschaft* relations	4
8. Common values or ethos	3
9. Separate institutions	3
10. Minority or subordinate status or majority or dominant status	2
11. Immigrant group	1
12. Other	5

The attributes mentioned most often are then: (1) common ancestral origin, (b) same culture, (c) religion, (d) race, and (e) language. It could be argued that religion, language, values and separate institutions can be subsumed under the category of culture or cultural traits.

Race, however, remains on a different level of analysis, referring to physical characteristics. Yet, looking at the definitions which include the race attribute, one could argue that in one sense race could be subsumed under cultural traits, especially if seen from the point of view of the subjective approach to definitions. Subjective definitions consider race as part of the individual's self-definition, and if self-definitions of a category of people remain the same over a period of time, they become part and parcel of the people's culture. On the other hand, if seen in biological genetic terms, race can be defined as referring to common ancestral origin and hence can be classified together with it.

With race, religion, language and some of the less frequently used attributes reclassified we can move towards a composite definition of ethnicity. The basic attributes would be common ancestral origin and the same cultural traits, the other attributes can be used as specifying the definition to apply to the North American experience. Since the attributes gathered here are taken from both the subjective and the objective definitions of ethnicity, our composite definition should allow for the possibility of both approaches. However, it does remain biased in the direction of the objective approach. Thus, we can define ethnicity as

> a group or category of persons who have common ancestral origin and the same cultural traits, who have a sense of peoplehood and *Gemeinschaft* type of relations, who are of immigrant background and have either minority or majority status within a larger society.

The definitions examined in this study, however, differ greatly in regard to which attributes are included and which ones are excluded. Thus among the definitions examined, 1 definition includes 7 of the above attributes, 1 definition includes 6 attributes, 2 definitions include 5 attributes, 4 definitions include 4 attributes, 4 definitions include 3 attributes, 7 definitions include only 2 attributes and 5 definitions include only 1 attribute. Three definitions include attributes not considered in the above list. The number and the type of attributes included in a definition depends on the purpose for which the author uses the definition. Ashley Montagu, for example, includes in his definition of ethnicity religion, language and separate social institutions, but excludes race, because the purpose in his use of the definition is to show that race as such is not an important criterion of human grouping (Montagu, 1962). Oscar Handlin includes only culture in his definition inasmuch as his work in which the definition is used attempts to show continuity of ethnic groups across generations. The emphasis hence is on transmission of culture (Handlin, 1957).

On the other hand, Milton Gordon includes in his definition race, religion and national origin. By this he does not want to say that they are all the same, but that they all share a core element which is a sense of peoplehood. By this he shows that ethnic groups, like religious groups and racial groups form subsocieties within the American society (Gordon, 1964). Shermerhorn also includes religion and race among his other four attributes. His work, however, deals with the problem of relations between subordinate and superordinate groups and ethnicity, religion and race having the common element of minority or majority status. All in all, in our sample of definitions, 10 definitions included religion and, 8 of these, in addition to religion, included also race.

Genus and Specific Difference

From the point of view of logic, the problem with including religion and race in the definition of ethnicity is that if they warrant, as I think they do, independent definitions of their own, then they have to be conceived as either subtypes of ethnicity or else they all, including ethnicity, have to be subsumed under a more generic category. This is in effect what distinguishes the subjective from objective definitions. If ethnicity is self-identification or identification by others, then religion or race are two specific ways in which persons can be identified as different. If seen as real groups, then ethnicity, religion and race can be subsumed under the more generic notion of either groups with a sense of peoplehood or minority groups or the like. This is in effect what both Gordon and Schermerhorn do. As was mentioned previously, a good definition is definition by means of genus and specific difference. This is the only way in which a definition can have explanatory usefulness. The aim of an ideally good definition is not to identify as many properties of the phenomenon studied as possible, but to identify the minimum number of properties under which a greater variety of properties could be subsumed, yet which would also clearly indicate which properties should not be included.

With this in mind we can go back to our composite definition of ethnicity and attempt to rephrase it.

The idea of common ancestral origin in the definition obviously has to be seen in relation to sharing of the same cultural traits. That is, it is not the common ancestral origin as such that is important here, for all human beings ultimately have common ancestry; it is the ancestors or their descendents who can be said to have possessed the same cultural traits, as distinguished from persons and their ancestors with different cultural traits. However, what common origin in this sense indicates is that a person is born into a group which shares certain cultural traits and therefore becomes socialized into them. The person, of course, has no choice as to the specific cultural group which provides for him the basic process of socialization. Such groups can be called involuntary groups as distinguished from associations in which one has a choice of membership. The genus for our definition therefore is the involuntary group. By including the socialization process as the basic element of the concept, involuntary group connotes also the sense of peoplehood and the *Gemeinschaft* type of relations as other related elements in the concept. Only one definition in our sample referred to this generic definition of the ethnic group. Breton and Pinard state: "A person does not belong to an ethnic category by choice. He is born into it and becomes related to it through emotional and symbolic ties" (Breton and Pinard, 1960).

The concept of involuntary group, however, includes besides ethnicity, also religious groups, racial groups, and social classes. For the most part, persons are born into all of these. What we need therefore is the specific difference to distinguish between them. This can be provided by the second major part of the composite definition, i.e., the same cultural traits. This, however, has to be modified to mean culture. Religious groups, social classes or racial groups as such do not imply a totality of cultural traits. None of these groups necessarily transmit all the cultural traits of society or, to put it differently, the members of an ethnic group are not necessarily at the same time members of the same religion, the same class or even the same race. Yet they all would share basically the same ethnic culture.

But it should be understood that in cases where members of the same ethnic group are also members of the same religion, the same race or the same social class, then ethnicity and these groups become coterminous, their boundaries become the same.

We can thus state our general definition of ethnicity as referring to an involuntary group of people who share the same culture. Besides being general, i.e., applicable to many societies, this definition takes the objective approach. Essentially, the reason for this is that if we at all assume that ethnicity has anything to do with culture, we then must assume some link with the socialization process and socialization process can take place only in real groups. The trouble with Max Weber's definition of ethnicity is that he assumes ethnicity to be belief in common ancestry because of similarities of customs and above all language, but he gives no reason at all why these similarities should be there in the first place, or more importantly, why they should persist over the span of generations. Hence if the criteria of ethnic identification are assumed to be related to any cultural patterns, one has to assume also a basis for the criteria to be rooted in the objective group processes. Just not any subjective criteria can be chosen to produce ethnic identification.

For the same reason our definition would exclude such cultural groups as artistic societies or even newly established communes or the like because such groups are not a product of the basic socialization process, i.e., they are not involuntary groups. It takes at least two generations for a group to become involuntary.

Definition of Ethnicity for North America

The general definition just presented, however, is not satisfactory when applied as stated to the societies of North America in which there are many persons of the second, third or even fourth immigrant generations who might have gone through the process of socialization within the larger society rather than the ethnic subsociety, who, as a result, may not share the culture with their ancestors, or even with their contemporaries who have been socialized into their ethnic group, but who nevertheless may have retained or even developed to a higher degree subjective identity with their ethnic group. Can one consider them as members of the ethnic group?

Too often it has been assumed that ethnic identity in North America is a temporary matter, i.e., that in time all "ethnics" assimilate and the ethnic group boundaries disappear. Likewise, it has often been assumed that the question of ethnic identity maintenance derives exclusively from the processes within ethnic groups themselves rather than the processes inherent in the society at large. Neither of these assumptions can be justified. Much evidence indicates that in North America ethnic indentities persist beyond cultural assimilation and that persistence of ethnic identity is not necessarily related to the perpetuation of traditional ethnic culture. Rather, it may depend more on the emergence of ethnic "rediscoverers," i.e., persons from any consecutive ethnic generation who have been socialized into the culture of the general society but who develop a symbolic relation to the culture of their ancestors. Even relatively few items from the cultural past, such as folk art, music, can become symbols of ethnic identity. Significantly, there seems to be a process of selection of items from the cultural past and rather than accepting the entire baggage of ethnic tradition persons from consecutive ethnic generations show a degree of freedom in choosing such items from the cultural past of their ancestors which correspond to their needs created perhaps by the specific character of relations in society as a whole (Isajiw, 1972).

It is in this connection that the subjective approach can be tied together with the objective definition. The important thing in linking the two approaches is that the subjective ethnic identification should not be seen as something arbitrary but as a phenomenon based on a real ancestral link between a person and a group which has shared a culture. I do not think that it would be realistic to assume that in a more general number of cases ethnic identification can be based on a purely imaginary link with any ancestors. Ancestral mythologies notwithstanding, ancestors usually are not identified at will.

The involuntary nature of the ethnic group is connected with *Gemeinschaft* type of relations among members of the group and as a result, on the psychological level, articulates with feelings of sympathy and loyalty towards members of the same ethnic group. This, we can say, forms the basis for ethnic boundaries from within the ethnic group. In societies such as the United States or Canada, where members of many ethnic groups have to interact and compete with one another, the existence of ethnic boundaries from within inevitably produces ethnic boundaries from without. As Barth has pointed out, persons will be identified by others as belonging to one or another ethnic group even if they do not actively share anymore any cultural patterns with that ethnic group as long as a link to their ancestors can be made. Identification by others in turn usually stimulates self-identification and may condition new forms of social organization. Hence, ethnicity is a matter of a double boundary, a boundary from within, maintained by the socialization process, and a boundary from without established by the process of intergroup relations. It is in terms of the relationship between these two boundaries that the differences between ethnicity in Canada and in the U.S. can be most fruitfully compared. I would suggest that the basic difference lies in the external boundaries. It is not so much a matter of faster or slower assimilation, and non-assimilation. More significantly it is a matter of how the various ethnic groups are perceived and identified by others in the two societies, but especially how they are perceived and identified by the power-holding, policy-making and influence-exerting bodies of the two societies. Thus the external ethnic boundaries would be reflected in the reasons and rationales behind specific immigration policies, cultural policies, and the like.

We can now add to our general definition of ethnicity a specific definition. Thus, ethnicity refers to:

> an involuntary group of people who share the same culture or to descendants of such people who identify themselves and/or are identified by others as belonging to the same involuntary group.

The advantage of this definition is that it makes possible a development of ethnic group theory and likewise makes possible explanation rather than mere description of the concrete ethnic group processes in Canada, United States, or similar societies. It allows for

(1)   development of typology of ethnic groups,
(2)   analysis of various ethnic group processes such as maintenance of ethnic identity, assimilation, etc.
(3)   development of a theory of intergroup relations based on the interaction between voluntary and involuntary groups, as for example voluntary groups can be seen as instrumental in the relations among involuntary groups.

This, however, goes beyond the scope of definition of ethnicity.

BIBLIOGRAPHY

Works Used for Analysis of Definitions of Ethnicity

Barth, Fredrick (1969), *Ethnic Groups and Boundaries,* George Allen and Unwin, London.

Berry, Brewton (1958), *Race and Ethnic Relations,* Houghton Mifflin Co., Boston.

Breton, Raymond and Maurice Pinard (1960), "Group Formation Among Immigrants: Criteria and Processes," *Canadian Journal of Economics and Political Science,* 26, 465-477.

Bloom, Leonard (1948), "Concerning Ethnic Research," *ASR,* 13, 171-182.

Dictionary of the Social Sciences, U.N.E.S.C.O. Gould, Julius and William L. Kolb (Eds.).

Francis, E. K. (1947), "The Nature of the Ethnic Group," *AJS,* 52, 393-400.

Glaser, Daniel (1958), "Dynamics of Ethnic Identification," *ASR,* 23, 31-40.

Glazer, Nathan and Daniel P. Moynihan (1963), *Beyond the Melting Pot,* M.I.T. Press, Cambridge, Mass.

Gordon, Milton M. (1964), *Assimilation in American Life,* Oxford University Press, New York.

Greeley, Andrew (1971), "Ethnicity as an Influence on Behavior," *in* Feinstein, Otto (ed.) *Ethnic Groups in the City,* Heath Lexington Books, Lexington, Mass. pp. 1-16.

Handlin, Oscar (1957), *Race and Nationality in American Life,* Little, Brown, Boston.

Handlin, Oscar and Mary Handlin (1956), "Ethnic Factors in Social Mobility," *Explorations in Entrepreneurial History,* **9,** 1-7.

Hatt, Paul (1948), "Class and Ethnic Attitudes," *ASR,* **13,** 36-43.

Hoult, Thomas Ford (1969), *Dictionary of Modern Sociology,* Littlefield, Adams, Totowa, N.J.

International Encyclopedia of the Social Sciences, Vol. 5, p. 167.

Kolm, Richard (1971), "Ethnicity in Society and Community," *in* Feinstein, Otto (ed.) *Ethnic Groups in the City,* Heath Lexington Books, Lexington, Mass., pp. 57-77.

Marden, Charles F. and Gladys Meyer (1968), *Minorities in American Society,* American Book Co., New York.

Montagu, Ashley (1962), "The Concept of Race," *American Anthropologist,* **64,** 919-928.

Nahirny, Vladimir C. and Joshua A. Fishman (1965), "American Immigrant Groups: Ethnic Identification and the Problem of Generations," *Sociological Review,* **13,** 311-326.

Naroll, Raoul (1964), "Ethnic Unit Classification," *Current Anthropology,* **5,** No. 4.

Pettigrew, Thomas F. (1971), "Ethnicity in American life: A Social Psychological Perspective," *in* Feinstein, Otto (ed.), *Ethnic Groups in the City,* Heath Lexington Books, Lexington, Mass. pp. 29-37.

Schermerhorn, R. A., (1970), *Comparative Ethnic Relations,* Random House, New York.

Shibutani, T. and K. Kwan (1965), *Ethnic Stratification: A Comparative Approach,* Macmillan Co., New York.

Theodorson, George A. and Achilles G. Theodorson (1969), *A Modern Dictionary of Sociology,* Thomas Y. Crowell Co., New York.

Warner, L. and L. Srole, (1945), *The Social Systems of American Ethnic Groups,* Yale University Press, New Haven, p. 28.

Weber, Max (1968), *Economy and Society,* Bedminister Press, New York, Vol. 1, Chapter 5.

Winick, Charles (1970), *Dictionary of Anthropology,* Littlefield, Adams, Totowa, N.J.

Isajiw, Wsevolod W. (1972), "The Process of Maintenance of Ethnic Identity: The Canadian Context", paper presented to the Black Caucus of the American Sociological Association, New Orleans, La.

Rosen, Bernard (1959), "Race, Ethnicity and the Achievement Syndrome," *ASR,* **24,** 47-60.

Chapter 2

Non-Native Ethnicity in Crow Lake*

David H. Stymeist

Crow Lake as a Complex Society

Crow Lake is divided and stratified in various ways. The social life of the town does not have a uniform pattern or texture, but is greatly varied. There are those who cling tenaciously to the teachings of an established religion, others who attend church regularly more for social than religious reasons, and some who are generally unconcerned with religion or religious activity. There are Roman and Greek Orthodox Catholics, Anglicans, Moslems, Baptists, members of the United Church, and Jehovah's Witnesses. Some people are closely associated with the bush, their major interests being fishing, hunting, and camping. Others pursue these activities to some extent, and still others are totally uninterested in the surrounding forests and lakes. In another area, there are those who eagerly accept the ideologies of capitalism and progress and work persistently for individual maximization. Others work simply to survive and regard their jobs as nothing more than a necessary evil, while a few float through life living from hand to mouth. All of these people live in the same community, interact with each other and pursue their aims independently, but in concert with others who do not necessarily share their aims.

*Reprinted from Ethnics and Indians, Toronto: PMA Books, 1975, by permission of the author and the publisher.

There is, then, no single pattern of life, no archetypal member of the community, no real unity in terms of aspirations, needs, standard of living, or cultural orientation. There are instead individuals and small knots of people who structure or attempt to structure a definite and at times consciously different pattern for their lives. However, they do not do this in a vacuum. They do not exist as isolates. All their desires to do what they want to do, have to do, or feel that they somehow should do exist within the framework of constraints and incentives set by the local and larger society.

Non-Native Ethnicity in Crow Lake

Ethnicity is one of the factors adding depth and variety to the existing social spectrum. It is one complex of ideas and relationships — real or assumed — that appears to be significant in the daily conduct of the community's life.

Evidences of ethnicity and indications of the apparent importance of ethnicity are not difficult to discover. On the walls of one of the town's hotels, for example, hangs a framed poem stitched on white linen:

> *Take a little bit of Welsh*
> *Now just a little bit*
> *Mix well with Irish Pluck*
> *And some Scottish Grit.*
> *Blend in England's sons*
> *From town and village sweet.*
> *And call the mixture Britain*
> *For its dashed hard stuff to beat!*

Walking down the main street one passes a Chinese restaurant in which several related families are gathered in the back talking in their native language and reading letters from relatives in China. In the pool hall Mike G. sits and reads an Italian-Canadian newspaper. From time to time he stands up and shouts advice to one of the players. Other Italians drop in to visit. On the street corners retired men stand talking to each other in Ukrainian or Finnish or Icelandic. The local chapter of the Canadian Legion holds a "Scotch Night" and an "Irish Night". The Catholic Women's League sponsors a "Pakistani Tea" and the Knights of Columbus a "Traditional Italian Spaghetti Supper". In a pub one man shouts to the barkeep: "What did this damn Frenchman order? Ex? Give me a Black Label. I'm not drinking any beer that these Frenchmen drink." He nudges the man next to him and his companions break into laughter.

From such observations one might assume that not only do discrete ethnic groups exist in Crow Lake, but that ethnicity itself is an important social parameter. It is slightly disconcerting to find upon closer examination, however, that the appearance of ethnicity is often no more than that: an appearance. The traditional view of the ethnic group assumes that members are regarded as "full-time ethnics"; that ethnicity, wherever it exists, canalizes social life; that, as Barth has said, ethnicity is "imperative in that it cannot be discarded and temporarily set aside by other definitions of the situation". (1969:17.) But in Crow Lake one finds that ethnic distinctions once made are not permanent; that certain people can make announced shifts in ethnic identity from time to time. Moreover, the ethnic dimension becomes a structuring principle only in some contexts and on certain occasions. Within the non-Indian segment of Crow Lake's population one does not find the existence of permanent, stable ethnic groups in which "ethnic identity is superordinate to most other statuses, and defines the permissible constellations of statuses, or social personalities, which an individual with that identity may assume" (Barth 1969:17). What one does find is a series of ethnic categories out of which, from time to time and place to place, "ethnic groups", quasi-groups, or assemblages are formed.

Distributions of Ethnic Memberships in the Community

Ethnic diversity among non-Natives is the general pattern in northern Canadian communities; Crow Lake is no exception. On the contrary, ethnicity appears especially pronounced. This is true perhaps because the community, as the main service centre of the immediate area, is able to provide a great variety of job opportunities which have attracted people of widely disparate origins. The town is proud of its "harmonious mixture" of peoples, a phrase used in 1968 by former Prime Minister Diefenbaker in his address to the graduates of the town's high school.

The core of the town's population is, as one might expect, Anglo-Saxon in origin: first, second, or third generation English, Irish, Welsh, and Scots people. But in addition, one may find Ukrainians, Russians, Yugoslavs, Poles, Finns, Swedes, Icelanders, Italians, French-Canadians, Chinese, Malays, Filipinos, Australians, West Indians, Germans, Portuguese, Pakistanis, Persians, Nigerians, Belgians, Austrians, and Americans. Some of these people are transients rather than permanent residents. This is especially true with regard to ethnic categories of more recent vintage: Pakistanis, Malays, Filipinos, etc. Other categories have a long, established history in the town.

The distribution of ethnicity in Crow Lake is itself interesting. According to the Dominion Bureau of Statistics Census of Canada, ethnic distribution in 1961 was as follows:

Population By Specific Ethnic Groups — 1961

British Isles	1101	Russian	5
French	211	Scandinavian	137

German	83	Ukrainian	247
Italian	264	Other European	188
Jewish	4	Asiatic	40
Netherlands	35	Native Indian	40
Polish	93	Other	5

Total   2453

The thoroughly mixed nature of the community's population is immediately obvious. However, if these figures are compared with similar figures taken from previous censuses, certain interesting points emerge.

In 1911, for example, the ethnic distribution of Crow Lake and the immediately surrounding area was much less completely diverse:

*1911 Census of Canada Transcontinental Railway Crow Lake to mile 10 district E.**

British Isles Races

English	202
Irish	91
Scotch	199
Other	4

Other European Races

German	29	Italian	308
Austro-Hungarian	331	Japanese	—
Belgian	—	Jewish	17
Bulgarian & Roumanian	39	Negro	5
Chinese	2	Polish	14
Dutch	1	Russian	303
Greek	—	Scandinavian	139
Hindu	—	Swiss	—
Indian	—	Unspecified	46

---

*The categories used here are census categories. It is interesting to note that certain categories differ from census to census. It is of even greater interest that "races" was the term used to denote ethnic categories. The information in these tables is reprinted here as it appears in the DBS Census of Canada 1911, 1921, 1931, 1941, 1961. (Figures unavailable for 1951 and 1971.)

In 1921 the pattern was as follows:

British Races

English	342
Irish	144
Scotch	209
Other	—
Total	1127

European Races

French	93	Hebrew	—
Austrian	69	Italian	97
Belgian	—	Polish	13
Dutch	9	Russian	16
Finnish	55	Scandinavian	39
German	25	Other	7
Greek	—	Ukrainian	—

Asiatic Races

Chinese & Japanese	6
Syrian	—
Indian	—
Negro	3
Other	—

And in 1931:

English	554	Hungarian	4
Irish	297	Italian	145
Scottish	357	Polish	72
Other	7	Russian	15
French	143	Roumanian	14
Austrian	13	Scandinavian	124
Belgian	1	Ukrainian	103
Czech & Slovack	2	Other	5
Dutch	15	Chinese & Japanese	10
Finnish	116	Other	—
German	68	Indian & Eskimo	—
Hebrew	21	Unspecified & Others	2
Total		2088	

In 1941:

English	398	Jewish	12
Irish	290	Netherlands	27
Scottish	306	Polish	83
Other	18	Roumanian	12
French	133	Russian	14
Austrian	4	Scandinavian	94
Belgian	—	Ukrainian	124
Czech & Slovack	2	Chinese	5
Finnish	64	Other	—
German	37	Indian & Eskimo	—
Hungarian	1	Other	2
Italian	121		

Total   1756

Problems and Implications of Existing Statistics

The reliability of these statistics may be questioned. The ethnic categories used to construct these tables are arbitrary and change from census to census. More importantly, such statistics are based on census data which can only be a rather cursory examination of the actual area of enquiry. Yet, even if partially inaccurate and misleading, such information does indicate the existence of certain regularities. There has been, first of all, a general persistence of ethnicity in Crow Lake through time. The ethnic mixture that so characterizes the community today was present, though in a somewhat different form, from the earliest days of the community.

In addition, although the percentage distribution of categories has fluctuated over time, the major ethnic categories have remained fairly constant, supplemented by a varying mixture of less numerically significant categories.

Percentage distributions:

	1911	1921	1931	1941	1961
English	11.0	30.0	26.5	22.6	—
Irish	4.9	13.7	14.2	16.5	—
Scottish	10.8	18.5	17.0	17.4	—
Other	.2	—	.3	1.0	—
British Isles	26.9	61.2	57.0	57.5	44.8
French	5.3	8.2	6.8	7.5	8.6
German	1.4	2.2	3.2	2.1	3.3

Italian	16.8	8.6	6.9	6.8	10.7
Jewish	.9	—	1.0	.6	.1
Netherlands	.05	.7	.7	1.5	1.4
Polish	.7	1.1	3.4	4.7	3.7
Russian	16.5	1.4	.7	.7	.2
Scandinavian	7.6	3.4	5.9	5.3	5.5
Ukrainian	—	—	4.9	7.0	10.0
Other European	2.5	.6	.2	.1	7.6
Asiatic	.1	.5	.4	.2	1.6

Meaning of Ethnic Distributions

What does this persistence of established patterns mean? Does it indicate the continued persistence of definite, discrete "ethnic groups" in community life? If one were to claim, as the census material seems to claim, that in 1961 6 percent of the population was Scandinavian and 11 percent Italian, would this statement accurately reflect the reality of the local situation?

Experience in Crow Lake eventually indicated that it would not. Gradually it became clear that such census data as exists indicates little more than how people thought about their own ethnic identities when they were answering the census questions. The resulting data did not necessarily reflect how people perceived and acted upon the ethnic dimension in their social lives. Emperical evidence, though not completely denying the implications of ethnic diversity, did not often support them.

It was clear, for example, that earlier patterns of residential segregation according to "ethnic group" affiliation were no longer operational. There were incidences of uneven ethnic distribution in various areas of the community, but the natural boundaries — the blocks and neighborhoods — did not have ethnic connotations. By 1972 the northwest sector of the community was no longer called "Swede Town" and the eastern section was no longer a "Central European" area.

The general pattern was one of uneven but thorough mixture. In a sample of three streets located in different areas of town, the following ethnic distribution was found:

Block A. "South Street"

English	Finnish
Swedish	Ukrainian
German	vacant
English	English
French	Ukrainian
English	Scots
Dutch	French

Block B. "Centre Street"

English	English
Finnish	Irish
Italian	Chinese
Irish	Czech
French	English
English	English
	English
	French

Block C. "North Street"

German	
Irish	
English	
French	English
Polish	English
Finnish	Scots

The point is that the ultimate nature of ethnicity in Crow Lake could not be deduced from census material, the implication of which is that the categories used in the data are meaningful boundaries in the social life of the community. The reality of the situation in Crow Lake, however, was much more complex.

The Ethnic Dimension as a Conceptual Structure

The ethnic dimension in Crow Lake begins most properly in the minds of the people of the community. Ethnicity, if it refers directly or indirectly to origin (as it does in Crow Lake) begins with the perception of differences in origin. The actual words "ethnicity" or "ethnic group" are not often used in the community. Instead, people refer to "nationalities". One's "nationality", used in this special sense, is seen as an integral part of his identity. In addition, it is assumed that every person has this dimension, an ethnic affiliation. This is perhaps the first and most significant general "law" of ethnicity in Crow Lake. The ethnic dimension is understood as a total system of identities within which each person has a place. And his place, or "nationality", is determined by his name or parentage, by his ultimate biological origin.

Ethnicity, as thus defined, is inescapable. From time to time someone will attempt to state that he is simply Canadian and not Italian-Canadian or Icelandic-Canadian. But even if he is of third or fourth generation immigrant stock, such claims are generally ignored. He is pressed about his ultimate "ethnic" origins, and will, in this position, usually acquiesce.

Categories inside Categories

As might be imagined, such a system of total ethnic membership is not left circulating in people's heads as an inexhaustable list of place names. It is instead codified and presented as a series of related social categories. Such a system, however, is not all-inclusive. It does not include the exact origin status of every individual in the community, but is instead a simplified list of geographical or political areas which serve as origin reference points. Thus, although certain families distinguish between Sicilians and Neopolitians, such a distinction is not current in the general social consciousness; to most people in the community the category that "fits" in this case is "Italian".

This system of social categories is not one-dimensional and linear, but layered. It reflects both different degrees of specificity, and current folk ideas of geographical and cultural connection which in a sense parallel the now dated culture-area approach in cultural anthropology.

Briefly, certain ethnic categories are nested inside other ethnic categories, the different levels corresponding to more or less specific identification of one's origin. The major, central categories are thus often expanded and diluted of specific meaning. For example, the central category "English" breaks down into the following categories:

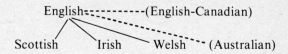

This system is interesting in various ways. The word "English" can be used to refer to an immigrant from London, a Canadian of English parentage, to the people of Britain as a whole, or to "English-speaking" people. Used this way, the term "English" subsumes the somewhat more precise categories that fall within its domain; it refers to and can imply a range of specific ethnic identities each of which can at other times and in other circumstances, stand alone. The term "Irish", therefore, is a highly precise term in the lexicon of ethnic conceptualizations in Crow Lake. To be categorized as "Irish" does not mean that one cannot be classified as "English" in other situations. But when "Irish" is used, it is meant in an exact sense which differentiates it from English, Welsh, and Scottish memberships. While related to the category "English" it exists at a different level of conceptualization.

Existing Possibilities of Multiple Affiliations

None of this in itself is surprising. However, in Crow Lake the nesting of ethnic categories is a central feature of the entire system. It operates at all levels and in all directions, and may take some surprising turns. The major non-Native ethnic categories current in the community are English, Finlander, Ukrainian, Chinese, Italian, Pakistani, German and French. Each of these contains sub-categories which may sometimes operate as separate categories. A few of these subordinate categories exist only as conceptual categories, relating to memberships that were represented in the past or perhaps will be represented in the future. Thus:

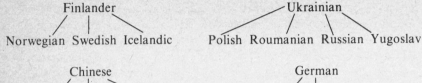

```
        Finlander                        Ukrainian
        /    |    \                    /    |    \
Norwegian Swedish Icelandic   Polish Roumanian Russian Yugoslav

        Chinese                          German
        /    |    \                      /    |
Japanese Malayan Filipino          Dutch Austrian etc.
```

The way this nesting system works is less a case of people agreeing that a "Pole" is in many ways similar to a "Ukrainian" than a kind of loose identification with the category "Ukrainian" of an individual whose ancestors were Poles.

An example of such a situation occurred one night in a local pub. J., an "Englishman", exclaimed: "What! Am I supposed to buy this worthless Uke a drink?" Somewhat later I purposely broke the rules of this interaction situation by asking D., the "Ukrainian", if he was actually Ukrainian. The answer was yes. "Well," I asked innocently, "what part of the Ukraine did your family come from?"

"They didn't. They came from Poland. I'm a Polack." D. in this situation was not really confused about his ethnicity. He was a second generation "ethnic"; his parents were both of the same ethnic category. Yet in this and in other interaction settings he chose to present himself as a Ukrainian and his companions chose to accept this definition of the situation.

The group at our table that night was well mixed: there were two "Englishmen" (both of whose great-grandparents were born in Canada), a "Frenchman" (a French-Canadian who spoke little French and whose parents had lived in Ontario all their lives), two "Ukrainians" (a third generation Ukrainian and a second generation Pole), and a "Finlander" (a second generation Norwegian). Under these circumstances, ethnic jokes and insults were rather broad in scope. They pertained to the larger, more visible social categories of ethnicity. Individual memberships were subsumed under the appropriate major category and people would defend "their" ethnic category, making jokes about the assumed specific ethnicity of others.

Somewhat later, however, C., a second-generation Ukrainian from Manitoba, referred to B., in a moment of minor irritation, as "that God damn Polack". While B., himself, would make disparaging comments from time to time as to the level of intelligence of those "Ukrainians". He distributed a photocopied drawing of what was identified as a "Ukrainian Target Pistol" — a Smithinski-Wesonovitch 32 caliber.

This was by no means an isolated occurrence. It was part of a general pattern that was often repeated and elaborated. It could, furthermore, reach levels bordering on the absurd. As in the case of one person of ultimate Scottish ancestry who claimed from time to time that he was a North American Indian, that "Indians are people that you whites will never understand". This man had lived with Indian people for many years and was well acquainted with the North. His periodic identification with Native people was neither completely accepted by the majority of the townspeople, nor completely denied. Similarly, it seemed that various Native people regarded him in a somewhat different light than other white men.

And yet, on occasion, this man would claim that he was Scottish or rather *"really"* Scottish. He was born and grew up in a rather isolated part of Scotland and came to Canada and the North as a young man. Periodically he maintained that he was more Scottish than the Anglo-Saxons of Edinburgh or Glasgow. Often he would make announced shifts in identity in the course of an evening. These shifts might occasionally be questioned, but no more seriously than in many less ambiguous cases.

The Attributing of Culture and Identity to Persons

The fact that the system allowed such announced shifts in identity is important. It indicates, first of all, that ethnicity in Crow Lake was a domain of identity relating to culture and to folk ideas of culture. Ethnic comments, labels and stereotypes usually centred on certain cultural traits or customs: food, dress, personal habits and proclivities. Secondly, ethnicity was something that was often more attributed than "real". The Scot/Indian mentioned above was obviously neither a "full" Indian nor a "full" Scot. His attitudes, activities, and orientations were all very much the same as those of the town's "Ukrainians", "Italians", "Finlanders" and "Chinese". In Crow Lake specific ethnicity was thus often attributed without being the source of a total, unchangeable identity or status.

Instead, certain "ethnic" cultural traits were continually being expanded into stereotypes and used indiscriminately in social interaction. A person was not simply regarded as an "Italian" or a "Finlander", but a whole range of supposedly specific phenomena were related to him because of his alleged ethnicity. These phenomena were either "really" ethnic or they were not, but they were often regarded as being ethnic in specific interaction situations.

For example, one day G. and B. were drinking coffee together and G. happened to make a gesture with his hands upsetting his cup slightly. B. jokingly said, "Christ, G., do all of you Frenchmen have to talk with your hands and spill things?" Earlier, however, the question of G.'s "nationality" had arisen. It had been stated that at one time G.'s family was French, but that he was not "really" French or even French-Canadian. Objectively, it was this earlier statement that was perhaps the more accurate.

Italians were supposed to like spaghetti and to make their own wine. When they did eat spaghetti or drink homemade wine, they were regarded by others as engaging in activities that were part of their cultural heritage. Similarly, since Ukrainians were alleged to prefer vodka over all other alcoholic beverages, when they drank vodka their ethnic membership was noticed and often commented upon. When they drank beer or rye, however, it was not. When Finnish people ate fish or enjoyed a sauna, their "ethnicity" was occasionally pointed out. However, many people other than Finns took saunas in Crow Lake, and many ate spaghetti and drank vodka even though they were neither Ukrainian nor Italian. The indication was that ethnicity was not simply perceived cultural difference or perceived differences of origin. It was instead an identity system, a structural system, with a certain existence and importance of its own.

The Ethnic Dimension as a Basis for the Development of Social Forms

Faced with endless repetition of this apparent ambiguity, I was willing to believe that the ethnic dimension in Crow Lake society was nothing more than a figment of the collective imagination. Some evidence, however, pointed to the contrary. Groupings did occur, from time to time, in which ethnic memberships became truly relevant. On these occasions ethnicity was not simply a theme of interaction but formed its base. Various ethnic categories sometimes formed real, though temporary, ethnic groups. Moreover, common ethnic membership did mean at times that there was "a sharing of criteria for evaluation and judgement", that "between them [persons of similar ethnicity] there was a potential for diversification and expansion of their social relationship to cover eventually all different sectors and domains of activity". (Barth 1969:15.)

One night at a party K., a transient, sat down to talk to M., a permanent resident. Both were "Icelandic" in origin and came from the same area of Manitoba. Later, K. told me what had taken place:

> Well I sat down to talk to M. You know that you had told me that he was Icelandic from the same area where I came from. So I wanted to talk to him. We were talking about his work for a long time, and then he asked me what I did. I told him that I was an entertainer and played in bars. Well, get this — he didn't believe me! He said, "Ah come on now." I was really taken back for a while and didn't know what to say. Finally I asked him where he came from. When he told me, you know, that he was from this place in northern Manitoba, I just said, "How are you?" in Icelandic. Well, Jesus Christ, you should have seen his face light up. From then on he believed everything that I said.

They talked for more than two hours, and at the end of the evening M. insisted on driving K. home even though he lived only a few blocks away.

Specific ethnicity, real or assumed, thus often had potentialities for real development. It could facilitate the formation of groups or quasi-groups. In the past there were several important ethnic organizations in Crow Lake. There was, for example, a Ukrainian Church Hall and a "Finn Hall". The second is no longer in existence and the first is in decline. Yet during the summer groups of "Ukrainian" women would gather in the largely disused

Church Hall to make perogies and cabbage rolls for sale. Groups of "Finlanders" would be invited to the homes of others to take saunas. The town's pool hall, owned and operated by an Italian, was the focus of an Italian social group. The players, most of them youths, would be of mixed ethnic backgrounds, but the older groups watching from the sidelines were all there because they were "Italians" and shared certain things in common. In addition, various organizations such as the Canadian Legion or the Knights of Columbus would hold "ethnic events" which are often attended by members of all categories but were focussed upon one specific category.

A Paradox in Folk Usages

Something of a paradox emerges at this point. Whereas certain behaviour is often wrongly attributed to specific ethnicity, in other cases the ethnic dimension can have a genuine effect on behaviour. Ethnic distinctions in the first instance are often regarded as minor and amusing. In the second case, however, they are regarded as being real distinctions upon which individual relationships can be built.

Gradients of Ethnic Memberships

This paradox cannot be resolved entirely for it encompasses at least two distinct definitions of the situation. It may, however, be clarified to some extent. First of all, there are considered to be degrees in the "quality" of ethnic membership. This gradient derives in part from the assumption that every person in the community has an ethnic dimension, an assumption which may be a remnant from the town's past, or simply a reflection of the larger social consciousness of the nation.

At one end of the scale are the "core" ethnics, people who possess and act out the cultural stuff of their origins a fair percentage of the time. Most core ethnics are older people. Next there are the "peripheral" ethnics, those who may be familiar with the language and customs of an ethnic category, but seldom if ever use them. This is the archetypal second generation. Finally, there are the "name" ethnics, people who are regarded as having an ethnic dimension simply because their ancestors are or are assumed to have been "ethnics".

Culturally, I am talking about assimilation, about first, second, and third generations. Structurally, however, all three — core, peripheral, and name ethnics — are or can be "real" ethnics, in that they are all encompassed within the same ethnic category system. This in itself has several important implications.

The Social Nature of Ethnicity in Crow Lake

In social terms ethnicity emerges in Crow Lake in two distinct patterns: as interaction between members of the same ethnic category (however defined) or as ethnic banter between members of different ethnic categories. The first kind of social interaction is largely informal. It may facilitate the temporary formation of ethnic groups or assemblages, but does not directly relate to members of other ethnic categories.

In the second pattern, however, interaction in a mixed ethnic setting is presented as social drama. By "drama" I mean a conscious performance through which the "actors" indicate that they are not to be taken seriously. Ethnic jokes and insults take place when the situation is defined as a reasonably friendly gathering of members of various ethnic categories. When the ethnic mix in a social situation reaches a certain level of complexity it is likely that a typical interaction set will be established and a social drama acted out (cf. Turner 1957).

An example of this kind of interaction set occurred during a fishing trip. Present were two Ukrainians — one name and one peripheral. The peripheral Ukrainian was in charge of buying the food for the trip and had brought, among other items, a commercially prepared garlic sausage which we all shared. Someone in our group commented that the sausage was good. Several others agreed, and then the peripheral Ukrainian, M., began: "Well, you boys can eat that crap if you want to, but P. (the name Ukrainian) and I know what *real* garlic sausage tastes like." Instantly, the definition of the situation had changed from a group of fishermen having lunch to a Ukrainian/non-Ukrainian confrontation. Moreover, it had changed so that we, the non-Ukrainians, were at a definite disadvantage. Not only were we guilty of eating inferior food, we were guilty of being unenlightened enough to enjoy it. All argument to the contrary — that if it tasted good to us it was good — was to no avail. They, the Ukrainians, knew what real garlic sausage was and we did not.

More was at stake than a simple display of one-upmanship. M. had not only placed "his" category temporarily above "ours", he had intelligently and skillfully established a defence against the stereotyped charge that "Ukrainians" eat strange food. None of us could ever make such a statement in the presence of C. or M. and expect to get away with it, even in jest. Immediately we would be reminded that since we couldn't tell the difference between good and bad garlic sausage our opinions were of no value whatsoever.

The Establishment of Equivalence Between Categories

The kind of situation illustrated in the above example may seem trivial, but it is typical of much of the "ethnic" interaction which occurs between members of different categories. Each category has associated with it a stock list of positive and negative stereotypes. A member of category B can attack a member of category C with a negative stereotype attached to all C's. The member of C can then retaliate with a corresponding attack on B, a recital of C's alleged positive characteristics, or a demonstration of how C's so-called weaknesses are actually strengths. Such exchanges are usually carried out in a spirit of good-natured fun — which perhaps has roots in earlier patterns of ethnic tension. The jokes can continue for hours and be repeated again and again. But eventually a rough equivalence between B and C is established. More importantly, an agreement is reached that the assumed stereotypes of each category are not to be taken seriously. As when J. (of ultimate Finnish origin) demonstrates at a party how a "Finlander pulls up his socks": he drops his trousers, pulls up his socks, and then puts his pants back on.

In Crow Lake, ethnic joking is essentially concerned with stereotypes, and it is significant that members of all ethnic categories have learned the stereotypes associated with other categories. An older, first generation Ukrainian woman, for example, stated one day that she thought well of the Dutch:

> Very clean people, very clean. I worked with a Dutch woman once in the hotel. Very clean, she always wanted everything to be so clean.

Interestingly, Mrs. Simcoe made a very similar observation about the Dutch in southern Ontario. In 1792 she wrote in her diary:

> Wed., June 27th — We passed Captain Duncan's house before we came to the Rapid Plat. — His wife is a Dutch woman and the house is excessively clean and neat.

> Thurs., June 28 — There are many Dutch and German farmers about here, whose houses and grounds have a neater and better appearance than those of any other people. (Robertson 1934:104-5)

The point is not that the Dutch are or are not "excessively clean and neat". Members of all ethnic categories in Crow Lake are familiar with the positive and negative stereotypes generally associated with many different ethnic categories. All are thus able to participate in ethnic banter — distributing insults and praise across a broad spectrum of ethnic affiliation.

Most core ethnics in Crow Lake are first generation immigrants and most peripheral and name ethnics are second and third generation respectively. The distinction should be made, however, between ethnic generation and chronological generation. Ethnic generation concerns the time of entrance into North America, while chronological generation refers to one's relative age in the age structure of the community. In this regard, the following may prove interesting.

The case concerns two families of the same ethnic category. Both families were founded by members born in the same specific European country. One, however, arrived in Crow Lake much earlier than the other. The first man immigrated to Canada in 1909 and into Crow Lake in 1914. The second immigrated to Crow Lake with his wife and young children in 1952.

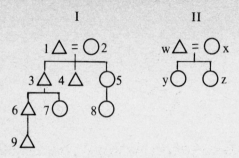

The details of the kin structure are not pertinent here. But it is important to note that the ethnic and chronological generations of the two families are not congruent.

Ethnic Generation

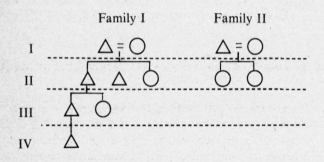

Chronological Generation

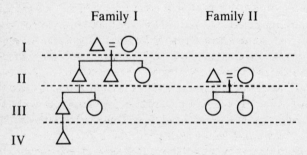

In terms of ethnic generation the distribution of persons is as follows:

1st	2nd	3rd	4th
1, (2) W, X	3, 4, 5, Y, Z,	6, 7, 8	9

But in terms of chronological generation the distribution of persons is significantly different:

1st	2nd	3rd	4th
1, (2)	3, 4, 5,	6, 7, 8,	9
	W, X	Y, Z	

W and X are of the same *ethnic* generation as 1 and 2, but they are of the same *chronological* generation as 3, 4, and 5. Ethnic and chronological generations do tend to correspond within a family, but it is significant that they do not necessarily correspond between families. W and X, who are core ethnics, are of the approximate ages of 3, 4, and 5, who are peripheral ethnics at best and are, more importantly, well established and respected in the community. Similarities in age and, to a lesser extent, origin unite them, and they are all friendly with each other. Adverse comments about the specific ethnicity of W or X would thus immediately become comments about 3, 4, and 5 as well.

The Ethnic Dimension as a Secondary Social Dimension Among Non-Natives in Crow Lake

It can be argued that ethnicity in the community is at once real and spurious. All people are considered "ethnics" in some sense, and whether core, peripheral, or name ethnics are placed within the same ethnic category system.

In the case of the two families analyzed above, comments about their ethnic category would refer to all members of both families. But in the community such comments cannot have general validity as it is obvious that the representatives of the category vary greatly in terms of occupation, background, age, income, and social position. Social networks are in fact formed more on the basis of common age than on common ethnic background. The overall process tends to be one in which name and peripheral ethnics mediate the image and position of core ethnics and the ethnic category as a whole. Negative stereotypes are continually contradicted by the reality of the situation in the community. Each major ethnic category is thus able to defend itself against the ideological allegations of members of every other category. This attack and defence and counterattack occurs constantly.

Ethnicity is now recognized not as the major factor in a person's identity, but as one factor among many. Because name and peripheral ethnics are, at best, only "part-time" ethnics culturally, the perception of one's ethnic dimension depends directly upon the definition of the situation at any given moment. Although ethnicity forms the basis for a system of social categories, it is not the core of a central and definitive system of social categories. The earlier congruence between occupation, ethnicity, and social class in

Crow Lake has declined progressively as the railroad ceased to be *the* single economic base of the settlement. This means today that W and X, although core ethnics, do not have to live in a certain part of town or earn a certain amount of money working at an established type of job. A statement of one's ethnic affiliation is no longer a statement of one's position in various occupational, educational, residential, or social class hierarchies.

Society in Crow Lake, though still ethnically mixed, is not a plural society in Furnivall's initial and classical use of the term. It is not a society in which "distinct social orders live side by side but separately within the same political unit", and where "the various sectors meet in the market. The highest common denominator of their wants is the economic factor." (1944:446, 449.)

A kind of "mosaic" may still be said to exist in Crow Lake but a different one from the somewhat romantic image conjured up by the term "Canadian Mosaic". The process of cultural assimilation has succeeded in blurring real ethnic distinctions while leaving the distinctions themselves extant as a system of social identities.

This proposition can be less easily proved than illustrated. In a sample of two distinct work groups, for example, the following ethnic mixture was observed:

Work Group I

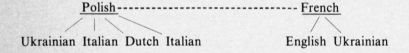

Work Group II

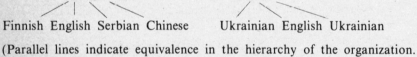

(Parallel lines indicate equivalence in the hierarchy of the organization. Descending lines indicate authority.)

In an illustration of segments of the personal networks of two people, a similar mixed pattern emerges. These were action sets in Mayer's (1966) use of the term. A certain activity was initiated by Ego. He then called friends and relatives who, in turn, contacted others. Solid lines from Ego indicate a direct invitation to the activity while dotted lines indicate an indirect invitation from people contacted directly by Ego.

I

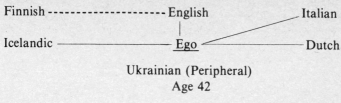

Ukrainian (Peripheral)
Age 42

II

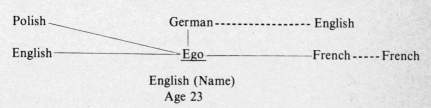

English (Name)
Age 23

And finally, in a sample of over one hundred marriages classified in time one finds:

Time Period	Number of Marriages	Intra-ethnic	Inter-ethnic
1913-1927	27	21	6
1927-1935	28	13	15
1936-1946	26	8	18
1959-1965	29	9	20

Classification of what was intra-and inter-ethnic marriage was made at a relatively high level in the conceptual system of ethnicity in Crow Lake: e.g., marriages between Poles and Ukrainians were considered to be intra-ethnic marriages. Marriages between Poles and Italians were considered to be inter-ethnic.

This increasing pattern of inter-marriage is significant. It adds to the evidence indicating that ethnicity, as a quality or attribute of community life, is apparent but no longer central among the non-Native sector of Crow Lake's population.

REFERENCES

Barth, Fredrik, *Ethnic Groups and Boundaries,* Boston: Little, Brown & Co., 1969.

Furnivall, John S., *Netherlands India: a Study of Plural Economy,* Cambridge: The University Press, 1939.

Robertson, J. Ross (ed.) *The Diary of Mrs. John Graves Simcoe,* Toronto: The Ontario Publishing Company, 1934.

Turner, Victor, *Schism and Continuity in an African Society,* Manchester: Manchester University Press, 1957.

Chapter 3

Divergent Patterns of Intergroup Living*

Chester L. Hunt and Lewis Walker

One of the paradoxical aspects of our times is that, even as improvements in communication and transportation make a world community conceivable and national sovereignty almost an anachronism, we have counter-movements which would divide up existing states and would multiply the number of units trying to perpetuate national sovereignty in an increasingly interdependent world. The argument seems plausible that our existing national units serve to fragment a world in which scientific endeavor is creating the potential basis for a world society. On the other hand, spokesmen for minority groups protest that their identity is threatened by forced incorporation within a larger state.

Complaints of the minorities — i.e., distinguishable groups that receive unequal and differential treatment — may be classified under two headings: (1) discrimination against the individuals of the minority group in favor of members of the majority groups and (2) threats to the validity and viability of the minority culture. Such problems form a basic component of many of the battles recorded in world history for several millennia, but probably have become more salient with the breakup of empires and the rise of nation states. The latter trend culminated in the process described by the late

*Abridged from *Ethnic Dynamics* (2nd edition), Holmes Beach: Learning Publications, 1978, by permission of the authors and the publisher.

American president, Woodrow Wilson, as "the self-determination of peoples."[1] Presumably the implication of Wilson's statement is that every group which considers itself a "people" should have the right to decide its own form of territorial and governmental organization. When the Ottoman and Hapsburg empires met defeat in World War I, it was taken for granted that their realms should be broken up rather than reconstituted, since they included a number of "nations" which had unwillingly been placed under a single government. Thus the Hapsburg Empire shrank to tiny Austria, and the Ottoman Empire to the nation of Turkey, while the rest of their territories were carved up into separate and independent states.

The process did not stop with the dissolution of the Hapsburg and Ottoman Empires, and the question of whether and how minorities can survive as parts of larger units is a live issue everywhere in the world today. In the United States, some blacks have despaired of the possibility (and perhaps the desirability) of real integration in American society and call for the erection of the "Republic of New Africa" on American soil. In Northern Ireland, the Protestant attempt to retain a portion of the island where they can be free from Catholic rule has led to charges of Protestant oppression of the Catholic minority. In Belgium there is a question whether it is really practical for Walloons and Flemish to try to coexist under the same governmental regime. In Nigeria, as well as in many other countries of Africa, the issue is whether or not several ethnically distinct groupings — tribes, "peoples", incipient nationalities — can be contained within the boundaries of a single state.

In many countries of the world, there are small minorities that have been strikingly successful in commerce and trade but are now threatened with expulsion from the countries which have become their home. In the Soviet Union, Communist theorists tried to construct a system which would combine specific ethnic identity with loyalty to an overall Communist regime. In the Republic of South Africa, few men are optimistic about the chances of constructing any type of arrangement by which blacks and whites can live in peace and harmony. One might find similar problems in nearly every country in the world.

Ethnicity and Social Structure

[Our] goal is to examine a number of such intergroup situations, and to determine whether each case is unique and specific or whether certain principles operate in many situations. In making this type of a survey, the focus will be on ethnicity rather than race per se and on patterns of social structure rather than on unique individual relationships or psychological perspectives.

Now a word as to what is meant by these terms. Our definition of ethnicity is taken from Gordon.[2] Gordon's definition is based on the American situation, but appears to have a wider applicability:

When I use the term "ethnic group," I shall mean by it any group which is defined or set off by race, religion, or national origin, or some combination of these categories. I do not mean to imply that these three concepts mean the same thing. They do not. Race, technically, refers to differential concentrations of gene frequencies responsible for traits which, so far as we know, are confined to physical manifestations such as skin color or hair form; it has no intrinsic connection with cultural patterns and institutions. Religion and national origins, while both cultural phenomena, are distinctly different institutions which do not necessarily vary concomitantly. However, all of these categories have a common social-psychological referent, in that all of them serve to create, through historical circumstances, a sense of peoplehood.[3]

This highly inclusive definition simply says that there are a number of factors which lead people to consider themselves (and to be considered by others) as an ethnic group. An ethnic group is a collection of people whose membership is largely determined by ancestry and which regards its place in society as being affected by its ethnicity. Thus the test of differences in physical appearance (frequently referred to as racial), national origin, or religion is not the difference per se, but whether this difference is considered socially significant. Some societies will disregard a rather wide range of differences in physical appearance, while others will relate social privileges to rather minute types of variations. Likewise, some societies will be greatly concerned about the national (or tribal) origins of the people in a given territory, while, to other societies, this will be a matter of indifference. Finally, religious diversity may simply indicate a variation in the interpretation of ultimate reality by various groups within the nation, or it may constitute a rigid dividing line which affects practically every phase of life. Sometimes ethnic differences are based upon a variation in all three of the criteria, physical appearance, national origin and religion; sometimes, upon one or two. In any case, what matters is not the nature of the difference, but the intensity of feeling about the importance of the difference, and the way in which this difference is associated with economic stratification, political power, and other elements of social structure.

Intergroup conflicts along racial lines have been so prominent in recent years that sometimes the term *race relations* is viewed as a synonym for *intergroup relations.* Since this is not the viewpoint of this particular book, some elaboration may be in order. If *race relations* were a synonym for *intergroup relations,* one would expect to find harmony in any society which is racially homogenous and conflict in any society which is racially heterogeneous. A brief look at the world indicates that such a proposition will hardly stand close examination. It is true that there are many cases of racial conflict, but it is also true that there are examples of conflict among those who are members of the same race. In Africa, one looking for social conflict would find it in the fierce warfare between Arabs and black Africans in the Sudan or in the seething discontent which pervades racial relationships in the Republic of South Africa. However, one would also find that one of the bloodiest civil wars of recent decades took place in Nigeria, while the combatants, although separated by ethnic affiliations, were all members of the Negroid race. Again, in Ireland or in Belgium, one would find Caucasians of similar appearance assailing each other with considerable bittterness.

Admittedly, the reverse cases, in which people who are racially different live together in a fair degree of peace and harmony, are more difficult to find. There are, however, some examples which can be cited. One could, for instance, point to the relatively harmonious and cooperative relationships existing between the British and black Africans in Northern Nigeria. Race relationships on the mainland of the United States have often been difficult but, in Hawaii, Caucasians, Polynesians, and Orientals have lived together in relative tranquility. Similarly, the "colored" inhabitants of Martinique and Guadeloupe seem to be happy with incorporation in the predominantly Caucasian French nation. Such examples are rare and may represent changing situations, but they do indicate that major friction between racial groups is not inevitable. Racial differences do frequently form lines along which intergroup conflict occurs. This pattern, however, is not always present, and there are many cases in which equally bitter conflict may occur among members of the same race.

It may be argued that racial differences, since they are rooted in physical heredity, are more durable than differences based on nationality, regional origin, or religious affiliation. This seems to be a self-evident truth, but the evidence in its favor is somewhat less than overwhelming. Those who assume that genetic heredity is a constant, forget that sexual attraction operates across racial lines and may largely replace the original peoples with a new hybrid strain. Mexico, where the majority of the populace are classed as mestizo, is a case in point. On the other hand, groups with a high degree of phenotypical similarity, such as the Flemish and Walloons in Belgium, have preserved a separate identity for centuries. In sum, groups whose identity is based on cultural distinctiveness sometimes survive for long periods, while groups identified by distinctive physical characteristics may diminish or even disappear.

Since there are no specific types of patterns which are associated with differences in race, as contrasted to religious, regional, or nationality differences, it seems best to place all types of fairly durable socially significant classifications under the ethnic rubric. However, not all authorities in the field are happy with this use of the term ethnic, and where the authorities whom we cite speak of *nationality,* or *regional, tribal, religious,* or *racial* differences, we shall follow their usage in our discussion.

Voluminous literature has appeared dealing with the psychodynamics of prejudices which grow out of ethnic conflict. There seems little doubt that our perception of the attitudes and actions of other individuals is shaped to a great degree by our respective ethnic affiliations. This ethnic stereotyping serves to justify the attitudes of our own group and to invalidate the attitudes or demands of other groups. It represents what Gunnar Myrdal referred to as "beliefs with a purpose."[4] There are also psychological problems which hinge on the relation between self-concept and group pride. These important problems having to do with individuals and individual attitudes, however, are not a major topic of concern in this volume, rather we are concerned with systems of group behaviour or, in other words, relationships in social structure. It is assumed, for present purposes, that psychological processes may be viewed as constants which operate in all types of human relationships. However, there are some patterns of relations between groups which appear, at least for the time being, to have produced a tolerable situation for all concerned, while there are other patterns in which severe conflict appears to be endemic.

The best description we have seen of social patterns is found in Gordon's discussion of social structure. Like many other terms used by sociologists, social structure has a variety of meanings, but its use in the present context is indicated by the following statement:

> By the social structure of a society we mean the set of crystallized social relationships which its members have with each other which places them in groups, large or small, permanent or temporary, formally organized or unorganized, and which relates them to the major institutional activities of the society, such as economic and occupational life, religion, marriage and the family, education, government, and recreation. . . . It is a large definition but a consistent one in that it focuses on *social relationships,* and social relationships that are *crystallized* — that is, which are not simply occasional and capricious but have a pattern of some repetition and can to some degree be predicted, and are based, at least to some extent, on a set of shared expectations.[5]

Perhaps one concrete example might indicate the significance of social structure. Blacks and whites in the United States frequently react psychologically to each other. This interaction results in stereotypes, prejudices, racially tinged notions of the self concept, and numerous other behavior patterns and attitudes which have been classified by psychologists and social psychologists. No study of American race relationships, however, can ignore the differences which came with one massive change in social structure — the shift from slavery to emancipation. Undoubtedly, many of the psychological processes operating during slavery have continued afterwards, but certainly the nature of race relations in the United States was drastically changed when blacks moved from the category of slaves to that of citizens.

To take another example, people of French ancestry and people of British ancestry interact in ways which produce various psychological reactions to the French or British labels that are probably somewhat similar in a great many circumstances, but French and British differences are far more salient in Canada, under a social system which maximizes their significance, than in the United States under a system which minimizes the importance of national ancestry.

Social Structural Patterns

As with most other types of sociological classification, there is no "right" number of classifications which is inherent in the nature of the phenomena.

The number of such classifications inevitably varies with the viewpoint of the writer and with the criteria which he uses. For our purposes, three main headings would seem to be adequate. These are segregation, cultural pluralism, and integration. These structural patterns are "ideal types" which are never found in their pure form in the real world. Indeed, Max Weber,[6] who is generally credited with developing the concept of the ideal type, argued that social scientists should even exaggerate significant features of social reality rather than describe them with photographic accuracy. The justification for this procedure is that thereby salient aspects of social life are brought inescapably to our attention for purposes of analysis. Admittedly the patterns of social structure we have mentioned will never be found in a form which is identical with their definitions. In spite of such disparity between these social structural patterns and reality, they are still of value if they direct our attention to significant features of intergroup relations.

Segregation. The segregated society is one in which contacts between various groups are restricted by law, by custom, or by both. It is assumed that the group differences, whether cultural or biological, are permanent in nature and determine one's total social role. The segregated society is organized on terms agreeable to the dominant ethnic group. This pattern is based on the premise that individuals have few rights apart from their ethnic group and that ethnic groups are unequal. Members of subordinate ethnic groups are allowed to engage only in the type of activities which are seen as contributing to the interests of the dominant group.

Cultural Pluralism. Cultural pluralism is similar to segregation in that a variety of cultures continue to exist in the society. It differs from segregation in the degree to which the dominance of any one ethnic group is recognized. In a situation of cultural pluralism all groups, theoretically, have equal rights. It is a system which flourishes best when each ethnic group in a society has a specific territory in which it is a numerical majority and when there is at least an approximate equality of economic development between groups. When there is a marked overlapping of territorial ethnicity or when there is a marked divergence of economic development, there are likely to be fears for group survival and charges of discrimination.

Internal peace in a nation which espouses cultural pluralism is facilitated when the various territorial districts of the nation at least approximate ethnic homogeneity. Such a situation makes it possible for the ethnic group to follow its own way of life without being harassed by either cultural competition or charges of discrimination against other ethnic groups. However, even territorial homogeneity may not eliminate conflict about economic discrimination. Territories are likely to be unequal in resources or in economic development, or in both, with the result that per capita incomes in the richer district may be several times those in the poorer. Even socialism is little help in avoiding this kind of disparity, since a poor territory cannot bring up low per capita incomes by redistributing nonexistent revenues. Consequently, the poorer territory will demand that the national government bring about economic parity between the regions and that it do this without giving "alien" (nonethnic) experts control over the depressed territories.

Acquiescence to such demands requires not only that the more prosperous regionally based ethnic groups share the wealth with ethnically distinguishable fellow countrymen but that in giving aid they limit the use of the most competent personnel in order to avoid charges of "internal colonialism." In addition to demanding a rare type of magnanimity from the wealthier ethnic groups such a decision also poses a dilemma for the national government — the choice between the most rapid economic development and the amelioration of the needy districts. Revenues are always in short supply and the national authorities usually desire to maximize the growth of the gross national product. Usually the already prosperous districts are best equipped to make use of additional investment, and it is here that scarce capital will yield the greatest return. A decision on this basis may be criticized as shortsighted, but demands on revenues are always greater than resources, and if the national government accepts a slower rate of overall economic growth it is even less able to help develop the poorer regions. On the other hand, if its developmental efforts are focused on the richer regions, the gap between them and the poorer areas will increase and the discontent of the less prosperous ethnic groups will grow. Problems of this type have emerged in most nations which follow patterns of cultural pluralism. Experience indicates that, while peaceful reconciliation of the economic demands of regionally based ethnic groups may not be an impossible task, it is certainly a difficult one.

A basic premise of cultural pluralism is that there is no need to sacrifice ethnic identity. Switzerland is frequently offered as a classic example of cultural pluralism. It is a nation characterized by a diversity of religion and national origin and by the complete absence of any one tongue which may be classified as the "Swiss language." Swiss are divided by national origin, religious affiliation, and language of common usage, and yet are united in their devotion to a Swiss nation which transcends these ethnic characteristics. There are few nations in which the path of cultural pluralism has been as tranquil as that of Switzerland or where differing ethnic identities could be combined with a common national loyalty with such apparent success. In fact, even the Swiss have at times had difficulty in maintaining this type of structure.

In spite of its difficulties, cultural pluralism is an attractive pattern, as it offers the hope of combining the preservation of ethnic distinctiveness with the advantages of coordination in a larger state.

Integration. Integration may be defined as a situation in which all citizens of the nation, or possibly even all members of the society regardless of citizenship, participate freely in all forms of social interaction without concern for ethnic affiliation. Integration differs from cultural pluralism in that it is not concerned with group privileges but with the rights of individuals. The integrated society is not directly concerned with ethnic group equality, inequality, survival, or disappearance. Its legal and social structure is not concerned with ethnicity. If ethnic groups survive this is because of the cumulative effect of individual choices rather than because of governmental guarantees to protect ethnically based institutions or privileges.

Integration differs from both cultural pluralism and segregation in that ethnic affiliation loses its salience in the social structure. The integrated nation may allow for some degree of cultural diversity, such as the toleration of religious differences in the United States, but its basic premise is a denial of any social obligation to preserve ethnic distinctions. Efforts to preserve special privileges on the basis of ethnicity are seen as a denial of integration and as an injustice to other ethnic groups. Likewise, efforts to preserve distinctive minority cultures tend to be regarded as separatist and divisive.

Minorities sometimes view this lack of protection for their cultures as tyranny, especially when their children are compelled to attend a school system which functions in terms of the majority culture. Some of the more cohesive and isolated minorities, such as the Amish and the stronger American Indian tribes, may succeed in maintaining a distinctive culture, but the general trend is toward homogenization. In the United States, this has meant the acceptance of a high degree of "Anglo-conformity"[7] which is most vividly seen in the dominance of the English language.

The philosophy of integration implies that individual frustrations will not furnish the basis for the development of ethnic grievances because salient attachment to the ethnic group has disappeared. This, however, is a process which, at best, takes a period of time and in the case of groups with distinctive physical traits or tenaciously held cultural patterns may never occur.

The question as to the extent to which integration is dependent on assimilation is illuminated by the distinction which Gordon makes between cultural and structural assimilation.[8] Cultural assimilation is seen as one of the subprocesses whereby members of the "guest" group become acculturated to the cultural patterns of the "host" society; in religion, for instance. General attitudes also come under the heading of cultural assimilation, and their direction influences the pace of structural assimilation even though not necessarily on a one to one ratio. Structural assimilation involves interaction at the primary group level between members of the "host" society and those of the "guest" group, i.e., widespread patterns of face-to-face relationships in clubs, organizations, and institutions of the "host" society.

Cultural assimilation threatens ethnic identity, but does not necessarily destroy it. Some individuals, for instance, may have largely forgotten their ancestral culture but yet restrict their group participation to those of their own ethnic background — or they may be excluded by those who claim ancestry which is either more prestigious or has been longer in the country. In other circumstances, structural assimilation, even including marriage, may occur before cultural assimilation is far advanced. In sum, assimilation is the basis of an integrated society, but assimilation is often incomplete and may not move at an equal rate at the structural and the cultural level.

We attempt to focus on patterns and hence on social structure rather than on attitudes, but attitudes and actions always interact and this is especially true in an integrated society. This interaction between attitudes and action patterns is the key to the understanding of Kenneth Clark's insistence on the difference between desegregation and integration.[9] Desegregation is the term applied to the removal of legal barriers which enforce ethnic segregation. Integration requires removal not only of legal barriers, but also of the prejudiced attitudes and social pressures which maintain ethnic barriers even after legal restrictions have been eliminated.

Gordon describes integration in terms of a social structural situation which would be impossible to approximate without the attitudinal changes which come from a lessening of prejudice:

> in social structural terms, integration presupposes the elimination of hard and fast barriers in the primary group relations and communal life of the various ethnic groups of the nation. It involves easy and fluid mixture of peoples of diverse racial, religious, and nationality backgrounds in social cliques, families (i.e., inter-marriage), private organizations and intimate friendships.[10]

Integration even approximating this description is certainly rare and thus (like the other patterns that we have considered), represents an "ideal type" rather than an actual situation. Nevertheless, the insistence that the individual, rather than the ethnic group, should be the focus of social and legal concern is a pattern with continuing appeal. . . .

Ethnic Patterns and the Drive for Equality

Since there are no national states without some variety of ethnic identification, the rejection of ethnic group rights in favor of individual rights appears to occur only when men feel either that their ethnic background is no handicap in the competition for success or that they can easily leave their ethnic identity and "pass" into the more favored group. Moreover, if the members of an ethnic group are doing well individually, the group as a whole achieves a higher status; conversely, the group is placed at a lower level if the proportion of individuals who are successful is low. Thus, the concept of "equal rights" merges into the demand for ethnic as well as individual social and economic equality.

While the structures which a segregated society erects to maintain the supremacy of the favored group are easy to recognize, it is much more difficult to delineate those which make for equality. Not only is true equality difficult to obtain, it is even hard to define the conditions under which true equality may be said to exist. Does true equality, for instance, mean equality before the law? Does it mean equality of opportunity? Does it mean equality of achievement? Does true equality assume that the various groups will be equally distributed in all areas of the nation's life, or are the demands for equality satisfied when the domains in which the members of different ethnic categories participate are different but considered approximately equal? In other words, does equality imply proportionate ethnic representation in every occupation? If some groups are underrepresented are others overrepresented?

It is seldom, if ever, true that all groups in a society will agree that true equality exists. For the segregationist this is not much of a problem, since he is ideologically committed to maintaining the superiority of his ethnic group. Even the segregationist, however, will speak of the benefits which his rule brings to the subordinate ethnic groups and will compare their situation with allegedly more unfavorable conditions elsewhere. Cultural pluralists find that absolute ethnic self-determination is frequently compromised by a national drive to eliminate or minimize inequality between regions. Integrationists shift the focus from the group to the individual, but, if many individuals identified with an ethnic group feel that society is unfair, then the whole structure of integration is in danger. Even though equality may be hard either to achieve or to define the drive for it is a constant factor in any pattern of ethnic relationships.

Ethnic Patterns in Operation

We said earlier that our structured patterns of ethnic behavior are "ideal types" never found in their pure form in the real world. Even though there is no perfect replication of the conditions implied in the definition, however, some countries do illustrate to some degree the patterns described. Any example may be faulted on the grounds of imperfect representation of the ideal type, but it is still from an examination of living societies that such concepts emerge as aids to social analysis. For this reason, we have taken a variety of societies which, to some extent, represent the types we have listed. Through an examination of these societies we may expect to gain further insight into the problems which arise under various patterns of intergroup relationships and, conversely, into the factors which contribute to the stability of these patterns.

INTEGRATION

Integration assumes that the problem of ethnic group conflict is solved through the adoption of a common identity and the disappearance of separate ethnic interests. To cite an example previously mentioned — if people cease to identify themselves as French and British, as has happened with the longtime descendants of these groups in the United States, then we may expect that there will be no conflict which runs along the lines of separate French and British identification. Integration, in other words, solves group conflict through the merger of separate groups into a common whole. Such a process is not necessarily inconsistent with a lingering consciousness of a distinct ethnic subcultural identity, but it assumes that such identity will be chiefly one of historical identification which does not have any great significance in terms of present interest.

Integration assumes a high amount of cultural assimilation such as the adoption of a common language and a considerable consensus on basic values and standards. Sharp cultural differences obviously tend to provide lines along which conflict can emerge and therefore appear to be inconsistent with effective integration.

A real question is whether the same observation applies to biological differences; that is, whether there can be a national unity along lines of integration in a nation which preserves two or more groups differing rather sharply in physical appearances. Two nations which appear, to a large extent, to have adopted the path of integration have followed different practices in this matter. In the United States, there has been widespread intermarriage between those of European ancestry; this has tended to bring about a biological as well as a cultural unification of the Caucasian population. Such intermarriage has occurred to a lesser degree between blacks and whites. One estimate is that as many as 21 percent of the Caucasian population of the United States may have some black ancestry and that perhaps as many as three fourths of blacks have some degree of white ancestry.[11] Most of this intermixture, however, apparently occurred during the days of slavery and the years immediately following Emancipation. At any rate, at the present time, in spite of a small number of people who may "pass" from one race to another, the majority of people in the United States can be rather easily categorized as white or nonwhite, and this situation does not appear to be changing with any degree of rapidity.

In Mexico, on the other hand, intermarriage has been so widespread that a mestizo population is dominant both numerically and socially. The black population has practically disappeared and pure Indians and pure whites constitute only a small minority. Thus Mexico represents a pattern of integration which includes both racial amalgamation (biological intermixture) and cultural assimilation, while in the United States amalgamation has not been pervasive enough to eliminate or greatly diminish recognizable racial categories.

SEGREGATION

Segregation, or a separation of racial groups by both law and custom, was for a long time the unchallenged practice in the southern part of the United States. In the 1970s it has been more starkly represented in the Union of South Africa and in Rhodesia than in other countries. In the United States, segregation was a part of the tactics used by white supremacists to overturn the reconstruction government after the Civil War. Between 1880 and 1910, laws were passed in many southern states ordering the separation of white and black in schools, libraries, restaurants, public transportation, and, in general, prohibiting the common use of any type of facilities when this use might imply an equality of the races.[12]

These practices of segregation were practically unchallenged until the 1950s, when a series of court decisions pronounced legalized segregation unconstitutional. At the same time, both in many state legislatures and in the national Congress, civil rights laws were passed which sought to outlaw segregation and discrimination in all the areas where, in a previous era, the law had commanded that segregation should be the practice. For some time, these laws and court decisions were largely formal procedures with little effect on day-to-day living and the practices of segregation which had been outlawed by judicial decisions continued to be the normal pattern in many communities. During the late 1950s and early 1960s, however, several forces narrowed the gap between theory and practice in a way that brought about significant change in black and white relationships. More effective enforcement of civil rights laws made it apparent that segregation placed one outside the legal order. Additional lawsuits by the NAACP (National Association for the Advancement of Colored People) produced additional court decisions which made it abundantly clear that no legal technicalities would be allowed to thwart the move toward equal rights. Finally, the demonstrations led by the Reverend Martin Luther King, Jr., dramatized the issue and gave evidence of mass support for the ideal of a desegregated society. By the end of the 1960s, formal public separation of the races in the use of public facilities had ceased to exist.

This does not mean that there is no longer separation between the races in the United States. Mutual suspicion and unfamiliarity of black and white do not vanish overnight. Many people will continue to pursue traditional patterns even though the force of both law and custom that support these patterns has been greatly weakened.

Nor have all of the events of social life reinforced the decision of the courts and legislatures in discouraging racial separation. In the cities two types of migratory movements have brought an actual increase in separate racial housing. The first movement is the migration of whites from the central cities to the suburbs, and the other movement is a massive black urban migration. The combined effect of these two population movements has made many central cities largely black in population. This development has been accompanied by a more critical attitude on the part of many blacks toward policies of integration and the adoption by some blacks of a separatist philosophy.

In spite of all the reservations which must be made, it still remains true that the general course of events in the United States since 1950 has been away from segregation. Formal legal rules requiring segregation have been scrapped in all cases, and all types of activities in which joint participation was once taboo are, to some extent, now the scene of integrated activity.

In the Republic of South Africa events have taken an exactly opposite course. When the Nationalist Party acquired control of South Africa in 1948, it adopted a formal stated policy to eliminate every possible vestige of integration and to make segregation the rule and practice as far as possible in South African life. To most observers, South Africa would already have seemed a segregated society before this time, but the aim of the Nationalists was to make segregation complete and total. South Africa has evolved an elaborate system of racial classification whereby people are issued cards indicating the racial category in which they belong. All political rights have been denied the nonwhite population, and hundreds of thousands of black Africans have been forcibly removed from supposedly white areas.

There are two major questions in the South African situation. One is how long a segregationist regime can be maintained by whites who are a minority of around 20 percent inside the Republic of South Africa, are a still smaller minority in the continent of Africa, and, in addition, are condemned by the bulk of world opinion. Another question is the viability of a program of segregation in a country with a rapidly growing economy where the demand for skilled personnel is beyond that which can be supplied by the white population. In any event, the Republic of South Africa and, to a slightly lesser extent, Rhodesia offer a case study of the results of the efforts to maintain segregation in a modernizing society.

CULTURAL PLURALISM

Cultural pluralism, according to Hoult, is "the doctrine that society benefits when it is made up of a number of interdependent ethnic groups, each of which maintains a degree of autonomy."[13] As we added earlier, this implies, in contrast to segregation, some degree of equality. Admittedly, though, it is seldom, if ever, true that all the various groups feel that they have equal privileges in the society. Under cultural pluralism, however, group relationships are so ordered that the extremes of inequality found in segregation are avoided and each group feels that it is gaining some benefit from association in the common society.

It should be added that such a feeling is not necessarily unanimous in any group and that it does not preclude the existence of extremists who feel that the sacrifices demanded by membership in a common society are so great that the group itself should secede and form a separate entity. The term cultural pluralism used in this way covers a wide and varied number of social patterns. In addition to Belgium, Switzerland, the Soviet Union, and Yugoslavia in Europe, there are examples in other continents. Canada, Malaya, and possibly Brazil could be so classified. There are also several African countries which have diverse, and apparently persisting, ethnic groups. So far, however, it is unclear whether the African trend is toward cultural pluralism or toward integrated societies based on assimilation to core cultures.

One of the most successful examples of cultural pluralism is the Republic of Switzerland. It is based on an arrangement whereby Swiss of Protestant or

Catholic religious beliefs and of German, French, and Italian descent live in districts which are, to a great extent, ethnically homogeneous, but which are united in a federal republic that proclaims a respect for the cultures of all its ethnic groups without insisting on the dominance of any.

Much more difficult and conflictive than the Swiss experience is that of the Kingdom of Belgium and the district of Northern Ireland. Both are examples of a situation in which a partition had been accepted in the efforts to end conflict through arrangement of territories in which, supposedly, ethnic conflict could be escaped. Belgium was a result of the division of an area which, at one time, embraced both the largely Protestant Netherlands and largely Catholic Belgium. Partition did, it is true, create a Belgium which is homogeneous with respect to religion but which included two national groups, the Flemish and the Walloons, who have lived together in a decidely uneasy relationship since that time. Northern Ireland was created at the time of the formation of the Irish Free State and was divided from the rest of the island in order to form an enclave in which Protestants might be free from Catholic rule. This partition did create an area in which Protestants were the majority, but it included a substantial Roman Catholic minority who came to resent bitterly what they regarded as classification as second-class citizens. Both Belgium and Northern Ireland may be regarded as examples of countries in which democratic cultural pluralism has seemingly failed to develop a society satisfactory to the contending groups.

The largest European country in which cultural pluralism is the official state policy is the Soviet Union. During the time of the Czars, the Russian government regarded the non-Russian minorities in the country as a menace to national unity. The government's answer to this problem was a program of forced assimilation known as "Russification." This program brought resentment and hostility from the minority groups, which constituted about half of the population of the empire, without producing the cultural assimilation sought. When the Communists came to power, in 1917, they denounced the Czarist regime as a "prison of the peoples" and announced a policy of cultural freedom for all the ethnic groups in the area. As a result, varied political units based on ethnic lines were developed which were subordinate to Moscow politically and economically, and which were not only allowed, but encouraged, to develop the language and arts indigenous to the particular culture. The Communists had proclaimed that ethnic conflict is the result of capitalistic oppression and would be absent in a socialist state. Thus an examination of intergroup relations in the Soviet Union may serve as a test case for examination of the hypothesis that ethnic quarrels are simply a manifestation of a capitalist social system.

Yugoslavia, although much smaller than the Soviet Union, also includes a variety of ethnic groups and has endeavored to maintain cultural pluralism through the establishment of "republics" constructed on ethnic lines. In Yugoslavia regional-ethnic autonomy has been carried into the economic field by a policy of decentralization which allowed individual enterprises controlled by workers' councils to make policy on wages and investment. The result has been a spurt of economic growth in the more industrialized regions, along with a growing gap between them and the agricultural areas.

The changing Yugoslav policies on centralism and local autonomy vividly illustrate the difficulty in maintaining a satisfactory pattern of cultural pluralism in a nation which has great differences in regional economic development. Two of the issues which emerge are (1) whether socialist equality implies equality between regions, and (2) whether a nation should submit to top-heavy centralized dictation in order to even out regional disparities. Along with the Soviet Union, the Yugoslav experience offers a case study of the opportunities and problems which arise when a noncapitalist, multi-ethnic state attempts to follow a policy of cultural pluralism.

The relations of the onetime colonial powers and their former subjects had elements of both integration and cultural pluralism. During the course of empire some degree of acculturation occurred, usually it was confined to a minority of the population who had the most intense interaction with the colonial power. There were, however, some cases in which the indigenous culture either was totally destroyed or survived only in small pockets and in which the postcolonial culture was an amalgam of the precolonial and the colonial cultures.

When the indigenous culture was not destroyed, there was usually at least a de facto cultural pluralism in which the colonial power conceded the legitimacy of some parts of the indigenous culture and social structure. After the withdrawal of colonial military suppression, the question still remained whether the inhabitants of the onetime colony should direct their major emphasis toward further assimilation of the culture of the "mother country" or should seek to strengthen what were regarded as indigenous cultural forms. This issue emerges sharply both in the newly independent countries and in those overseas territories which have chosen to retain their links with the imperial country. The assimilation of the colonial culture, incidentaly, does not necessarily predispose a country to forgo independence nor does a distinct culture necessarily dictate political separatism. Rather, the question seems to be whether the relationship between the two territories is regarded as inhibiting and stifling or as promoting the welfare of the inhabitants of the former colony. The empires were usually edifices maintained by force which were quickly destroyed as soon as a native elite developed a national consciousness. There are, however, some exceptions to this cycle of colonialism succeeded by nationalism and, consequently, by independence and separation from the imperial country. In the United States this can be seen in the case of Hawaii, in which the predominantly non-Caucasian people of a distant Pacific island have accepted statehood for Hawaii. A somewhat different example is also afforded by the Commonwealth of Puerto Rico, the majority of whose inhabitants prefer a link with the United States although there is a small and fervent independence party.

Hawaii would probably be considered an example of integration, with the various Oriental and Polynesian groups functioning as subcultures in which people acknowledge the necessity of conforming to an American core culture even as they struggle to maintain some elements of their traditional heritage.

In Puerto Rico, on the other hand, Spanish is still the language of basic education and a Latin culture coexists with Yankee practices and values. It is a somewhat uneasy kind of coexistence with many Puerto Ricans fearful that their political links with the United States may threaten Latin culture — a fear most vividly expressed in the independence party which, as yet, represents only a small minority of the island's people.

One of the most striking examples of a onetime colony which has expressed a preference for an organic relationship with the imperial country rather than independence is found in the case of Martinique and Guadeloupe. Martinique and Guadeloupe contrast rather sharply with the African territory of Senegal. Senegal was also the scene of an assimilative French colonial policy which attempted to bring Africans into a relationship with France in which French culture would be assimilated and French political ties accepted. The Senegalese, though, decided that, however strong the French influence might be, their real destiny lay in independence. Martinique and Guadeloupe are in the West Indies, and they also contrast sharply with other West Indian islands of roughly similar economic and ethnic attributes which had been under the British control and which opted for independence at the first opportunity.

Colonialism was one method of bringing other peoples under the rule of Europeans. Another method which, in a sense, accomplished the same objective was that of the migration from former colonies to European countries. During the colonial periods there was a small trickle of immigration from the colonies to France and Britain, and after the end of World War II this flow of immigrants from the former colonies sharply increased. Whatever their overseas policies, neither France nor Great Britain had a history of racial intolerance at home, and ethnocentric colonial attitudes were assumed to be historical anachronisms with no present viability. France and Britain were both inclined to look with some bewilderment at countries such as the United States in which racial prejudices and discrimination seemed rife. However, a sudden increase in their non-European population brought problems of many types.

Turning away from Europe, let us look at Africa, where the boundaries of most national states reflect the strategic or economic concerns of former colonial powers rather than African ethnic distinctions. Indeed, one of the main problems of several African states is the gross lack of corrrelation between political and ethnic boundary lines. Several ethnic groups commonly live within the same national boundary lines and yet also spread beyond the national limits. To mention only a few cases: Hausa- and Yoruba-speaking peoples are not confined to Nigeria, Swahili-speaking groups are found in several East African nations, and significant numbers of Somali comprise minority populations in Ethiopia and Kenya.

In discussing African populations, "tribalism" is often used as a term indicating any kind of ethnic distinction. The "tribe" may be a diffuse category of several million people with no common government, a cohesive band of a few hundred, or any number in between. Actually, Africa has had as great a variety of governmental entities as Europe. These include empires ruling diverse peoples, as in the case of the Egyptians, Ethiopians, and Songhai; collectivities often referred to as nations, such as the Zulu and the Ashanti; kingdoms comparable to smaller European states, such as Buganda or the six Hausa kingdoms; city states, several of which flourished among the Yoruba; along with thousands of small tribal units found throughout the continent. Colonialism paid little attention to any of these patterns and developed a network of territories with little relation to indigenous African ethnicity.

When independence movements developed in Africa the leaders generally accepted the boundary lines agreed upon by the European colonial powers. The result is that practically every country in Africa includes a number of ethnic groups, practicing different customs, speaking different languages, and following different religions. Often an ethnic group spread beyond the country's borders and its identification with any of the newly independent nations was weak. Similarly, there was frequently little sense of any common bond with other ethnic groups in the same country, a situation similar to that often found in Europe.

The leaders of African governments seek to foster a national consciousness which will supersede ethnic loyalties, but this is a different task. Ethnic rivalries were in fact, exacerbated by a differential assimilation of European culture. Some ethnic groups were heavily exposed to Western education and technology, while others followed a traditional pattern of life with little intrusion from the outside world. In Nigeria, competition between the highly westernized Ibo and Yoruba and conflict between both of them and the Hausa-Fulani stimulated dissension which erupted in a bloody civil war. It was a war watched with much anxiety by the rest of Africa. This anxiety was based partly upon sympathy and concern for the contending groups and also upon a fear that similar conflicts might erupt elsewhere from the pluralist ethnic basis on which all African nations were erected.

Africa is also one of the areas which saw the development of cultural pluralism on the basis of religious precepts. The expansion of Islamic territory from a tiny portion of the Middle East to North Africa, Asia, and Europe brought about a type of cultural pluralism which followed the precepts laid down in the Islamic law. This type of society found its most outstanding expression in the Ottoman Empire, which allowed the Turks to rule an area running in a sort of semicircle from Cairo to the Balkans for a period of over 500 years. It was an empire in which, although the political power was exercised by those of Turkish nationality, the basic distinction was between Muslims and those outside of the faith. Ideally the infidels would accept conversion, but, in practice, this did not always follow and some arrangements had to be made for the dissenting minority. In addition to considerations of expediency, tolerance of those who rejected the faith was justified on the ground that Christians and Jews were also "People of the Book" and therefore shared some elements of Islam.

The resulting accommodation was known as the *millet* system, in which each religious group was allowed to have autonomy in its own territory although required to pay tribute to the Muslim ruler. This system had nearly constant discontent, saw occasional massacres, and yet retained a degree of peace in an area of the world which, since the end of the Ottoman Empire, has often been involved in conflict.

Still another type of cultural pluralism is that in which ethnicity is rather sharply correlated with economic function. In societies of this type, it is common for a minority ethnic group to be successful in commercial undertakings which appear risky to the majority group. The social contribution of this minority group does not, however, serve to facilitate their acceptance by the majority. Usually they thrive best in a colonial regime in which the government is more concerned with economic development than with the ethnic identity of those engaged in economic activities. When independence occurs, the ethnic majority then sees the minority persons who constitute the commercial middle class as a group occupying economically profitable positions which should be held by members of the majority group.

Frequently there are legal provisions, such as ratification of the United Nations' Human Rights covenants or the extension of citizenship to non-indigenous inhabitants, which would seem to guarantee certain rights to the despised minority. These legal restrictions are usually broken or ignored while various governmental measures are taken to drive the "aliens" out of the economy and to replace them with indigenous inhabitants. Two situations which contrast sharply with respect to history and ethnic composition but which represent a somewhat similar experience in this regard are offered as test cases. These are the Indian minority in Kenya and the overseas Chinese minority in the Philippine Islands.

One might question placing these, and similar situations, under the rubric of cultural pluralism, since both the Indians in Kenya and the Chinese in the Philippines have suffered discrimination. Such discrimination conflicts with the previous statement that, in a situation of cultural pluralism, all groups, theoretically, have equal rights. In Kenya and the Philippines not only is there inequality, but also an unstable type of ethnic relationship, since it is possible that eventually discrimination may reach the point at which the minority is unable to function or is either massacred or deported. These are not just academic possibilities, but actions which have occurred in the past and could take place again. The Chinese in the Philippines had been nearly wiped out by massacres in previous centuries. In Kenya, after independence in 1963, thousands of Indians left the country fearing that they would be unable to make a living under the restrictions imposed by the Kenya government, and a few were actually deported. A similar Indian minority in Uganda has been deported en masse.

In addition to a preference for limiting the number of ethnic patterns we are using, there are three reasons for considering marginal trading peoples, such as the Indians in Kenya and the Chinese in the Philippines, as examples of cultural pluralism. First, there have been periods in the past when these commercially successful minorities did not experience discrimination to any great extent. Second, the majority refuses to acknowledge that the minority has suffered discrimination, since their average economic condition is usually better than that of the majority or dominant group. Finally, many societies face the question of determining their policy toward nonassimilable minorities which constitute marginal trading peoples. As mentioned earlier, our ethnic patterns are "ideal types" and there are no situations which fit the definitions perfectly. Since the marginal trading peoples have an identity which is expected to persist for a relatively long period, since they usually experience at least some intervals when they enjoy equal rights, since they often prosper to a greater extent than the majority in spite of discrimination and are found in countries both with and without formal discrimination, it seems justifiable to include them under the cultural pluralism rubric.

General Issues in Cultural Pluralism. An examination of these varied instances of cultural pluralism will raise many questions. For instance, is it possible for minority groups to be secure in a country in which democratic procedures allow the majority to take whatever repressive measures it sees fit? Related to this is the question whether a peaceful type of pluralism requires the acceptance by minorities of the dominance of one particular group which will serve as a core group in the society. An issue already mentioned is whether the course of intergroup adjustment is easier in a country in which the social ownership of the means of production has lessened the rivalries which are alleged to be inherent in a capitalist economy. A final question which occurs in all examples of cultural pluralism is the extent to which it is possible to maintain a separate ethnic identity while giving allegiance to a common society.

Conclusion

We have attempted to describe briefly the various patterns of intergroup relations and some of the results which occur in countries which attempt to follow them. In one sense, every experience is unique; in another sense, every human experience is an aspect of the universal situation. It may well be that we shall not only learn something about the factors involved in integration, segregation, and cultural pluralism, but that we shall also become aware of universal requirements which affect the course of human associations in all the varied patterns which may develop.

NOTES

[1]Woodrow Wilson, "Pueblo Speech on the League of Nations," ". . . the sacredness of the right of self-determination, the sacredness of the right of any body of people to say that they would not continue to live under the government they were then living under . . ." cited in the Staff of Social Sciences of the University of Chicago (eds.), *The People Shall Judge,* Chicago: University of Chicago Press, 1949, p. 387.

[2]Milton M. Gordon, *Assimilation in American Life: The Role of Race, Religion and National Origins,* New York: Oxford University Press, 1964.

[3]*Ibid.,* pp. 27-28.

[4]Gunnar Myrdal, *American Dilemma,* New York: Harper & Bros., 1944, pp. 101-6.

[5]Gordon, *Assimilation in American Life,* pp. 30-31.

[6]H. H. Gerth and C. Wright Mills, *From Max Weber, Essays in Sociology,* New York: Oxford University Press, 1958, pp. 59-60.

[7]Stewart G. Cole and Mildred Wiese Cole, *Minorities and the American Promise,* New York: Harper and Brothers, 1954, pp. 135-40.

[8]Gordon, *Assimilation in American Life,* pp. 71-72.

[9]Kenneth B. Clark; "Desegregation: The Role of the Social Sciences," *Teachers College Record,* 62 (October 1960): pp. 16-17.

[10]Gordon, *Assimilation in American Life,* p. 246.

[11]Robert P. Stuckert, "African Ancestry of the White American Population," *Ohio Journal of Science,* 58 (1958): pp. 155-160, and John H. Burma, "The Measurement of Negro Passing," *American Journal of Sociology,* 52 (1946): pp. 18-22.

[12]C. Vann Woodward, *The Strange Career of Jim Crow,* Fair Lawn N.J.: Oxford University Press, 1957.

[13]Thomas Ford Hoult, *Dictionary of Modern Sociology,* Totowa, N.J.: Littlefield, Adams & Co., 1969, p. 239.

Chapter 4

A Societal Theory of Race and Ethnic Relations*

Stanley Lieberson

"In the relations of races there is a cycle of events which tends everywhere to repeat itself."[1] Park's assertion served as a prologue to the now classical cycle of competition, conflict, accommodation, and assimilation. A number of other attempts have been made to formulate phases or stages ensuing from the initial contacts between racial and ethnic groups.[2] However, the sharp contrasts between relatively harmonious race relations in Brazil and Hawaii and the current racial turmoil in South Africa and Indonesia serve to illustrate the difficulty in stating — to say nothing of interpreting — an inevitable "natural history" of race and ethnic relations.

Many earlier race and ethnic cycles were, in fact, narrowly confined to a rather specific set of groups or contact situations. Bogardus, for example, explicitly limited his synthesis to Mexican and Oriental immigrant groups on the west coast of the United States and suggested that this is but one of many different cycles of relations between immigrants and native Americans.[3] Similarly, the Australian anthropologist Price developed three phases that appear to account for the relationships between white English-speaking migrants and the aborigines of Australia, Maoris in New Zealand, and Indians of the United States and Canada.[4]

*Reprinted from *American Sociological Review* 26:6 (1961), by permission of the author and the publisher.

This essay seeks to present a rudimentary theory of the development of race and ethnic relations that systematically accounts for differences between societies in such divergent consequences of contact as racial nationalism and warfare, assimilation and fusion, and extinction. It postulates that the critical problem on a societal level in racial or ethnic contact is initially each population's maintenance and development of a social order compatible with its ways of life prior to contact. The crux of any cycle must, therefore, deal with political, social, and economic institutions. The emphasis given in earlier cycles to one group's dominance of another in these areas is therefore hardly surprising.[5]

Although we accept this institutional approach, the thesis presented here is that knowledge of the nature of one group's domination over another in the political, social, and economic spheres is a necessary but insufficient prerequisite for predicting or interpreting the final and intermediate stages of racial and ethnic contact. Rather, institutional factors are considered in terms of a distinction between two major types of contact situations: contacts involving subordination of an indigenous population by a migrant group, for example, Negro-white relations in South Africa; and contacts involving subordination of a migrant population by an indigenous racial or ethnic group, for example, Japanese migrants to the United States.

After considering the societal issues inherent in racial and ethnic contact, the distinction developed between migrant and indigenous superordination will be utilized in examining each of the following dimensions of race relations: political and economic control, multiple ethnic contacts, conflict and assimilation. The terms "race" and "ethnic" are used interchangeably.

Differences Inherent in Contact

Most situations of ethnic contact involve at least one indigenous group and at least one group migrating to the area. The only exception at the initial point in contact would be the settlement of an uninhabited area by two or more groups. By "indigenous" is meant not necessarily the aborigines, but rather a population sufficiently established in an area so as to possess the institutions and demographic capacity for maintaining some minimal form of social order through generations. Thus a given spatial area may have different indigenous groups through time. For example, the indigenous population of Australia is presently largely white and primarily of British origin, although the Tasmanoids and Australoids were once in possession of the area.[6] A similar racial shift may be observed in the populations indigenous to the United States.

Restricting discussion to the simplest of contact situations, i.e., involving one migrant and one established population, we can generally observe sharp differences in their social organization at the time of contact. The indigenous population has an established and presumably stable organization prior to the arrival of migrants, i.e., government, economic activities adapted to the environment and the existing techniques of resource utilization, kinship, stratification, and religious systems.[7] On the basis of a long series of migration studies, we may be reasonably certain that the social order of a migrant population's homeland is not wholly transferred to their new settlement.[8] Migrants are required to make at least some institutional adaptations and innovations in view of the presence of an indigenous population, the demographic selectivity of migration, and differences in habitat.

For example, recent post-war migrations from Italy and the Netherlands indicate considerable selectivity in age and sex from the total populations of these countries. Nearly half of 30,000 males leaving the Netherlands in 1955 were between 20 and 39 years of age whereas only one quarter of the male population was of these ages.[9] Similarly, over 40,000 males in this age range accounted for somewhat more than half of Italy's male emigrants in 1951, although they comprise roughly 30 per cent of the male population of Italy.[10] In both countries, male emigrants exceed females in absolute numbers as well as in comparison with the sex ratios of their nation. That these cases are far from extreme can be illustrated with Oriental migration data. In 1920, for example, there were 38,000 foreign-born Chinese adult males in the United States, but only 2,000 females of the same group.[11]

In addition to these demographic shifts, the new physical and biological conditions of existence require the revision and creation of social institutions if the social order known in the old country is to be approximated and if the migrants are to survive. The migration of eastern and southern European peasants around the turn of the century to urban industrial centers of the United States provides a well-documented case of radical changes in occupational pursuits as well as the creation of a number of institutions in response to the new conditions of urban life, e.g., mutual-aid societies, national churches, and financial institutions.

In short, when two populations begin to occupy the same habitat but do not share a single order, each group endeavors to maintain the political and economic conditions that are at least compatible with the institutions existing before contact. These conditions for the maintenance of institutions cannot only differ for the two groups in contact, but are often conflicting. European contacts with the American Indian, for example, led to the decimation of the latter's sources of sustenance and disrupted religious and tribal forms of organization. With respect to a population's efforts to maintain its social institutions, we may therefore assume that the presence of another ethnic group is an important part of the environment. Further, if groups in contact differ in their capacity to impose changes on the other group, then we may expect to find one group "superordinate" and the other population "subordinate" in maintaining or developing a suitable environment.

It is here that efforts at a single cycle of race and ethnic relations must fail. For it is necessary to introduce a distinction in the nature or form of subordination before attempting to predict whether conflict or relatively harmonious assimilation will develop. As we shall shortly show, the race relations cycle in areas where the migrant group is superordinate and indigenous group subordinate differs sharply from the stages in societies composed of a superordinate indigenous group and subordinate migrants.[12]

Political and Economic Control

Emphasis is placed herein on economic and political dominance since it is assumed that control of these institutions will be instrumental in establishing a suitable milieu for at least the population's own social institutions, e.g., educational, religious, and kinship, as well as control of such major cultural artifacts as language.

MIGRANT SUPERORDINATION

When the population migrating to a new contact situation is superior in technology (particularly weapons) and more tightly organized than the indigenous group, the necessary conditions for maintaining the migrants' political and economic institutions are usually imposed on the indigenous population. Warfare, under such circumstances, often occurs early in the contacts between the two groups as the migrants begin to interfere with the natives' established order. There is frequently conflict even if the initial contact was friendly. Price, for example, has observed the following consequences of white invasion and subordination of the indigenous populations of Australia, Canada, New Zealand, and the United States:

> During an opening period of pioneer invasion on moving frontiers the whites decimated the natives with their diseases; occupied their lands by seizure or by pseudo-purchase; slaughtered those who resisted; intensified tribal warfare by supplying white weapons; ridiculed and disrupted native religions, society and culture, and generally reduced the unhappy peoples to a state of despondency under which they neither desired to live, nor to have children to undergo similar conditions.[13]

The numerical decline of indigenous populations after their initial subordination to a migrant group, whether caused by warfare, introduction of venereal and other diseases, or disruption of sustenance activities, has been documented for a number of contact situations in addition to those discussed by Price.[14]

In addition to bringing about these demographic and economic upheavals, the superordinate migrants frequently create political entities that are not at all coterminous with the boundaries existing during the indigenous populations' supremacy prior to contact. For example, the British and Boers in southern Africa carved out political states that included areas previously under the control of separate and often warring groups.[15] Indeed, European alliances with feuding tribes were often used as a fulcrum for the territorial expansion of whites into southern Africa.[16] The bifurcation of tribes into two nations and the migrations of groups across newly created national boundaries are both consequences of the somewhat arbitrary nature of the political entities created in regions of migrant superordination.[17] This incorporation of diverse indigenous populations into a single territorial unit under the dominance of a migrant group has considerable importance for later developments in this type of racial and ethnic contact.

INDIGENOUS SUPERORDINATION

When a population migrates to a subordinate position considerably less conflict occurs in the early stages. The movements of many European and Oriental populations to political, economic, and social subordination in the United States were not converted into warfare, nationalism, or long-term conflict. Clearly, the occasional labor and racial strife marking the history of immigration of the United States is not on the same level as the efforts to expel or revolutionize the social order. American Negroes, one of the most persistently subordinated migrant groups in the country, never responded in significant numbers to the encouragement of migration to Liberia. The single important large-scale nationalistic effort, Marcus Garvey's Universal Negro Improvement Association, never actually led to mass emigration of Negroes.[18] By contrast, the indigenous American Indians fought long and hard to preserve control over their habitat.

In interpreting differences in the effects of migrant and indigenous subordination, the migrants must be considered in the context of the options available to the group. Irish migrants to the United States in the 1840's, for example, although clearly subordinate to native whites of other origins, fared better economically than if they had remained in their mother country.[19] Further, the option of returning to the homeland often exists for populations migrating to subordinate situations. Jerome reports that net migration to the United States between the midyears of 1907 and 1923 equaled roughly 65 per cent of gross immigration.[20] This indicates that immigrant dissatisfaction with subordination or other conditions of contact can often be resolved by withdrawal from the area. Recently subordinated indigenous groups, by contrast, are perhaps less apt to leave their habitat so readily.

Finally, when contacts between racial and ethnic groups are under the control of the indigenous population, threats of demographic and institutional imbalance are reduced since the superordinate populations can limit the numbers and groups entering. For example, when Oriental migration to the United States threatened whites, sharp cuts were executed in the quotas.[21] Similar events may be noted with respect to the decline of immigration from the so-called "new" sources of eastern and southern Europe. Whether a group exercises its control over immigration far before it is actually under threat is, of course, not germane to the point that immigrant restriction provides a mechanism whereby potential conflict is prevented.

In summary, groups differ in the conditions necessary for maintaining their respective social orders. In areas where the migrant group is dominant, frequently the indigenous population suffers sharp numerical declines and their economic and political institutions are seriously undermined. Conflict often accompanies the establishment of migrant superordination. Subordinate indigenous populations generally have no alternative location and do not control the numbers of new ethnic populations admitted into their area. By contrast, when the indigenous population dominates the political and economic conditions, the migrant group is introduced into the economy of the indigenous population. Although subordinate in their new habitat, the migrants may fare better than if they remained in their homeland. Hence their subordination occurs without great conflict. In addition, the migrants usually have the option of returning to their homeland and the indigenous population controls the number of new immigrants in the area.

Multiple Ethnic Contacts

Although the introduction of a third major ethnic or racial group frequently occurs in both types of societies distinguished here, there are significant differences between conditions in habitats under indigenous domination and areas where a migrant population is superordinate. Chinese and Indian migrants, for example, were often welcomed by whites in areas where large indigenous populations were suppressed, but these migrants were restricted in the white mother country. Consideration of the causes and consequences of multi-ethnic contacts is therefore made in terms of the two types of racial and ethnic contact.

MIGRANT SUPERORDINATION

In societies where the migrant population is superordinate, it is often necessary to introduce new immigrant groups to fill the niches created in the revised economy of the area. The subordinate indigenous population frequently fails, at first, to participate in the new economic and political order introduced by migrants. For example, because of the numerical decline of Fijians after contact with whites and their unsatisfactory work habits, approximately 60,000 persons migrated from India to the sugar plantations of Fiji under the indenture system between 1879 and 1916.[22] For similar reasons, as well as the demise of slavery, large numbers of Indians were also introduced to such areas of indigenous subordination as Mauritius, British Guiana, Trinidad, and Natal.[23] The descendents of these migrants comprise the largest single ethnic group in several of these areas.

McKenzie, after observing the negligible participation of the subordinated indigenous populations of Alaska, Hawaii, and Malaya in contrast to the large numbers of Chinese, Indian, and other Oriental immigrants, offers the following interpretation:

> The indigenous peoples of many of the frontier zones of modern industrialism are surrounded by their own web of culture and their own economic structure.

Consequently they are slow to take part in the new economy especially as unskilled laborers. It is the individual who is widely removed from his native habitat that is most adaptable to the conditions imposed by capitalism in frontier regions. Imported labor cannot so easily escape to its home village when conditions are distasteful as can the local population.[24]

Similarly, the Indians of the United States played a minor role in the new economic activities introduced by white settlers and, further, were not used successfully as slaves.[25] Frazier reports that Negro slaves were utilized in the West Indies and Brazil after unsuccessful efforts to enslave the indigenous Indian populations.[26] Large numbers of Asiatic Indians were brought to South Africa as indentured laborers to work in the railways, mines, and plantations introduced by whites.[27]

This migration of workers into areas where the indigenous population was either unable or insufficient to work in the newly created economic activities was also marked by a considerable flow back to the home country. For example, nearly 3.5 million Indians left the Madras Presidency for overseas between 1903 and 1912, but close to 3 million returned during this same period.[28] However, as we observed earlier, large numbers remained overseas and formed major ethnic populations in a number of countries. Current difficulties of the ten million Chinese in Southern Asia are in large part due to their settlement in societies where the indigenous populations were subordinate.

INDIGENOUS SUPERORDINATION

We have observed that in situations of indigenous superordination the call for new immigrants from other ethnic and racial populations is limited in a manner that prevents the indigenous group's loss of political and economic control. Under such conditions, no single different ethnic or racial population is sufficiently large in number or strength to challenge the supremacy of the indigenous population.

After whites attained dominance in Hawaii, that land provided a classic case of the substitution of one ethnic group after another during a period when large numbers of immigrants were needed for the newly created and expanding plantation economy. According to Lind, the shifts from Chinese to Japanese and Portuguese immigrants and the later shifts to Puerto Rican, Korean, Spanish, Russian, and Philippine sources for the plantation laborers were due to conscious efforts to prevent any single group from obtaining too much power.[29] Similarly, the exclusion of Chinese from the United States mainland stimulated the migration of the Japanese and, in turn, the later exclusion of Japanese led to increased migration from Mexico.[30]

In brief, groups migrating to situations of multiple ethnic contact are thus subordinate in both types of contact situations. However, in societies where whites are superordinate but do not settle as an indigenous population, other racial and ethnic groups are admitted in large numbers and largely in accordance with economic needs of the revised economy of the habitat. By contrast, when a dominant migrant group later becomes indigenous, in the sense that the area becomes one of permanent settlement through generations for the group, migrant populations from new racial and ethnic stocks are restricted in number and source.

Conflict and Assimilation

From a comparison of the surge of racial nationalism and open warfare in parts of Africa and Asia or the retreat of superordinate migrants from the former Dutch East Indies and French Indo-China, on the one hand, with the fusion of populations in many nations of western Europe or the "cultural pluralism" of the United States and Switzerland, on the other, one must conclude that neither conflict nor assimilation is an inevitable outcome of racial and ethnic contact. Our distinction, however, between two classes of race and ethnic relations is directly relevant to consideration of which of these alternatives different populations in contact will take. In societies where the indigenous population at the initial contact is subordinate, warfare and nationalism often — although not always — develops later in the cycle of relations. By contrast, relations between migrants and indigenous populations that are subordinate and superordinate, respectively, are generally without long-term conflict.

MIGRANT SUPERORDINATION

Through time, the subordinated indigenous population begins to participate in the economy introduced by the migrant group and, frequently, a concomitant disruption of previous forms of social and economic organization takes place. This, in turn, has significant implications for the development of both nationalism and a greater sense of racial unity. In many African states, where Negroes were subdivided into ethnic groups prior to contact with whites, the racial unity of the African was created by the occupation of their habitat by white invaders.[31] The categorical subordination of Africans by whites as well as the dissolution and decay of previous tribal and ethnic forms of organization are responsible for the creation of racial consciousness among the indigenous populations.[32] As the indigenous group becomes increasingly incorporated within the larger system, both the saliency of their subordinate position and its significance increase. No alternative exists for the bulk of the native population other than the destruction or revision of the institutions of political, economic, and social subordination.

Further, it appears that considerable conflict occurs in those areas where the migrants are not simply superordinate, but where they themselves have also become, in a sense, indigenous by maintaining an established population through generations. In Table 1, for example, one can observe how sharply the white populations of Algeria and the Union of South Africa differ from those in nine other African countries with respect to the per cent born in the country of settlement. Thus, two among the eleven African countries for which such data were available[33] are outstanding with respect to both racial turmoil and the high proportion of whites born in the country. To be sure, other factors operate to influence the nature of racial and ethnic relations. However these data strongly support our suggestions with respect to the significance of differences between indigenous and migrant forms of contact. Thus where the migrant population becomes established in the new area, it is all the more difficult for the indigenous subordinate group to change the social order.

TABLE 1

Nativity of the White Populations
of Selected African Countries, Circa 1950

Country	Per Cent of Whites Born in Country
Algeria	79.8
Basutoland	37.4
Bechuanaland	39.5
Morocco[a]	37.1[c]
Northern Rhodesia	17.7
Southern Rhodesia	31.5
South West Africa[b]	45.1
Swaziland	41.2
Tanganyika	47.6
Uganda	43.8
Union of South Africa	89.7

Source: United Nations, *Demographic Yearbook*, 1956, Table 5.

Note: Other non-indigenous groups included when necessary breakdown by race is not given.
[a]Former French zone.
[b]Excluding Walvis Bay.
[c]Persons born in former Spanish zone or in Tangier are included as native.

Additionally, where the formerly subordinate indigenous population has become dominant through the expulsion of the superordinate group, the situation faced by nationalities introduced to the area under earlier conditions of migrant superordination changes radically. For example, as we noted earlier, Chinese were welcomed in many parts of Southeast Asia where the newly subordinated indigenous populations were unable or unwilling to fill the economic niches created by the white invaders. However, after whites were expelled and the indigenous populations obtained political mastery, the gates to further Chinese immigration were fairly well closed and there has been increasing interference with the Chinese already present. In Indonesia, where Chinese immigration had been encouraged under Dutch domain, the newly created indigenous government allows only token immigration and has formulated a series of laws and measures designed to interfere with and reduce Chinese commercial activities.[34] Thompson and Adloff observe that,

> Since the war, the Chinese have been subjected to increasingly restrictive measures throughout Southeast Asia, but the severity and effectiveness of these has varied with the degree to which the native nationalists are in control of their countries and feel their national existence threatened by the Chinese.[35]

INDIGENOUS SUPERORDINATION

By contrast, difficulties between subordinate migrants and an already dominant indigenous population occur within the context of a consensual form of government, economy, and social institutions. However confused and uncertain may be the concept of assimilation and its application in operational terms,[36] it is important to note that assimilation is essentially a very different phenomenon in the two types of societies distinguished here.

Where populations migrate to situations of subordination, the issue has generally been with respect to the migrants' capacity and willingness to become an integral part of the on-going social order. For example, this has largely been the case in the United States where the issue of "new" vs. "old" immigrant groups hinged on the alleged inferiorities of the former.[37] The occasional flurries of violence under this form of contact have been generally initiated by the dominant indigenous group and with respect to such threats against the social order as the cheap labor competition of Orientals in the west coast,[38] the nativist fears of Irish Catholic political domination of Boston in the nineteenth century,[39] or the desecration of sacred principles by Mexican "zoot-suiters" in Los Angeles.[40]

The conditions faced by subordinate migrants in Australia and Canada after the creation of indigenous white societies in these areas are similar to that of the United States; that is, limited and sporadic conflict, and great emphasis on the assimilation of migrants. Striking and significant contrasts to the general pattern of subordinate immigrant assimilation in these societies, however, are provided by the differences between the assimilation of Italian and German immigrants in Australia as well as the position of French Canadians in eastern Canada.

French Canadians have maintained their language and other major cultural and social attributes whereas nineteenth and twentieth century immigrants are in process of merging into the predominantly English-speaking Canadian society. Although broader problems of territorial segregation are involved,[41] the critical difference between French Canadians and later groups is that the former had an established society in the new habitat prior to the British conquest of Canada and were thus largely able to maintain their social and cultural unity without significant additional migration from France.[42]

Similarly, in finding twentieth-century Italian immigrants in Australia more prone to cultural assimilation than were German migrants to that nation in the 1800's, Borrie emphasized the fact that Italian migration occurred after Australia had become an independent nation-state. By contrast, Germans settled in what was a pioneer colony without an established general social order and institutions. Thus, for example, Italian children were required to attend Australian schools and learn English, whereas the German immigrants were forced to establish their own educational program.[43]

Thus the consequences of racial and ethnic contact may also be examined in terms of the two types of superordinate-subordinate contact situations considered. For the most part, subordinate migrants appear to be more rapidly assimilated than are subordinate indigenous populations. Further, the subordinate migrant group is generally under greater pressure to assimilate, at least in the gross sense of "assimilation" such as language, than are subordinate indigenous populations. In addition, warfare or racial nationalism — when it does occur — tends to be in societies where the indigenous population is subordinate. If the indigenous movement succeeds, the economic and political position of racial and ethnic populations introduced to the area under migrant dominance may become tenuous.

A Final Note

It is suggested that interest be revived in the conditions accounting for societal variations in the process of relations between racial and ethnic groups. A societal theory of race relations, based on the migrant-indigenous and superordinate-subordinate distinctions developed above, has been found to offer an orderly interpretation of differences in the nature of race and ethnic relations in the contact situations considered. Since, however, systematic empirical investigation provides a far more rigorous test of the theory's merits and limitations, comparative cross-societal studies are needed.

NOTES

[1]Robert E. Park, *Race and Culture,* Glencoe, Ill.: The Free Press, 1950, p. 150.

[2]For example, Emory S. Bogardus, "A Race-Relations Cycle," *American Journal of Sociology,* 35 (January, 1930), pp. 612-617; W. O. Brown, "Culture Contact and Race Conflict" in E. B. Reuter, editor, *Race and Culture Contacts,* New York: McGraw-Hill, 1934, pp. 34-47; E. Franklin Frazier, *Race and Culture Contacts in the Modern World,* New York: Alfred A. Knopf, 1957, pp. 32ff.; Clarence E. Glick, "Social Roles and Types in Race Relations" in Andrew W. Lind, editor, *Race Relations in World Perspective,* Honolulu: University of Hawaii Press, 1955, pp. 243-

262; Edward Nelson Palmer, "Culture Contacts and Population Growth" in Joseph J. Spengler and Otis Dudley Duncan, editors, *Population Theory and Policy,* Glencoe, Ill.: The Free Press, 1956, pp. 410-415; A. Grenfell Price, *White Settlers and Native Peoples,* Melbourne: Georgian House, 1950. For summaries of several of these cycles, see Brewton Bern, *Race and Ethnic Relations,* Boston: Houghton Mifflin, 1958, Chapter 6.

[3]Bogardus, *op. cit.,* p. 612.

[4]Price, *op. cit.*

[5]Intra-urban stages of contact are not considered here.

[6]Price, *op. cit.,* chaps. 6 and 7.

[7]Glick, *op. cit.,* p. 244.

[8]See, for example, Brinley Thomas, "International Migration" in Philip M. Hauser and Otis Dudley Duncan, editors, *The Study of Population,* Chicago: University of Chicago Press, 1959, pp. 523-526.

[9]United Nations, *Demographic Yearbook,* 1957, pp. 147, 645.

[10]United Nations, *Demographic Yearbook,* 1954, pp. 131, 669.

[11]R. D. McKenzie, *Oriental Exclusion,* Chicago: University of Chicago Press, 1928, p. 83.

[12]See, for example, Reuter's distinction between two types of direct contact in E. B. Reuter, editor, *op. cit.,* pp. 4-7.

[13]Price, *op. cit.,* p. 1.

[14]Stephen Roberts, *Population Problems of the Pacific,* London: George Routledge & Sons, 1927.

[15]John A. Barnes, "Race Relations in the Development of Southern Africa" in Lind, editor, *op. cit.*

[16]*Ibid.*

[17]Witness the current controversies between tribes in the newly created Congo Republic. Also, for a list of tribes living on both sides of the border of the Republic of Sudan, see Karol Józek Krótki, "Demographic Survey of Sudan" in *The Population of Sudan,* report on the sixth annual conference (Khartoum: Philosophical Society of Sudan, 1958), p. 35.

[18]John Hope Franklin, *From Slavery to Freedom,* second edition, New York: Alfred Knopf, 1956, pp. 234-238, 481-483.

[19]Oscar Handlin, *Boston's Immigrants,* revised edition, Cambridge, Mass.: The Belknap Press of Harvard University Press, 1959, Chap. 2.

[20]Harry Jerome, *Migration and Business Cycles,* New York: National Bureau of Economic Research, 1926, pp. 43-44.

[21]See, George Eaton Simpson and J. Milton Yinger, *Racial and Cultural Minorities,* revised edition, New York: Harper & Brothers, 1958, pp. 126-132.

[22]K. L. Gillion, "The Sources of Indian Emigration to Fiji," *Population Studies,* 10 (November 1956), p. 139; I. M. Cumpston, "A Survey of Indian Immigration to British Tropical Colonies to 1910," *ibid.,* pp. 158-159.

[23]Cumpston, *op. cit.*, pp. 158-165.

[24]R. D. McKenzie, "Cultural and Racial Differences as Bases of Human Symbiosis" in Kimball Young, editor, *Social Attitudes,* New York: Henry Holt, 1931, p. 157.

[25]Franklin, *op. cit.,* p. 47.

[26]Frazier, *op. cit.,* pp. 107-108.

[27]Leo Kuper, Hilstan Watts, and Ronald Davies, *Durban: A Study in Racial Ecology,* London: Jonathan Cape, 1958, p. 25.

[28]Gillion, *op. cit.,* p. 149.

[29]Andrew W. Lind, *An Island Community,* Chicago: University of Chicago Press, 1938, pp. 218-229.

[30]McKenzie, *Oriental Exclusion, op. cit.,* p. 181.

[31]For a discussion of territorial and tribal movements, see James S. Coleman, "Current Political Movements in Africa," *The Annals of the American Academy of Political and Social Science,* 298 (March 1955), pp. 95-108.

[32]For a broader discussion of emergent nationalism, see, Thomas Hodgkin, *Nationalism in Colonial Africa,* New York: New York University Press, 1957; Everett C. Hughes, "New Peoples" in Lind, editor, *op. cit.* pp. 95-115.

[33]United Nations, *Demographic Yearbook,* 1956, Table 5.

[34]B. H. M. Vlekke, *Indonesia in 1956,* The Hague: Netherlands Institute of International Affairs, 1957, p. 88.

[35]Virginia Thompson and Richard Adloff, *Minority Problems in Southeast Asia,* Stanford, Calif.: Stanford University Press, 1955, p. 3.

[36]See, for example, International Union for the Scientific Study of Population, "Cultural Assimilation of Immigrants," *Population Studies,* supplement, March 1950.

[37]Oscar Handlin, *Race and Nationality in American Life,* Garden City, New York: Doubleday Anchor Books, 1957, Chap. 5.

[38]Simpson and Yinger, *op. cit.*

[39]Oscar Handlin, *Boston's Immigrants, op. cit.,* Chap. 7.

[40]Ralph Turner and Samuel J. Surace, "Zoot-Suiters and Mexicans: Symbols in Crowd Behavior," *American Journal of Sociology,* 62 (July 1956), pp. 14-20.

[41]It is, however, suggestive to consider whether the isolated settlement of an area by a racial, religious, or ethnic group would be permitted in other than frontier conditions. Consider, for example, the difficulties faced by Mormons until they reached Utah.

[42]See Everett C. Hughes, *French Canada in Transition,* Chicago: University of Chicago Press, 1943.

[43]W. D. Borrie assisted by D. R. G. Packer, *Italians and Germans in Australia,* Melbourne: F. W. Cheshire, 1954, *passim.*

II.

Ethnic Group Differences: Persistence and Change

Chapter 5

The Persistence of Native Values*

Thomas R. Berger

The native peoples of the North have values that are in many respects quite different from our own. These values are related to the struggle for survival waged by their ancestors, and they persist in their struggle today to survive as distinct peoples.

There is a tendency for us to depreciate native culture. Many white northerners have argued that the native way of life is dying, that what we observe today is a pathetic and diminishing remnant of what existed in the past. The argument arises as much from our attitudes toward native people as from any process of reasoning. We find it hard to believe that anyone would wish to live as native people do in their homes and villages. We show indifference, even contempt, for the native people's defence of their way of life. We tend to idealize those aspects of native culture that we can most easily understand, or that we can appropriate to wear or to place on a shelf in our own homes. We simply do not see native culture as defensible. Many of us do not even see it as a culture at all, but only as a problem to be solved. But we must learn what values the native people still regard as vital today. Only then

*Reproduced from *Northern Frontier, Northern Homeland* by Thomas R. Berger by permission of the author, the Minister of Supply and Services Canada, and James Lorimer & Co., Publishers, Toronto 1977.

can we understand how they see their society developing in the future, and what they fear the impact of a pipeline and an energy corridor on that future will be.

The Native Concept of Land

The native people of Canada, and indeed indigenous people throughout the world, have what they regard as a special relationship with their environment. Native people of the North have told the Mackenzie Valley Pipeline Inquiry that they regard themselves as inseparable from the land, the waters and the animals with which they share the world. They regard themselves as custodians of the land, which is for their use during their lifetime, and which they must pass on to their children and their children's children after them. In their languages, there are no words for wilderness.

The native people's relationship to the land is so different from that of the dominant culture that only through their own words can we comprehend it. The native people, whose testimony appears throughout this chapter . . . are people of all ages, from teenagers to the very old.

Richard Nerysoo of Fort McPherson:

> It is very clear to me that it is an important and special thing to be an Indian. Being an Indian means being able to understand and live with this world in a very special way. It means living with the land, with the animals, with the birds and fish, as though they were your sisters and brothers. It means saying the land is an old friend and an old friend your father knew, your grandfather knew, indeed your people always have known . . . we see our land as much, much more than the white man sees it. To the Indian people our land really is our life. Without our land we cannot — we could no longer exist as people. If our land is destroyed, we too are destroyed. If your people ever take our land you will be taking our life. [C1183ff.]†

Louis Caesar of Fort Good Hope:

> This land it is just like our blood because we live off the animals that feed off the land. That's why we are brown. We are not like the white people. We worry about our land because we make our living off our land. The white people they live on money. That's why they worry about money. [C1790]

Georgina Tobac of Fort Good Hope:

> Every time the white people come to the North or come to our land and start tearing up the land, I feel as if they are cutting our own flesh because that is the way we feel about our land. It is our flesh. [C1952]

Susie Tutcho of Fort Franklin:

> My father really loved this land, and we love our land. The grass and the trees are our flesh, the animals are our flesh. [C684]

---

†Editors' note: This bibliographic citation refers to pages in the transcript of the community (C) or formal (F) hearings of the Mackenzie Valley Pipeline Inquiry.

Joe Betsidea of Fort Franklin:

This land is our blood. We were born and raised on it. We live and survive by it. Though I am young, this is the way I feel about my land . . . we the people of the North know our land and could find minerals and be a millionaire one day. But the creator did not make us that way. [C761ff.]

Ray Sonfrere of Hay River:

I need and love the land I was born and raised on. Many people find meaning in different things in life. Native people find meaning in the land and they need it and they love it. . . . Sometimes you stand on the shore of the lake, you see high waves rolling onto shore, and it's pushed by winds you can't see. Soon it's all calm again. In the winter you see flowers, trees, rivers and streams covered with snow and frozen. In the spring it all comes back to life. This has a strong meaning for my people and me and we need it. [C552]

Norah Ruben of Paulatuk:

As the sea is laying there, we look at it, we feed from it and we are really part of it. [C4456]

Marie Moosenose of Lac la Martre:

We love our land because we survive with it. It gives us life, the land gives us life. [C8227]

Charlie Gully of Fort Good Hope:

We talk so strongly about our land because we depend so much on it. Our parents are gone now. Our grandparents [are gone] but we still live on the same land that they did, so it is just like they are still living with us. I was born in 1926 and my father died in the year 1947, but the land is still here and I still could use it the way my father taught me to, so to me it is like my father is still alive with me. [C1918ff.]

Isadore Kochon of Colville Lake:

This is the land that we make our living on. . . . We make our living the simple way, to fish on it, to hunt on it and to trap on it, just live off the land. . . . This land fed us all even before the time the white people ever came to the North. To us it is just like a mother that brought her children up. That's how we feel about this country. It is just like a mother to us. That's how serious it is that we think about the land around here. [C8309ff.]

Joachim Bonnetrouge of Fort Providence:

We love the Mackenzie River, that's our life. It shelters us when it storms and it feeds us when there is hunger. It takes care of its children, the native people. [C7839]

Eddie Cook of Fort Good Hope:

Why do I go back to my land? Because I love and respect my land. My land was my supplier of food. It was my teacher, my land taught me. It taught me education which I could not learn in the white man's books. [C2037]

The Land as Security

The native people in every village made it quite clear to me that the land is the source of their well-being today and for generations to come. This is how Bertram Pokiak of Tuktoyaktuk talked about the land in the best years of the fur trade, 40 years ago:

> In Aklavik a lot of fur them days, just like you white people working for wages and you have money in the bank, well my bank was here, all around with the fur. Whatever kind of food I wanted, if I wanted caribou I'd go up in the mountains; if I wanted coloured fox, I went up in the mountain; in the Delta I get mink, muskrat; but I never make a big trapper. I just get enough for my own use the coming year. Next year the animals are going to be there anyway, that's my bank. The same way all over where I travelled. Some people said to me, "Why you don't put the money in the bank and save it for future?" I should have told him that time, "The North is my bank." But I never did, I just thought of it lately. [C4234]

Pierre Tlokka told the Inquiry at Fort Rae:

> I don't think that I will end up being like a white man or act like one. The white people they always have some money in the bank. I will never have any money in the bank. The only banking I could do is something that is stored in the bush and live off it. That's my bank. That's my saving account right there. [C8030]

The deep and abiding value of the land as the basis for the native people's long-term security is still central to native society. At Tuktoyaktuk, Inuit witnesses told the Inquiry of the proposal they had made to the federal government for a land freeze in the Cape Bathurst and Eskimo Lakes region to protect this land pending settlement of the Inuit claims. Jimmy Jacobson explained the thinking behind it:

> Lots of us Eskimos, they talk about Cape Bathurst and Eskimo Lakes. We thought that Eskimo Lakes and Cape Bathurst should be just like a reserve, kept free, not just keep it free for two or three years, [but] completely, have it for a reserve in case the pipeline come up; [then] we got something to go back on to keep our good hunting grounds, because if that pipeline ever come up, the people will be only rich for one or two years. They won't have money for years and years because most of the people after they work on the pipeline they bound to go and have a heck of a good time, most of them, and come back broke. They got to fall back on something. It's something that will be good to keep for the young people because they got to go back to hunting and fishing for sure. [C4255]

The Land as the Basis of Identity, Pride and Self-Respect

The native people's identity, pride, self-respect and independence are inseparably linked to the land and a way of life that has land at its centre.

Jean Marie Rabiska, a trapper in his twenties, addressed the Inquiry at Fort Good Hope:

> I am strictly a trapper. I was born and raised in the bush. When I was seven years old, that is when I first started learning about bush life. I used to watch my brothers come back from the trap line. They would bring back marten and when they would go hunting, they would always bring back a moose or caribou. They

are good hunters and trappers. They seldom failed when hunting, and I used to envy them because they were good in the bush life. Ever since that time I had one thing in my mind: I wanted to be a trapper. From then on, I tried hard to learn the ways of bush life. I learned most everything from my mother. She is a tough woman when it comes to bush life. Through hardships and good times, we always stuck it out. We seldom complained for complaining is not the way of a true trapper.

My Mum, she did a good job. She made a good trapper out of me. She taught me to follow in the footsteps of my ancestors. Today I stand out among trappers and I am proud of it. [C2013]

Paul Pagotak addressed the Inquiry at Holman, through an interpreter:

He wants to see the Eskimos live the way they are for quite some time. He wants to see the children of the children on the land supporting themselves from the land. We don't have money among ourselves but our pride in living off the land is one thing we don't want taken away. [C3937ff.]

Even native people, who are not themselves hunters and trappers but who make their contribution to native society in other ways, see their identity and pride as people as linked to the land. Mary Rose Drybones, the social worker at Fort Good Hope, made this point quite clear:

I am proud at this moment to say that my father was a real Dene because he made his living off the land for us. There was no welfare at that time. He died in 1953 and left a memory for me and my brother to be true Dene and we are still, and we would like to keep it that way. [C1940]

There is one other important characteristic of the native people's relationship to land. Traditionally there was no private or individual ownership of land among the Dene and the Inuit. They have always believed that all the members of a community have the right to use it. That is why indigenous people do not believe they have the right to sell the land. It is not so much a limitation upon their rights over the land; it is rather something to which the land is not susceptible. Gabe Bluecoat of Arctic Red River addressed the Inquiry on this subject:

The land. Who made it? I really want to find out who made it. Me? You? The government? Who made it? I know [of] only one man made it — God. But on this land who besides Him made the land? What is given is not sold to anyone. We're that kind of people. What is given to us, we are not going to give away. [C4587]

Social and Political Values

Dene and Inuit societies have also developed important values that centre on the welfare of the group or community. They are values that have survived many changes and are still strong today.

The values of egalitarianism has important implications for the way decisions are made within native society. George Barnaby of Fort Good Hope, Vice-President of the Indian Brotherhood of the Northwest Territories, explained this tradition:

No one can decide for another person. Everyone is involved in the discussion and . . . the decision [is] made by everyone. Our way is to try and give freedom to a person as he knows what he wants. [F22003]

At the community hearings of the Inquiry, I discovered what Barnaby meant. In the native villages there was an implicit assumption that everyone shared in forming the community's judgment on the pipeline.

Those who wonder why the feelings of the native people have not previously appeared as strongly as they do now may find their answer in the fact that the native people themselves had substantial control over the timing, the setting, the procedure and the conduct of the Inquiry's community hearings. The Inquiry did not seek to impose any preconceived notion of how the hearings should be conducted. Its proceedings were not based upon a model or an agenda with which we, as white people, would feel comfortable. All members of each community were invited to speak. All were free to question the representatives of the pipeline companies. And the Inquiry stayed in a community until everyone there who wished to say something had been heard. The native people had an opportunity to express themselves in their own languages and in their own way.

Egalitarianism in northern native communities is closely linked with the people's respect for individual autonomy and freedom. Peter Gardiner, an anthropologist who spent a year among the Dene of Fort Liard, spoke to the Inquiry of his experience:

> Living with the people, you can see that they try to act with respect, even toward people who are young, or people who are confused, or people who are different; they are tolerant beyond anything white Canadians ever experience. When the people here give freedom to one another, they give equality. Then, many of us have a lot to learn from the people. . . . These are values that other Canadians can appreciate. They are ancient values though, and we should not see them as a result of our better teachings. [C1705ff.]

The Sharing Ethic

The tradition of sharing is seen by native people as an essential part of their cultural inheritance. Joachim Bonnetrouge told the Inquiry at Fort Liard:

> We do not conquer, we are not like that. We are sharers, we are welcomers. [C1718]

Joe Naedzo at Fort Franklin:

> We native people, we help each other. We have good words for each other. And we share the things that we have with each other. I am not talking just for Fort Franklin. This happens throughout all of the North. . . .
> When we visit another community, you never buy food. You don't have to buy the food. I went to visit Fort Good Hope with a dog team for five days. My dogs were fed and I was fed, I had a place to stay. And on the return trip, they gave me food for the dogs. They gave me enough food to make sure that I [could] come home. . . .
> In this community, if one hunter went out hunting and got five to ten caribou, that person feeds everybody. They share that whole meat until it is all gone with

everybody. That is the way the native people live among each other. They share.
It is the same thing for fishing. If a person went out fishing and got some fish, that person shares it with the community. We help each other. That is how our life continues. We share all the time.

Our ancestors have taught us a lot of things. They have taught us how to make life continue. They teach you that for your neighbours, when they are in need and when you are in need, the neighbours will feed you. Take care of each other and share with each other. [C810ff.]

Louis Norwegian at Jean Marie River.

If a person kills one moose, he shares and shares alike, and everybody have some amount, no matter how big the people around here. This is still carried out. If they kill one moose, everybody get a share of it. . . . If they go to fish, a few of them go to the lake and get some fish, everybody gets the same amount of fish. That's just the way we live here, at Jean Marie. [C2855ff.]

It is not only among the Dene that sharing is highly valued. In the Inuit communities the people told me the same thing.

Alexandria Elias at Sachs Harbour:

Long ago people helped one another all the time. They used to go down to Kendall Island every summer, and they go there for whaling, and lots of people go there. Once they got a whale everybody got together and ate. Nobody ever looked down on one another, everybody helped one another, the poor, and who had some and who didn't have. They never try to beat one another or try to go against one another. They were all just like one big family. . . .

The Delta used to be as full of people then, and [I] never ever remember government ever helping them. They never ever asked for government help. Everything they got was what they got themselves and what they shared with one another . . . [I] never ever remember being poor. [I] didn't know what poor meant. [C4066ff.]

The observations of anthropologists provide additional support for the persistence of the sharing ethic in present-day native society. Joel Savishinsky, in *Kinship and the Expression of Values in an Athabascan Bush Community*, a study of the people of Colville Lake, writes:

In addition to generosity in terms of food, the people's concept of inter-dependence and reciprocity extends into matters of hospitality, cooperation, and mutual aid. People adopt and care for one another's children, help each other in moving to and from bush camps, get one another firewood in cases of immediate need, do sewing for each other, camp with one another for varying periods in the bush, and also offer each other assistance for mending and operating boats, motors, chain saws and other equipment. Generosity, therefore, covers both goods and services, and these two aspects often are interchangeable in terms of reciprocity involved in the people's behaviour. [p. 47]

Although the tradition of sharing is still regarded as vital, it has of course undergone some adaptation, particularly over the last 20 years with the movement of the native people into permanent settlements. Thus, in the larger communities, a single moose may not be distributed among every single household, but it will be shared within the extended family group. Even in the larger communities, however, wherever circumstances and the magnitude of the kill allow, communal distribution is still practised.

The native people have described not only how sharing and generosity characterize relations among themselves, but also how they have characterized their relations with whites. They told the Inquiry how, during the days of the fur trade, they shared with the traders their knowledge and their food, both of which were indispensable to the traders' survival in the North. This is how Philip Simba of Kakisa Lake remembers those days:

> When the first snow comes, they come into camp and the Hudson's Bay [manager] has at least 12 men working for him. Each man had a team of six dogs. These people went and got the moose. This was provided to the Hudson's Bay for his food. In the winter time they provided him with rabbits and all that. This is how they helped the Hudson's Bay. That's how he grew rich on the misery of the people, I guess. That's how come he's got a beautiful store today. [C7930]

Joe Naedzo at Fort Franklin told how native people extended the same generosity to some of the white trappers that came into the North:

> The native people don't only share among themselves. There was one white man who lived among us. His name was Jack Raymond. He went to Johnny Hoe River with us. He had no money. He had five pounds of flour and that is supposed to last him for the whole year that they spent at Johnny Hoe River. . . . Before the end of November there was no flour. . . .
> At the time . . . there was a lot of people living in Johnny Hoe. And Jack Raymond and his family had no more food. And they had only six dogs left. And for five months we shared our food with him. From January to April we fed them, we fed their dogs. And then at the end of April, with their six dogs, they went to Port Radium to find job.
> They have a job and they make money. But we never asked them to pay us back for all the five months that we took care of them. This is what our ancestors taught us. You know the kind of sharing we had with Jack Raymond. . . . The white man and the native people, no difference, we share our food. [C814ff.]

Many native people expressed the view that, although they have extended to white strangers the same generosity with which they have traditionally treated each other, the white man has not reciprocated.

Gabe Bluecoat of Arctic Red River told the Inquiry:

> Us people, Arctic Red River people, if a white man come and asked to stay with us, sure, right away we'd say, "Yes, yes, my friend." The white people, why can't they be like that? Everything they do is money, money, money. Why don't they be our friends and use everything, share everything, just the same as the other? Why don't they do that? It's always money. It really makes me feel bad. [C4588ff.]

Native people have also commented with some bitterness on the lack of reciprocity which they say has characterized our dealings with the mineral resources of the North. Cecile Modeste of Fort Franklin expressed the sentiments of many native people in the North:

> In Port Radium, radium was discovered. In Norman Wells oil was discovered. In Yellowknife gold was discovered. All of these discoveries were [made] by Indian people. But all of the people who have discovered those minerals and stuff like that, the ways of making money, have died poor. They have died really poor. And those, the white people who have come in — we just go ahead and let them have all of these things, we never say anything about getting money back. . . .

But now it has come to a point where they are deciding to take the whole land. Then we have to say something about it. [C633ff.]

The Role of the Elders

There exists among the native people a special respect for the old. The elders are their historians, the keepers of their customs and traditions. They are respected for what they are, for the experience and the knowledge that their age has given them, and for all that they can in turn give to others. George Barnaby put it this way:

> Respect for the old people is another law, since all the laws come from the teaching by our elders, from stories that give us pride in our culture, from training since we are young; we learn what is expected of us. Without this learning from the elders our culture will be destroyed. [F22003]

The role of the elders and the respect they receive are important in the native people's attempts to deal with the problems that face them today. René Lamothe told the Inquiry at Fort Simpson about the activities of the Koe Go Cho Society, a community resource centre that serves the educational, cultural and social needs of the native people of Simpson. He explained the central role of the elders in the society's activities:

> We don't look at senior citizens' homes as they are looked at in the South or by the industrial economy. . . . The reason for having senior citizens here is a service to them of course. If they choose to come here there would be no charge to them. We would ask them to come as leaders of the people, as people who have the knowledge of the ways of life of the people to teach to the young here. They would come, not as people who have no further productive reality in the existence of the people, but as the crucial element, the age which passes on the life to the young. One of the perspectives of life that is lacking in the industrial economy, which is a very real thing. . . . in the Indian world, is the fact that we are born every day, and that every little bit of information that we learn is a birth. As we learn the way of life from the old, as we get older, we understand different things, we hear a legend, we hear it again, we hear it again, we hear it again, and every time at a given age this legend takes on new meaning.
>
> So the senior citizens by their presence, their knowledge of the past, of language, of songs and dances, of the legends, the material aspects of their culture, such as the building of canoes, snowshoes, this kind of thing, will be very instrumental in creating the spirit, the atmosphere in which the culture thrives. The senior citizens will be present to give moral support to the adults in alcohol rehabilitation. They will be present to assist the research and information crews to build a library of native folklore. Their presence in the education system as it is developing will make it possible for them to take up their rightful and ancestral role as teachers of their people. [C2698ff.]

Native Leadership

Until the signing of the treaties and the establishment under the Indian Act of the chief and band council model of Indian government, the Dene had no institutionalized political system as we understand it. However, as they made clear to the Inquiry, they did have their own ways of governing themselves. Chief Jim Antoine of Fort Simpson told the Inquiry:

> Before 1921 people used to live off the land along the rivers ... my people at that time were a nation. They had their own leaders, they had elders who gave direction, they had learned men who knew how to cure people and give good directions to the people, so that they could continue living off the land. [C2619]

Joe Naedzo, of the Fort Franklin Band, told the Inquiry:

> In those days, too, the government wasn't there to tell them how to do this and that, to survive. So the Indian people chose leaders and these leaders were the government for the people. They decided in what way the people should go this year, what to do before the winter comes. . . . These chosen leaders were the government. [C640]

When the Dene were still living in semi-nomadic extended-family groups, their leaders were the most respected hunters. The acceptance of their leadership rested on the deference of others to their wisdom and judgment and on their ability to provide for the group. Guidance was also provided by the shamans, men knowledgeable in spiritual and psychological matters. Leadership, however, was not usually autocratic; it respected the basic egalitarian structure of the group. Dr. June Helm, an anthropologist who has specialized for many years in Northern Athabascan society, described its nature in a paper written in 1976:

> The traditional Dene leader . . . is, on the basis of his superior abilities, consensually recognized by the group to serve as organizer, pacesetter and spokesman for the group. He is not the "boss" or independent decision-maker in group matters, as the Euro-Canadian might surmise. [*Traditional Dene Community Structure and Socioterritorial Organization*, p. 20, unpub.]

The Dene told the Inquiry about some leaders of the past. The Dogrib people of Fort Rae spoke of their great Chiefs Edzo and Monfwi, and the Loucheux people of Fort McPherson talked of the guidance given by Chief Julius. Both Chief Monfwi and Chief Julius were respected leaders when Treaty 11 was signed in 1921, and they became the first chiefs of their respective peoples under the system of elected chiefs instituted by the Indian Act.

Because no treaties were ever made with the Inuit, and because they were not brought within the framework of the Indian Act, they have not developed an institutionalized system for electing leaders. However, Inuit witnesses told the Inquiry that they, too, had their traditional leaders. Frank Cockney at Tuktoyaktuk described through an interpreter how, as a young man, he came to be aware of these leaders:

> At one time Eskimos used to get together in Aklavik after ratting and just before it was whaling season time. . . . He said he was big enough to understand, and that was the first time he saw the Indians there. And the Indians and the Inuit used to mix together, and that was the first time he also found out that there were chiefs. And he said the Eskimo Chief was Mangilaluk and there was other people there that got together with the Indians, Muligak and Kaglik, that was the

Eskimo leaders. He said the other Indian people he found out only later were Paul Koe and Jim Greenland and Chief Julius. He said he used to wonder how they always got together, but later he found out they were making plans about their land. . . . He found out only later, even though he didn't see them very often, that the older people always used to get together. They always planned how they would look after their land, so he said now, after he grew up, he knew it's nothing new that people plan about their land and how they look after it. It was done a long time ago also. [C42512ff.]

Charlie Gruben also told the Inquiry at Tuktoyaktuk about Inuit leadership:

> When we were young we had a Chief Mangilaluk. He tell us not to kill this and that. We don't do that because we want to listen to our chief, so good, we don't overkill. It was better than game wardens we got today, I think. That's the way the people used to handle their game that time. We don't kill game just for the sport, we just kill what we need and that's it. [C4254ff.]

Mark Noksana, one of the men who took part in the five-year reindeer drive from Alaska to the Mackenzie Delta in the 1930s, told the Inquiry how the wise judgment of William Mangilaluk had continued to serve the Mackenzie Delta Eskimos. He explained that Mangilaluk had been asked by government representatives whether the Eskimos wanted to take and receive treaty money like the Indians:

> [Mangilaluk] heard of some reindeer in Alaska. There was no caribou at all here in Tuktoyaktuk. You have to go far down to Baillie Island to get your caribou. No caribou at all at that time. . . . So the chief asked the government if he could get the reindeer from Alaska for the Eskimos. See, they don't want no money. He says money is no good to him. That's what he told me. He said he'd rather get reindeer so that he can have meat all the time for the new generation coming. . . . That's what happened. . . . I'm glad about it because the reindeer this year has been a real help to the Delta people at Tuk, McPherson, Arctic Red, Aklavik. There is no caribou on the west side this year. The reindeer have been real helpful for the people in the North. If it wasn't for the reindeer brought here, a lot of them would have been hungry for meat at Tuk, all these places, this year. [C4273ff.]

In the last few years the structure of native leadership seems, at first glance, to have changed. In many villages the Dene have elected young men to be their chiefs, and young people now play an essential role in the development of native political organizations. On closer analysis, however, the structure of leadership today can be seen to be continuous with traditional ways. In the old days, native leaders were chosen for their ability as hunters and as spokesmen in dealings with the white man. Today, the young and educated Dene and Inuit, who have learned to speak English and to articulate their aspirations to the outside world, have been chosen as leaders in the contemporary struggle for survival.

As leaders, however, the young people look to the elders for guidance. They seek to blend the knowledge they have acquired through education with the knowledge of the elders. Isidore Zoe, Chairman of the Settlement Council of Lac la Martre, a man in his early twenties, explained to the Inquiry the role of the new leadership:

My position is to go between the young and the old. It is the sort of thing like you compare from the old to the young generation to see what is suitable for both. . . .

We young people are the ear of the old people, to listen to what has been said. We hear what the politicians say — to pass it on to old people, in order for them to support and to make decisions.

We young people are the eyes of the old people, to see what is happening down South, what we read, and to compare what is the best for the Dene people.

We young people are the tongue of the old people . . . to say what they have to say. [C8197ff.]

Conclusions

There have been great changes in the life of the native people, particularly in the last 20 years, but they have tried to hold fast to the values that lie at the core of their cultures. They are striving to maintain these values in the modern world. These values are ancient and enduring, although the expression of them may change — indeed has changed — from generation to generation. George Erasmus, President of the Indian Brotherhood of the Northwest Territories, told the Inquiry at Fort Rae:

We want to be our own boss. We want to decide on our land what is going to happen. It's not as some people keep referring to as looking back. We are not looking back. We do not want to remain static. We do not want to stop the clock of time. Our old people, when they talk about how the Dene ways should be kept by young people, when they talk about stopping the pipeline until we settle our land claims, they are not looking back, they are looking forward. They are looking as far ahead into the future as they possibly can. So are we all. [C8068]

One of the greatest fears of young native people is that the impact of the pipeline will reduce to little more than a memory the values by which their parents and grandparents have lived. Bella T'Seleie spoke to the Inquiry at Colville Lake:

I was born in Fort Good Hope in 1953. When I was three years old my mother caught T.B. and was taken away. I was taken care of by the people of Good Hope. The people there are like that. If a kid doesn't have a mother, it is everybody's responsibility to make sure this kid doesn't starve . . . the kid is not taken off to some home, you know, to strangers either. I was kept by many families until my foster parents . . . learned about my situation. They weren't young and they had three children alive and they already had three younger girls who died. But they are kind people and they knew that I needed help, so they adopted me.

For the rest of my childhood I was raised in Colville Lake. In the summer we lived in fish camps, always working together making dry fish, cutting wood, and I look back on those days as really happy. I was happy. . . .

I look at Colville Lake today . . . [the people] still have their own lives; they still have their pride. I don't want my people to have nothing but memories of what their life used to be. . . .

There's a lot of young people, like myself, that want to have something other than memories. That's why we want control of what's going to happen to us and our lives in the future. I think about all that and I know that we are one of the last people to have our own land and still have our own kind of life in the world. I think the government and oil companies should consider that, after all they've done to the native people in the South, they should know that it doesn't work. It didn't work for them. They are not happy people; they are not proud people. All they have is memories. [C8329ff.]

The native people of the North insist that they have the right to transmit to future generations a way of life and a set of values that give coherence and distinctiveness to their existence as Dene, Inuit and Metis. Frank T'Seleie, then Chief of the Fort Good Hope Band, expressed his hope for the future of his people:

> Our Dene nation is like this great river. It has been flowing before any of us can remember. We take our strength, our wisdom and our ways from the flow and direction which has been established for us by ancestors we never knew, ancestors of a thousand years ago. Their wisdom flows through us to our children and our grandchildren, to generations we will never know. We will live out our lives as we must, and we will die in peace because we will know that our people and this river will flow on after us.
>
> We know that our grandchildren will speak a language that is their heritage, that has been passed on from before time. We know they will share their wealth and not hoard it, or keep it to themselves. We know they will look after their old people and respect them for their wisdom. We know they will look after this land and protect it, and that 500 years from now, someone with skin my colour and moccasins on his feet will climb up the Ramparts and rest, and look over the river, and feel that he, too, has a place in the universe, and he will thank the same spirits that I thank, that his ancestors have looked after his land well, and he will be proud to be a Dene. [C1778]

It may be asked why I have devoted so much space to these statements of native values. It may be said that the task that is at hand is the development of the North. But I have given this space to the native people's own words because they felt it was essential to say these things. By these statements the native people have affirmed their belief in themselves, their past and their future, and the ideals by which they seek to live. These are the values and the principles that must underlie the development of the North.

Chapter 6

The Acadian Society of Tomorrow: The Impact of Technology on Global Social Structure*†

Marc-Adélard Tremblay

Introduction

The traditional social structure and economic institutions of Acadia have recently been considerably affected by technological change and severe economic recessions. Unlike many countries which have successfully made the change from a traditional to a technological social structure, Acadian society has remained largely unchanged, at least in the development of its economy. The French Shore in Nova Scotia can hardly, by any standards, be considered industrial or urbanized. However, although the Shore has always been isolated from other centres of French culture, it has suffered some of the more undesirable consequences of industrialization due to the influence of surrounding areas which have been affected by modernization. Thus, in spite of the fact that the Shore has not itself been industrialized, the survival of the Acadian culture is seriously threatened by lack of economic development and massive migration of its youth to industrial centres.[1]

*Reprinted from *Anthropologica* 8:3 (1966), by permission of the author and the publisher.

†This chapter has been translated by the author. It first appeared as an article in *Anthropologica* under the title "La société acadienne en devenir: l'impact de la technique sur la structure sociale globale," 8, No. 2 (1966), 329-350. It appears as special chapters in M.-A. Tremblay and M. Laplante, *Famille et parenté en Acadie,* Ottawa: National Museum, 1971.

In practically every Acadian community, the occupational structure indicates a close economic dependence upon the rest of the province and Canada as a whole. In all the settlements, a number of industrial workers hold jobs in a neighbouring city during the week and return home only on the weekends.[2] Some work in other Canadian provinces or in the United States and return to visit their relatives only two or three times a year. To a large extent, these demographic shifts have coincided with the disappearance of a subsistance economy and have allowed for the mixing of values, new standards of living, and new lifestyles.

All these changes and the consequent effects that they have had on all levels of the social structure once again compel the Acadians to face the survival of their cultural traditions in southwestern Nova Scotia. But this time, the threat is more serious than previously. Although the indications of cultural change are not as explicit as in the past, they are nevertheless more solidly embedded in the everyday life patterns of the individual. Policies to reduce the impact of change are equally hard to outline and, in any case, do not have unanimity of purpose.

There are some modern elements that do not threaten the Acadian cultural traditions and are considered positive factors of progress, whereas others contradict the most fundamental themes of Acadian sentiment patterns. Acadians in leadership positions are divided among themselves as to the formulation of a general survival strategy and put forward divergent cultural orientations without knowing their relevance. In brief, we can say that the Acadian group does not have the basic instrumentation necessary for its socio-cultural reorganization. It also does not possess the essential techniques for reducing the continual outflow of its youth and for counter-influencing the powerful acculturating force of the mass media, that is, in general for counteracting the processes of acculturation.

We will attempt to follow the internal influences of these exogenous dynamisms of change in their respective development within the main segments of the total social structure, that is, occupational structure, social organization, and ideology.

Occupational Structure

Economic development has had its greatest impact upon occupational structure. Changes can be seen in a sharp decline of work activities in the primary sector of the economy: lumbering, farming, and in-shore fishing. It is not that these industries have stopped operating, but on the contrary, they have been reorganized for mass production. In the majority of cases, the updating of production techniques has not originated with the Acadians, but with outside English-speaking industrialists who took advantage of technological change by using local resources to return profitable gains, especially in times of economic recession.

A substantial decrease in the number of employees in the extraction industries is another result of economic and technical changes. Until recently, the great majority of the Acadian labour force was engaged in that sector. The economic evolution along the French Shore has therefore introduced at least two new trends: unemployment and the necessity to find work outside the community.

These two phenomena are closely linked as individuals migrate from their home communities to seek work. Unemployment, of course, has not been distributed equally through all social strata. Unskilled workers in the fishing and lumbering industries were the most severely affected. In 1952, close to three fifths of the workers in these occupational categories had been unemployed for varying lengths of time during the preceding twelve months.[3] Those in newer jobs, such as machine operators and truck drivers, as well as the white-collar workers have suffered little from unemployment.

Unemployment and the pattern of work outside the community have created numerous shifts in population. The demographic components of the Shore have remained fairly stable since 1910 and, since there has been very little immigration into the area, the natural growth of the population has been absorbed by departures. The migration of youth seeking work and of nuclear families has always been a threat to the survival of Acadian culture.

Until the twenties the Acadians looked to the U.S.A. and especially the New England states for employment. At about that time, with the introduction of new restrictive American immigration laws, families tended to move toward the industrial centres of the province. Since the end of the Second World War, this migration has spread to the other provinces and many Acadian migrants now leave to settle in large Canadian industrial centres. Most people, however, find it hard to settle in new locations, so that it is only after having examined the alternatives and having made a few compromises that migrants finally arrive at a decision to move.

In addition to problems of survival and of unemployment, traditions of out-county work and the departure of many young people and of whole families have introduced numerous difficulties for those who remain in the county.

Social Organization

FAMILY STRUCTURE

Economic and technological changes have not only transformed work patterns and the job market but they have also brought to an end the subsistence economy upon which family organization used to depend. Firstly, the family has lost its independence. Although the family network was never really self-sufficient, it is no longer able to meet even its basic needs in the new money economy. The increased relevance of monetary exchanges, the control of markets and jobs by large industrial corporations, the appearance of modern needs, and the lack of appropriate training and resources that could lead to the introduction of new mass production techniques have all served to outmode the traditional subsistence economy.

The family holding is no longer sufficient to provide a living for all household members. Moreover, the family land has been substantially reduced in size through traditional inheritance patterns which required the splitting up of property between all masculine descendants. The splitting up of holdings ceased for most families at the turn of this century, but in the case of families which owned large farm holdings and lumber lots, this inheritance practice survived up to the forties. Land under cultivation and farm woodlots can barely feed a restricted household. Therefore it comes as no surprise that children aim at earning their living outside the community.

These trends substantially altered family and kinship patterns. The extended family headed by the patriarch survived up to about 1920. From 1920 to 1940, the *famille souche* prevailed, that is, the family consisting of the husband, his wife, married son and his children living under the same roof. Finally, since the Second World War, the conjugal family has been the predominant model.

The breakdown of such a family system has brought about numerous changes. The patriarch has lost his former prestige in the family as the sole repository of power. The authority is now in the hands of the head of the restricted family and, since he has to be away from home for varying periods of time, his wife has acquired new power privileges.

The Acadian mother has always been highly regarded in the household, for she is responsible for teaching the children ethical values. Because of the frequent absence of the father, her new role in the household appears mainly to be bringing up the children, setting up networks of social relations, and defining the needs and aspirations of the family.

APPEARANCE OF A CLASS SYSTEM

Technological and economic changes also contributed to the birth of a class system. Even though we cannot as yet refer to clearcut social strata, there are indications of the emergence of several subgroups. Standard of living is one of the criteria that can be used to identify these groups. If we leave aside a small minority of professionals and businessmen who were more fortunate in traditional Acadian society, the other occupational categories used to share the same socio-economic status and the community as a whole took care of its poor. Moreover, a strong egalitarian ideology prevented great differences in lifestyle and restrained the more ambitious plans for betterment of a few members of the community.

But since the appearance of new value systems which place greater importance on material well-being, the differences in income are easier to notice because they are reflected in the quantity and quality of material goods purchased by families. The lower social classes also have aspirations toward greater equality with the more affluent, although there are still disparities in the goods bought with available income. Variations in income allow for differentiation in lifestyles but individuals who share the same standard of living tend to group themselves in the same voluntary organizations, political parties, and recreational activities.

The social hierarchy is also shown in the increasing number of jobs which have become available in the French Bay as the secondary sector of the economy grew in importance. The increasing number of workers in the service industries has accentuated class differences. Within the latter sector, most occupational functions require higher levels of education or more advanced training and therefore command better pay.

For a long time the Acadians have had a strong interest in education and Acadian leaders have promoted this interest among the population. But until the appearance of new occupations, higher education was almost exclusively reserved for priests and the other liberal professions such as doctors, dentists, and teachers. Besides, few Acadians who completed higher grades could find an opening in their own community. Thus, with the growth of a tertiary sector, a new social grouping has emerged: that of the administrators and civil servants who are responsible for providing new services.

Economic development and the emergence of social class have been accompanied by a number of significant social changes. These included the raising of educational levels and the appearance of new indigenous elites who displaced the existing Irish and Anglo-Saxon leadership. There was also a cultural renewal centred upon the establishment of municipal organizations interested in nationalistic pursuits. Finally, the appearance of economic differentiation is reflected in the lifestyles of Acadian families which is also another indication of class distinctions.

The class system has broken down the equalitarian ideology and accordingly challenged one of the most fundamental sentiments of the Acadian culture. It has also drawn a clearcut line between the sacred and the secular in defining with greater precision the specific responsibilities of the religious leader. If we attempt to underscore the special impact of this emerging class system upon the total social system we have to mention the splitting of Acadian society into two distinct groups: a new minority power elite that has appropriated all the symbols associated with wealth, and a growing majority of individuals who are left behind and are frustrated in their economic goals and social aspirations.

LEADERSHIP STRUCTURE

The very existence of an economically depressed group within the community challenges the survival of the Acadian "nation." Recent studies on the acculturation of the Acadians in some mixed communities of Stirling County show that it is the Acadian group with low standards of living, little schooling, and a low-class position that is the most attracted by English values and most readily relinquishes the corresponding traditional Acadian values.[4]

On the other hand, concern about the survival of the Acadian culture has become more closely connected with the higher classes. A national consciousness and the promotion of nationalistic sentiments are phenomena which first appeared at the end of the nineteenth century.[5] The idea of a spiritual and ideological community of all Maritime Acadians was promoted at conventions which provided the opportunity for an ethnic consciousness to develop. It convinced them that this "little nation," dispersed over the eastern Maritimes could ensure its perpetuation only if it undertook to take its own destiny in hand and create social institutions capable of protecting their rights and of promoting their objectives. In those days their survival still seemed providential and the Acadian mission in the Maritime Provinces was openly announced and national goals and programs were developed.

The fight for survival was undertaken at a time when the leadership was unchallenged by members of Acadian society. Today, the Acadian elite feel that it is almost compulsory to support the cause. A new leadership has been established through social organizations initially started to promote the survival of the group (La Société Nationale de l'Assomption, Le Collège St-Jean-Eudes, Acadian festivals, and various organizations whose aim is to improve education and regenerate Acadian customs) and through the efforts of those who have had to create and reinforce ties between communities committed to Acadian renewal. The Acadian revivalism is an ideology which aims at reinforcing Acadian power and influence along the French Shore and in the Atlantic Provinces. This, of course, necessitates specialized associations and new channels for communication to exert pressure upon the various governments in order to ensure new legislation favourable to the Acadian minority group. To co-ordinate their involvement, Acadian leaders, both lay and religious, must keep in touch with those who strive toward the same goals in other provinces.

New groups and new goals called for more leaders to fill available posts in community life. However, the modern leaders do not rouse the interest and respect associated with leadership functions in traditional Acadian society. Among much of the population the predominant attitude is one of passivity and resistance to change and to the new class of leaders who are working toward economic development and more nationalistic endeavours. The elite has diversified itself in order to incorporate new fields of activities and to meet the need for more formal decisions. But at the same time the leadership has lost some of its strength because it no longer has the unanimous support of the community nor spontaneous agreement even among those various specialized organizations which have similar objectives.

Dependence upon the outside environment, especially in the economic field, has forced local leaders to expand outside the boundaries of the local community and to endorse a kind of nationalism that needs to be well organized if it is to be spread to all Acadian communities. The fight for survival has become a full-time and highly specialized job for the more affluent.

But ideological distortions are beginning to appear that would further separate those with high socio-economic status from other Acadians. Those for whom making a living consumes all their energies are becoming conscious of the fact that it would be an easier undertaking if one were to join the dominant Anglo-Saxon group. The survival ideology does not seem to involve them, which explains their greater sensitivity to alien values. In comparison, the ruling class, which has severed itself from the larger society through better education, greater social prestige, and new lifestyles, continues to strive toward group survival in the name of the whole group. Leaders are still admired because of their ability to achieve personal success. In the new social context, however, access to leadership functions is not so much related to inherited status as to acquired individual capabilities. The one who shows special skills, initiative, and interest for a public function becomes a candidate for one of the leadership roles. Contributions to the fight for survival can then be understood partly as an effort on the part of those who have received more than others or who have had better opportunities to participate in community development but also partly as an effort to consolidate a class position. In mixed areas at the present time, the gap between the ideology of the leaders and that of the larger population continues to widen and is coupled with an increasing influence of the leaders.[6]

Ideology

IDEOLOGY AND EVENTS IN ACCULTURATION

The influence of economic and technical changes touch both directly and indirectly upon ideology. In the Acadian case, previous studies have dealt with levels of social structure through an analysis of shared sentiments which set forth the dominant values and norms of the group as well as outline fundamental attitudes on major issues.

Changes in Acadian sentiments can be interpreted as consequences of changes which occurred in other aspects of social life. We have already introduced the main chain of reactions without pursuing them to their final limits. Let us first summarize this series of consequences before coming to the question of value and ideological changes.

The first aspect to be considered is that of acculturation.[7] Acculturation levels, of course, differ in the various communities of the Bay. Some communities still get their inspiration from traditional indigenous value systems and reject alien values, whereas other localities have reached high acculturation levels.[8] We have already established that the appearance of a class system depending on the socio-economic status of the individual has worked toward establishing a new social stratum, the economically depressed, and that this particular social class increased with the growth of a monetary economy. Those at the lower end of the economic scale have a tendency to acculturate faster so that as unemployment contributed to the lowering of standards of living, it also indirectly favoured the acculturation process by forcing individuals to move into alien cultural environments.

We have already mentioned the impact of migratory moves on family life. These exogenous work patterns have increased French-English contacts and led to assimilation of new values. The same observations apply to young workers who have moved away from their home towns and thus enlarged their possibilities for mate selection. In quite a number of instances mixed English-Acadian marriages have been a primary factor behind Acadian acculturation. On the other hand, those who returned to the French Shore to settle after many experiences of outside work have themselves often been in conflict with their co-religionaries. They could draw comparisons and consequently interpreted Acadian values from a new perspective. These conflicts have caused some doubt and anxiety and represent the onset of a serious confrontation within Acadian culture. Furthermore, this stress is usually found among Acadians with below-average wealth who are at the centre of opposing forces. The younger generation, which is more acculturated and more sensitive to new values, is also tending to pull Acadians away from their culture of origin toward incorporation into the great American and English patterns. The Acadian leaders, however, continue to attempt to neutralize these new influences by proposing traditional culture models, but do not, in fact, improve their condition.

This inferiority, however, is not easily accepted, especially since material belongings and the size of one's bank account have become important criteria for measuring social prestige. The former primacy of the spiritual and the religious world view is contradicted by new values which call for short-term benefits, rest on models of living founded upon material well-being, and emphasize the conspicuous consumption of available goods and services. The Acadian has remained somewhat ambiguous in his self-evaluation of both his moral superiority and his material inferiority. If this ambiguity is to be resolved, it seems that it will tend more in the direction of striving toward economic betterment than in attempting to accentuate a spiritual outlook on life. It is toward this end that Acadian leaders are now working. They want to take over their own economy and to better equip the workers with the kind of skills that will allow them to undertake the new economic, technical, and administrative functions. Thus, in the new socio-economic context, the fundamental sentiment of group survival and its providential character and related spiritual mission has ceased to be as influential as it was in the past.

Techniques for survival have undergone parallel changes. An important concept has been that language was the sole guardian of the faith and that if these two elements remained interconnected and unchanged, survival would be ensured. Now, in a centre like Portsmouth, for instance, where Acadians account for 40 percent of the total population, more than half of the Acadian families use the English language in the home and about one third of them have lost their mother tongue altogether. These figures were collected ten years ago and one could hypothesize that the language situation has suffered additional setbacks since then. The highly acculturated Acadians feel inferior and attempt to make members of the English majority forget their ethnic history. They have accepted a religious pluralism which according to their view reflects the parity of all churches.

Although Portsmouth is a particular case, it reflects a general tendency to challenge the formerly undisputed supremacy of the spiritual. To the average Acadian, religion is no longer the sole important endeavour in life: more and more, he values upward social mobility, political leadership, and material success. In practice, religion and its main prescriptions have become less influential.

In traditional Acadia, group cohesion, efficient leadership, profound respect for those in authority positions, and betterment of schooling were the main techniques for survival. Many of these means are no longer as efficient as they were in the past and they are tending to become even less influential. Social cohesiveness is really threatened by class differences and by conflicts which arise between those who have outside experiences and those who have never left their home region. Family solidarity is already an ideal of the past as it has been eroded by the departure of family heads to work in industrial centres, the out-migration of the youth, and the new role of women in the household. With the exception of a few families, kinship ties no longer bind people together as before and families have built new networks of social relations. Leadership problems, as we have seen, are accentuated by the departure of the young who cannot use their knowledge or talent along the Bay. These problems are also related to the breach between the ideology of the survival-oriented leaders and that of the common people which is tied to personal success or subsistence. Consequently, those who occupy positions of authority do not command the same respect and are thus incapable of obtaining a concensus. Finally, although educational levels have risen, the departure of trained people has prevented education from being an appreciable factor in Acadian survival.

The sum of these changes at the level of shared sentiments and of group ideology would lead one to believe that Acadian society in Nova Scotia is profoundly influenced by new values. At the moment, it is easier to state that the old structure is disappearing than to foresee the nature of an emerging social structure.

The Future Outlook for Acadian Culture

ETHNIC CONSCIOUSNESS CRISIS

We did not hesitate to mention in 1960 that the Acadians of the French Bay had survived in spite of forces and external pressures from the dominant English Protestant group. In the face of strong pressures to assimilate, the group has held on to its most authentic values (those which distinguish the Acadians from the English). They have built a socio-cultural universe within which it is possible to maintain values that contradict those of the power group. These values stemmed from everyday activities through which the Acadians of the Bay found all the necessary elements to create a self-sufficient cultural tradition. They felt protected against the encroachments of Anglo-Saxon culture by a strong indigenous tradition that was well adapted to local living conditions. All these various dynamisms make it possible for us to understand, in part, the overall social processes which made survival possible.

But new tendencies were arising as early as 1960, (new value profiles, new linguistic patterns, etc.) which fit into the culture patterns of the majority group. In our estimation, four factors can explain these accelerated changes.

A Greater Dependence upon the Outside for Economic Subsistence. The French Shore does not have the internal resources required to develop its economy. This has led to a dependence upon outside economic activities and a climate of economic insecurity among workers. This dependence has forced many workers to hold jobs in Anglo-Saxon environments and the local economic leaders have been led to initiate regular administrative and financial transactions with English corporations. In all exchanges in which the Acadians must transact with English producers they are considered their inferiors.

The disappearance of the subsistence economy has also created deep rifts within the extended family, between various family units, and even among members of the same nuclear family. This is seen in the youth who wait for the first opportunity to move to a city. Migration affects young and old as it encourages the infiltration of alien values into Acadian society.

The New Mass Media. Even though English and Acadians associate daily in the new urban work settings, the two groups do not have as intimate and authentic a relationship as that created by innovations within the mass media. For some time, movies, popular magazines, and English newspapers have penetrated French towns without creating abrupt or spectacular changes. However, the relatively new medium of English television has in a decade brought about more changes among youth than all previous media. The "small screen" brings directly into the homes the fundamental North American values of love, marriage, religion, work and leisure, and human relations which are in conflict with traditional Acadian values. Also, watching TV from three to five hours a day reduces the opportunities for communicating and expressing oneself in French in the home. It is too early as yet to grasp fully the impact that such a daily contact with English culture will have on the Acadians. Undoubtedly television is a socializing agency which presents values and ideals that compete with those set up by other child-training agencies such as parents, school, and church. To what extent it will widen the generation gap and accelerate changes in value systems and attitudes among youth is a question which we do not, as yet, have enough empirical data to answer.

The Widening Gap between the Nationalistic Ideology Professed by the Elites and the Attitudes and Behaviour of the Population. In the fifties, new local elites contributed to the revival of the national ideology in two ways. First, the glorious past of their ancestors, stressed in such festivities as those which were held in the historic village of Grand Pré to celebrate the bicentenary of the Acadian Expulsion, was used as a powerful pole of national identity. In sharp contrast, the predestined future of the group in the Atlantic Provinces was considered conditional on the improvement of schooling and of standards of living so that the young intellectuals, industrialists, traders, and white-collar workers could take over the leadership.

Although leaders proposed schemes to revitalize the group, there was a weakening of national activities. Tired of taking upon themselves the onerous tasks of leadership, the elites are now marking time and enjoying the comfort and peace they feel they deserve as a reward for past efforts. At the same time, there is less sensitivity to issues of national interest and more emphasis is placed upon material acquisition. They feel that the greater victories have been won: the preservation of their mother tongue, the free practice of religion, the use of the French language in schools, and the establishment of an Acadian diocese in Nova Scotia. People do not understand why the group should have to bear new hardships at a time when most families voluntarily deprive themselves of essential goods to send their children to institutions of higher learning and to technical schools. The latter seldom return home to put their trade or professional skills to use which is detrimental to the development of new leadership and also to the efforts of the present leaders. Moreover, the nationalistic ideology has not been able to regenerate itself or to integrate itself in daily problems. Neither labourers nor white-collar workers see how the fact of being an Acadian and therefore different from others could be of any use to them in their relationships with their foremen and employees. In effect, covert social norms compel them to adopt alien behaviour models.

During important events, the traditional elites profess their faith in Acadian culture, but one has the impression that most Acadians feel progressively less involved in their messages and prefer to remain on the sidelines. The old nation of Acadia does not attract the youth who are too involved with their future and their material prospects in economically prosperous urban centres.

The Family has Ceased to be a Sanctuary that Mirrors the National values. Initially it was an interest in the function of the family in Acadian society that prompted us to study the impact of technological changes upon kinship structures and kinship relations. Young people first learned of their traditional heritage at home as the older generation were concerned not only to teach traditional values, but also to relate the history of preceding generations whose names and deeds were known as far back as the original settlers. Also the frequent large family gatherings encouraged a feeling of solidarity and of the unity of the small group within a larger society. This foundation in the kinship structure gave rise to a feeling of identification with their national symbols.

With the breakdown of the extended family generations became more divided. This generation gap reflects a new power structure within the family setting, but, more important for our purposes, it also severed the present generation from its historical past. Young families are building their future not so much on the basis of traditional or historical teaching but rather from the standpoint of aspirations stemming from the norms of success and upward mobility transmitted by the mass media. Thus the family is no longer able to safeguard national values for most families are too caught up in the process of change and the acquisition of material goods to have time to re-examine and re-interpret their traditional heritage and their functions as a family. The younger families are too interested in their television programs, their leisure activities, and in other peer-group undertakings to take an interest in a past which is temporally and psychologically distant. As far as they are concerned, everything has to be restructured because the modern world differs so drastically from the traditional.

We have mentioned only some of the more important factors in the new crisis in Acadian ethnic consciousness. However, from our viewpoint, these factors are more influential now than ever before because they are leading toward the building of a mass society which is gradually dissociating itself from its identification with its ethnic origins and is moving away from its traditional nationalistic value system toward that of the English Protestant culture.

SOME ELEMENTS OF RESTRUCTURING

Although fresh empirical data does not enable us to make any predictions about the survival of the Acadians in this region, we can pinpoint the most fundamental challenges to modern Acadia in order to grasp the full meaning of what is happening and bring into the open some of the critical elements in the new situation.

SOME FUNDAMENTAL PROBLEMS IN MODERN ACADIA

1. The economic underdevelopment of Acadian communities and of the Atlantic Provinces;
2. The progressive assimilation of Acadian groups living in mixed areas and in predominantly English Protestant environments;
3. The ethnic sentiment pattern is, in many respects, ambiguous. The leaders have not as yet stated ethnic aims that conform closely to daily activities;
4. High geographical mobility of workers within the province and between provinces;
5. The massive out-migration of the youth to industrial centres and the problems that this raises from the standpoint of leadership continuity and of the maintenance of cultural traditions; and

6. Industrialization and urbanization have brought about greater social differentiation which is reflected in the objective, socio-cultural characteristics of the Acadians as well as in their overt value patterns. We do not think it is feasible for a new leadership to integrate all these tendencies in a policy for action.

CRITICAL ELEMENTS OF THE ACADIAN FUTURE

It seems evident that the family has become ill-equipped to take over the survival functions of the group. Two facts lead to this conclusion: firstly, the family is no longer an isolated, self-sufficient social unit or a microcosm of the larger society; and secondly, the new family structure has not only developed new types of social relationships within itself, but also does not encourage an historical consciousness, nor does it allow for a spontaneous adherence to past teachings. Within that social context, the promotion of ethnic values depends upon the creation of new institutional structures, such as, economic development, higher levels of schooling, the democratization of elites, and a new arrangement of social space.

Economic Development. The French Bay must become a viable economic unit again, not only able to absorb its own labour force but also to become a pole for further development. This would presuppose that the Acadians could exert a greater control over the regional economy than they have up to the present, and that they could undertake new economic developments using available resources, modern manufacturing techniques, and local participation.

A Higher Level of Education. We have noted that the highly educated and those who receive the best occupational training tend to migrate to the city. All Acadians from the region should be able to remain in school as long as possible and get the training best suited for the labour market. Higher schooling would encourage the growth of a stronger economic and intellectual elite, but drastic measures would be needed to keep the educated in the area. The consolidation of schools is a step in the right direction.

The Democratization of Elites. Traditional elites are being challenged because they express values that are less and less understood by the people. If there could be pluralism in leadership, new leaders might appear who can better identify themselves with the socio-economic aspirations of individuals. Their contemporary world view, expertise, and economic aspirations are concrete assets which can bring about a renewed interest in national objectives. The lay teachers, who are closer to young students, are in the best position to arouse interest in and understanding of an ethnic ideology.

The Arrangement of Social Space. For many years the Acadians have conceived the larger territory of the Bay as a supra-parochial territorial unit. Organizations such as the Acadian Association for Education and the St.-Malo Board of Trade have been established on a wider geographical base and have achieved important results. This principle could be applied in many other fields of activities to regroup efforts and expertise. Why could we not work toward urbanizing some small centres that would eventually become poles of economic development and demographic growth?

Unless some of these suggestions are put into practice, it seems likely that the rural French Bay will soon become an anachronism and an easy prey to assimilation into the larger industrial society whose social institutions are better suited to the various facets of modernism and industrial technology.

NOTES

[1]See Marc-Adélard Tremblay, "Les Acadiens de la Baie Française: L'Histoire d'une Survivance," *Revue d'Histoire de L'Amérique Française,* 15, No. 4 (1962), 540-541.

[2]In the summer of 1962, about two hundred family heads from the Bay spent five days a week in Halifax where they work.

[3]Technological change has accelerated the disappearance of traditional jobs for which the Acadians were well equipped. They have been unable to learn the trades of industrial society which could absorb many workers. This double lag — the displacing of traditional trades and the inability of workers to adapt to the requirements of the urban job market — has been at the origin of the high unemployment rates that we observe today along the Shore.

[4]M.-A. Tremblay, "The Acadians of Portsmouth: A Study in Culture Change" (Ph.D. Thesis, Cornell University, Ithaca, 1954). See also, C. C. Hughes et al., *People of Cove and Woodlot,* New York: Basic Books, 1960, pp. 73-78.

[5]Camille Richard, "L'Idéologie de la Première Convention Nationale Acadienne" (M.A. Thesis, Université Laval, Québec, 1960).

[6]Francine Chartrand, "L'Idéologie de la Survivance chez les Acadiens de Portsmouth" (M.A. Thesis, Université Laval, Québec, 1963), p. 2.

[7]I am here referring to the theoretical framework that guided our studies on the acculturation of Acadians. See Marc-Adélard Tremblay, "Le Transfert Culturel: Fondement et Extension dans le Processus d'Acculturation," *Anthropologica,* 4, No. 2 (1962), 293-320.

[8]The main factors which led to the cultural dissociation process are the following: social isolation from French centres of civilization; the predominantly Anglo-Protestant mass media; frequent and continuous cross-cultural contacts; migratory experiences; mixed marriages; the neutral school; and the hierarchy of the diocese (Irish before 1955). There are fewer factors which reduce the impact of acculturation; the parish, family and kinship networks, and the cultural orientations of local elites. For a study of the levels of acculturation of Portsmouth, Pulp Creek, and Northport Acadians see, Marc-Adélard Tremblay, "Niveaux et Dynamismes d'Acculturation des Acadiens à Portsmouth," *Anthropologica,* 3, No. 2 (1961), 1-50.

Chapter 7

Language and Ethnic Community Survival*†

Jeffrey G. Reitz

Language retention is a main theme of ethnic politics in Canada. Spokesmen for ethnic minorities view with alarm the failure of the second and third generations to learn the ethnic language. They issue demands for publicly supported language schools and other facilities needed to keep the language alive. "Language loyalty" also has been a concern of many American ethnic group organizations, though they function in the context of considerably less public sympathy (see Fishman, et al., 1965).

What is the real significance of language retention in ethnic communities? Does its significance lie primarily in its intrinsic value as an expression of

---

*Reprinted from *The Canadian Review of Sociology and Anthropology,* Special Issue, 1974, by permission of the author and the publisher.

† The data used in the analysis are drawn from a survey commissioned by the Secretary of State, Ottawa. The data were first used as the basis for a comprehensive report on *Non-official Languages in Canada,* by K.G. O'Bryan, J.G. Reitz, and O. Kuplowsky, which is being published by the Queen's Printer. Permission to use the data for the purposes of the paper was generously granted by the Office of the Secretary of State. The paper was prepared independently of the original project, and of course responsibility for its contents lies solely with the author. Thanks are due to Raymond Breton, Lorne Tepperman, and James Turk for their valuable comments on an earlier draft.

traditional ethnic culture? Or is language retention really also an important key to the survival of the ethnic community itself? There is much literature devoted to the relation between language and culture, but the relevance of language retention to ethnic community survival and change is only beginning to be explored. The purpose of this paper is to pose the issue rather sharply, and to examine some relevant survey data on Canadian ethnic minorities having immigration histories spanning several generations.

One body of theory argues that the possession of a common language by a group constitutes a powerful social force binding that group together. This is one of the functions of language listed by Edward Sapir (1933). For Sapir, language is not only a vehicle for the expression of thoughts, perceptions, sentiments, and values characteristic of the group; language also represents a fundamental expression of collective social identity. "The mere fact of a common speech serves as a peculiarly potent symbol of the social solidarity of those who speak the language" (Sapir, 1933:159). It would follow that language retention may serve to maintain feelings of ethnic kinship. Descendants of immigrants who do not learn their ancestral language are not exposed to a powerful force for ethnic group solidarity.[1]

Hertzler (1965) emphasized the double implication of this theory. Language knowledge, by serving as a basis for ethnic solidarity, in effect defines the boundaries of the ethnic group. It defines who is included in the ethnic group and who is excluded. Immigrants' sons and daughters who fail to learn the ancestral language are not merely lax in their appreciation of certain ethnic values. In the eyes of bilinguals, they are almost deviant, and in any case they are denied full participation in the ethnic community. Social exclusion of such "deviants" may weaken the group itself, a possibility mentioned in several studies of specific ethnic communities. For example, Lemaire (1965:268) in his study of Franco-Americans in New England, observes that "instead of being the 'keeper' of the faith that it once was, the French language had become an instrument of religious ignorance." Hertzler devotes a chapter each to what he calls the "centripetal" and "centrifugal" functions of language.

Language retention, or bilingualism, is not a key independent variable in most conventional sociological literature on assimilation. For example, Gordon (1964) analyses the effects of social interaction between ethnic insiders and outsiders. The main hypothesis is that cultural assimilation (adoption of the cultural patterns of the host society) results from structural assimilation (entrance into equal participation in the social structure of the host society). If Sapir's theory is correct, then language knowledge should be included as an important independent variable affecting the process of assimilation, or at least as an intervening variable which affects the relation between structural assimilation and cultural assimilation. This would include the possibility that structural assimilation leads to cultural assimilation because it undermines bilingualism, and the possibility that under certain circumstances structural assimilation may be compatible with bilingualism, leading to the persistence of a degree of ethnic solidarity.

It would be a mistake, of course, to see language retention as some kind of universal functional prerequisite to the maintenance of an ethnic community. Few would agree with Weinstock (1969:16) who finds it "difficult to imagine how an ethnic group could maintain its solidarity without a language of its own." In the first place, low social standing and social exclusion as analysed by Gordon may symbolize and reinforce ethnic distinctiveness whatever its effect on language retention. Skin colour is undoubtedly relevant to the maintenance of the Black community in the United States. For Jews, religion and culture affected by a long history of oppression and anti-semitism are at least as important as language in providing a basis for solidarity. Barth (1969:14) lists many possible cultural symbols of ethnic cohesion, including language, but also dress, life style, and basic value orientations. Mention is sometimes made of the political situation in the homeland (for example, Ukrainians in North America are alleged to be unified by a common concern with Soviet policies of cultural annihilation in the Ukraine). Even the desire in a modern bureaucratic society for particularistic associations outside the family may be relevant. The persistence of ethnicity without language, as implied for example in Hansen's (1962) "principle of third generation interest," is certainly feasible, even though the meaning of ethnicity may change considerably from one generation to the next (cf. Glazer and Moynihan, 1963:13; Nahirny and Fishman, 1965a and 1965b:355). The task is to determine the relative impact of each of these and other conditions on assimilation.

Research Requirements

To find out whether ethnic language retention is actually a basis for social solidarity in particular ethnic groups, one must consider the separation of cause from effect. In an ethnic group undergoing partial or total assimilation, various ethnic characteristics are likely to be highly intercorrelated, whatever the causal relations among them. Language retention may be highly correlated with ethnic community participation because it is a result of ethnic solidarity, rather than because it is a cause.

Two recent Canadian studies exemplify this methodological problem. Both studies produced correlations between language retention and ethnic community maintenance, but the authors reached opposite conclusions about causal priority. Lieberson's (1970:245-248) study of *Language and Ethnic Relations in Canada* contains a brief analysis in which language retention is treated as causally prior. For nine ethnic groups (including British and French) Lieberson examined the association between mother tongue and residential segregation. He concluded that language retention serves to maintain residential segregation (religion was a control variable). Vallee and Shulman (1969) also presented data relating language retention to community structure, but they treated language retention as the dependent variable. The study concerned French-Canadian communities outside Quebec, and the community variables included residential segregation and the organization strength of the ethnic community. On the basis of the correlations they found, they concluded that ethnic community structure influences language retention. Clearly, more detailed data are needed to assess the actual causal sequences, and specifically to find out whether language retention has any independent effects on ethnic community maintenance.

The appropriate research device for dealing with such problems is the panel study. Unfortunately, an appropriately designed panel study in this case would have to extend over at least two decades in time. Ethnic languages generally are learned in early childhood (if at all), and we are interested in whether adult participation in the ethnic community is affected by language knowledge independently of other factors likely to be strongly associated with language learning.

The present study relies on cross-sectional survey data, which can be used to improve on previous studies in two ways. First, we can compare generational groups. If ethnic community participation is weaker in the second and third generation, we can determine to what extent this weaker participation is accounted for by the failure of second and third generation ethnic group members to learn the ethnic language. Of course it must be kept in mind that each generational group today represents a different historical period of immigration. The parents of today's second generation may not be adequately represented by today's immigrant generation.

The use of retrospective questions asking respondents to reconstruct their own past experiences obviously raises the problem of selective and distorted recall. However, such questions in certain circumstances can produce useful information. In this study, responses to retrospective questions will be analysed to reach conclusions about the relative importance of language learning and other socializing influences in the parental family.

Survey Data on Four Ethnic Groups in Canada

The study focuses on urban Canadians of Italian, German, Ukrainian, and Polish origin. These four groups are the largest urban ethnic minorities in Canada[2] and each has an immigration history extending from before the First World War up to the recent past. Thus each group contains many persons in the second and third generation, as well as many recent immigrants (cf. Royal Commission on Bilingualism and Biculturalism, 1970:17-32).[3] Since the Second World War, Canada has experienced immigration from many sources, and its urban centres, particularly Toronto, now have a large number of active ethnic communities. In 1970, half of the household heads in Toronto had been born outside Canada, and one-third had mother tongues other than English or French (Richmond 1972:15-17). Members of nearly all of the non-English groups are concerned with the survival of their ethnic community and in particular with the fate of their mother tongue in Canada. But this study deals only with four groups in which it is possible to study intergenerational change in fairly large representative samples.

The characteristics of the four groups suggest that language retention may be particularly important to their ethnic solidarity. In many respects the groups are similar to English Canadians and have become fairly well integrated into Canadian society. They are white, usually Christian, and share with most other Canadians a European heritage. The groups are distributed throughout the urban Canadian occupational structure, although they are somewhat less well represented in professional and financial occupations than are the English, Jews, and Asians (Porter, 1965:87).[4] Only Italians have any significant occupational disadvantage at the moment. This may be attributed at least in part to the lower occupational level of a large number of the very recent Italian immigrants.

The sample was selected to represent all members of the four ethnic groups over 18 years of age living in Montreal, Toronto, Winnipeg, Edmonton, and Vancouver in 1973.[5] A double-sample procedure was employed. The first phase consisted of city-wide stratified sampling in each of the five cities. City-wide sampling was necessary to ensure adequate representation for all ethnic group members. Although some residential segregation does exist, many ethnic group members do not live in ethnic neighborhoods. This sample was interviewed to determine ethnic origin, using the Canadian census criterion of ethnicity (ethnic or cultural ancestry on the male side). A second phase of sampling selected those found to be in one of the eligible ethnic groups. The main interview was conducted with only the second-phase sample (N = 1319). The over-all interview completion rate was 64 per cent. A weighting procedure was devised so that the data may be used to represent the sample universe. The weighting procedure takes account both of differential sampling probabilities and of differential interview completion rates in the various sample strata (weighted N = 959,097). Table I presents the group-by-group sample breakdown. For comparative purposes Table I also presents a 1971 census special tabulation for the sampled population. The population estimate based on the sample does exceed the census enumeration by 17.9 per cent. In part, this excess might be attributable to continued immigration between 1971 and 1973, or to errors in the census enumeration itself. The main sampling-error possibility is over-sampling among immigrants. This does not pose a major problem for the analysis, since generational groups are treated separately.

Interviewing was conducted by the York University Survey Research Center in the spring of 1973. About 83 per cent of the interviews were conducted in English; the rest were conducted by bilingual interviewers, using an appropriate translation of the interview schedule.

Four generational groups will be distinguished. There is the usual distinction between immigrants, second generation (native-born children of foreign or mixed parentage), and third generation. However, immigrants in the sample comprised 64 per cent, and it is desirable to distinguish two subgroups. Most of the immigrants came to Canada as adults. However, about one in four were children when they arrived. These "childhood

TABLE I
SAMPLE CHARACTERISTICS; 1973 FIVE-CITY ETHNIC GROUP SURVEY

Ethnic group	1973 Sample		1971 census*	Percentage by which weighted sample estimates exceed census enumeration
	N	Weighted N		
Italian	359	382,499	299,470	+27.7
German	347	303,876	250,500	21.3
Ukrainian	338	181,656	169,880	6.9
Polish	275	91,066	93,830	-2.9
Total	1319	959,097	813,680	+17.9

* From a special tabulation of the 1971 Census of Canada for ethnic
  group members 18 years of age and over in Montreal, Toronto,
  Winnipeg, Edmonton, and Vancouver.

immigrants" grew up in Canada, and are perhaps more like second generation persons actually born in Canada than they are like the adult immigrants. Table II presents the distribution over four generational categories for each ethnic group.

Detailed attention was given to the measurement of language knowledge. However, no tests of such knowledge were administered. Instead, respondents were asked their mother tongue, and their current ability to understand, speak, read, and write in the ethnic language (Lieberson, 1966). In the analysis, two language-knowledge variables will be used: (1) *Current language knowledge*. Respondents were classified either as fluent (good self-rated ability to understand, speak, read, and write in the ethnic language), as having some knowledge of the ethnic language (but not fluent), or as having no knowledge of the ethnic language at all. (2) *Mother tongue*. Respondents were asked which language they first learned in childhood and still understand.

Solidarity with the ethnic group is measured using responses to questions about current participation in the ethnic community. Eleven different aspects of ethnic community participation are included. Three explicitly involve use of the ethnic language: (1) *Language use in speaking*. Respondents were asked how often they speak in the ethnic language. (2) *Language use in reading the ethnic press*. Respondents were asked whether they had read any ethnic newspapers or bulletins written in the ethnic language during the previous year. (3) *Language use in church*. Respondents associated with a church were asked what languages are used in the church services.

The eight other aspects of participation may or may not involve use of the ethnic language: (4) *Ethnic identification*. Respondents were asked: "How do you usually think of yourself; as a (Italian, German, Ukrainian, Pole), or a (. . .)-Canadian, or a Canadian-(. . .), or what? (5) *Ethnic endogamy*. Married respondents were asked the ethnicity of their spouse. (6) *Close ethnic ties*. Respondents were asked: "Do you maintain close ties with other (. . .) in

TABLE II
PERCENTAGE OF ETHNIC GROUP MEMBERS IN EACH GENERATION CATEGORY

Generation	Ethnic group				Total
	Italian	German	Ukrainian	Polish	
Adult immigrant	63.7	48.5	20.5	33.9	47.8
Childhood immigrant	18.0	14.3	14.4	14.6	15.8
Second generation	13.8	17.6	44.3	40.9	23.3
Third generation (and later)	4.6	19.6	20.8	10.6	13.0
(N)	(382499)	(303876)	(181656)	(91066)	(959097)

Canada?" (7) *Ethnic friendships.* Respondents were asked the ethnicity of their three closest friends. (8) *Association with an ethnic church.* Respondents associated with a church were asked about the ethnic composition of the church membership. (9) *Residence in an ethnic neighbourhood.* Respondents were asked about the ethnic composition of their neighbourhood. (10) *Membership in ethnic organizations.* Respondents were asked about the ethnic composition of the organization in which they are most active (other than churches, unions, or professional organizations). (11) *Reading the ethnic press in English or French.* Respondents were asked whether they had read any ethnic newspapers or bulletins written in English or French during the previous year.

In the multivariate analysis, gamma is used as the measure of association. All the variables are ordinal, having two, three, or four categories (cf. Mueller, et al., 1970:279-292). The N used to calculate gamma varies as a result of non-response to particular interview questions.

Generational Differences in Ethnic Characteristics

Second and third generation Italians, Germans, Ukrainians, and Poles in urban Canada have definitely moved away from the ethnic community. "Canadianization" is a term not frequently heard in connection with the New Canadians, and many regard it as undesirable. But in fact there is very limited retention of language and most other ethnic characteristics among the children and grandchildren of immigrants.

Generational trends in language knowledge are presented in Figure I. Adult immigrants are of course quite fluent in their mother tongue. Childhood immigrants generally report their mother tongue to be the ethnic tongue, but less than half are fluent. In the second generation, fluency is down to 11 per cent, although over 80 per cent do retain some knowledge of their ethnic language. And by the third generation, almost none are fluent, and less than 40 per cent retain any knowledge of the ethnic language at all.

Intergenerational language loss is paralleled by intergenerational withdrawal from the ethnic community. This withdrawal is reflected not only in language use (also represented in Figure I), but also in most other aspects

FIGURE I. *Language-Related Ethnic Characteristics, by Generation. Italians, Germans, Ukrainians, and Poles are Combined.*

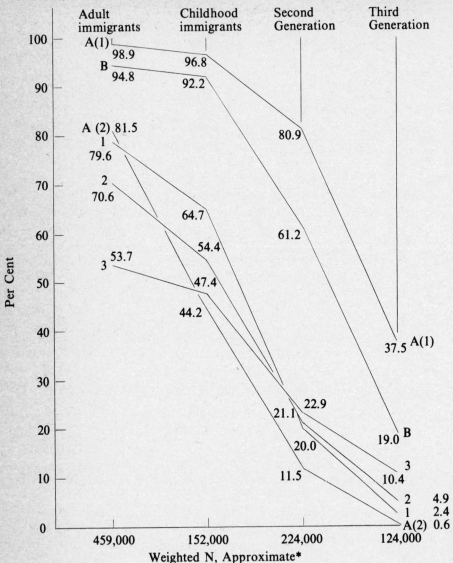

DEFINITIONS:

A(1) / Percentage having at least some knowledge of the ethnic language (see text)

A(2) / Percentage fluent in the ethnic language (see text)

B / Percentage whose mother tongue is the ethnic language

1 / Percentage speaking the ethnic language "every day"

2 / Percentage having read any ethnic newspaper or bulletin written in the ethnic language during the previous year

3 / Percentage associated with a church in which the ethnic language is used in the services

*Actual *Ns* used to calculate percentages vary as a result of missing data.

FIGURE II. *Other Ethnic Characteristics, by Generation, Italians, Germans, Ukrainians, and Poles are Combined.*

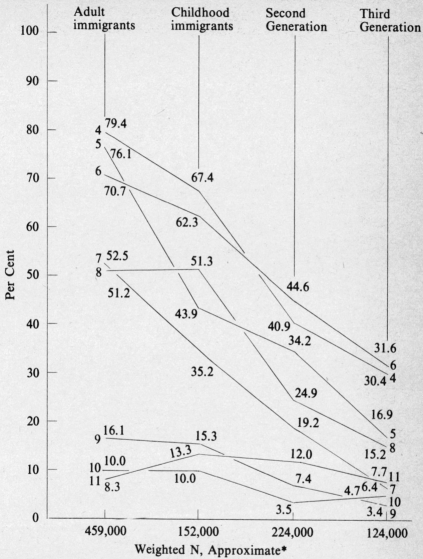

DEFINITIONS:
4 / Percentage identifying self with ethnic label (e.g., Italian, Italian-Canadian, Canadian of Italian origin)
5 / Percentage having a spouse in the ethnic group
6 / Percentage maintaining close ties with the ethnic group
7 / Percentage whose three closest friends are all in the ethnic group
8 / Percentage associated with a church in which more than half of the members are in the ethnic group
9 / Percentage living in a neighbourhood in which residents are mostly in the ethnic group
10 / Percentage whose main organizational membership (other than religious-

or occupation-related organizations) is in an organization in which more
than half the members are in the ethnic group

11 / Percentage having read any ethnic newspaper or bulletin written in English
or French during the previous year

*Actual Ns used to calculate percentages vary as a result of missing data.

of ethnic community participation (see Figure II).[6] Ethnic community
participation drops off less sharply than language knowledge, in part because
such participation among adult immigrants is not as universal as language
knowledge. Both reach a low level in the third generation. The most
widespread ethnic characteristics in the third generation are the possession
of some language knowledge, the claim to be maintaining close ties, subjective
ethnic identification, and having the ethnic tongue as mother tongue. All of
the specific behaviours representing ethnic participation are reported by fewer
than 20 per cent of the third generation respondents. (Note that there is no
evidence of any increased "third generation interest" in ethnicity, in terms of
any of the various measures of ethnic community participation.)

Similarities in generational trends among the four ethnic groups are more
significant than the differences. In Table III, the generational trends for each

TABLE III
EFFECT OF GENERATION ON ETHNIC CHARACTERISTICS, BY ETHNIC GROUP
(GAMMA)

	Ethnic group				
Ethnic characteristics	Italian	German	Ukrainian	Polish	Total (See also Figs. I, II)
Ethnic language:					
1. Current knowledge	.781	.932	.827	.809	868
2. Ethnic mother tongue	.921	.819	.812	.687	.839
Ethnic language use:					
1. Speaking	.822	.817	.749	.746	.794
2. Reading ethnic press	.596	.773	.783	.781	.729
3. Church	.562	.479	.543	.693	.490
Other characteristics:					
4. Ethnic identification	.580	.617	.344	.540	.587
5. Ethnic endogamy	.808	.490	.573	.533	.657
6. Close ethnic ties	.457	.426	.300	.523	.443
7. Ethnic friendships	.534	.416	.476	.537	.500
8. Assoc. with ethnic church	.468	.280	.606	.650	.431
9. Res. in ethnic nbhd.	.173	−.154	−.124	−.150	.079
10. Memb. of ethnic org.	−.054	.453	.560	.647	.292
11. Reading ethnic press (in English or French)	.227	−.073	−.068	.163	−.077
(Weighted N, approximate)*	(382,000)	(304,000)	(182,000)	(91,000)	(959,000)

*Actual N's used to calculate gamma vary as a result of missing data.

ethnic group are summarized using gamma for the relation between generation and each ethnic characteristic. The effect of generation on language knowledge is quite strong in each ethnic group, ranging from 0.781 for the Italians to 0.932 for the Germans. Generational trends in ethnic community participation are also very similar in all four ethnic groups. There are some variations from group to group depending upon the type of participation. For example, the effect of generation on ethnic identification is relatively low among Ukrainians and relatively high in the other three groups. On the other hand, the effect of generation on ethnic church attendance is relatively high both among Ukrainians and Poles, and relatively low among Germans and Italians. Over-all, there is no clear tendency for any group to leave the ethnic community more rapidly than the others. In the remainder of the analysis the four ethnic groups will be combined.

Bilingualism and Ethnic Solidarity in the Second and Third Generation

To find out whether language loss has any effect in reducing ethnic solidarity, we will begin by looking at the relation between language knowledge and ethnic community participation within each generational group. Interest focuses mainly on the second and third generations, and in fact the adult immigrants will be excluded from most of the analysis, since language knowledge among them is universal. It is important here to have in mind the fact that a basic knowledge of an ethnic tongue usually is acquired, if at all, in the very early years of life (before age five at the latest).[7] Language knowledge therefore precedes in time the ethnic community participation measured for the study. Any relation between language knowledge and participation at the individual level would reflect an effect of language knowledge on participation, rather than the reverse.[8]

The relation between language knowledge and ethnic community participation within each generational group is shown in Table IV. In each generational group, an ethnic group member who learns the ethnic language (as a child) is far more likely to participate in the ethnic community (as an adult). Two-thirds of the gammas are over 0.500. Of course, forms of participation explicitly involving use of the ethnic language are the most strongly related to language knowledge. The significant fact is that language knowledge is strongly related to all other forms of ethnic community participation as well.

Notice that there is no difference by generation in the importance of language knowledge as a determinant of ethnic community participation, despite the sharply reduced level of language knowledge in the later generations. As language knowledge becomes less widespread, it does not become less relevant to ethnic cohesion. If anything, the effect of language knowledge is increased in the later generations. The increased effect is particularly evident in the case of membership in ethnic organizations, and attendance at ethnic churches, forms of participation which perhaps require the greatest individual initiative, and in which language use may be most strongly enforced.

The findings suggest that the failure of second and third generation children to learn the ethnic language is an important link in the sequence leading to deterioration of ethnic solidarity from one generation to the next, and that if conditions existed which prevented "language shift," the ethnic community would more likely survive in succeeding generations. The extent to which this is true can be seen in Table V, where gamma measures the effect of generation on ethnic community participation within groups having acquired particular levels of language knowledge. It is quite clearly the case that at each level of language knowledge, generation has relatively little effect on participation. While the data are a bit erratic, the effect of generation is reduced in all cases, and is as often negative as positive.

TABLE IV
EFFECT OF ETHNIC LANGUAGE KNOWLEDGE ON ETHNIC COMMUNITY
PARTICIPATION, BY GENERATION; ADULT IMMIGRANTS EXCLUDED (GAMMA)

		Generation		
Aspect of ethnic community participation	*Total*	*Childhood immigrants*	*Second generation*	*Third generation*
Ethnic language use:				
1. Speaking	.934	.747	.895	.999
2. Reading ethnic press	.877	.518	.913	.989
3. Church	.700	.391	.700	.677
Other characteristics:				
4. Ethnic identification	.610	.473	.458	.631
5. Ethnic endogamy	.642	.672	.572	.532
6. Close ethnic ties	.658	.533	.700	.606
7. Ethnic friendships	.565	.535	.506	.503
8. Assoc. with ethnic church	.698	.373	.670	.785
9. Res. in ethnic nbhd.	.360	.359	.265	.402
10. Memb. of ethnic org.	.633	.224	.806	.950
11. Reading ethnic press (in English or French)	.300	.417	.330	.073
(Weighted *N,* approximate)*	(500,000)	(152,000)	(224,000)	(124,000)

*See note to Table III.

Independent Effects of Language Learning in the Parental Family

The centrality of language in ethnic community participation is established by the analysis so far, but we are not yet in a position to draw firm conclusions about the Sapir theory. Ethnic-language learning in childhood is bound to be highly associated with other socializing experiences which influence later ethnic allegiance. If such experiences are not perfectly correlated with language retention, then it is possible to analyse their independent effects.

TABLE V
EFFECT OF GENERATION ON ETHNIC COMMUNITY PARTICIPATION, BY KNOWLEDGE OF THE ETHNIC LANGUAGE (GAMMA)

		Knowledge of ethnic language		
Aspect of ethnic community participation	*Total (from Table* III)	*Fluent*	*Some knowledge*	*No knowledge*
Ethnic language use:				
1. Speaking	.794	.277	.586	**
2. Reading Ethnic Press	.729	.171	.474	**
3. Church	.490	.092	.488	**
Other characteristics:				
4. Ethnic identification	.587	.279	.385	-.279
5. Ethnic endogamy	.657	.281	.415	.010
6. Close ethnic ties	.443	-.160	.226	-.209
7. Ethnic friendships	.500	-.033	-.317	.105
8. Assoc. with ethnic church	.431	-.165	.391	-.098
9. Res. in ethnic nbhd.	.079	.282	.228	.087
10. Memb. of ethnic org.	.292	.042	-.101	**
11. Reading ethnic press (in English or French)	-.077	-.337	-.251	-.186
(Weighted *N*, approximate)*	(959,000)	(467,000)	(361,000)	(131,000)

*See note to Table III.
**Insufficient number of non-tied pairs.

Which other socializing experiences are relevant? Religion is sometimes mentioned as an institution which helps bind ethnic communities together. It might be expected that early religious training would encourage later participation in the ethnic community. However, the present study finds that early religious training has only a small over-all effect in this direction. Among respondents who grew up in Canada, church attendance while growing up is not at all related to the maintenance of close ties with the ethnic community in the adult years (gamma = 0.030). Of the eleven measures of ethnic community participation, reading the ethnic press in the ethnic language is most strongly affected by early church attendance (gamma = 0.142).

A more direct measure of early experiences relevant to ethnicity is needed. Respondents (except adult immigrants) were asked: "Would you say your parents hoped you would maintain ties with other (Italians, Germans, Ukrainians, Poles)?" Just over half (59 per cent) replied "yes." These responses will be used to measure parents' efforts on behalf of ethnic retention in general. The responses are strongly associated with respondents' reports on their actual maintenance of close ethnic ties (gamma = 0.672).

The two childhood experiences — language learning and having parents who encouraged ethnic solidarity — are closely related (gamma = 0.774), but since the association is not perfect, the independent effects of each on adult behavior can be analysed.[9] Some respondents did not learn the ethnic language despite their parents' hopes that they would maintain ethnic ties. This may happen when parents attach more importance to non-linguistic aspects of ethnicity, or when the community environment makes effective language teaching difficult. Other respondents learned the ethnic language despite their parents' hopes that they would assimilate. This may happen when the parents themselves do not speak English well, and tend to use the ethnic language around the house despite their own desire to assimilate.

TABLE VI
EFFECT OF KNOWLEDGE OF THE ETHNIC LANGUAGE ON ETHNIC COMMUNITY PARTICIPATION, BY PARENTAL ATTITUDES TOWARD ETHNIC PARTICIPATION; ADULT IMMIGRANTS EXCLUDED (GAMMA)

Aspect of ethnic community participation	Total from Table IV)	Did parents hope you would maintain ethnic ties?	
		Yes	No
Ethnic language use:			
1. Speaking	.934	.849	.978
2. Reading ethnic press	.877	.793	.890
3. Church	.700	.521	.738
Other characteristics:			
4. Ethnic identification	.610	.450	.448
5. Ethnic endogamy	.642	.638	.173
6. Close ethnic ties	.658	.605	.317
7. Ethnic friendships	.565	.550	.318
8. Assoc. with ethnic church	.698	.429	.728
9. Res. in ethnic nbhd.	.360	.232	.133
10. Memb. of ethnic org.	.633	.496	.602
11. Reading ethnic press (in English or French)	.300	.229	.298
(Weighted *N*, approximate)*	(500,000)	(257,000)	(178,000)

*See note to Table III.

The effect of language knowledge on ethnic community participation, within groups whose parents had similar attitudes toward ethnicity, is shown in Table VI. Language learning (in childhood) has a strong effect on adult ethnic community participation, whether or not parents had hoped for the retention of ethnic ties. The actual effect of language knowledge is somewhat less than appeared to be the case on the basis of zero-order relationships in Table IV, but it is strong nevertheless. These findings provide striking confirmation for Sapir's theory that language knowledge in itself can be a powerful force for ethnic group solidarity. Whatever the intentions of parents, children raised in an environment conducive to language retention are far more likely to remain within the ethnic fold than those who are not.

TABLE VII
EFFECT OF PARENTAL ATTITUDES ON ETHNIC COMMUNITY PARTICIPATION, BY KNOWLEDGE OF THE ETHNIC LANGUAGE; ADULT IMMIGRANTS EXCLUDED (GAMMA)

Aspect of ethnic community participation	Knowledge of ethnic language			Total
	Fluent	*Some knowledge*	*No knowledge*	
Ethnic language use:				
1. Speaking	**	.386	**	.717
2. Reading ethnic press	**	.374	**	.747
3. Church	.161	.462	**	.672
Other characteristics:				
4. Ethnic identification	.478	.572	.030	.664
5. Ethnic endogamy	.682	.565	−.050	.651
6. Close ethnic ties	.556	.602	.044	.672
7. Ethnic friendships	.458	.375	−.095	.502
8. Assoc. with ethnic church	**	.653	**	.726
9. Res. in ethnic nbhd.	.373	.282	.014	.357
10. Memb. of ethnic org.	**	.718	**	.874
11. Reading ethnic press (in English or French)	.268	.104	**	.312
(Weighted *N*, approximate)*	(94,000)	(281,000)	(125,000)	(500,000)

*See note to Table III.
**Insufficient number of non-tied pairs.

The empirical relation between reported parental attitudes and actual ethnic retention is interesting, though difficult to assess. In the first place, the relation is due in part to the effect of parental attitudes on language retention. Table VII shows that the relation between parental attitudes and ethnic community participation is less strong when examined among persons having similar levels of language knowledge. Note in addition that the effect of parental attitudes appears to be contingent upon their children learning the ethnic language. Among respondents having no knowledge of the ethnic language, the effect of parental attitudes in encouraging ethnic solidarity is virtually nil. This interesting finding suggests that efforts to awaken ethnic consciousness will encounter serious difficulties once major bases of ethnic solidarity have been lost.

The effect of language retention is itself conditional upon parental attitudes, but even when parental attitudes are negative, a significant effect exists. The specific form of this conditional relation depends upon the type of participation. Detailed cross-tabulations of the three variables involved will help clarify their mutual interrelation. In Table VIII the dependent variable is maintenance of close ethnic ties. The effect of language retention on this variable is quite strong, and it is strongest when parents are reported to be in favour of maintaining such ties. The effect of parental attitudes is fairly strong under conditions which foster at least some language retention, but it is otherwise negligible.

TABLE VIII
PERCENTAGE MAINTAINING TIES WITH OTHER ETHNIC GROUP MEMBERS IN CANADA, BY PARENTAL ATTITUDES AND KNOWLEDGE OF THE ETHNIC LANGUAGE; ADULT IMMIGRANTS EXCLUDED

Knowledge of the ethnic language	Did parents hope you would maintain ethnic ties?	
	Yes	No
Fluent	81.5 (67888)	55.7 (9719)
Some knowledge	58.3 (168937)	25.8 (76871)
No knowledge	20.1 (20460)	18.7 (91243)

Weighted N = 435,118

Implications for the Analysis of Ethnic Communities

Survey data on Canada's four largest urban ethnic minorities support Sapir's theory that language retention promotes ethnic group cohesion. Language is important to ethnic communities not merely as an expression of traditional ethnic culture; the data suggest that ethnic language retention is a cornerstone of the ethnic communities themselves. Failure to learn the ethnic language leads to failure to participate in the ethnic community, and this to a large extent explains reduced participation in the second and third generations. Language loss is a well-founded concern of ethnic community leaders, however difficult might be its prevention.

These results have some specific implications for the analysis of ethnic communities. Since ethnic community survival, change, and assimilation may be so drastically affected by language retention, any relevant theory should deal specifically with the linguistic dimension. Ideas developed in sociolinguistics have a direct bearing here. Fishman's (1965a; 1965b) earlier reviews emphasized the importance of separate social domains in which only ethnic language use is permitted. "Unstable intragroup bilingualism" exists if "either available language may be employed under most circumstances, between most interlocutors, at will" (Fishman, 1965a:143). Evidently, in Canada's urban areas conditions needed for stable intragroup bilingualism among Italians, Germans, Ukrainians, and Poles have not existed, at least in the past. The home is of course one potential ethnic language domain. In data collected for this study, the use of the ethnic language in the parental home is extremely strongly related to language retention (gamma = 0.911). English or French (usually English) has gradually displaced household use of other languages. Outside the home, the situation is less clear cut. Ethnic schools had been attended by 25 per cent of the sample, mostly from homes in which the ethnic language was used regularly. Among persons from such homes, ethnic school attendance had little additional effect on language retention.

Failure to maintain ethnic language domains might result from cultural assimilation, but other possible reasons should be explored. Why, for example, do parents choose not to use the ethnic language in their home, other than because of a weakening of their own ethnic attachments? They may be afraid that to deemphasize learning of the official languages, especially English, would jeopardize their children's social and economic future in Canada. A dilemma may exist between seeking mobility for the children and maintaining the ethnic language. One solution could be to stress the non-linguistic aspects of ethnicity. This solution might satisfy parents in the short run, but contribute to the deterioration of the ethnic community in the long run.

Another implication of this study concerns the efforts of ethnic communities to mobilize participation. These efforts probably are structured along linguistic lines. The data in this study show the relevance of parental attitudes in the mobilization of bilingual children, but conditions outside the home undoubtedly also are relevant. Nahirny and Fishman (1965a) emphasize how difficult it is to persuade children of the value of ethnicity. Their imagery is not one of the ethnic family defending its traditions against the alien culture outside; it is rather one of the parental generation defending (and attempting to propagate) its traditions against the alien culture their children acquire in the outside community. Parental encouragement for bilingual children to maintain ethnic ties may be effective only when the community environment also is generally supportive of ethnic retention.

Efforts to mobilize non-bilinguals are more problematic and may signal basic changes in the ethnic community. Several studies in the Fishman, et al. (1965) volume suggest that an organizational segregation often develops along language-knowledge lines. Our findings suggest that the English- or French-speaking branches are likely to atrophy unless they cultivate additional bases for ethnic interest, or begin to shift away from an exclusively ethnic focus.

Possible bases for ethnic solidarity without language still require more detailed study. It remains to be seen whether the social dynamic of ethnic persistence will develop in distinctive ways in an avowedly "multicultural," but still not multilingual, Canadian society.

NOTES

[1]In this connection, Weinreich (1967:100) has discussed the link between language loyalty and various types of "group élans" including nationalism (see also Barker, 1972; and Deutsch, 1966).

[2]There are more Canadians of Dutch origin than Canadians of Polish origin, but the Dutch tend to live outside the major urban centers.

[3]Italian immigrants in Canada tend to be more recent arrivals than the German, Ukrainian, and Polish immigrants. The latter groups arrived primarily in the first decade after the Second World War. Italians resumed immigration during the mid-fifties, and have continued to come in large numbers since then.

[4]Porter's occupational data include both urban and non-urban residents. If agricultural workers are excluded, the occupational positions of the Germans, Ukrainians, and Poles are quite similar to those of the general population.

[5]See O'Bryan, Reitz, and Kuplowsky (forthcoming) for details on the sampling. The sample for the main study includes ten ethnic groups.

[6]The apparent exception is for reading the ethnic press written in English or French. Few adult immigrants engage in this activity, probably because of their relative lack of facility with English and French.

[7]Of the respondents who grew up in Canada (i.e., not adult immigrants), and who reported an ability to carry on a conversation in their ethnic tongue (this included 65 per cent), only 4.7 per cent had acquired that ability after the age of five.

[8]Still it will be necessary to separate effects of language learning itself from the effects of other early socializing experiences which also may influence adult ethnic community participation. This will be the object of the second part of the data analysis.

[9]The "effects" of parents' attitudes may be exaggerated by the use of a retrospective question as a measure. However, our main interest is in the independent effects of language learning, and not in the actual size of the effect of parental attitudes.

REFERENCES

Barker, George C., *Social Functions of Language in a Mexican-American Community,* Tucson: The University of Arizona Press. Original publication in 1947; 1972.

Barth, Fredrik, "Introduction", in Fredrik Barth (ed.), *Ethnic Groups and Boundaries: The Social Organization of Cultural Difference,* Boston: Little, Brown and Company, 1969.

Deutsch, Karl W., *Nationalism and Social Communication: An Inquiry into the Foundations of Nationality,* (Second Edition), Cambridge: The MIT Press, 1966.

Fishman, Joshua A., "Bilingual Sequences at the Societal Level", *On Teaching English to Speakers of Other Languages,* 1965a, 139-144.

_____ "Language Maintenance and Language Shift as a Field of Inquiry", in: Fishman, et al., 1965[b]: 424-458.

Fishman, Joshua A., Vladimir C. Nahirny, John E. Hoffman, and Robert G. Hayden, *Language Loyalty in the United States: The Maintenance and Perpetuation of Non-English Mother Tongues by American Ethnic and Religious Groups,* The Hague: Mouton and Company, 1965.

Glazer, Nathan, and Daniel Patrick Moynihan, *Beyond the Melting Pot: The Negroes, Puerto Ricans, Jews, Italians, and Irish of New York City,* Cambridge: The MIT Press, 1963.

Gordon, Milton M., *Assimilation in American Life: The Role of Race, Religion, and National Origins,* New York: Oxford University Press, 1964.

Hansen, M.L., "The Third Generation in America", *Commentary,* 1962, 14:492-500. Original publication in 1938.

Hertzler, Joyce O., *A Sociology of Language,* New York: Random House, 1965.

Lemaire, Herve-B., "Franco-American Efforts on Behalf of the French language in New England", in: Fishman, et al., 1965:253-279.

Lieberson, Stanley, "Language Questions in Censuses", *Sociological Inquiry,* 1966, 36:262-279.

———— *Language and Ethnic Relations in Canada,* New York: John Wiley and Sons, 1970.

Mueller, John H., Karl F. Schuessler, and Herbert L. Costner, *Statistical Reasoning in Sociology,* (Second Edition), Boston: Houghton Mifflin Company, 1970.

Nahirny, Vladimir C., and Joshua A. Fishman, "American Immigrant groups: Ethnic Identification and the Problem of Generations", *Sociological Review,* 1965[a], 13:311-326.

———— "Ukrainian Language Maintenance Efforts in the United States", In: Fishman, et al., 1965[b]:318-357.

O'Bryan, Kenneth G., Jeffrey G. Reitz and Olga Kuplowsky, *Forthcoming Non-official Languages in Canada,* Ottawa: The Queen's Printer.

Porter, John, *The Vertical Mosaic: An Analysis of Social Class and Power in Canada,* Toronto: The University of Toronto Press, 1965.

Richmond, Anthony H., *Ethnic Residential Segregation in Metropolitan Toronto,* Toronto: York University Institute for Behavioral Research, 1972.

Royal Commission on Bilingualism and Biculturalism, *Report, The Cultural Contribution of the Other Ethnic Groups* (Book IV), Ottawa: The Queen's Printer, 1970.

Sapir, Edward, "Language", *Encyclopedia of the Social Sciences,* Volume IX, 1933:155-168. New York: The Macmillan Company.

Vallee, Frank G. and Norman Shulman, "The Viability of French Groupings outside Quebec", in: Mason Wade (ed.), *Regionalism in the Canadian Community,* Toronto: University of Toronto Press, 1969.

Weinreich, Uriel, *Languages in Contact: Findings and Problems,* The Hague: Mouton and Company. Original publication in 1953; 1967.

Weinstock, S. Alexander, *Acculturation and Occupation: A Study of the 1956 Hungarian Refugees in the United States,* The Hague: Martinus Nijhoff, 1969.

Chapter 8

Contrasts in the Prewar and Postwar Japanese Community in British Columbia: Conflict and Change*†

Victor K. Ujimoto

The meaning of the term "community" can vary in its basis as well as in degree, and, thus, it has been difficult for urban sociologists to agree on a satisfactory definition. In general, the problem stems from lack of agreement on a given definition because of the varying degrees of emphasis placed upon the geographic and social aspects to be described. Hillery (1955:III) observes that "to the extent that the degree of consensus is in doubt, to that extent must one remain uncertain whether different things are being described or whether the same thing is merely viewed from different vantage points". Thus, it should be noted in our comparative description of Japanese communities in British Columbia before and after the Second World War that extreme care must be exercised in selecting and in describing those component features which characterized the Japanese community.

One way to delineate the principal components of any community would

*Reprinted from *The Canadian Review of Sociology and Anthropology* 13:1 (1976), by permission of the author and the publisher, Fitzhenry and Whiteside Limited.

†Revised version of a paper presented to the CSAA Regional Symposium "British Columbia: Power and Conflict," University of Victoria, Victoria, B.C., February, 1974. I am grateful to Professor Raymond Breton and the assessors of the CRSA for their valuable comments and suggestions in improving the original paper.

be to select those features or characteristics most frequently noted by the various authors in their definition of a community. One such attempt has been the analysis of ninety-four definitions of community by Hillery (1955:III-23) in which he was able to specify social interaction as one necessary element for the definition of a community. Hillery noted that not all definitions examined specified the necessity of a specific geographic area or the notion of a territorial entity in which that social interaction should occur. Since Hillery's study, several authors, for example, Goode (1957:194), Martindale (1960:133), and Westhues and Sinclair (1974:12), have excluded the territorial criteria from their definition of a community. In contrast, Reiss (1959:118), Schnore (1967:92), Gans (1970:298), and Hawley (1971:10) entertain the idea that a community consists of a group of people sharing a common and bounded territorial space. Other essential elements such as common needs, shared institutions, and a sense of group consciousness tend to be acceptable to most authors. From the survey of the literature then, it becomes evident, as observed by Warren (1972:2), that depending on the dimensions selected as crucial ones, different conceptions of a community emerge.

In this article, I intend to explore and attempt to explain selected variations with reference to the Japanese communities in British Columbia. In particular, I will note the differences in the social organization of the Japanese collectivity. In the Japanese community as it existed in Vancouver prior to the Second World War, the territorial criteria were applicable. A specific geographic area or territorial space was a physical reality and a concomitant result was that various social units were also territorially defined. For example, certain kinds of Japanese businesses were concentrated in the Powell Street area and were referred to as "Little Tokyo" by both Japanese and Occidentals. LaViolette (1948:75) noted that "Little Tokyo" was more than a physically segregated area and that it was also recognized as a "frame of mind" which stemmed from the highly systematized and interdependent social relations that existed between the Japanese family, religious groups, trade associations, welfare and promotional activities, and extended kinship organizations. In addition to the Japanese business community located along Powell Street, Young, Reid, and Carrothers (1938:71) identified two other predominantly Japanese areas which were located south of False Creek and which accounted for over 50 percent of the Japanese collectivity outside the Powell Street area. Although it was also shown that the Japanese were scattered throughout the Fraser Valley and the various coastal areas, Young, Reid, and Carrothers (1938:23) have noted that 19,281 of the 22,205 Japanese in British Columbia were located in census divisions 4 and 5 which were mainly in the city of Vancouver.

In contrast, the 1971 census of Canada listed the total Japanese Canadian population in British Columbia as 13,590 with 5,045 residing in the city of Vancouver. In terms of the number of households, a more recent survey (JCCA:1974) revealed that there were only 2,941 households in British Columbia with Vancouver, North Vancouver, and West Vancouver accounting for 1,755 of the total. Richmond had 515 households, Burnaby 232, and Surrey 121. With the exception of Kamloops and Kelowna collectivities, other Japanese-Canadian communities in British Columbia consisted of less than fifty households each. Not only was the total Japanese-Canadian population in British Columbia considerably less than it was before the Second World War, the Japanese Canadians were not concentrated in specific censal or bounded territorial locations but were widely dispersed throughout the Greater Vancouver and Lower Mainland regions of British Columbia. A concomitant development was that it discouraged the formation of effective social networks for individual, familial, and prefectural or clan social relations.

In order to account for the differences in both the demographic distribution and composition of the Japanese in British Columbia, and for subsequent differences in their social organizations, a descriptive account of the major factors which contributed to these differences between the Japanese community before and after the Second World War will now be provided.

The Prewar Japanese Community: Conflict and Change

The Japanese community in Vancouver before the war consisted of a large, cohesive, and well unified collectivity, and several factors should be noted in order to account for the extensive social interactions that occurred within the community. One important element was that both sponsored and group migration were quite extensive. For example, one early visitor to Canada was Gihei Kuno, a carpenter from Mio village. He came to Canada in 1877 and was so impressed by the salmon fishing on the west coast that he encouraged many Mio villagers to migrate to Canada (Fukutake, 1962:149). Subsequently, these early immigrants sponsored their relatives into the country. Mass emigration also occurred in association with the construction of the Canadian Pacific Railway. The general tendency of the Japanese immigrants to make money and then to return to Japan was not limited only to the Japanese fishermen but also extended to the Japanese labourers who came to Canada under contract to work on the construction of the railway. Japanese immigrants were later engaged in the boat-building, lumbering, and mining industries, but sponsorship played an important role in securing employment in these occupations.

Another factor which contributed to the social cohesion of the prewar Japanese immigrants stemmed from the fact that they were all victims of a rather hostile political climate at the time. In 1907, the United States government passed legislative measures which prohibited Japanese immigrants from entering the United States. This resulted in a further mass influx of Japanese immigrants to Canada, and the concomitant increase in hostility and prejudice eventually gave rise to conflicts which culminated in the Vancouver race riots of 7 September, 1907 (Sugimoto, 1972:92-126). The Canadian government appointed a royal commission and the first gentlemen's agreement restricted Japanese immigrants to Canada to the following four classes of people (Adachi, 1956:4): (1) returning immigrants and their wives and children; (2) immigrants engaged by Japanese residents in Canada for bona fide personal or domestic service; (3) labourers under special contracts approved by the Canadian government; and (4) immigrants brought under contract by Japanese resident agricultural holders in Canada. The continuation of the sponsored immigration of relatives and prefectural associates facilitated the establishment of a network of social organizations and the formation of what Breton (1964:193-205) calls the institutional completeness of ethnic communities. The prewar Japanese community in Vancouver was able to sustain commercial and noncommercial organizations, and both social and business transactions were conducted in Japanese on the basis of traditional authority structures based on the principle of social obligations and responsibilities. It must be stressed that all of this was possible because of the homogenous nature of the collectivity, that is, they were all *issei*, or first generation Japanese, and thus the usual problems associated with language and the observance of traditional customs were practically nonexistent.

The fact that there was a large Japanese population characterized by a common language, religion, and similar occupations, mainly non-professional, also meant that it was possible to form various social organizations. Friendship groups and prefectural associations numbered approximately eighty-four units in Vancouver in 1934 (Young, Reid, and Carrothers, 1938:108), and these organizations provided the cohesion to keep both formal and informal social networks intact in the Japanese community. Miyamoto (1972:224) notes that "the *kenjinkai* or prefectural association not only served as a means of drawing workers into particular businesses and training them, but also provided a network of relations that sustained the economy and determined its patterns". Association members were able to secure social and financial assistance from the prefectural associations and this fact, together with the strongly cohesive nature of the Japanese family, enabled the early Japanese immigrants to retain their competitive power in numerous service-oriented business enterprises. It was precisely this highly cooperative institutional structure of the early Japanese community which later precipitated an open conflict with the members of the host Canadian society. This conflict between the members of the Japanese community and Canadian society further reinforced the social organization and group solidarity of the Japanese community.

The forced breakdown of the Japanese community organization occurred with the outbreak of the Second World War and the resulting mass evacuation of all persons of Japanese ancestry from the coastal areas of British Columbia. One of the consequences of the proclamation of the War Measures Act was that Japanese families, both citizens and aliens, were relocated to various centres in the interior of British Columbia, and in Alberta, Manitoba, and Ontario. After the relocation, those who elected to return to Japan renounced their Canadian citizenship and were repatriated. The real victims of this episode were the Canadian-born Japanese who were still minors at this time: they could exercise no option and just followed their parents back to Japan. After the war, very few Japanese Canadians returned to British Columbia, and the Japanese collectivity in Vancouver never regained its previous level of social and business activity.

The Postwar Japanese Community: Changing Composition of the Population

Since the end of the Second World War, the number of immigrants of Japanese origin in Canada has increased steadily (see Table I). During the initial five-year period after the war, only thirty-seven Japanese immigrated to Canada (Kalbach, 1970:426). However, with the passing of the 1952 Immigration Act and subsequent amendments (Immigration Act, 1968) the number of postwar Japanese immigrants since 1952 has totaled more than 8,691. Of this total, approximately a third settled in British Columbia, mainly in the lower mainland region of the province and, excluding the concentration in Ontario, constituted the second largest collectivity of Japanese immigrants in Canada. Although immigration from Japan has increased gradually in the past few years, it has not reached the level of immigration established before the war, and Japanese immigrants to Canada number considerably less than Chinese and Indian immigrants. Comparative data are shown in Table II.

TABLE I
NUMBER OF JAPANESE IMMIGRANTS
ENTERING CANADA, 1946-74

Year	Number	Year	Number
1946*	3	1960	169
1947	2	1961†	114
1948	6	1962	141
1949	13	1963	171
1950	13	1964	140
1951	3	1965	188
1952	7	1966	500
1953	49	1967	858
1954	73	1968	628
1955	102	1969	698
1956	124	1970	785
1957	185	1971	815
1958	193	1972‡	684
1959	197	1973	1020
		1974	810

*SOURCE: Kalbach (1970:426-7), ethnic origin
†SOURCE: *Immigration Statistics,* Department of Manpower and Immigration, by country of citizenship
‡SOURCE: *Quarterly Immigration Statistics,* Department of Manpower and Immigration, by country of citizenship

TABLE II
JAPANESE, CHINESE, AND EAST INDIAN IMMIGRANTS TO
CANADA, 1941-74

Five-year period	Japanese	Chinese	East Indian
1941-45*	5	0	5
1946-50*	37	2,654	356
1951-55*	234	11,524	837
1956-60*	868	10,407	2,557
1961-65†	861	11,785	8,576
1966-70‡	3,504	23,218	25,349**
1971-74	3,329	13,580	35,845**

*SOURCE: Kalbach (1970:43)
†SOURCE: *Canada Year Book,* 1941 to 1970, by ethnicity
‡SOURCE: *Immigration Statistics,* 1966 to 1974 inclusive, Department of Manpower and Immigration, Ottawa, by citizenship
**Categorized as Indian citizenship

The 20 December 1957 amendment to the 1952 Immigration Act enabled non-Canadian residents in Canada to sponsor the admission of immigrants from Asia. However, a recent study of postwar Japanese immigrants who reside in the greater Vancouver area (Ujimoto, 1973:35-9) has revealed that most relative-sponsored immigrants were admitted to Canada prior to the Immigration Act amendment and that less than 10 percent of the postwar Japanese immigrants were sponsored by relatives in Canada. This fact provides a partial explanation for the lack of kin-oriented social networks within the Japanese collectivity, which is in contrast with the vast network of social affiliations which existed within the prewar Vancouver Japanese community. Another explanation for the lack of social interaction and group solidarity within the postwar Japanese collectivity in British Columbia is that the first generation Japanese, or *issei,* has aged and many of the original leaders now lack the power and community influence to bridge the immense cultural gaps between the first generation, second generation (*nisei*), and third generation (*sansei*) Japanese Canadians. One may expect at least some form of social organization or a network of social affiliations to become established within the postwar Japanese immigrant collectivity; however, this has not happened because of the diverse nature of the immigrant groups, such as the *kika nisei* (returned second generation), the *yobiyose* (sponsored immigrant), and the *gijutsu imin* (technical immigrant).

The *kika nisei* or the "returned second generation" were those Japanese Canadians who were repatriated during the Second World War and who later returned to Canada. The *kika nisei* were usually sponsored by relatives who resided in Canada. It is extremely difficult to determine whether the *kika nisei* were officially included in the Canadian government immigration statistics for the period 1946 to 1952, since it was only after the 1952

Immigration Act that a Canadian citizen resident in Canada was able to sponsor a wife, husband, or unmarried dependent under twenty-one years of age. It is quite conceivable that the forty or so Japanese immigrants who entered Canada between 1946 and 1951 (Table I) were those who had earlier renounced their Canadian citizenship due to political considerations. There are, of course, numerous factors to be taken into account before one may attach the "immigrant" label to the *kika nisei.* However, that is beyond the immediate concern of this article and it will suffice to note that the *kika nisei* constituted one group of Japanese frequently included under the rubric of postwar Japanese immigrants.

Until 1965, postwar Japanese immigrants to Canada were mostly sponsored by relatives, a category enabling people who lacked both educational experience and occupational skills to enter Canada. This usually resulted in the employment of the Japanese immigrant in his or her sponsor's family occupation or in some other makeshift work arrangement within the Japanese collectivity. The only Japanese community in British Columbia where the people share a common and bounded territorial space is Steveston. It had its origin in the mass transplantation of a fishing village from Mio-mura, Wakayama Prefecture, Japan. Emigration from Mio-mura reached its peak in 1926 (Fukutake, 1962:152). Consequently, after the Second World War, a number of sponsored immigrants came to reside in the Steveston and Richmond areas and were employed in the fishing industry.

Sponsored Japanese immigrants were also destined to the various agricultural areas of southern Alberta, Manitoba, and Ontario. Perhaps, next to those immigrants who were employed in the fishing industry, the immigrants in the various agricultural occupations constituted the second largest group of sponsored immigrants to Canada.[1] The remainder of the sponsored immigrants did not immediately enter the labour force: this group includes children, housewives, and "picture-brides" to provide a few examples.

With the establishment of the Canadian visa office in Tokyo in 1966, a vigorous advertising campaign was launched in Japan to attract highly qualified technical and professional people. It was a great success as evinced by the nearly threefold increase in immigration for that year (see Table I). There were significant differences between those Japanese immigrants who entered Canada after 1966 and those who had arrived previously. Japanese immigrants to Canada after 1966 were known as *gijutsu imin* or literally translated "technical immigrants". Unlike their predecessors, the *gijutsu imin* consisted of both professional and technical people: they were highly educated, had several years of experience in their own occupations, and were able to converse in English. The *gijutsu imin* therefore did not have to rely upon the social organizations of the Japanese-speaking community and tended to establish a network of social affiliations in the host Canadian society.

A very transitory but active form of social network affiliation which exists among the Vancouver Japanese collectivity centres around the postwar Japanese immigrants who had already been introduced to each other through the English-language orientation course held in Tokyo prior to emigration. There are approximately fifteen to twenty-five candidates per orientation course and during the month of intensive language training, a very cohesive group of friends can be established. Although Japanese immigrants to Canada tend to be more individualistic than those remaining in the collectivity-oriented Japanese society, it appears that a group spirit can be rekindled by the English orientation course. This is manifested by the course membership group photos, course outings and picnics, and, sometimes, group travel to Canada.

Another source to be considered for the formation of the Japanese immigrant social network is the environment which surrounds the Japanese Immigrant Reception Committee at the YMCA. Although this group meets only once a week, those immigrants who experience difficulty in obtaining employment return to the YMCA week after week to exchange their unemployment experiences. Others, who have experienced nothing but a full week of frustration trying to converse in English, return to the YMCA to release their frustrations in a tongue in which they are more able to articulate their feelings.

Affiliations established through these two sources do not tend to be stable and lasting. Classmates in the English orientation course soon disperse to various geographic locations depending on where they obtain employment. Similarly, for those immigrants whose social contacts were established through the Japanese Immigrant Reception Committee, attendance at the YMCA meetings decreases markedly once employment has been secured. Thus, the reception committee is frequently without a resource person to assist and advise new immigrants.

Not all Japanese immigrants to Canada attend the English orientation courses held in Tokyo. Less than 13 percent of the total number of immigrants to Canada are channelled through these courses (Japan Emigration Service, 1972:1). For most Japanese immigrants, this source of future social ties does not exist and contacts which do occur with other Japanese immigrants will be found through the Japanese Immigrant Reception Committee. However, many Japanese immigrants do not make any contact with the reception committee unless they encounter extraordinary difficulties in finding work. Some even make a deliberate effort to stay away from other Japanese immigrants and limit their affiliations to Canadians. Once employment is secured by Japanese immigrants, social relationships tend to be directed towards their new acquaintances made at their place of work. The formation of new social contacts is sometimes facilitated by the fact that Japanese immigrants in the technical trades can make their job skills available off the job. It is not uncommon for a radio technician or an auto mechanic to be asked by a neighbour or friend to do some repair work, perhaps in exchange for some other service or goods. Such social relations now occur beyond the boundaries of the immigrant's own ethnic collectivity, whereas in the prewar Japanese community, patterns of mutual assistance were manifested only in the Japanese community.

Discussion of Observed Differences

It has been observed that before the Second World War the Japanese community was an institutionally complete, self-sustaining collectivity of Japanese immigrants. Their social organization was based on shared needs as well as on a sense of group consciousness. The immigration policy of the time stressed sponsorship and this reinforced the kinship and social network ties of the immigrant group. Group solidarity within the ethnic collectivity was further strengthened by a common and bounded territorial space. The highly systematized and interdependent social relations within this space were based upon the principle of social and moral obligations and traditional Japanese practices of mutual assistance such as the *oyabun-kobun* (parent-child) and *sempai-kōhai* (senior-junior) relationships. The *oyabun-kobun* relationship promoted non-kin social ties to be formed on the basis of a wide ranging set of obligations (see Ishino, 1953:696 and Nakane, 1970:42-3). Similarly, the *sempai-kōhai* relationship was based on a sense of responsibility whereby the *sempai* or senior member assumed the responsibility of overlooking the social, economic, and religious affairs of the *kōhai* or junior member. Such a system of social relations provided for a cohesive and well-unified collectivity which possessed a high degree of competitive power in the economic sphere. The rapidly increasing competitive economic power held by the minority ethnic collectivity gave rise to racial conflict with the members of the host Canadian society. This external hostility further strengthened the social consciousness of the Japanese community.

It has been suggested that, in contrast to the prewar Japanese community, the postwar collectivity of Japanese Canadians and Japanese immigrants who currently reside in British Columbia and in the Greater Vancouver area in particular does not appear to have a sense of community as described by such elements as common needs, shared institutions, and a sense of group consciousness. Several factors can be delineated to account for this difference. The changes in immigration regulations during the postwar period permitted individuals to apply for landed immigrant status without relying on kin or other forms of sponsorship. Also, the postwar emphasis on professional and technical immigrants provided for less reliance upon the established social organizations of the Japanese-speaking community in order to secure employment. Unlike their predecessors, postwar immigrants were able to converse in English and this enabled them to assimilate much more readily into the host Canadian society. All of these factors assisted the Japanese immigrants in establishing their networks of social affiliation more in the host society and not so much, if at all, within the older generation of Japanese immigrants and the Canadian-born *nisei* and *sansei* collectivities.

Unlike the prewar *issei,* the *nisei* and *sansei* shared some common characteristics with those of the *gijutsu-imin.* They were highly educated, were mostly employed in the professional and technical occupations, and were fluent in English. These characteristics, in addition to the fact that the social and political climate of the postwar era provided for greater social mobility for the *nisei, sansei,* and *gijutsu-imin,* contributed to geographic mobility as well. Thus, in great contrast with the prewar Japanese community, for the postwar community the notion of bounded territorial locations no longer existed to the same extent.

The geographic dispersal of the Japanese Canadians and the Japanese immigrants hindered the formation of social affiliations, but another very important element which contributed to the decrease in social interaction and in the sense of Japanese group consciousness stemmed from the fact that the *issei* had gradually lost the power and community influence to bridge the cultural gaps between successive generations of Japanese Canadians. The traditional Japanese concepts of filial piety, social and moral obligations as expressed by such terms as *oya koko, on,* and *giri,* which were at one time the basis for family cohesion and group solidarity, no longer conveyed the same meaning and importance to the Canadian-born. The lack of a workable common language especially between the *issei* and *nisei* further complicated and hindered the transmission of the traditional Japanese values and customs on to the *sansei.*

The cultural values emphasized by the *issei* of an earlier period no longer seemed important to the postwar *issei* immigrants. The change in the type of Japanese immigrant to Canada in recent years undoubtedly reflects to some extent the educational and social transformations of modern Japan since 1945. The individualistic nature of the postwar Japanese immigrant certainly provides a vivid contrast to his collectivity-oriented predecessors. Apart from the varying degree of emphasis on traditional Japanese values and customs, the use or nonuse of the Japanese language itself is another very important element associated with the lack of social interaction between members of the Japanese collectivity. This is especially true between the postwar Japanese immigrants and the Japanese Canadians. The Japanese language consists of numerous forms of honorifics associated with the traditional rules of propriety and dependent on one's social status; even informal conversations may not take place between people of different status. The Anglicized Japanese or "pigeon Japanese" spoken by the *nisei* or *sansei* further widens the cultural and language gulf which exists between those Japanese educated in Japan and the Canadian-born.

An important factor to be considered to account for the differences in education as well as in the degree of skills possessed by the postwar Japanese immigrants would be the effects of the Canadian government immigration policies before and after the Second World War.[2] It will be noted that before the war Japanese immigrants were allowed into Canada mainly to satisfy the demand for cheap contract labour by the Canadian corporations

(Young, Reid, and Carrothers, 1938:10) and thus government policy did not stress the qualifications of immigrants. However, since 1945, the Canadian government has made vast revisions in the immigration regulations and in the selection system which reflect the demand for skilled immigrants. It is suggested that the realities of political control and the ideology of the government in power are extremely important facets to be considered when examining international migration (Hawkins, 1972:10).

Conclusion and Future Research Considerations

The differences in the social organization of the prewar and postwar Japanese communities can be attributed to several factors which basically are the result of the changing composition of the Japanese population after the Second World War. The prewar Japanese community consisted of a relatively homogenous collectivity of Japanese immigrants possessing a common language and religion and an understanding of the traditional beliefs and customs. All of these factors contributed to the formation of a collective consciousness and to the subsequent establishment of an institutionally complete ethnic community. In contrast, the postwar Japanese population consisted of several diverse groups, the *issei, nisei, sansei,* and the *gijutsu-imin.* The language spoken by the *issei* reflected the vocabulary of a past era. The vocabulary of the *nisei* and *sansei* was a mixture of English and Japanese. The postwar immigrants spoke the "modern" Japanese and they looked down upon the "illiterate" Japanese Canadians. This lack of an acceptable common language tended to create serious misunderstandings between the *issei, nisei, sansei,* and *gijutsu-imin.* Because of the language barriers, the *nisei* and *sansei* did not fully appreciate the traditional Japanese values and customs and this alone may be a major contributing factor for the lack of communication between the Japanese Canadians and the postwar Japanese immigrants.

Although variations in the demographic composition of the postwar Japanese collectivity impeded the formation of social networks, it can be argued that the acceptance of the *nisei* and *sansei* into the professional and salaried positions of the Canadian occupational structure no longer necessitated the formation of an institutionally complete social organization similar to the Japanese community of the prewar period. Similarly, the postwar immigrants, by virtue of their educational, technical, and professional skills, were able to secure employment in Canada without too much reliance on the network of personal affiliations.

In the present study, it was not possible to examine the patterns of social participation in voluntary associations by Japanese Canadians. However, our data on postwar Japanese immigrants revealed that participation in the network of personal affiliations such as family and friendship networks, and in activities such as reading and studying, occurred more frequently among immigrants who were still in the process of adjustment and who required household essentials to be purchased than among those who were able to participate in forms of social activities requiring financial resources. This finding indicates the priority given by the immigrant to the purchase of essential household goods over participation in voluntary associations and in activities requiring money; it further illustrates the fact that the system of social obligations and mutual assistance rendered to the newcomers by those already established no longer exists as it once did in the prewar Japanese community.

The finding that social participation in any given sphere of activity is strongly influenced by both employment and the availability of material goods to the Japanese immigrant tends to reinforce Porter's thesis (Porter, 1968:63) that there exists an "entrance status" to be assumed prior to the acceptance of the immigrant into the status level commensurate with the occupation held before emigration. This implies, for example, that a doctor who is unable to qualify for medical practice in Canada will have a lower level occupational role until the professional requirements are met. Entrance status also implies that, regardless of occupational status, an immigrant of a given ethnic group is subject to the "processes of assimilation laid down and judged by the charter group" (Porter, 1968:64). It remains for a later study to determine whether or not postwar Japanese immigrants have been able to move out of entrance status to equality status.

It has been observed that the low proportion of relative-sponsored Japanese immigrants to Canada accounted for the lack of kin-oriented social networks. However, our study did not adequately assess the effects of the ethnically homogenous collectivities on the social relationships of the Japanese immigrants, *issei, nisei,* and *sansei.* Although the prewar Japanese community provided us with an example of an extremely well-organized structure, it was evident that collective power was manifested only in the social and economic spheres of activity and seldom in the political domain. Nevertheless, the potential threat to the members of the host Canadian society was of sufficient magnitude to create a conflict situation. In this regard, historical data provide some convincing evidence to support the hypothesis advanced by Breton (1974:23) that "the greater the organized capacity for concerted action of an ethnic collectivity or its potential for it, the more it is likely to represent a threat to other collectivities and, as a consequence, the more the very existence of a corporate organization and/or the conditions necessary for its formation and maintenance, become objects of conflict and ones over which power is exercised". In contrast, the widely dispersed aggregates of Japanese Canadians of the postwar period may represent the other end of the continuum in that they possess an extremely limited sense of ethnic identity and collective purpose. These observations readily suggest the need for further research of a much larger sample of Japanese Canadians. It is recommended that an eastern Canadian setting be selected for the proposed study, preferably Toronto, where the Japanese-Canadian and postwar Japanese immigrant population is considerably greater than it is in metropolitan Vancouver.

Another important reason for suggesting Toronto as a possible setting for a further study of Japanese-Canadian social relationships is that the relocation of Japanese Canadians to the Toronto area at the outbreak of the Second World War resulted in a highly cohesive social group and a concomitant development was the institutionally complete ethnic community (Breton, 1964). The presence of the Japanese Canadian Cultural Centre, Japanese newspapers, Japanese churches, and Japanese language schools will undoubtedly affect the social relationships of the Toronto Japanese Canadians. The suggested study will provide valuable comparative information between the two largest Japanese-Canadian collectivities in Canada.

NOTES

[1]An attempt was made to obtain statistical information from the Department of Manpower and Immigration on sponsored Japanese immigrants to Canada, such as their intended occupation and destination in Canada. Unfortunately, this information was not available due to the confidential nature of other data on the microfilm of the immigrant application form.

[2]With reference to immigration to Canada in general, Ziegler notes that the new immigration regulations introduced in 1967 reinforced the trend to select well educated and skilled immigrants. It is also observed that 30 percent of all immigrants were in the professional, technical, and managerial occupations, and relatively few immigrants were destined to work in the primary industries such as agriculture, mining, and forestry. See Ziegler (1972:2-3).

REFERENCES

Adachi, Ken, *A History of the Japanese Canadians in British Columbia,* Toronto: Japanese Canadian Citizens Association, 1956.

Breton, Raymond, "Institutional Completeness of Ethnic Communities and the Personal Relations of Immigrants", *American Journal of Sociology,* 1964, 70:193-205.

————— "Types of Ethnic Diversity in Canadian Society", Paper presented to the Eighth World Congress of Sociology, University of Toronto, Toronto, Ontario, 1974.

Canada Statistics Canada, *Census of Canada, Volume 1, Part 3, Bulletin 1.32, Population, Ethnic Groups,* Ottawa: Information Canada, 1971.

Fukutake, Tadashi, *Man and Society in Japan,* Tokyo: University of Tokyo Press, 1962.

Gans, Herbert J., "The Suburban Community and its Way of Life", in Robert Gutman and David Popenoe (eds), *Neighborhood, City and Metropolis,* New York: Random House, 1970.

Goode, William J., "Community Within a Community: the Professions", *American Sociological Review,* 1957, 22:194.

Hawkins, Freda, *Canada and Immigration: Public Policy and Public Concern,* Montreal: McGill-Queen's University Press, 1972.

Hawley, Amos H., *Urban Society: An Ecological Approach to New York:* Ronald Press, 1971.

Hillery, G. A., "Definitions of Community: Area of Agreement", *Rural Sociology,* 1955, 20:111-23.

Ishino, Iwao, "The Oyabun-Kobun: a Japanese Ritual Kinship Institution", *American Anthropologist,* 1953, 55(5):695-707.

Japan Emigration Service, *Japan Emigration Service Statistics,* Tokyo: Kaigai Iju Jigyo Dan, 1972.

Japanese Canadian Citizens Association, *Greater Vancouver J.C.C.A. Bulletin,* 1974, 15(2).

Kalbach, Warren E., *The Impact of Immigration on Canada's Population,* Ottawa: Dominion Bureau of Statistics, 1970.

LaViolette, Forrest E., *The Canadian Japanese and World War II,* Toronto: University of Toronto Press, 1948.

Martindale, Don, *American Social Structure,* New York: Appleton-Century-Crofts, 1960.

Miyamoto, S. Frank, "An Immigrant Community in America", In Hilary Conroy and T. Scott Miyakawa (eds), *East Across the Pacific,* Santa Barbara: CLIO Press, 1972.

Nakane, Chie, *Japanese Society,* Berkeley: University of California Press, 1970.

Porter, John, *The Vertical Mosaic,* Toronto: University of Toronto Press, 1968.

Reiss, Albert J., "The Sociological Study of Communities", *Rural Sociology,* 1959, 24:118-30.

Schnore, Leo F., "Community", In Neil J. Smelser (ed.), *Sociology: An Introduction,* New York: John Wiley, 1967.

Sugimoto, Howard, "The Vancouver Race Riots of 1907: a Canadian Episode", In Hilary Conroy and T. Scott Miyakawa (eds), *East Across the Pacific,* Santa Barbara: CLIO Press, 1972.

Ujimoto, K. Victor, "Post-War Japanese Immigrants in Canada: Job Transferability, Work, and Social Participation", PHD dissertation, University of British Columbia, 1973.

Warren, Roland L., *The Community in America,* Chicago: Rand McNally, 1972.

Westhues, Kenneth, and Peter Sinclair, *Village in Crisis,* Toronto: Holt, Rinehart and Winston, 1974.

Young, Charles H., H.R.Y. Reid, and W.A. Carrothers *The Japanese Canadians,* Toronto: University of Toronto Press, 1938.

Ziegler, Edgar, "Manpower Challenges of the 1970's", *Canada Manpower Review,* 1972, 5:1-8.

Chapter 9

The Organization of Secular Education in a Chassidic Jewish Community*†

William Shaffir

. . . Today too, Pharaoh the King of Egypt still exists in the guise of the mores and norms of the country, in the guise of the demands that Jewish children should be cast into the mold of the behavior patterns and customs of the land. Our children, says the modern Pharaoh should immerse themselves and be submerged in the river, in whatever will ostensibly provide them with economic sustenance. Jewish children should be placed within the walls of Pithom and Ramses, the treasure cities of Egypt; they should be wholly involved in those matters which symbolize the economic power and most intensive pre-occupation of the land. . . . Consequently we must stand with the greatest fortitude against his decrees and educate our children in the spirit of Eternal Israel.

Practically, this means that at the time when we are involved with the education of Jewish children it is not only unnecessary, but actually forbidden to immerse them in the paganism of the land. It is prohibited to overwhelm children with concern about the pursuit of adult economic and occupational goals. The sole way of life is a complete and thorough Torah education — with the "Torah of Life." (by the leader of the Lubavitcher chassidim in Di Yiddishe Heim, Vol. 10, No. 4:15).

*Reprinted from *Canadian Ethnic Studies* 8:1 (1976), by permission of the author and the publisher.

†I am indebted to Berkeley Fleming for valuable comments on an earlier draft of this paper.

Religious communities typically view public education as a sustained threat to their distinctive lifestyle and seek to offset its potential influences (Gutwirth, 1970; Poll, 1962; Redekop, 1969; Rubin, 1972). This is accomplished by organizing the secular curriculum to ensure that it does not conflict radically with the contents of the children's religious education (Peters, 1971; Shaffir, 1974). Viewed as an agent of social disorganization that will adversely affect the future of the religious community, the public school has traditionally served as the battleground between the school authorities and the leaders of the religious community (Hostetler, 1968).

Religious communities resist public education because they believe that the school's secularizing and assimilative influences contradict the group's way of life. They view the secular educational process as a primary mechanism through which the surrounding society's culture is absorbed by the young. Brief excerpts from studies about religious communities reveal the basic apprehensions:

> The American high school would break down this needed period of isolation by taking the youth away from the family farm and by teaching him to identify with non Amish associates. . . . The public high school also teaches ideas that are foreign to the Amish culture and not appreciated by the community. The "way of life" of the high school is feared perhaps even more than the curriculum itself. If the child is removed from the community for most of the working hours of the day there is virtually no chance that he will learn to enjoy the Amish way of life (Hostetler, 1968: 195). (from a study on the Amish).
> . . . We feel that farming and higher education are not compatible. We feel our calling is to till the soil. This keeps us together and keeps us in the simple life. If the six years that we conduct are done well, the person learns all he needs to farm and be successful at it. If he can learn to read, "figure" . . . and read the Bible, he has all he needs, for farming need not be learned out of books. It can be learned by practising. Look at how well the Mennonites have done here. They are being copied wholesale by the world. And this was not learned out of books, but through diligent work and practise (Redekop, 1969: 78). (from a study on the Mennonites).
> We recognize the value of an education but also see its evil when stripped of Christ's teachings. Our children have not learned respect for God, for home, for elders. They have gained a little knowledge, but they have no fear of God in their hearts. They have no conscience. We can't appeal to them any more (Young, 1932: 147-48). (from a study on the Molokans).
> What concerns community leaders most is the possibility that the exposure of the youngsters to strange people and materials may be an avenue for undesirable acculturation, a gap in the isolating wall they try to build around the young until they grow up and are ready to deal with the environment from the more favorable vantage point of adulthood and full-fledged incorporation in the community (Sobol, 1972: 150). (from a study on the Satmarer chassidim).

As the outside agency that has penetrated the religious community most powerfully, community members must actively address themselves to the assimilative influences posed by secular education.

This essay examines how a religious community of Lubavitcher chassidim attempts to minimize their children's exposure to contradictive materials during their secular learning. Some background information about the community's schools is presented, followed by the views of the Lubavitcher chassidim and their leader — the *Rebbe*[1] toward secular education. The organization of the Lubavitch schools and their curricula is then discussed, focussing on the secular program. In conclusion, the hiring practices for secular teachers and the careful screening of the secular curriculum by the school principals are discussed. While the data mainly centre on the Labavitcher chassidim, data reflecting how other chassidic groups in Montreal deal with the dilemma posed by secular education are also provided.

Background

The discussion is based on observation of a community of Lubavitcher chassidim in Montreal, Quebec. The data on secular education were gathered through participant observation in the community from late 1969 to 1971. Further information was obtained from discussions with parents, teachers, school administrators, and by reading material on education published by this chassidic group. While much of my data is based on the Lubavitcher chassidim, my information on other chassidic groups derives from research that I undertook for a one year period beginning in the summer of 1969.

The chassidim are a religious movement within the framework of Jewish laws and practices, but with their own unique customs and traditions. Their everyday way of life is circumscribed by religious ideas and principles which differentiate them from other Jewish minority groups, both orthodox and non-orthodox. Not unlike other religious communities, to maintain their distinctive way of life all chassidic groups attempt to insulate themselves both socially and culturally from the larger community. The commonly referred to "chassidic community" (Poll, 1962) consists, in fact, of a number of different chassidic groups, each with a loyalty and devotion to its own leader, or *Rebbe*. With their headquarters in Brooklyn, New York, and communities in many parts of the world, the Lubavitcher chassidim comprise one segment of the chassidic community. The Lubavitch community in Montreal dates back to 1941 when upon the arrival of nine Labavitcher students to the city, a school for religious studies for boys — the Lubavitcher Yeshiva — was organized. The curriculum centred on religious instruction and students were instructed on how to behave in an orthodox Jewish manner. The community organized a school for girls — the *Bays Rivkeh* — in 1955. Today both schools include a nursery, kindergarten, and grades 1 through 11, thus matching the organizational framework of other public schools in the city. Whereas the Yeshiva maintains a *Bays Medresh* — A Rabbinical College — which provides further education to the high school graduates and from which ordained Rabbis, ritual slaughterers, and teachers are graduated, the *Bays*

Rivkeh's program finishes with Grade 11 and graduates must leave for New York or Paris if they wish to pursue more advanced studies at a Lubavitch Teachers Seminary.

The two schools in the community have approximately 550 students. In the Yeshiva, attended by nearly 350 students ranging from nursery to Grade 11, only 30 per cent are from Lubavitch families. The remainder come from Sephardic and Ashkenazic homes — 33 and 37 per cent respectively. A roughly similar breakdown is to be found in the *Bays Rivkeh*. Of the 200 students, 75 per cent are from non-Lubavitch backgrounds equally divided between students of Moroccan and Canadian origin.

Both the administrators at the two schools, and parents sending their children there, see themselves as providing the students with a certain kind of Jewish education. Although the Jewish curriculum in the Lubavitcher schools and several other non-Lubavitch schools is similar, Lubavitcher regard their schools as being qualitatively different. The major difference, claim Lubavitcher, lies in the manner in which Jewish studies are presented. Whereas they are taught in the Yeshiva as a way of life grounded in Torah, they are approached in many other Jewish day schools as part of the Jewish culture and tradition, principally as a series of facts to be recalled.

The Rebbe's Views on Secular Education

Lubavitcher consider that the Jewish curriculum in many Jewish schools does not influence the students in the way that a Torah education should. In fact, a main selling point of the two Lubavitch schools is that the students will be exposed to *Yiddishkayt* (refers to Jewish way of life within traditional Judaism) in its traditional sense and that any compromise of the Torah's precepts will neither be practised nor encouraged.

The Lubavitcher *Rebbe* has addressed himself on several occasions to the importance of a Torah education. A number of the *Rebbe's* discourses, as well as articles in *Di Yiddishe Heim*, (Literally, *The Jewish Home*; a Lubavitch publication) have urged parents to fulfill their obligation by providing their children with a thorough Jewish education. "It is ludicrous to begin thinking of a child's education six months before his *Bar Mitzveh*," the *Rebbe* once declared at a chassidic gathering, "it must begin in earliest childhood." On a separate occasion the *Rebbe* stated:

> One of the greatest frailties in contemporary Jewish life is the complacency toward the true Torah education of our youth. . . . In our generation we have become the unfortunate witnesses of the tragic fruits of this complacency — intermarriage and assimilation. Parents who neglected the Torah education of their children thinking that matters would somehow take their proper course without it, or that it just wasn't that important — without realizing the consequences — have become victims of devastated homes and disgraced families because of their children's behavior. Elements foreign to Torah way of life beckon the Jew to come and share their society. But the Jew can never

acquiesce to this society, for a Jew cannot survive in a life devoid of Torah, just as a fish cannot live without water (Teachers Programme, 1969: 392).

The present Lubavitcher *Rebbe's* emphasis on Torah education has led some Lubavitcher to expose their children only to such an education. While some of these Lubavitcher admit the possible benefits of a secular education, they are also quick to point to its potential dangers. These dangers centre on exposure to ideas which conflict with a religious interpretation of the creation and development of the universe. Although the *Rebbe* continually emphasizes the importance of a religious education, he does not specifically discourage secular learning for all of his followers. Lubavitcher claim that the *Rebbe* is opposed to secular education "where it is not needed". On the other hand, the *Rebbe* has adopted a definitely negative attitude toward a follower's pursuit of a college education. As one reads through the *Rebbe's* argument, one can understand how some Lubavitcher may have extended his views to refer to secular learning even at the primary school level. From a copy of a letter written by the *Rebbe* we are told:

> . . . There is a well-known parable for this, about the boy who strayed from the road and later found himself in the midst of the woods. He got there by making a small false step off the road, which led to another, and yet another.
>
> The conditions and environment in a country such as this call, therefore, for an even greater spiritual reinforcement of the Jewish boy and girl than even before and elsewhere. This reinforcement must be of such strength and duration that the Jewish child will always be conscious of the fact that no matter what the environment is, he is the bearer of the sacred tradition of the Divine Torah and Mitzvoth, and belongs to a people that is holy and different. For this, it seems essential that right from earliest childhood to adolescence the Jewish child should receive the fullest possible Jewish education, throughout his formative years.
>
> Hence when a Jewish boy completes his compulsory education, it is an absolute must that for a couple of years, at least, he should dedicate himself to the exclusive study of the Torah and sacred subjects, in a most conducive atmosphere of a Yeshivah, without distraction of secular studies, all the more so as the teenage years are crucial and formative and of lasting effect, in the cyrstallization of the character.
>
> This would have been my opinion even if the college entailed no more than the distraction of secular studies. Actually there is much more involved. Theoretically a college and its faculty should not try to impose any particular views, much less a way of life, on the students. Actually, however, the student cannot help being impressed on the conscious and subconscious level, by the views, outlook and way of life of his professors. These, as well as the whole atmosphere of a college are unfortunately not compatible with the Jewish way of life, and frequently if not always quite contradictory to it . . . Needless to say, the whole atmosphere of college is in violent conflict with the Shulchan Aruch way of life — whereby the Jew is totally committed . . . to the Torah and Mitzvoth and the service of G-d[2], as is written "You shall know Him in all your ways". . . . In other words, the Jewish boy (or girl) entering college, yet desiring to retain the Jewish way of life in accordance with the Torah,

finds himself tossed about in the raging waves of conflict between two contradictory worlds.

He is at a further disadvantage in finding himself in a minority camp, since those sharing his views and convictions are few on the college campus, while the forces pulling in the opposite direction are overwhelming; forces he must confront at every turn — among the student body, faculty members, textbooks, newspapers and periodicals. It is very doubtful whether even an adult and mature person who is subjected to such "shock treatment" day after day, would not be shaken; how much more so a teenager.

When Weiner (1969), during a personal audience with the *Rebbe* asked: "But you too have studied in two worlds, and your Hasidim are rather proud of the fact that you once attended the Sorbonne. Why then do you discourage them from studying in the 'other world'?" the reply was:

> Precisely because I have studied, and I know what the value of the study is, I recognized its usefulness. If there are people who think they can help God sustain the world, I have no objection. We need engineers and chemists, but engineering and chemistry are not the most important things. Besides, to study does not mean only to learn facts. It means exposure to certain circles and activities which conflict with a believer's values and faith. It's like taking a person from a warm environment and throwing him into a cold water shock treatment several times a day. How long can he stand it? In addition, studies in college take place at the age when a man's character is not yet crystallized, usually before the age of thirty. Exposure then is dangerous (1969: 174).

The *Rebbe's* attitude toward secular education is characterized by two underlying thoughts: first, that secular studies inevitably expose the person to secular ideas which may be in conflict with his religious upbringing; second, that attention to secular studies detracts from the most important task, that of acquiring knowledge of the Torah.

The Schools and their Curricula

The curriculum in both the *Bays Rivkeh* and the Yeshiva are structurally similar in that approximately three and a half hours each are officially devoted to religious and secular studies. The Hebrew curriculum is studied in the morning. This is not because secular teachers are not available in the morning, but rather reflects the greater importance attached to the *Limudai Kodesh* — the Hebrew studies. As one teacher remarked: "Hebrew studies are always in the morning. It's more important and the child is more impressionable then and he's more alert." Those enrolled in the secular program in both schools follow the curriculum outlined by the Protestant Board of Greater Montreal with which the schools have gained affiliate status. In return for following the provincial regulations governing the administration of secular education, the schools receive a subsidy from the government for each child attending secular classes.

While a secular curriculum is readily available in both schools, one finds that norms governing attendance of the classes for boys and girls differ.

that norms governing attendance of the classes for boys and girls differ. Such norms reflect the different expectations concerning both the amount and kinds of religious knowledge males and females must acquire in order to fulfill their respective religious obligations. The males are expected to be familiar with many more religious precepts than females and consequently must concentrate more on religious studies. A boy's curriculum schedule must, therefore, be more closely and carefully organized than a girl's to ensure he makes adequate progress in religious studies. As a result, while all girls attend the secular studies program in the *Bays Rivkeh,* two educational streams are pursued concurrently at the Yeshiva. Along with the large majority of students that attend both religious and secular study classes, a minority of students from so called "hard-core" Lubavitch families refrain from learning secular subjects and sometimes assume negative feelings for those who do.

Parents whose sons begin school by only receiving a Jewish education are not necessarily opposed to every form of secular learning. In certain instances their sons might begin to attend the secular program at a later date:

> My son who is thirteen and a half went to Grade 1 at nine years old, he skipped Grade 2 because I helped him with his phonetic sounds at home. My second son went straight into Grade 3, skipped out Grade 4, and then continued 5 as a normal. My youngest who is eight is still going to Jewish full-time.

In other cases, a tutor is hired to instruct the boy in certain secular subjects that it is thought will be important to him later on. One woman admitted that her boys had private lessons when they were "in the higher grades". Another said: ". . . when they are about thirteen to sixteen they may get lessons in arithmetic, reading, and writing."

Except for those who do not attend secular classes, students both at the Yeshiva and *Bays Revkeh* find the school day divided between religious and secular studies. While the practical emphasis between the two is balanced, greater philosophical importance is attached to the religious curriculum. One of the principals explains:

> Let's say, I insist and I try to see to it that all girls take the Provincial exams and we are trying to equip them to pass. High marks on the one hand. On the other hand, I am definitely not promoting college entrance. I definitely think that every girl who finished high school should rather go to teacher's seminary, if she has some flair for it, and get more knowledge in Hebrew studies, and also get professional instruction on psychology and methods of teaching. . . . And besides, what's going on on campus now, who would dare to direct any of his kids to this environment?

It is precisely the religious curriculum, in which students are taught the importance of practising and living the traditions of Judaism, that sets the Lubavitch schools apart from other Jewish parochial schools in Montreal. While the schools' secular programs are patterned on the one outlined for public schools, the religious curicula are intended to help mold the students' characters and attitudes.

Although many public education institutions emphasize the relationship between level of educational achievement and occupational role in adulthood, Lubavitcher do not regard their schools in this way. While they do recognize the advantages to be gained from secular schooling, they are quick to emphasize that a university education is hardly a guarantee for successful occupational placement and performance. For instance:

> I can give you an example of myself. . . . I never started Grade 1 (secular) and I think I'm finding my way around life. I'm not stuck. I never started Grade 1 because when I was supposed to start the *Rebbe* came out with the big campaign. . . . no English whatsoever. . . . And no one of my age group got any English education. One picked it up by hanging around in the community, and the other picked it up by looking in books himself. . . . but everyone ended up knowing English one way or another. And no one can say that any became a *shlemazel* or a *goilem* (fool) and couldn't get a job because of this. Success in work doesn't have to do with how long you study English subjects.

It is generally believed that success in one's work or occupation is forthcoming regardless of college and university attendance. As a Lubavitcher emphasizes, the critical variable to be considered is whether or not the person "has a head on his shoulders":

> . . . There was once an article in the Reader's Digest about the proportion of jobs, whether college actually adds anything to the job or not, and they came to the conclusion that college really does nothing for a job. But if we look at it statistically, we find very simple that 90 percent of the people that go to college end up with fantastic jobs and the *shlemazolim* (unlucky persons) that don't go to college end up with nothing. So it must be college, right? But the answer is not true. Who goes to college? Someone who has a head on his shoulders. A guy that has no head doesn't go. That's it. Now this same *shlemazel*, if he has a head, and did not go to college, would find the same job. On the other hand, the *shlemazel* who goes to college without a head wouldn't find a job. So it is not college that is doing it, it's actually the head.

In summary, Lubavitchers' interest in attracting non-orthodox students to their school has been largely responsible for the organization and maintenance of well-developed secular departments. While recognized as necessary, the secular curriculum is not intended to whet the student's intellectual appetite to pursue secular studies at a more advanced level. Instead, the main emphasis in both schools is on inculcating the young with a desire to accept the significance and centrality of orthodox Judaism as a guide to everyday life. In line with other religious minorities, Lubavitcher expect their schools to serve as a bastion against undesirable acculturation. As such, special attention must be devoted to hiring the secular staff and screening the curriculum.

Hiring Teachers and Screening the Curriculum

Finding teachers to fill the positions in the schools' Jewish departments should theoretically, present little difficulty as the community is able to train its own teachers. Those presently teaching in the Yeshiva are ordained Rabbis, the majority of whom are Lubavitcher and have taught there for many years. If younger teachers are desired, the graduates of the *Bays Medresh* are considered to have the necessary background knowledge to teach. The recruitment of younger teachers to the Yeshiva is, however, problematic. The Lubavitch philosophy, emphasizing the dissemination of orthodox Judaism, has always held a special attraction and appeal to young married couples. Many, consequently, prefer to seek positions in less well-established Jewish communities in which their "success" is more noticeable. A Lubavitcher expressed the problem this way:

> There is in Lubavitch, the *Rebbe* stresses this very much, the desire to go out and create something. So, it's strange to say, but a boy would rather go to the other *ek* (corner) of the *velt* (world) and start from scratch than to come to an established school and feel like the fifth wheel to the wagon. The capable boys . . . would rather work somewhere in a Lubavitch house with students than to come here.

As for the *Bays Rivkeh*, high school graduates are encouraged to attend a Lubavitch teacher's seminary and return to join the school's Jewish department. The school has, apparently, succeeded in its efforts as the entire Jewish department's staff is comprised of *Bays Rivkeh* graduates.

Although the community does experience some difficulty in recruiting staff for the Jewish departments, it has, in fact, been able to produce enough of its own teachers. Such, however, is not the case with staffing the secular departments, as graduates of both schools are discouraged from pursuing their secular studies. The following comments illustrate that while Lubavitcher recognize the many benefits of having their own kind staff the secular departments, the risks involved in Lubavitcher students continuing their secular education to the necessary level are believed to offset any such advantages:

> You see, I feel that you have no right to expose somebody to danger. You never know what will be the outcome if somebody goes to college. It would be very nice (if secular teachers came from within the community). But, then again, you're going into the conflict that we don't want to expose our girls to the university and that makes it very hard. You just can't do it. You can't have teachers if they're not going to go to university. And the university is a dangerous place, especially, I think, for our children who have been so cloistered all their life. To let them out like that, they have to be very strong-minded not to get pushed around and not to be pushed onto the wrong paths.

The formal qualifications of the teachers are likely to vary; some have both a university degree and a certified teacher's diploma whereas others may have only one or the other. All teachers are hired on a part-time basis, which again creates problems in finding sufficient suitable staff. While some of the other chassidic groups, for example the Satmarer and Tasher, consider a person's religious observance as an important criterion for hiring secular staff, the Lubavitch approach to this matter is more tolerant. As a Yeshiva administrator said: "In Lubavitch when we want someone to teach mathematics, we're first concerned with his mathematical capabilities." A teacher in the Yeshiva, supporting this view, remarked:

> . . . if you could get secular teachers that were observant, it would be much better. But we can't get this. We don't have it. When we are looking for teachers, we are looking for the best quality teachers. We prefer they should be male teachers.

Yet, on the basis of discussion with teachers and administrators of both schools, it appears that in addition to formal qualifications, less formal considerations are also important. Commenting on the potential problems of hiring non-religious Jewish teachers, a *Bays Rivkeh* administrator states:

> . . . sometimes it's even worse than a Gentile. Their not being religious sometimes makes more conflict. A Gentile woman comes in and she knows she's not allowed to say anything, do anything, and that's it, because it's two different worlds, while a Jewish girl thinks "Well, I'm religious enough, I can tell these kids anything," and that's where all the trouble starts.

The aforementioned comments point to what may be regarded as the ideal appointment to the secular staff: a Jew with a teacher's diploma who not only attended a religious school but also practises the tenets of traditional Judaism. For such a teacher, remarked one of the principals:

> . . . it would be easier to control the material which she is presenting. I mean, let's not kid ourselves. Even in a secular department we have to watch our steps. In the textbooks there are things that are contradictory. . . So, therefore, it is my duty to see that the teachers should remember not to get into controversial problems at a certain stage where the kids are not yet ready to digest them properly.

As such teachers are difficult to recruit, secular staff are expected to remain strictly within the limits of their subject and not influence the children unnecessarily (Poll, 1962: 173).

A striking feature of secular education among the chassidim is the degree to which the subject matter is screened. The rationale for this is succinctly expressed by Rubin:

> What concerns community leaders most is the possibility that the exposure of the youngsters to strange people and materials may be an avenue for undesirable acculturation, a gap in the isolating wall they try to build around the young until they grow up and are ready to deal with the environment from the more favorable vantage point of adulthood and full-fledged incorporation in the community (1972: 150).

One way this screening is done is by issuing a handbook containing instructions to teachers informing them of proscribed areas of discussion with students. A teacher at an orthodox girls' school, which included girls from chassidic families, remarked:

> . . . at the beginning of the year the Rabbi made up a manual for all teachers.

A section of this manual was devoted to explaining to teachers what we must not teach. . . . It said something to the effect of: everything contrary to Jewish religion must not be taught . . . such as evolution. Anything philosophical and contrary to Judaism must not be taught. Sex is absolutely out. If a teacher feels a serious need to communicate these ideas to the students, then she is to consult the Rabbi first, but under no circumstances is free discussion to be allowed in the classroom.

In some cases explicit verbal instructions are given by the principal. For example, a university graduate who was teaching chassidic boys from various chassidic groups had this to say:

He (the principal) told me a few things that I shouldn't be discussing with the kids. Things that would conflict with the religious beliefs. . . . Don't talk in terms of time, long periods of time, because they just won't believe you. They all just sort of block it out or they'll challenge you . . . because the earth has been in existence for a certain amount of time for them and if you talk in terms of millions of years. . . .

Along with such instructions, the reading material is inspected to ensure that both the written and pictorial content of books will not suggest or imply anything contrary to what orthodox Jews are expected to know. Thus, for example, certain areas of discussion are not only intentionally avoided, but all references to them are forbidden. A secular teacher at a Hungarian chassidic Yeshiva recalled:

Now, when . . . the _____ (name) *Rebbe* wanted them to learn English, even in the higher classes, they had to learn from certain books that were approved by them. For instance, if there was a picture of a woman, even a cartoon picture, anything, if didn't matter whether she had a long skirt on or not, it had to be marked in black. And I told the _____ (name) *Rebbe* that if I marked it in black the boys will be more curious, but this had nothing to do with it. It had to be marked off. All the *Rabonim* (Rabbis) saw that, even for the youngsters, every single illustration was taken out and all references to women were taken out.

Writing about the Satmarer, Rubin notes:

For example, one of the tasks imposed on the principal is a continuous combing of the textbooks for potentially subversive content (e.g., love stories or pictures), a task to which he devotes a great deal of his available time (1972: 151).

In addition, some chassidic schools limit the secular educational experience to the classroom. While school assignments may extend secular studies to the home, organized extra-curricular activities are discouraged. The following was recounted by a teacher in a Hungarian chassidic school:

I wanted to take my kids to the museum and to the Redpath (museum) and it had to go through the Council and it was refused just like that — they just wouldn't allow it. Also I wanted to start a library. It was refused, ostensibly, you know, on technical grounds that there wasn't enough room in the school. . . . They didn't know which books I would bring in and they thought the threat was too great and it would be too much trouble anyway, so they said to forget it. . . . Their list of priorities didn't include their kids reading anything like Hardy Boys mysteries, or anything to get them interested in reading.

In contrast to the secular departments in other chassidic schools in Montreal, Lubavitch schools' secular curricula closely follow the guidelines outlined for all public schools. As such guidelines permit flexibility, in that certain subjects are mandatory and others are optional, the Lubavitch schools' curricula do not include biology which is believed to contain views that are contradictory to an orthodox Jewish conception of the nature of the universe. The following incident illustrates this:

> It happens that I was teaching . . . at the time and we were studying personal health, and I was just surprised how little girls knew about the human body. This was in high school. And I was discussing this with the principal and I just mentioned to him that for science I was surprised that the girls didn't study biology instead of chemistry. It certainly would interest them more and it's certainly more directly applicable to them. And the answer was: chemistry is more objective and it's more specific, whereas with biology you could get into various views and various theories, and the easiest way was to stay away from it.

Nonetheless, the schools' administrators recognize the need to screen the subject matter and to be fully aware of the discussions and arguments that teachers wish to enter with their students. This, they claim, is to avoid situations in which material contradictory to the students' religious beliefs is brought into the open. As a Lubavitch administrator emphasized: "Teachers are told in the beginning two things they are not supposed to discuss — one is religion and the other is politics." Another administrator remarked:

> We told them that anything that has to do with religion, they should leave up to the Hebrew teacher. Last year we had a problem ... . the girls in one of the classes were discussing with their teacher things about their body and the discussion seemed to have gone quite well. But one of the little girls went home and told her mother "Oh boy, what we had in school today" and it bounced back. And the teacher was told: "Look, anything except your spelling and arithmetic don't touch, that's all. If the children want to know anything, let them go and ask their mothers. The discussion might be perfectly healthy and normal, but these children are brought up differently. . . ."

When asked if his staff was presented with instructions proscribing consideration of certain topics, one of the principals replied:

> I don't make it so formal, but while talking to a teacher I give the teacher to understand, and, besides, as she has three hours in the afternoon to cover English language, composition, spelling, arithmetic, geography, there's so much to do before coming to these problems. And let's say that you take a kid and you'll tell him in Grade 5 or 6 how dinosaurs lived ten million years ago, his concept of time is so limited that it actually wouldn't enlighten him. It might mix him all up. I see no educational purpose in it even from a secular point of view . . . I just say: "Don't get involved in problems that clash with religious beliefs. . . ." On the contrary, I do believe that kids should

not even be involved in these abstract discussions at all because their concept of time and numbers at this age is so limited and they only take it religiously. They believe because the teacher told them so.

While material considered openly contradictory to orthodox Judaism can easily be avoided or deleted from the curriculum, there is greater concern about students' exposure to subtle contradictory influences that may sway them against their religious upbringing. A Lubavitch woman remarked that:

> Today you can't help but head into it (evolution) wherever you are. Thank G-d, for our children it's not disastrous, because they feel G-d created the world. O.K., there's a problem, so the problem exists, but G-d created the world. I mean no one's arguing that. So really, the problems aren't too great for our children. Their belief, by the time they reach it, is strong enough. I'm much more afraid of the things that are not strongly contradictory to *Yiddishkayt* (Orthodox Judaism) that would endanger the child. (For example) things like, talking about physical enjoyments in life in a book that makes it sound so good and cushions it up so well. You know, romanticized. That is what I would be much more afraid of as influencing my child than anything else. I think that in any scientific beliefs a child, by that time, has enough Torah within him to keep him well-rooted.

The readers children use are also inspected to ensure that stories or passages in novels either related to other religions or in direct conflict with traditional Jewish beliefs are not studied in class. For example:

> The literature books today are just impossible. Well, at least Shakespeare, half of it is not understood, so they don't know what's coming off. But Mordecai Richler, or any of the others, I mean their books are just impossible for girls to read. _____ (name) tries to censor them as much as possible and to bring in only material that's both acceptable to the Quebec Board and also to us. It's very difficult to find.

Whereas in some chassidic schools such negatively defined content is deleted with a black pen, it is simply replaced with another story in the two Lubavitch schools:

> The reader series, if they are from the Protestant School Board, are oriented to the Protestant School Board's way of thinking. So, therefore, sometimes, when they plan that a book should be finished in Grade 1 or in Grade 2, right in the middle of the book where they consider the children will be three months after school begins, there'll be stories about Christmas and, about Père Noel. We just replace it by something else. I don't replace the pages. I just tell the teacher: "Don't get into these stories, leave this story, take another one." So the children can still read it. You cannot close the child. Anyway the child goes out in the street and he sees this Père Noel. On the other hand, in the Hebrew department, the child gets this: this is not for me, this has nothing to do with me.

Although the secular curriculum is closely supervised, Lubavitcher realize the difficulties inherent in shielding the student from all potentially dangerous secular influences. Thus, while such influences are viewed as the inevitable accompaniments of a secular curriculum, it is expected that they will be offset by the schools' Hebrew departments. For instance:

> . . . There is a direct influence and an indirect influence. The direct influence for instance, evolution, doesn't bother the children because we discuss it with them and it has no influence. But there is an indirect influence and you can't help it; for instance, a way of life described in a book. You can take (secular studies) or leave it. There's no way you can avoid (secular influences). It's impossible. . . . You see, the child is exposed to it in the street, in the newspapers, everywhere. . . . We must help the child understand the situation. For example, in secular studies they read about the Crusaders. So in the Hebrew department they explain to the children that there were plenty of Jewish communities wiped out by them. But still in the books they are heroes. We don't expect that the secular teacher will explain it to them, but the Hebrew teacher will.

In addition to the screening efforts of the schools, parents consider it their responsibility to be aware of what goes on in their children's English classes, and may petition the principal to change what they think necessary. For example:

> An important way that such negative influences could be avoided or controlled and checked is for the parents to take an interest in what their children are studying. . . . And even my youngest, who is only in elementary school, came home with a view of something that the teacher said. I didn't like it, so I referred it back to the principal and she checked on her. . . . If you get an irreligious teacher, not only could she be plain irreligious, but she might have some negative or cynical views about religion . . . and she doesn't even try to control its coming out. Now if she's teaching very young children, that's very bad. And I think it's only through parent-teacher communications, or parent interest in what's going on, that you can check this. . . .

Conclusion

To ensure its persistence the religious community must actively address itself to the assimilative influences in the larger society which threaten especially the young. These influences are typically regarded as corruptive and antithetical to the community's way of life. Aware of the public school's influence over the students, members of religious communities become concerned about the conflicts that their children will encounter when exposed to these schools' curricula. In response to this concern active efforts are initiated to retain a measure of control over the secular educational process.

In contrast to ethnic-based communities, those communities organized around a religious base have more successfully maintained their distinctive lifestyle, and have ensured that the young are socialized into the community's way of life. To accomplish this goal, such communities create a way of life that is both tenable and attractive to the members, in order to disinterest them from leaving while, at the same time, committing them to stay. The community must effectively impress upon its members that the surrounding society's seemingly attractive features are, in fact, potentially harmful to their distinctive lifestyle.

A feature characterizing communities is the property of intentionality. Restricting our discussion to religious and ethnic-based communities, we notice this property to be different in degree in both. Religious-based communities are highly intentional and are characterized by a series of strategies intended to maintain the community's distinctive identity. As efforts are organized specifically for this purpose, religious communities are largely successful at resisting the assimilative influences of the larger society, since group members are socialized to become integrated into the community's way of life. Ethnic-based communities, on the other hand, are less intentional. Such communities are not organized for the specific purpose of persistence and are not coordinated to effectively resist assimilation. These two kinds of communities can be distinguished in terms of active and passive resistance to assimilation. Active resistance to assimilation includes the organization of a series of institutions and activities to resist both the person's and the community's immersion into the surrounding culture. Passive resistance to assimilation, however, refers to the efforts of an individual or a family not to adopt the dominant culture. Unlike religious communities, efforts are not coordinated to ensure survival over time.

In the course of studying communities organized around a religious base we are able to closely examine how identity shaping mechanisms are utilized to ensure that the community's distinctive identity is maintained. The studies of such communities might profitably serve as a reference point for those interested in understanding the changes that occur within and among ethnic communities and their members.

NOTES

[1]The word refers to the religious, charismatic leader of a chassidic group. From the Lubavitch headquarters in Brooklyn, New York, the Lubavitcher *Rebbe* directs the affairs of the Lubavitch movement throughout the world. To his chassidim the *Rebbe* represents the essence of Lubavitch. The *Rebbe*'s followers recognize him as a central figure in their lives and are eager to accept his views and practise his directives. An appreciation of any chassidic group requires that the reader understand the chassidim's relationship to their *Rebbe*.

[2]The practice of spelling God in this form is based on a prohibition of obliters ing God's name. This would occur if, for example, the paper on which the word were written would be discarded or destroyed.

REFERENCES

Gutwirth, J., *Vie Juive Traditionnelle: Ethnologie D'Une Communauté Hassidique,* Paris: Les Editions De Minuit, 1970.

Hostetler, J.A., *Amish Society,* Baltimore: The John Hopkins Press, 1968.

Peters, V., *All Things Common: The Hutterian Way of Life.,* New York: Harper & Row, 1971.

Poll, S., *The Hasidic Community of Williamsburg,* New York: The Free Press of Glencoe, Inc., 1962.

Redekop, C.W., *The Old Colony Mennonites: Dilemmas of Ethnic Minority Life,* Baltimore: The John Hopkins Press, 1969.

Rubin, I., *Satmar: An Island In the City,* Chicago: Quadrangle Books, 1972.

Shaffir, W., *Life In a Religious Community: The Lubavitcher Chassidim In Montreal,* Toronto: Holt, Rinehart and Winston of Canada, Limited, 1974.

Weiner, H., *9½ Mystics: The Kabbala Today,* New York: Holt, Rinehart and Winston, 1969.

Young, P.V., *The Pilgrims of Russian-Town,* Chicago: The University of Chicago Press, 1932.

Lubavitch Publications, *Di Yiddishe Heim,* New York: Council Neshai Ub'Nos Chabad, Teachers programme, London: Lubavitch Foundation, 1969.

III.

Ethnic Inequalities

Chapter 10

The Canadian Corporate Elite: Ethnicity and Inequality of Access*

Wallace Clement

In Canada, as in many modern societies built on conquest and immigration, ethnicity is interwoven into the class system so that it provides advantages to the conquerors while keeping the conquered and newly-arrived at the bottom of the so-called "opportunity structure". Two elite systems based on the two chartered groups provide their members with differential access to the elite with the "third force" of other ethnic groups not even having an elite of their own which operates in the national arenas of economic power.

The Historical Participation of Ethnic Groups in the Economic Elite[1]

Commerce in New France was dominated by merchants from France (Pritchard, 1972) but Conquest by the English in 1755 drove most of these early entrepreneurs back to their mother country and they were replaced in economic activities by British immigrants (Guindon, 1968). Strengthened through their ties with Britain, the Anglo elite dominated commerce while the French lacked the advantages of capital and market

---

*Reprinted from *The Canadian Corporate Elite,* Toronto: Macmillan, 1975, by permission of the author and the publisher.

access associated with the Empire. The trans-Atlantic alliance between Canadian and British mercantilists effectively stifled mobility into dominant economic activities for others. For example, Tulchinsky's study of the Montreal business community from 1837 to 1853 finds few French-Canadians in commercial occupations. They tended to be concentrated in medical and legal professions (1972: 132-133). Further evidence of Anglo dominance is provided by Acheson's detailed study of the industrial elite in Canada between 1885 and 1910 which again finds French and "third" ethnic groups under-represented. French-Canadians had only seven per cent of the elite positions in 1885 and this dropped to six per cent in 1910 in spite of their representing about 29 per cent of the population. About 16 per cent of the population was accounted for by "third" ethnic groups, but only four and three per cent, respectively, of the industrial elite. Porter found only 6.7 per cent of the economic elite to be French-Canadian (a third of the population by then) while "third" ethnic groups represented insignificant numbers in the elite (but one fifth of the Canadian population) and the remainder were Anglos (1965: 286). In other words, since the Conquest and through the next two centuries until mid-way into the present century, French-Canadians and "third" ethnic groups have been effectively restricted in their access to top decision making positions in the Canadian economy.

Why have there been so few French and "third" ethnic group members in the upper levels of economic power? Since the Conquest, Canada's economic development relied heavily on British capital and markets. Early migrants from the United Kingdom tended to bring their own capital plus contacts with the financial houses of Britain. Using primarily British portfolio investment, first and subsequent generations of Anglo extraction were able to establish and maintain a commercial empire which eventually provided them with autonomy and control in financial, transportation and utilities sectors of the economy. This indigenous capitalist class formed a closed circle of powerful and wealthy men who excluded outsiders, among whom were included French-Canadians and newly-arriving ethnic groups. Control of the economic sector has remained with Anglos over the years because of their ability to gain access to sources of capital. More recently, the Canadian economy has become continental in focus and the Canadian Anglos were established in a stronger position linguistically and through their accumulated capital to transform their power into an alliance with the United States industrial capitalists. As a society based on conquest and immigration, Canada developed a high correlation between ethnicity and social class (hence Porter's title, *The Vertical Mosaic*). With this strong relationship, it is difficult to distinguish between the effects of social class and ethnic origin for mobility into the economic elite. Regardless, the combined effects have been sufficient to maintain Anglo dominance in the upper class and in elite positions within the economy.

TABLE 34
Proportion of Ethnic Representation in
the Economic Elite, 1951 and 1972

	Economic Elite		Canadian Population	
	1951	1972	1951	1971
Anglo	92.3%	86.2%	47.9%	44.7%
French	6.7	8.4	30.8	28.6
Other	1*	5.4	21.3	26.7
TOTAL	100%	100%	100%	100%
N	(760)	(775)		

*Porter says .78 per cent of his sample is Jewish; other 'third' ethnic groups "were hardly represented at all" (1965:286).

French-Canadians[2]

Although French-Canadians constitute just under one third of the Canadian population, only 65 members of the current economic elite could be classified this way, making the French component of the elite only 8.4 per cent. In 1951, Porter found 51 French-Canadians representing only 6.7 per cent of the elite at that time. This means a net increase of only 14 more French-Canadians or 1.7 per cent more of the elite population over the past twenty years. These have not been uneventful years in French-Anglo relations; quite the contrary, they were supposed to contain the "new awakening" (a loaded phrase which somehow assumes the French have themselves been their own barrier to gaining equality and not their position vis à vis the dominant Anglos) and the "quiet revolution" of the 1960's and the not-so-quiet revolution of recent years. In spite of ideological statements to the contrary, the French have not made significant inroads into the economic world.

Some may argue that the French may not have made it to the very top of the corporate world but they have at least made gains in the middle range and smaller corporations. Once again, the evidence is to the contrary. A recent study based on 12,741 names of executives from some 2,400 companies operating in Canada listed in the 1971 *Directory of Directors,* found only 9.48 per cent to be French-Canadian (Presthus, 1973:56). This is only about one per cent more than are to be found in the economic elite and includes many corporations much smaller than the 113 dominant ones which are the basis of this study.

As is evident in Table 35, French-Canadians have made some ground over the past twenty years with their proportion of the elite increasing slightly while their proportion of the population fell slightly. Nevertheless, they still remain very much under-represented in both periods, in fact,

TABLE 35
**Index of Ethnic Representation* in
the Economic Elite, 1951 and 1972**

	Economic Elite	
	1951	*1972*
Anglo	1.93	1.93
French	0.22	0.29
Other	0.05	0.20

*A figure of over 1.00 denotes over-representation and an index below 1.00 shows under-representation. This index is arrived at by dividing the population into the elite representation thus standardizing over time for changes in the ethnic composition of the population. It is a ratio of the ethnic proportion in the elite divided by the corresponding proportion of the Canadian population for the same time. The basic data is drawn from Table 34.

almost as under-represented by 1972 as "other" ethnics. In the process, however, the Anglos have not lost any ground. From Table 34 it appears that Anglos have declined but the drop from 92.3 per cent in 1951 to 86.2 per cent in 1972 is deceptive. In fact, when compared to the decline in the population base, as in Table 35, the apparent decline disappears. For Anglos the index of representation is identical for each period (1.93 in 1951 and 1972). In other words, their decline in the proportion of the total Canadian population and the change can be explained simply in demographic terms and is not due to inroads made by either French or "third" ethnics.

One of the key issues of French-Anglo relations is the different proportions of French in the various elites. It has already been stated that they represent only 8.4 per cent of the current economic elite. This is still well below the 13.4 per cent Porter found for the bureaucratic elite in 1953 and the 21.7 per cent of the political elite from 1940 to 1960 (1965: 389,441). Moreover, it is well below the French proportion found in the current state elite by Dennis Olsen, who says 23.2 per cent of the bureaucratic elite in 1973 and the 24.7 per cent of the political elite between 1961 and 1973 are French (Clement and Olsen, 1974). It is evident in comparison with the two state elites that they have a much higher French representation, although still never reaching their proportion of the population. This suggests that the historical division of labour between the two charter groups is still very much in evidence.

It was already stated that only three French-Canadians (3.9 per cent) were included in the group of elite members who have survived twenty years or more in the economic elite. This suggest they lack the same historical continuity in the corporate world as do Anglos. With access to the upper levels of the economic domain so dependent upon inheritance of position through both capital and social networks, it is understandable that French-Canadians are under-represented in the present elite. Previous generations of French-Canadian elites did not accumulate large amounts of capital, consequently, they were not able to transfer the same privileges to their offspring as were the Anglos. This is not to say that there is not a well-defined class structure within French Canada; it only means that that structure is not primarily based on control over economic institutions. At the top of the French class structure there are only a few families — like the Simards — who control very tightly what French corporate activity there is.

The class structure of French Canada is even more rigid than for all Canada, as was suggested in the earlier findings on regionalism. In fact, while 59.4 per cent of the elite as a whole are upper class, 87.6 per cent of the French in the elite have this distinction. Part of this is due to the effect of the classical college system and this being included as a criteria of upper class. However, even when only those born at or near the top (which excludes private schools) are examined, it is found that 50.8 per cent of the French are in this category compared to 46.8 per cent of the Canadian born elite as a whole. Only one French-Canadian has less than middle class origins and he was born in the United States. While there may not be a great deal of room for many French-Canadians in the economic elite as it now stands, there is certainly room made for the upper class French. This difference will be returned to later but for now it may be suggested that the different ethnic participation in the elite may not be due to "discrimination" but in fact may be a product of the different sizes of the various classes in each of the ethnic groups. That is, it may be that the French have a proportionately smaller upper class compared to their population base than do the Anglos and their 8.4 per cent proportion of the economic elite may resemble their proportion of the Canadian upper class.

The French tend to be younger than the elite as a whole but this reflects their higher class origins rather than their only slightly increased participation in the corporate world. While 18 per cent of the entire Canadian born elite was born before 1905, only 11 per cent of the French fell into this category; forty per cent of the French were born after 1920 compared to 29 per cent of the entire elite born in Canada. Most of the 65 French were born in Quebec (58) with only four in Ontario, two in the U.S. and one in France. This suggests that almost 90 per cent of the French-Canadians had avenues into the elite within the institutional structure of Quebec society.[3] There is a difference with respect to compradorization between the French and others in the elite. While 76.9 per cent of the French are indigenous elites, this is 4.1 per cent more than the non-French. The major difference is between the U.S. comprador group where only 7.7 per cent of the French are found but 18 per cent of the non-French. To some extent, this accounts for the higher French proportion of upper class since the Anglos have experienced greater compradorization and, as has been shown, this means greater mobility for the middle class.

A major avenue of mobility for French-Canadians into the economic elite has been through connections with the state. Of the French in the current elite, there are three Senators, an additional three from the political elite, including two former federal elite members and Jean Lesage, a former Premier, and three from the bureaucratic elite. Between them, they account for 14 per cent of all the French in the economic elite. In addition, seven have close relatives who are in the state elite and 19, not included in any of the categories listed thus far, sit on key government boards or organizations such as crown corporations. Altogether this includes 54 per cent of all the French in the elite. This suggests that the French have been successful in using the state as a means for access to the economic elite and that they have strong relations with the state after gaining access.

Law, one the major institutional links between the corporate and state systems, is also a major avenue of mobility for French-Canadians. There are 16 associated with law firms (24.6 per cent) and an additional 12 who have law degrees (18.5 per cent) representing a total of 43 per cent of the French members of the elite with training in law. This in considerably more than the one third of the French-Canadians in the 1951 economic elite trained as lawyers or the 19 per cent of the entire 1971 economic elite with training in law.

Education has been important for French-Canadian members of the elite with 75.4 per cent attending private schools, particularly the College Ste. Marie and College-de-Brèbeuf, with 11 members of the current elite attending each of them. Common educational experience within the upper class educational institutions of Quebec makes for lasting association; for example, four members of the elite attended both classical colleges mentioned above and all went on to the University of Montreal, with two of them now sitting on the board of Royal Trust together. University education has also been important to French-Canadian elites, with 83 per cent attending university (54) of which 43 went on to advanced degrees including 28 in law and 13 in commerce, of which six went to Harvard. Of the 54 attending university, 22 have their first degrees from the University of Montreal, eight at each of McGill and Laval, and four at the University of Ottawa with 12 going elsewhere.

Club life is important among French-Canadians with only eight of the 65 not reporting any club membership. Most popular is St. Denis, with 27 elite members (41 per cent). There are 43 per cent of the French-Canadians who belong to one of the six national exclusive men's clubs with 17 belonging to the Mt. Royal, 19 to the St. James and five to the Rideau, but only one to each of the three Toronto clubs. This illustrates that there is a high degree of social separation at the club level between the French-Canadians and Anglos outside Quebec, although they do come together in the Montreal clubs.

"Third" Ethnics

Although over one quarter of Canada's population is made up of ethnic groups other than the two charter groups (26.7 per cent), they have almost no representation in the economic elite, except for Jews. From the non-charter groups, there are only 32 Jewish-Canadians (4.1 per cent) and 10 from other "third" ethnic groups (1.3 per cent). In 1951 there were only six Jews (.78 per cent) in the elite thus indicating they have made significant inroads into the elite over the past twenty years. None the less, "third" ethnic groups still remain the most under-represented ethnic category in the elite, as can be seen in Table 35. They have made limited gains in the elite while simultaneously their proportion of the Canadian population also increased by over five per cent in the last twenty years.

There are, however, several factors associated with the Jewish representation worth noting. It has already been discussed that most of the inroads have been on their "own account", indicating that the avenue of mobility into the elite has not been through established corporations but through firms which have been established and grown to national scope within one generation. A closer examination of the firms with which they were associated explains why they are 4.1 per cent of the elite and only 1.4 per cent of the population. Of the 32 Jews, 28 are associated with one of the five corporations, with one of five a long established corporation in the beverage industry, three in trade and one primarily in real estate. These are tightly-held family firms with only six families accounting for 25 of the 32 Jewish members of the elite. Outside these family firms, Jews have much less economic power in dominant financial corporations, holding only five of the dominant bank directorships (2.4 per cent) and two dominant insurance directorships (1.2 per cent). In other words, their representation in financial corporations is well below their proportion of the entire economic elite.

Outside the board room there is not very much participation by Jews in the private world of the economic elite, with only two belonging to one of the six national exclusive men's clubs. There are, however, Jewish clubs to which they belong, particularly the Montefiore with 10 members and the Elmridge with eight. Rosenberg provides an excellent discussion of the Jewish cultural and social associations, mentioning in particular that "the Montefiore Club is the second home of the vast majority of Jewish community leaders" (1971: 143-144). In an earlier discussion, Rosenberg provided a detailed discussion of Jewish participation in various corporate sectors; the essence of his discussion, as with the findings of the present study, is that Jews have not, and do not, play a dominant role in the economic elite in Canada. Their participation is, for the most part, peripheral to the economic elite and located in the high risk sectors of trade and real estate (1939: 215). Although in proportion to their representation in the population Jews are over-represented in the elite, this participation is so confined to a very few family firms that it does not give an adequate indication of their participation in the elite as a whole.

Although not exclusively, there is a tendency toward social separation in the philanthropic, cultural and honourific activities of the Jewish members of the elite. These are for the most part institutions associated within the Jewish tradition and community. With few exceptions these 32 individuals are more correctly understood as an elite of the Jewish community, separate yet interlocking in a peripheral way with the national Anglo-dominated elite.

While Jewish-Canadians are somewhat over-represented in terms of their population base, other "third" ethnics are extremely underrepresented with only 1.3 per cent of the elite and 25.1 per cent of the Canadian population. Members of the other "third" ethnic groups stand in sharp contrast to the Jews. With one exception, the 10 members of the elite from other "third" ethnic groups are not participants in the cultural or philanthropic associations of their ethnic groups and unlike the Jewish members are not associated with a particular set of elite corporations. The only case of overlap is two members on the CNR, a federal crown corporation. Unlike the Jews who have made it on their own account within Canada, members of these other ethnic groups have mainly transported family businesses from elsewhere to Canada (for example, Bata, Prentice and Koerner from Czechoslovakia) or transferred their high class position to Canada within multinational corporations (for example, A.A. Franck of Genstar). In other words, these few members of other ethnic groups have not, for the most part, "made it" within Canada but have been horizontally mobile from high class positions outside Canada.

Implications of Ethnic Representation in the Economic Elite

Ethnic representation in the economic elite satisfies neither of the two "official" models of Canadian society — "biculturalism" and "multiculturalism". Neither in the 1951 or 1972 economic elite was there anything close to approaching the proportions required to say there was sufficient French representation for the bicultural model; nor was there sufficient "third" ethnic participation for the multicultural model. The conclusion must be that the economic elite is characterized by Anglo dominance in both periods. The limited "third" ethnic penetration which has occurred with Jewish-Canadians has not been through integration with the dominant Anglos; rather, it has been by creating a parallel elite within a few corporations which for the most part are separate from the mainstream of economic power. Members of other "third" ethnic groups remain virtually absent from the elite, never reaching close to two per cent while about a quarter of the Canadian population. Later, the issue of ethnic representation in the elite will be raised in connection with the mass media and the relationship between language, legal and capital bases of power by the various ethnic groups will be examined.

NOTES

[1] Parts of the following analysis also appear in a report submitted to the Secretary of State by Clement and Olsen, entitled "The Ethnic Composition of Canada's Elites, 1951 to 1973" (May, 1974). The historical perspective is a summary from Chapter Two.

[2] There is, of course, an issue as to the "degrees of Frenchness" actually apparent in the 65 members of the elite defined here as French. The criteria used to decide whether a person was to be categorized as French include: (i) membership in French-speaking clubs, (ii) association with known French social service of philanthropic organizations, (iii) ethnic origin of the father, (iv) mother and (v) wife, if their name appeared in (vi) *Biographies Canadiennes Françaises*, (vii) if educated in French-speaking institutions, particularly the classical colleges and French-speaking universities, (vii) if Catholic in religion, (ix) birth in Quebec or known settlements of French in the rest of Canada and (x) an historically French name. These ten criteria tend to cluster so that a person meeting one of the criteria usually has the rest as well. In marginal cases, if the person met any three of the ten criteria they were considered to be French. This means that some of those included were educated in English-speaking schools, has a mother who was Anglo and in several cases, wives who were Anglo (including an Eaton!)

[3] The Desmarais brothers of Sudbury are a notable exception.

REFERENCES

Acheson, T.W., "Changing Social Origins of the Canadian Industrial Elite, 1880-1910," *Business History Review,* XLVII, no. 2 (Summer, 1973).

Clement, Wallace and Dennis Olsen, "The Ethnic Composition of Canada's Elites, 1951 to 1973". Report submitted to the Secretary of State (May 1974).

Porter, John, *The Vertical Mosaic,* University of Toronto Press: Toronto, 1965.

Presthus, Robert, *Elite Accommodation in Canadian Politics,* Macmillan: Toronto, 1973.

Pritchard, James, "Commerce in New France", Macmillan, ed. (1972).

Rosenberg, Louis, *Canada's Jews: A Social and Economic Study of the Jews in Canada,* The Bureau of Social and Economic Research, Canadian Jewish Congress, 1939.

_____, *The Jewish Community in Canada,* Two Volumes, McClelland & Stewart: Toronto, 1971.

Tulchinsky, G., "The Montreal Business Community, 1837-1853", Macmillan, ed. (1972).

Chapter 11

French-English Relations as a Social Problem: Present Inequalities*

Raymond N. Morris and C. Michael Lanphier

In this chapter we adopt the "objective" definition of a social problem and compare anglophones with francophones in their economic and political roles. The existence of inequalities in individual, collective and cultural rights can sometimes be measured from existing data. This can be illustrated by comparing anglophone and francophone incomes. If *individual rights* are equal in this setting, there will be no differences between the income distribution for anglophones and the income distribution for francophones *who have the same qualifications.* Differences in experience, diligence, education and competence justify differences in income. To establish that individual rights were unequal, we would need to make careful comparisons in which such differences were held constant.

If *collective rights* are equal, there will be no differences between the income distribution for anglophones and the distribution for francophones *regardless of their qualifications.* Each ethnic group will be *proportionally* represented in the highest and in the lowest income brackets: if these each contain ten per cent of all anglophones they will also contain ten per cent of all francophones. The case for collective rights assumes that neither group has inherently superior talents.

---

*Reprinted from *Three Scales of Inequality,* Don Mills: Longman Canada Ltd, 1977, by permission of the authors and the publisher.

If *cultural rights* are equal, each ethnic group will be represented by *the same number of persons* in the economic elite; if it contains two thousand anglophones it will also contain two thousand francophones. It will be apparent, then, that when there are relatively few francophones, the establishment of equal *collective* rights will give them greater *individual* rights than anglophones have, because the group is the unit to which equal status is being granted, and not the individual. In this instance the award of equal *cultural* rights will give francophones greater *collective* rights than anglophones have. This pattern will be reversed where francophones are in the majority numerically.

Differences in Economic Rights

We first review briefly the data bearing on individual, collective and cultural economic rights. Major studies of individual economic rights were undertaken for the Royal Commission on Bilingualism and Biculturalism.[1] Dofny's survey of engineers in Montreal studied differences in their incomes and employment patterns. He found some evidence of unequal individual rights. Anglophones had significantly higher incomes than francophones — among those who worked for the same type of firm; among those in the same age-range and specialty; and among those holding administrative positions in large firms.[2] A Montreal study by Raynauld, Marion and Béland reached similar conclusions: in quite a few though not all occupations, males of British ethnic origin earned more than comparable males of French ethnic origin.[3] Nation-wide comparisons by the same authors showed that among unskilled workers with primary education, those of French origin earned 95% as much as those of British origin. For clerical and skilled workers with secondary education, the percentage fell to 90. For managers, professionals and sales workers with post-secondary education, it fell further to 86%.[4] Beattie and Spencer's research on federal civil servants showed that anglophones' incomes rose faster than those of comparable francophones.[5]

Collective economic rights have been much more frequently studied, because they involve simpler tabulations. Dofny and Raynauld *et al.* found much stronger differences when such factors as education were not held constant. In 1961, on the average full-time male employees of French ethnic origin in Canada earned only 79% as much as similar persons of British ethnic origin. Within Quebec alone, the corresponding figure was 64%, and within Montreal 67%.

Inequalities in collective rights can also be seen in the occupational distributions for anglophones and francophones. For Quebec in 1970, the Gendron Commission found that 36% of anglophone employees were in administrative or professional occupations, compared with 23% of francophones. Thirteen per cent of anglophones were labourers, as against 29% of francophones.[6] This pattern of an anglophone management and a francophone work force occurred in the construction, primary and manufacturing industries. Public utility services and finance were in anglophone hands at all levels, while by contrast public administration and commerce were in francophone hands at all levels.[7]

Francophones have formed less than 10% of the economic élite for the last hundred years.[8] Those who reach the economic élite tend to be clustered at the lower echelons, as senior managers rather than as company presidents.[9] Ownership of Quebec industry is largely in the hands of anglophones, especially in those sectors of the economy which offer the best wages, have the highest productivity, and are most likely to expand.[10] With only slight overstatement, Saint-Germain talks of two sectors in the Quebec economy. One has in the past been stagnant, francophone-owned, and oriented to local markets and cheap labour; the other generally dynamic, anglophone-owned and oriented to the exploitation of cheap raw materials for international markets.[11]

This section concludes with a few words about cultural rights. Inequality of cultural rights can be assessed directly, if there is evidence that anglicisation is important for the success of francophones, and that "francisation" is not important for anglophones. De Brouwer found signs that the former was true in business in Quebec, but his evidence was not conclusive.[12] The Royal Commission asserted strongly, on the basis of interviews with francophones, that anglophone culture was necessary for success at the higher levels of the federal civil service.[13]

Differences in Political Power

Three areas of political rights will be discussed briefly: representation, power and civil service employment. In terms of Parliamentary representation, anglophones and francophones have the same individual rights to vote and seek office. Collective rights are assured insofar as francophones are represented proportionately in decision-making bodies. This is the case in Parliament, though they have tended to be under-represented in the Cabinet and in the Supreme Court.[14] Within Quebec, francophones are now over-represented in the National Assembly, and in the provincial Cabinet. In other provinces, they generally have disproportionately few representatives.

The cultural rights of francophones have not matched those of anglophones since they became a minority numerically. The question of cultural rights comes to the fore when francophones seem to be uniting behind one proposal and anglophones behind another. While such issues have rarely come to a head, the fear of being outvoted on an important issue is a real one for francophones. Anglophones for their part fear that francophones exercise an informal veto power which is tantamount to equal cultural rights.[15]

The distribution of political power, individually and collectively, is much more difficult to measure. Federally, francophones have often maximised their collective power by voting solidly and sometimes overwhelmingly for a single party, while anglophone votes have been split among several parties. The majority party, in consequence, has often contained a strong francophone contigent, and the government has been sensitive to francophone points of view. In the Quebec National Assembly the situation is reversed. Where francophones' votes are split between several parties, block voting by anglophones[16] can influence the outcome in some two-fifths of the seats.[17]

Given the situation of francophones as a provincial majority but a federal minority, the issue of provincial as against federal rights takes on special overtones in Quebec. While anglophones have at times been the strongest fighters for provincial powers, they rarely portray themselves as a distinct nation within Canada, in the sense that many francophones do.[18] Practical matters such as the licensing of cable TV operators quickly acquire symbolic overtones and raise the question of Quebec's status in Confederation. Underlying what seem to be squabbles over protocol are different conceptions of the role of the federal government toward Quebec. Claude Morin summarizes these as follows:

> In the eyes of French-speaking Quebeckers, Ottawa and Quebec have no authority over each other: each administration is autonomous in its own areas of jurisdiction; sometimes their activities are complementary and if conflicts arise, the Government of Quebec is *a priori* in the right. Furthermore, to Quebeckers the federal government is traditionally English, and is usually seeking ways to intervene in areas outside its jurisdiction. . . . All politicians in the English language provinces agree that it is up to Ottawa to establish the broad policies of the country, to set "national" norms, in short to exercise all the authority usually vested in the government of a country, on condition, however, that it does not interfere unduly with their current programmes.[19]

Collective and individual rights in the civil service were carefully studied by the Royal Commission.[20] In 1965, 22% of all civil servants were of French mother tongue. Most were bilingual, for their promotions depended heavily on knowledge of English;[21] there were few bilinguals of English mother tongue. Procedures for recruiting and retaining francophones were less successful than those for anglophones, and the system functioned to train French speakers in anglophone ways of working. The inequalities in promotion were reduced by a policy of "parachuting" francophones with little civil service experience into high-level positions.[22] Since the middle 1960s, a massive programme of language training has been undertaken. This has had some effect in decreasing inequalities in individual and collective rights, as we shall see in Chapter 16; but critics argue that it seeks to teach French to anglophones now in high positions, rather than to improve the skills and promotion chances of francophones.[23] There are still indications that Ottawa remains a "foreign capital" to many Quebec francophones,[24] and that little progress has been made in equalising cultural rights. Within Quebec, the situation tends to be reversed: few anglophones are found among Quebec civil service or Montreal municipal employees.

Differences in the Status of the Languages

The relative status of the two languages also reveals the extent of inequality. The Royal and Gendron Commissions selected three contexts in which to examine language inequalities: employment, the market place and education. At work, most ambitious francophones are obliged to learn English whereas few ambitious anglophones are obliged to learn French — even in Quebec. Carlos' study in Quebec found that for jobs which involved little reading or writing, most communication was in French and the onus of becoming bilingual fell mainly on anglophones. As the proportion of written communication rose, the burden of bilingualism shifted to francophones, particularly for secretarial or management work.[25] The demands of companies and clients outside Quebec could not explain the full extent to which English was dominant.[26] The onus in "mixed conversation" was still on the francophone to use English, thereby assuming a disadvantage.[27] Even when the anglophone was the subordinate and the francophone the superior,[28] this convention was often observed. English remains the dominant language of management, even in areas of Quebec where most of the population is francophone.[29] Anglophone businessmen find it almost impossible to imagine that French could ever become the language of management in the province, an opinion echoed by many francophone business leaders in spite of the existence of major exceptions such as Hydro-Québec.[30]

The Gendron Commission then examined the status of the two languages in the market places of Quebec. Large commercial or governmental organisations provide box-office and telephone service to the public in both languages. Private and non-commercial organisations catering predominantly to one group have learned to offer certain services in the other language upon demand.[31] The likelihood of obtaining good service in one's own language deteriorates as one moves from standard forms and common requests to personal letters or requests of a specialised nature.[32]

In impersonal situations, the status of the languages is unequal. Very rarely in an anglophone province does one find goods for sale with labelling or instructions in French only. In Quebec, however, over 40% of francophones recalled buying something with instructions in English only. Packaging legislation obliges manufacturers to use bilingual labels only on a limited range of goods such as food stuffs. On other items such as major appliances or toys the labelling is often in English only — even in Quebec City, where anglophones constitute under 5% of the population. The Quebec government's Bill 22 is attempting to change this over a five-year period by insisting that the material in French be given equal prominence if not priority.[33]

Finally, the different conceptions of minority rights can be observed in education. The Royal Commission *Report* took as its ideal the system in Quebec, where cultural rights have been relatively equal. Each language group has organised its own schools and universities. Freedom of choice currently permits a small proportion of francophone and nearly all non-francophone immigrants' children to attend English-language schools, while a small proportion of anglophones attend French-language schools. This situation has been more advantageous to the numerical minority in the province, the anglophones, than either equal collective or individual rights would have been.

In the other provinces, cultural and collective rights have been very unequal: the official ideal has been gradual if not rapid assimilation. Students in grades one and two in areas heavily populated by francophones have usually been taught in French; but until recently their instruction was expected to be in English for grade three, and beyond. Schooling in French, however, often continued unofficially in higher grades.[34]

Educational policy for francophones in the anglophone provinces parallels in certain respects that afforded to mentally or physically handicapped children: integration as rapidly as possible for the mildly "disadvantaged," with special schools for those more seriously handicapped. Far from seeing it as a valuable heritage, these provinces have in effect treated French-Canadian culture as an impairment, to be overcome quickly.

Changes have come hesitantly. In Quebec there has been growing pressure on the government to give official priority to the French language in education and to reduce the cultural and collective rights of anglophones.[35] In the anglophone provinces three changes have occurred simultaneously; their long-run effects are not yet clear. First, French has ceased to be required for university entrance, and thus for jobs requiring a degree. Consequently the numbers studying it in high school have tended to drop.[36] Second, more anglophones are coming to view French as an economic asset for their children.[37] The numbers studying French in primary school are therefore growing.[38] Third, bilingual and French education has increased in scope. Ontario has increased the autonomy of the French-language committees of anglophone school boards. Manitoba now allows parents a choice of language of instruction. New Brunswick offers instruction in French at all levels, though some researchers doubt that it matches English-language education in quality.[39]

Anglophones and Francophones in the Larger Stratification System

The discussion of rights has pinpointed one recurrent theme. In many situations, anglophones show goodwill toward francophones as individuals, and believe they accord them equal individual rights; at the same time they stubbornly refuse to grant them the equal collective and cultural rights which francophones equally stubbornly seek. In consequence higher prestige and value are still attached to anglophone than to francophone culture; being anglophone itself grants a significant advantage in seeking economic and political power in most parts of Canada.[40]

Although our discussion has focused only on anglophones and francophones, other groups are obviously involved in this system of social stratification. Americans occupy a higher position than anglophone Canadians; Indians and Inuit a lower position than francophone Canadians. Immigrants who were already culturally similar to anglophones and who could speak English have become part of the anglophone group. The situation has been more ambiguous for immigrants who were culturally similar to francophones and who knew neither French nor English. The earlier generations of Italian immigrants in Montreal, for example, oriented themselves toward the francophones, who were immediately above them in the stratification system. More recent arrivals, and the descendants of the earlier Italian immigrants, have oriented themselves more toward the anglophones whose culture may now appear within their reach.[41]

In a stratified system, each group tries to "catch up with" the group which is immediately above it, to retain the allegiance of its present members, and to prevent those groups which are below it from catching up. This process fosters the retention of group distinctiveness. The uppermost group responds to its nearest rival group by denying it the collective and cultural rights which it enjoys itself. Traditional anglophone strategy, toward francophone nationalism and claims for equal collective and cultural rights, is characterised by a refusal to accord higher status to francophone culture than to those of immigrant groups. Traditional francophone strategy toward immigrant groups in turn draws an equally clear line between "founding" and "immigrant" groups, between "official" and "non-official" languages.

Each language group strives to maintain its status and boundaries. Individuals may accept this group goal as their own and become "nationalists," resisting threats of "foreign domination," i.e., of a situation in which the power and attraction of a rival group is such that their own group has difficulty in keeping the allegiance of its members and in attracting recruits from lower status groups. Nationalists assert that the distinctiveness of their group — its unique history, culture and set of heroes — should be defended at some personal sacrifice.[42] Alternatively, members may reject this goal for themselves, trying to shed their culture and if necessary migrate in order to succeed as individuals who have shed their old partisanship. In this case they might describe themselves as "internationalists"[43] or become nationalists of the group which they aspire to join.

The most visible groups are those immediately above and immediately below one's own; accordingly they conflict most intensively and are least likely to form alliances.[44] Appeals for a "united front" of English- and French-speaking Canadians to resist American cultural, economic or political "domination" have generally fallen on deaf ears. Each group places an important premium on defending its position and culture against the other. They are unable to agree on a strategy for mutual defense or on their relations with each other inside a mutual defense organisation. Each tends to propose an alliance on its own terms.[45]

In summary then, to accord equal individual rights, while denying equal collective and cultural rights, maintains a stratification system in which one group and its culture is widely regarded as inferior to the other. While anglophones defend the boundaries and superior status of their group against francophone claims for equality, francophones for their part defend their own status and boundaries against the claims of other ethnic groups. On the group level, then, each veritably practises a double standard, claiming collective and cultural equality with the one above, while denying such equality to the one below.

On the individual level, meanwhile, members of a group try to acquire the culture of the group immediately above their own, or to promote their own group's collective and cultural rights while themselves retaining its culture.

NOTES

[1] Royal Commission (1968), IIIA; Dofny (1970); Raynauld *et al.* (1967).

[2] Dofny (1970), pp. 17-19, 40. Only one or two of these factors could be controlled at the same time.

[3] Royal Commission (1968), IIIA, p. 68. The respondents were comparable in age, education and source of income. Ethnicity was not a factor in explaining income differences between those of French and Other ethnic origins.

[4] Raynauld *et al.*, (1967), Appendice Statistique, Tableaux 169, 170; Lanphier and Morris (1974), p. 61; Raynauld *et al.*, (1975), p. 224.

[5] Beattie and Spencer (1971); Beattie (1975), p. 187.

[6] Gendron Commission (1972), I, p. 73.

[7] *Ibid.,* I, p. 113.

[8] Clement and Olsen (1974); Falardeau (1965), pp. 41-44.

[9] de Brouwer (1973), p. 37.

[10] Royal Commission (1968), IIIA, ch. 4.

[11] Saint-Germain (1973), pp. 20-48. An exception to this is described in Gold (1973).

[12] de Brouwer (1973), pp. 97, 113-136, 139, 323.

[13] Royal Commission (1968), IIIA, pp. 195, 241, 256-59; Beattie (1975), ch. V.

[14] Clement and Olsen (1974), p. 15.

[15] This has happened in discussions on "repatriating the constitution": Smiley (1972), pp. 9-11. The proposed veto powers were, however, to be available to other (groups of) provinces besides Quebec.

[16] The 1972 CROP poll found that 85% of Quebec anglophones who stated their voting intentions chose the Liberals: Pinard (1973), p. 122. There was much less block voting in the 1976 election.

[17] "October 29th: Another Choice for Quebec," CBC, Oct. 24, 1973; R. Barberis, *Le Jour,* Sept. 4, 1974.

[18] L. Dion (1973b), p. 255; Laurendeau (1961).

[19]C. Morin (1973a), pp. 210-211; Bellavance et Gilbert (1971), pp. 116-19.

[20]Royal Commission (1968), IIIA, chs. VI-XII.

[21]*Ibid.,* pp. 120-30.

[22]Beattie (1975), p. 130.

[23]*Toronto Star,* April 4, 1973; L. Dion, *Le Soleil,* March 30, 1974.

[24]Ward (1960), p. 266; Rolland (1970), pp. 87-88; *Toronto Star,* Sept. 4, 1975. The exceptions tend to be those who were born in the area and who enter secure, lower-level routine jobs: Beattie (1975), pp. 74-76.

[25]Gendron Commission (1972), I, p. 107.

[26]Carlos (1973), pp. 73-74.

[27]Gendron Commission (1972), I, pp. 65, 91-93, 135, 204.

[28]*Ibid.,* p. 91.

[29]Royal Commission (1968), IIIB, pp. 460-61.

[30]de Brouwer (1973), pp. 78, 214; Royal Commission (1968), IIIB, pp. 494-503.

[31]Gousse (1973).

[32]Complaints about lack of service in one's own language can be made to the Commissioner of Official Languages if they involve the federal civil service or Crown corporations such as Air Canada. Otherwise it is unlikely that any law is being broken.

[33]*Toronto Star,* Jan. 28, 1976, highlights some of the resultant regulations.

[34]Royal Commission (1968), II, chaps. III, V.

[35]Some English-language educational expenditures were cut back by the provincial government where they exceeded the corresponding French-language expenditures: *Toronto Star,* Oct. 16, 1973.

[36]*Toronto Star,* June 13, 1973, Sept. 18, 1975.

[37]Macnamara and Edwards (1973), pp. 14-15, 25.

[38]*Toronto Star,* April 24, 1973, Sept. 18, 1975.

[39]Dufour (1973), pp. 45-75; Even (1972), p. 277.

[40]Byers (1969), p. 16.

[41]Gendron Commission (1972), III, p. 63; Boissevain (1971), pp. 45-47. The inference about reachability is our own.

[42]Groulx (1969).

[43]This outlook, we suspect, often accompanies the international job mobility which Richmond calls "transilience."

[44]There may be a situation of balance here, in which relationships between adjacent groups are mainly negative while those two positions apart have much more positive ties: Davis (1966).

[45]Rocher (1973) pinpoints the major threat as American (pp. 94-95), notes that francophones and anglophones see each other as an obstacle in meeting it (p. 104),

and firmly rejects the "bilingualism and multiculturalism" banner as a basis for rallying Canadians (pp. 119-26).

BIBLIOGRAPHY

Beattie, C. and Spencer, B.G., "Career Attainment in Canadian Bureaucracies," *American Journal of Sociology,* Vol. 77, (1971).

Beattie, C., *Minority Men in a Majority Setting,* Toronto: McClelland & Stewart, 1975.

Bellavance, M. et M. Gilbert, *L'opinion publique et la crise d'octobre,* Montréal: Ed. du jour, 1971.

Boissevain, J., *The Italians in Montreal. Social Adjustment in a Plural Society,* Ottawa: Information Canada, 1971.

Byers, N., "Dualism and Pluralism," paper presented to the Canadian Sociology and Anthropology Association meetings, York University, 1969.

Canadian Broadcasting Corporation, *"October 29th: Another Chance for Quebec",* (Oct. 22, 1973).

Carlos, S., *L'utilisation du francais dans le monde du travail du Québec,* Etude E3 de la Commission Gendron, Québec: Editeur Officiel du Québec, 1973.

Clement, W. and D. Olsen, "Official Ideology and Ethnic Power," paper presented to the American Sociological Association meetings, Montreal, 1974.

Davis, J. A., "Structural Balance, Mechanical Solidarity and Interpersonal Relations" in J. Berger et al. (eds.), *Sociological Theories in Progress,* Vol. 1. Boston: Houghton Mifflin, 1966.

de Brouwer, J-C., *Le francais langue de travail: ce qu'en pensent les élites économiques du Québec,* Etude E12 de la Commission Gendron, Québec: Editeur Officiel du Québec.

Dion, L., "Quebec and the Future of Canada", in D. C. Thomson (ed.), *Quebec Society and Politics,* Toronto: McClelland & Stewart, 1973.

Dofny, J., *Les ingénieurs canadiens-francais et canadiens-anglais à Montreal,* Ottawa: Information Canada, 1970.

Dufour, A., *La législation récente en matière linguistique dans les provinces d'Ontario, du Manitoba et du Nouveau-Burnswick,* Etude E2 de la Commission Gendron, Québec: Editeur Officiel du Québec, 1973.

Even, A., "Domination et développement au Nouveau-Brunswick," *Recherches sociographiques,* Vol. 13, (1972).

Falardeau, J-C, "L'origine et l'ascension des hommes d'affaires dans la société canadienne-française", *Recherches sociographiques,* Vol. 6, (1965).

Gendron Commission, *Report,* 3 vols., Quebec: Official Printer, 1972.

Gold, G. L., "Voluntary Associations and a New Economic Elite in a French Canadian Town" in Gold, G. L. and M-A Tremblay (eds.) *Communities and Culture in French Canada,* Toronto: Holt, Rinehart & Winston, 1973.

Gousse, C., *Pratiques et usages linguistiques de la clientéle québécoise en rapport avec ses organismes de service,* Etude E18 de la Commission Gendron, Québec: Editeur Officiel du Québec, 1973.

Groulx, L., "If Dollard were Alive Today" in R. Cook (ed.), *French Canadian Nationalism,* Toronto: Macmillan, 1969.

Lanphier, C. M. and R. N. Morris, "Structural Aspects of Differences in Income between Anglophones and Francophones," *Canadian Review of Sociology and Anthropology,* Vol. 11, (1974).

Laurendeau, A., "Le Canada: Une Nation ou Deux?" in *Congress on Canadian Affairs. The Canadian Experiment. Success or Failure?* Québec: Les Presses de l'Université Laval, 1961.

Le Jour, Montréal. Aug. 7, 1974 - Oct. 6, 1975.

Le Soleil, Québec. April 30, May 1, 1973; March 30, 1974; March 1, 1975.

Macnamara, J. and J. Edwards, *Attitudes to Learning French in the English-Speaking Schools of Quebec,* Study E8 for the Gendron Commission. Quebec: Official Publisher, 1973.

Morin, C., "The Gospel according to Holy Ottawa" in D. C. Thomson (ed.) *Quebec Society and Politics,* Toronto: McClelland & Stewart, 1973.

Pinard, M. "The Ongoing Political Realignments in Quebec" in D. C. Thomson (ed.), *Quebec Society and Politics,* Toronto: McClelland & Stewart, 1973.

Raynauld, A. et al., *La répartition des revenus selon les groupes ethniques au Canada,* Rapport à la Commission Royale, 1967.

Raynauld, A. et al., "Structural Aspects of Differences in Income between Anglophones and Francophones: A Reply", *Canadian Review of Sociology and Anthropology,* Vol. 12, (1975).

Rocher, G., *Le Québec en mutation,* Montréal: Hurtubise HMH, 1973.

Rolland, S. C., *The Second Conquest. Reflections II,* Montreal: Chateau Books, 1970.

Royal Commission on Bilingualism and Biculturalism, *Report,* 4 vols., Ottawa: Queen's Printer, 1968.

Saint-Germain, M., *Une économie à libérer,* Montréal: Les Presses de l'Université de Montréal, 1973.

Smiley, D. V., *Canada in Question,* Toronto: McGraw-Hill, 1972.

Toronto Star, Nov. 1, 1971 - October 1, 1975.

Ward, N. "The National Political Scene" in M. Wade (ed.), *Canadian Dualism,* Toronto: University of Toronto Press, 1960.

Chapter 12

The Social Standing of Ethnic and Racial Groupings*†

Peter C. Pineo

Ethnicity is generally understood to be an active ingredient in the present Canadian social stratification system, but the precise role it plays is only partially understood. Porter has addressed the issue of the extent to which ethnic and racial groups within Canada differ in socio-economic status, as measured by income, educational attainment, and occupational status (1965, 1971). Less is known about the extent to which ethnic group membership can directly influence the social standing of an individual. That is, is ethnicity an evaluated status in itself?

Nor is this a settled issue in the US literature. Three different positions can be found. Some see ethnic and racial groups as ranked but the rank wholly derivative of differences in the socioeconomic standing of the groups. This would seem to be the sense of Greer's statement: 'When we refer to ethnic groups we are, more often than not, communicating quite

*Reprinted from *The Canadian Review of Sociology and Anthropology* 14:1 (1977), by permission of the author and the publisher, Fitzhenry and Whiteside Limited.

†I wish in particular to acknowledge the help of John Porter who was a full collaborator in all but the analysis and write-up phase of this work. I am also indebted to various granting agencies, including the Canada Council, and to the staff of NORC which designed the study we replicated. Norman Shulman provided helpful comments, and Christine Kluck Davis provided research assistance.

specific implications about income and status in this society' (1974:19). In Milton Gordon's influential work, ethnic groups are seen principally as forming a horizontal differentiation cutting across socioeconomic status (1964:50). That is, they are non-status groups. A third position, adopted by Shibutani and Kwan is that ethnic groups are ranked in their own right and form a stratification system paralleling that of socioeconomic status. They write: 'In the United States today one's social status depends upon his position in two coexisting systems of social stratification: class and ethnic' (1965:33). A review of these positions has been provided by Jackson and Curtis (1968:125-6). They note that the most persuasive evidence that ethnic and racial groups form a ranked order in the public mind is provided by Bogardus in his work on social distance scales (1959). Yet this work has not settled the matter since the Bogardus scale deals with the more specific question of the admissibility of individuals into intimate social interaction.

Religious affiliation, cultural dissimilarity, etc., can create *social distance* between groups which do not greatly differ in social status; the Jews and British in contemporary Canada could be an example. What is demonstrated in this paper is that using a more general evaluative criterion, 'social standing' rather than social intimacy, also elicits a ranking of ethnic and racial groups, showing consensus as do the Bogardus results but differing from them in some details.

The evaluative criterion of 'social standing' is the same as is used in studies of the evaluation of occupations, the 'occupational prestige' studies. Its appropriateness has recently been thoroughly reviewed (Goldthorpe and Hope, 1972; Ridge, 1974). While highly critical of the tradition of using the word 'prestige' for these studies, these authors nonetheless appear to conclude that the criterion of 'social standing' does capture a broad and general evaluation of social status. As Ridge notes: 'A measure of "occupational prestige" is relevant *only* if it can be taken as a statement of where occupations stand in a social value hierarchy . . . There is good reason to believe that public-opinion surveys of the social standing of occupations provide just such a measure' (1974:3). By extension, then, the location of ethnic and racial groups in a value hierarchy can also be measured by using the stimulus of 'social standing.'

To test if the stimulus of 'social standing' would elicit a ranked ordering of racial and ethnic groups, 393 adult Canadians, forming a national sample, were asked to sort cards printed with the names of 36 ethnic, racial, and related groups. To provide a baseline for comparison, the same 393 were asked, at a different point in the interview, to sort in an identical manner 204 cards bearing occupational titles. With the social standing of the occupations and of the racial and ethnic groups measured in an identical way it is possible to ask a series of questions about how similar the ranking of ethnicities and racial groups is to the ranking of occupations. Are people as willing to rank ethnic and racial groups as they are occupations? Is there as much consensus? Is the range of rankings as great? Do subgroups within Canada agree about the ranking of ethnicities and racial groupings as fully as they do about the rankings of occupations?

Procedures

The details of the fieldwork for this study are available elsewhere (Pineo and Porter, 1967). To elicit the evaluations of racial and ethnic groups the following question was asked:

> Canada is a country made up of many different kinds of people. Some of these groups of people have higher social standing than others do. Here is a card with the name of one such group on it. Please put that card in the box at the top of the ladder if you think that group has the highest possible social standing. Put it in the box at the bottom of the ladder if you think that group has the lowest possible social standing. If it belongs in between, just put it in the box that comes the closest to representing the social standing of that particular group of people.

After the first card was placed, the interviewer was to go on to say:

> Here are a few more groups. As you did before, just put them in the boxes on the ladder which match the social standing you think these groups have. Place them the way you think people actually treat these groups, not the way you think they *ought* to treat them.

Except for the final sentence, this instruction is identical to the one eliciting the sorting of occupational titles.

The sorting of both the ethnicities and the occupational titles was made upon a cardboard 'ladder' with spaces numbered from 1 to 9. The scores were then transformed (using the formula $X = 12.5 X - 12.5$) so that they ran from zero to 100, the common form of presenting prestige scores.

English-Canadian Rankings of Ethnicities and Racial Groupings

The English Canadians in the sample appeared able to rank the ethnic titles given to them, and the resulting rank order of the groups contains few surprises.[1] It closely resembles the ranking generally felt to exist in the US (see, for example, Knoke and Felson, 1974). Western and North European origins, which in the US would be called the 'old immigrants,' are at the top; Eastern and Mediterranean, the 'new' immigrants,' further down; coloured and Asiatics at the bottom. The actual scores, with standard deviations, are given in Table 1, organized in these broader origin categories. For 19 of the groups in Table 1, Bogardus social distance scores from US college students are also available; the rank order by social distance and by social standing for these groups is high ($R = .95$). Only the Jews and Scots are to any degree out of rank (Bogardus, 1967:152).

The range from the lowest to the highest score in Table 1 is considerable.

English Canadians got the highest score, at 83.1; Negroes were given the lowest, at 25.4. But this is not quite so great a range as that used in the sorting of the occupational titles. In that sorting task, English Canadians gave 88.7 to provincial premier and 14.3 to newspaper peddler.[2] This is the first of several clues indicating that the ethnic rankings have a weaker statistical form than do the occupational rankings.

The 'don't know' rates provide a second clue. They are consistently somewhat higher for the ethnicity titles than for the occupational titles. The typical no-answer rate for an ethnic ranking was over 10 per cent while for occupations it was only 6.3 per cent. While people have, or think they have, sufficient information to rank quite exotic occupations, they appear less able or willing to rank certain of the smaller ethnic groups. Thus 16 per cent did not rank 'Lithuanians,' 15.7 per cent did not rank 'Icelanders,' and 12.7 did not rank 'Finns.' The title 'People of Foreign Ancestry' was left unranked by 13.7 per cent; it was possibly considered too broad a category. The smallest no-answer rates were for titles 'English,' 'Scots,' and 'English Canadians'; 7.3 per cent, 7.7 per cent, and 7.6 per cent respectively. Some 9 per cent declined to rank themselves; that is, the title 'People of My Own Ethnic Background.' By implication, then, 91 per cent must have felt they had some identifiable, rankable ethnicity themselves, despite the fact that 'Canadian,' as opposed to English Canadian or French Canadian, was not included as a title and therefore not suggested as an ethnicity. In general, however, these no-answer rates are not so high, by the ordinary standards of survey research, as to lead to any serious concern about the meaningfulness of the ethnicity rankings.

A third clue that the ranking of ethnicities has not quite the same structural firmness as the occupational rankings is that the standard deviations in the rankings of ethnicities are higher. The average standard deviation for the ethnicity rankings was 24.1; only around 20 of the whole 204 occupational titles, even with the French rankings included, had standard deviations this high (Pineo and Porter, 1967). This means there is less consensus within English Canada about the rankings of ethnic groups than there is about the occupations. No ethnic groups had low standard deviations; the lowest was for the title 'English' at 20.1, followed by 'English Canadians' at 20.5. Many occupations had standard deviations below 20 points. This suggests that one source of the lack of consensus is a tendency for people to base the scale around differing midpoints; such a tendency would contribute to uniformly high standard deviations. That is to say, there may be a tendency to shift the whole ethnicity ranking up or down the scale more than there is to shift the whole occupational ranking. But this cannot explain away the whole effect because there are also some exceptionally high standard deviations: 28.3 for Canadian Indians, 27.8 for French Canadians, 28.0 for Jews, and 26.1 for Negroes. Lack of familiarity with the group does not seem to be the issue; the standard deviations for Finns and Lithuanians are quite low. Rather it would seem to be that groups felt to suffer some degree of

TABLE I
RANKING OF ETHNICITIES BY ENGLISH-SPEAKING CANADIANS

Ethnic groups in origin categories	Mean rank	SD
Charter group members and related groups		
British	81.2	21.4
English	82.4	20.1
English Canadians	83.1	20.5
French	60.1	24.8
French Canadians	56.1	27.8
Irish	69.5	22.8
Scots	75.2	22.1
Western and North European		
Belgians	49.1	22.9
Danes	52.4	23.7
Dutch	58.7	22.6
Germans	48.7	25.2
Icelanders	45.6	24.7
Norwegians	55.3	22.8
Swedes	56.6	23.3
Swiss	55.7	21.9
Mediterranean and Central European		
Austrians	49.6	22.2
Czecho-Slovaks	41.2	22.9
Finns	47.6	22.7
Greeks	39.9	23.7
Hungarians	42.6	22.6
Italians	43.1	25.0
Jews	46.1	28.0
Lithuanians	41.4	21.9
Poles	42.0	22.4
Roumanians	42.1	23.5
Russians	35.8	26.2
Ukrainians	44.3	22.6
Non-Caucasian groups		
Canadian Indians	28.3	28.3
Chinese	33.1	25.4
Coloureds	26.3	26.2
Japanese	34.7	25.3
Negroes	25.4	26.1
Not ethnicities		
Catholics	70.1	25.6
Protestants	75.3	23.4
People of Foreign Ancestry	50.1	24.6
People of my own Ethnic Background	74.4	24.9

(*N* = 300 cases less the number not ranking each title)

overt discrimination, especially the more visible racial groupings, are the ones on which the lack of consensus is greatest.

There is, then, evidence that Canadians can rank ethnicities but that the consensus and knowledge about them are not quite so great as about occupations. The theorem that consensus implies social importance suggests that the ethnic ranking has not the same structural importance as the occupational ranking.

The ranking itself, as noted, has few surprises in it. The English and English Canadians did extremely well. With ethnicity ranks of 82.4 and 83.1 respectively, their ethnicity earns them, if one plays the game that the scales are transposable, about the same rank as being a member of the Canadian cabinet. They are followed, not unexpectedly, by Scots and Irish, although the fall off in rank is fairly swift, down to 75.2 for the Scots and 69.5 for the Irish. Following the Irish there is another dead spot in the scale, this time of almost 10 points. Thus English Canadians give a special status to these of British origin. The concept of charter group status, as used by Hughes (1952:137) seems appropriate.

Pineo and Porter suggested, in their analysis of occupational rating (1967:31), that a tendency to give inordinantly high ratings to the very top jobs might be a statistical representation of the 'elitist' pattern which Lipset suggested was important in Canadian society (1963:chap. 7). They note that only a small tendency of this kind is found in the occupational rankings. Here, in the ethnicity rankings, the effect *is* found, and it is of considerable magnitude. It is tempting to speculate that the expected elitist pattern may in fact exist in the realm of ethnic rather than socioeconomic status. There is no indication in the literature that the same exceptional status is given to any us ethnic group; in fact there is no colloquial term quite like 'English Canadian' in the us. Bogardus provides a social distance score for 'Americans (us White)' and it is not markedly ahead of the balance (1959:152).

The rating of the French Canadians, at 56.1 puts them near on the scale to the Dutch and Scandinavians. This is the traditional 'old immigrant' group described in us literature, and the ranking of them is about as expected. They are all ranked higher than the general title 'People of Foreign Ancestry,' suggesting they might be considered among the 'most desirable' immigrants. That the French Canadians should be seen by the English only as 'desirable immigrants' is ironic, but it also should be noted that as the major minority group in Canada their status undoubtedly vastly exceeds that of the blacks in the us.

Belgians and Germans rank slightly below the title 'People of Foreign Ancestry' and also slightly below the logical midpoint of the scale, 50.0. These too would be among those called 'old immigrants' in the us and their rank in Canada may be somewhat lower than one would expect. The lower ranking of the Germans may be a clue that international politics and warfare, operating perhaps through the media, can affect the status of an ethnic group within Canada. The Russians, an important international enemy at the time of the study, were given an extraordinarily low rank of 35.8.

The 'new immigrants' from Eastern Europe and the Mediterranean are closely bunched with those from the Baltic between 47.6 and 39.9. Again this would resemble the us pattern.

The Jews are not found 'at the bottom' as suggested for the us by Knoke and Felson (1974:631). Actual data which are presented below show them to be more in the middle of the hierarchy in the us, the same place as in Canada. They are not at the bottom in the Bogardus results either, but are, as might be expected, lower in social distance rank than in social standing (1967:152).

The Japanese and Chinese rank low, at 34.7 and 33.1 respectively. Finally, Canadian Indians, at 28.3, the coloured at 26.3, and the Negroes at 25.4 enjoy a social standing about equivalent to the occupational rank of a construction labourer or railroad section hand. Clearly the non-whites are felt to be very much at the bottom, visibility apparently accentuating the phenomenon.

Ratings of ethnic groups in the United States were collected in an identical manner and at approximately the same time as the Canadian ones. Scores for some 19 ethnic groups are now available for comparison with the Canadian ones. The high degree of similarity is shown by a rank order correlation between the two sets of .95. The two rankings are shown in Chart I.

The chart reveals one matter which the rank order coefficient would hide — that is the tendency to give a sort of elite ethnic status to those of British origin is, as we suggested, a distinctively English-Canadian pattern. The title 'British' was rated 81.2 in Canada and only 65.5 in the United States. In general, the us scores cluster much more closely together, suggesting less differentiation in the rankings of ethnic groups in the us than in Canada, perhaps since the period of heavy immigration is further back in us than Canadian history.

The only other major differences between the two sets of scores involved specific groups, although there may be a tendency in Canada to give systematically lower ratings to Eastern European and Mediterranean ethnicities. Among the specific titles, both Germans and Italians are much lower in Canada. This may be a legacy of the Second World War, in which Canada was more greatly committed than the us. On the other hand, the status of French Canadians is appreciably higher among English Canadians than Americans (56.1 as compared to 50.9).

Variation Within English Canada

In three tests so far, involving the incidence of no answers, the range and the size of the standard deviations, the amount of knowledge and degree of consensus surrounding the ranking of ethnicities is found to be lower than that of occupations. A fourth test can be made. One can compute correlation coefficients representing how similar the rankings were in different social categories within English Canada. Did women rank them in the same way as men? Did low and high income groups rank them similarly? This is a test traditionally applied to occupational prestige rankings, and the result, in that

CHART I
HIERARCHY OF ETHNIC GROUPS IN THE US AND ENGLISH CANADA

United States (N = 445)		*English Canada* (N = 300)
	81	British
	80	
	79	
	78	
	77	
	76	
	75	Scots
	74	
	73	
	72	
	71	
	70	Irish
	69	
	68	
	67	
British	66	
	65	
	64	
	63	
Irish	62	
	61	
	60	French
Scots, French	59	Dutch
Germans, Dutch	58	
	57	Swedes
Norwegians	56	French Canadians
Swedes	55	Norwegians
	54	
	53	
Danes	52	Danes
Finns, French Canadians	51	
Italians	50	
	49	Germans
	48	Finns
	47	
Jews	46	Jews
Hungarians	45	
Poles	44	
Lithuanians	43	Italians, Hungarians
Czechs	42	Poles
Greeks	41	Lithuanians, Czechoslovaks
	40	Greeks
	39	
	38	
	37	
Russians	36	Russians

SOURCE OF US DATA: Laumann (1973:46)

case, is uniformly high correlations which are offered as evidence of consensus.

By this test the amount of consensus in the rankings comes very close to the amount found in examining occupational rankings. The correlations were .99 for five variables comparing respondents from differing community sizes, comparing men and women, comparing those under and over 40 years of age, comparing those with any rural experience with those with none and comparing blue with white collar workers. The correlation was somewhat smaller for three other variables: between education levels it was .97; between income groups it was .98; and in comparing Catholics and Protestants it was .96.

The results seem inconsistent. The standard deviations were appreciably higher than those for the occupational ranking but the correlation coefficients are only slightly lower. The standard deviations imply some substantial dissensus within English Canada; the correlation coefficients suggest only moderate dissensus. In fact what has happened is that the dissensus which exists is not between the several social categories chosen for examination, and this reveals the limitation of this fourth test of consensus. As has been noted in the work dealing with occupational prestige, establishing that there is no important disagreement between major social categories is a very special test of dissensus (Burshtyn, 1968:176). It does not rule out the possibility of considerable individual variation within the categories or disagreement between less significant social categories. Those who have designed this test in the past must have adopted the position that dissensus across major, established social categories is theoretically and practically the more significant variety.

Inspection of the ratings given those of low and high education and those of low and high income, two variables producing correlations less than .99, reveals no obvious pattern. One might have expected simple effects of 'liberalism' among the better educated and also that the income differences were derivative of this. But while the better educated English Canadians gave some 10 extra points to Japanese, and 9 extra to Jews, no extra points were given to Negroes or Canadian Indians. If liberalism does operate at all it operates to increase the standing of most. On the average, ethnic titles were ranked some five points higher by the better educated, and this did not include the top charter group ethnicities which were ranked at about the same level by both the less and better educated. So the pattern for the better educated is that most ethnicities are lifted some five or six points closer to the charter groups. Exceptions were the Negroes and Indians, and also the Italians, who dropped one point. The French Canadians also were not raised. Certain Scandinavian ethnicities were given much higher ratings by the better educated; Danes were ranked 58.4 by the better educated and 45.9 by the less well educated. The better educated, then, see a society with the charter group ethnicities well up at the top, most continental European ethnicities somewhat higher than they are seen by the less educated, but the most deprived groups still very much at the bottom. Possibly, the better educated are simply showing a greater capacity to describe the society accurately. Or, if this is projection, Canadian education serves to liberalize attitudes to most continental European and Asian ethnicities but not Negroes, Indians, Italians, or French Canadians.

Examination of the difference between the income groups suggests that the basic pattern is the same. The ratings given by high income people are virtually identical to those given by the highly educated (r = .995).

The comparison of Catholic and Protestant respondents yielded the third correlation which was less than .99. Catholics rate Catholics higher and Protestants lower, of course. Catholics give themselves 75.2 points and the Protestants 69.1; Protestants give themselves 79.2 and the Catholics 68.8. Similarly, certain highly Catholic ethnicities are given higher points: Italians are rated 48.3 by the Catholics and 40.5 by the Protestants. The effect is less great in the ratings of French Canadians: Catholics give them 58.3 while the Protestants give them 54.2.

The clearest difference in the rankings given by English Catholics is that they give lower rankings to the charter groups. English get 78.0 from the Catholics while the Protestants give them 84.0. English Canadians get 79.3 rather than 84.2. Scots get 67.7 rather than 77.9.

Finally, the English Catholics are the first group identified which shows a sense of being second class citizens. The title 'People of My Own Ethnic Background' was given a ranking of only 63.7 by the English Catholics. The Protestants rated themselves 80.0. Evidence that this low rating of themselves by the Catholics has even further complexities in it lies in a continuingly high standard deviation: 26.9. Among the English Catholics there remains a diversity in self-image. In contrast there is much less variation among the Protestants: the standard deviation is only 21.5. The standard deviations were high for the majority of the rankings given by English Catholics, averaging to 26.2. The English Catholic population appears to be a quite heterogenous component of Canadian society.

Even when the correlation is nearly perfect there can be a difference in the ratings, as virtually all tend to be higher in one group than another. There were such differences. Respondents under 40 tended to give ratings averaging 4.5 points higher than the older. White collar respondents gave ratings averaging 4.0 points higher than blue collar workers, which is consistent with the tendency for higher income and highly educated respondents to give higher ratings. Other differences were minute. Women gave slightly higher ratings than men: Protestants slightly higher than Catholics. Those with rural backgrounds and those now living in communities under 30,000 gave slightly lower ratings.

Rankings by French Canadians

French Canada provides the only minority group sufficiently large in this sample for a direct investigation of how the members of a specific group modify the ethnic ranking system in response to their own status. The rank order given the groups by French Canadian respondents is quite different from that given by English Canadians; the correlation coefficient is only .84 (or .83 for 32 pure ethnicity titles.) By the standards of occupational prestige studies this is a very low correlation and it shows clearly that the statistical treatment of the data does not guarantee high correlations.[3]

The ratings by English and French are given in Chart II. The general shape of the ranking by French Canadians puts virtually all non-English, non-French ethnicities further down the rank. Western and Northern Europeans were ranked around an average of 52.8 by the English and 41.1 by the French. Mediterranean and Central Europeans were ranked around 43.0 by the English and 37.1 by the French. Non-Caucasians were ranked around 29.5 by the English and 27.0 by the French. The specific title 'People of Foreign Ancestry' was ranked 50.1 by the English and 38.9 by the French. French Canada is not a nation of new immigrants and foreign ethnicities are somewhat down-graded.

A second observation may be quickly made. The French do not agree with the English about where they themselves belong in the order. The French rank themselves at the top, giving themselves exactly the same score as they do the English: both ethnicities were ranked at 77.6. The tie, of course, suggests a model of a Canada formed of two equal founding races. This is the kind of image of Canada which underlay the Report of the Royal Commission on Bilingualism and Biculturalism. The commission apparently caught the main currents of thought in this respect within French Canada, at the time at least. Canada's problem, perhaps, is that this image is not shared by English Canada.

It must be noted that the extraordinary high ranking given to charter group ethnicities — those of British origin — by English Canadians is not found to be the pattern in the French Canadian responses. Rather they give the highest group only around 77.

While these broad patterns to the French responses are clear and perhaps expectable, closer inspection of the French ratings reveals details which to an English Canadian seem peculiar. The Scots, for example, are much lower than the English. Finns and Danes are ranked with Canadian Indians. Norwegians are tied with Poles. The very categories in which English Canadians and Americans apparently think about ethnicity, such as Scandinavian, Eastern European, etc., seem to disappear as their component ethnicities are scattered through the list.

It is quite possible that the problem is one of sample size. Only 93 French Canadians were given this ranking task to do. This may be a sufficient number to reveal the general pattern of the ranking within French Canada but not sufficient to look at the specific ranking given to the smaller ethnic groups.

As well, there is some evidence that French Canadians are, quite understandably, less familiar with some of the smaller ethnicities and hence less able to rank them. Don't-know rates for certain ethnicities are quite high:

CHART II
HIERARCHY OF ETHNIC AND RACIAL GROUPS IN ENGLISH
AND FRENCH CANADA

English Canada (N = 300)		French Canada (N = 93)
English Canadians (83.1)	83	
English (82.4)	82	
British (81.2)	81	
	80	
	79	
	78	
	77	French Canadians, English Canadians
	76	Catholics (77.6)
Protestants (75.3) Scots (75.2)	75	
My own ethnic background (74.4)	74	My own ethnic background (73.7)
	73	
	72	French (72.4)
	71	English (71.0)
Catholics (70.1)	70	
Irish (69.5)	69	
	68	
	67	
	66	British (66.0)
	65	
	64	
	63	
	62	
	61	
French (60.1)	60	
	59	
Dutch (58.4)	58	
Swedes (56.6)	57	Scots (56.5)
French Canadians (56.1) Swiss (55.7)	56	
Norwegians (55.3)	55	Irish (55.2) Protestants (54.8)
	54	
	53	
Danes (52.4)	52	
	51	Italians (51.3)
People of Foreign Ancestry (50.1)	50	Dutch (49.7)
Austrians (49.6) Belgians (49.1)	49	
Germans (48.7) Finns (47.6)	48	
	47	
Jews (46.1) Icelanders (45.6)	46	
	45	Belgians (45.3) Swedes (44.8)
Ukrainians (44.3)	44	Swiss (44.4)
Italians (43.1) Hungarians (42.6)	43	Jews (43.10)
Poles (42.0) Roumanians (42.1)	42	
Lithuanians (41.4) Czecho-Slovaks	41	
(41.2) Greeks (39.9)	40	Germans (40.5) Ukrainians (40.0)
	39	People of Foreign Ancestry (38.9)
	38	Hungarians (38.4) Poles (38.0)
	37	Norwegians (38.0) Austrians (37.5)

Russians (35.8)	36	
Japanese (34.7)	35	
	34	Roumanians (33.9) Greeks (33.5)
Chinese (33.1)	33	Russians (33.2) Icelanders (32.9)
	32	Canadian Indians (32.5) Czecho-
	31	Slovaks (32.4) Finns (32.3)
	30	Danes (32.2)
	29	Lithuanians (29.1)
Canadian Indians (28.3)	28	Japanese (27.8)
	27	Coloureds (26.5)
Coloureds (26.3)	26	
Negroes (25.4)	25	Chinese (24.9) Negroes (23.5)

20.4 per cent failed to rank Icelanders; 20.4 failed to rank Finns; 17.2 failed to rank Roumanians; and 16.1 failed to rank Danes. Thus, some of the titles which seem most peculiarly ranked are also ones for which the don't-know rates suggest there is less information within French Canada. When it came to some better known ethnicities, the don't-know rates were much lower: Chinese, 6.5; French Canadians, 6.5; English Canadians, 6.5.

While the don't-know rates, then, are fairly high, they can be put in perspective. In ranking some of the religion titles in a separate rating task also in the same study, the don't-know rates among the French became enormous. For the title Christian Scientists, 43.0 per cent failed to rank; for Mormon, 46.2 per cent; for Seventh Day Adventists, 49.5 per cent; and for Lutherans, 38.7 per cent. From this perspective, then, it would seem that French Canadians feel they do have some substantial knowledge about the smaller ethnic groups, at least in comparison with their knowledge about certain religious groups.

Another test that was applied to the rankings by English Canadians can also be applied to the French. That is, are the standard deviations particularly high? The average standard deviation for the French was 23.8, for the English, 24.1. The rankings from French Canada cannot be dismissed as mere statistical noise; where they do rank, they appear to rank with as much consensus as do the English. (In ranking religions the standard deviations differed more: 24.3 for the English; 25.8 for the French.)

High standard deviations and high don't-know rates do not appear to indicate the same thing. For ethnicities such as 'Finns' and 'Danes,' where the don't-know rate is high, the standard deviations are not particularly high. Rather the standard deviations within French Canada tend to be high for titles with rather low don't-know rates, suggesting they represent true differences of opinion rather than lack of information. There are high standard deviations for the title 'English,' for 'Protestants,' for 'Germans,' and 'Jews.'

Consensus Within French Canada

The final test of consensus, that of comparing the responses of major subgroupings within the society, can also be applied to the French-Canadian responses, although here sample sizes become quite small and interpretations risky.

Despite the small size of categories, the resulting correlation coefficients are quite substantial. They are listed in Table II, with the size of the smaller category in the comparison also included. No correlation is less than .95 despite category sizes as low as 16 cases. On balance, there is evidence here that the consensus within French Canada closely approaches but does not equal that within English Canada. Again, as in English Canada, the dissensus across socio-economic categories of income and education appears the greatest, although the category sizes are dangerously low here. There is considerable agreement between those with and those without rural background and between those in bigger cities and the others. The strength of the rural-urban distinction in French Canada has apparently considerably diminished since the 1930s when Hughes (1944) did his field work. Finally, there is a hint of possibly greater male-female differences in French than in English Canada.

The differences in the overall average rank given are not great — of about the same magnitude as in English Canada and varying in direction.

Detailed inspection of the ratings given specific titles is unwise with such small categories. A few quick points may be made. Generally, the title 'English Canadian' was rated about the same by all components of French Canada. It was highest, at 82.8, among those with higher incomes and lowest, at 74.4, among those with rural backgrounds. In contrast, the rating given 'French Canadian' varied more extensively. It was highest, at 85.2 among the highly educated, and lowest, at 72.9, among those now living in smaller communities.

In fact, the 85.2 rating given by the better educated is sufficiently greater than the 75.5 given by the less educated to achieve statistical significance. Also the 84.3 given by those in communities of 30,000 or more is significantly

TABLE II
A TEST OF CONSENSUS WITHIN FRENCH CANADA:
CORRELATION COEFFICIENTS REPRESENTING
THE AMOUNT OF CONSENSUS BETWEEN MAJOR
SOCIAL CATEGORIES WITHIN FRENCH CANADA

Variable	Size of smaller category	Correlation
Education	16	0.951
Income	29	0.961
Occupation	18	0.958
Size of community	32	0.962
Ruralness	43	0.970
Gender	37	0.958
Age	39	0.972

greater than the 72.9 given by those living in smaller communities. Thus a favourable self-image is more common among the more sophisticated, educated, and urban French Canadians than in the balance.

Again, for the French as well as the English, we are left with the paradox that while higher standard deviations imply some dissensus, a check for its source using a list of standard sociological categories does not prove successful. Alternative axes of dissensus must exist. For the French we have one clue. The standard deviations are low among those with higher socio-economic status and the more urban, but remain high in the balance. The dissensus largely exists among the less sophisticated component of the society. Some titles, such as English, English Canadian, and Jews do not follow this rule, however.

Conclusions

It is found that when asked to do so the Canadian public is able to rank ethnic and racial groupings according to their 'social standing.' That is, the rank ordering of ethnic and racial groups that is found in the social distance studies is also found when a more general measure of social status is the evaluative criterion. For English Canada the resulting order resembles that of Bogardus in most details; for French Canada it is substantially different.

By most tests, however, the degree of knowledge and consensus shown in performing the ranking is less than that shown when occupations are ranked. Considering that the ranking of occupations appears a much more arduous task, including 204 separate titles rather than 36, it is striking that the respondents apparently found the rating of the ethnic and racial groups the more difficult. In so far as the assumption that consensus (and knowledge) implies social importance is valid, the ranking of ethnic and racial groupings appears to be a less crucial element in Canadian social structure than the ranking of occupations.

The actual rankings given to groups were found to be of interest. The 'elite status' given to British groups by English Canadians, the close similarity of English-Canadian and US results, the large differences in the ratings by French and English respondents are examples.

Finally, it remains to be determined the extent to which the ranking of ethnic and racial groups is or is not a simple epiphenomenon of the socioeconomic status of the groups. Work on this question has been begun in another publication (Pineo, 1976).

NOTES

[1]For brevity, the term ethnicity (and ethnic group) is used frequently to encompass both ethnic and racial groupings.

[2]The source for these and other occupational rankings is Pineo and Porter (1967).

[3]Could the small size of the francophone sample have produced this 'low correlation'? For comparison, 30 pairs of randomly selected subsamples were drawn from the occupational ranking section of the study. The subsamples had 30 cases in each. Treated in the usual statistical manner, with means calculated for each occupation and the ranks intercorrelated between each pair, the resulting Pearsonian correlations averaged about .955 and none were less than .94. Sample size has some effect but not enough to produce the correlation of .84.

REFERENCES

Bogardus, Emory S., *Social Distance,* Yellow Springs, Ohio: Antioch Press, 1959.

_____ "Comparing Racial Distance in Ethiopia, South Africa and the United States," *Sociology and Social Research,* Vol. 52 1967:149-56.

Burshtyn, H., "A Factor-Analytic Study of Occupational Prestige Ratings," *Canadian Review of Sociology and Anthropology,* Vol. 5(3) 1968:156-80.

Goldthorpe, John H., and Keith Hope, "Occupational Grading and Occupational Prestige," Pp. 19-72 in Keith Hope (ed.), *The Analysis of Social Mobility: Methods and Approaches,* Oxford Studies in Social Mobility Working Papers: I, Oxford: Clarendon Press, 1972.

Gordon, Milton M., *Assimilation in American Life,* New York: Oxford University Press, 1964.

Greer, C. (ed.), *Divided Society: The Ethnic Experience in America,* New York: Basic Books, 1974.

Hughes, Everett Cherrington, *French Canada in Transition,* Chicago: The University of Chicago Press, 1944.

Hughes, Everett Cherrington, and Helen MacGill Hughes, *Where Peoples Meet: Racial and Ethnic Frontiers,* Glencoe, Illinois: The Free Press, 1952.

Jackson, E.F., and R.F. Curtis, "Conceptualization and Measurement in the Study of Social Stratification," Pp. 112-49 in H.M. Blalock, jr, and A.B. Blalock (eds.), *Methodology in Social Research,* New York: McGraw-Hill, 1968.

Knoke, David, and Richard B. Felson, "Ethnic Stratification and Political Cleavage in the United States, 1952-68," *American Journal of Sociology,* Vol. 80(3) 1974:630-42.

Laumann, Edward O., *Bonds of Pluralism: The Form and Substance of Urban Social Networks,* New York: John Wiley & Sons, 1973.

Lipset, Seymour M., *The First New Nation,* New York: Basic Books, 1963.

Pineo, Peter C., "Social Mobility in Canada: the Current Picture," *Sociological Focus,* Vol. 9(2) 1976:109-23.

Pineo, Peter C., and John Porter, "Occupational Prestige in Canada," *Canadian Review of Sociology and Anthropology,* Vol. 4(1) 1967:24-40.

Porter, John, *The Vertical Mosaic: An Analysis of Social Class and Power in Canada,* Toronto: University of Toronto Press, 1965.

_____ "Research Biography of a Macrosociological Study: The Vertical Mosaic," Pp. 149-81 in James S. Coleman, A. Etzioni, and John Porter (eds.), *Macrosociology: Research and Theory,* Boston: Allyn and Bacon, 1971.

Ridge, J.M., Introduction, Pp. 1-7 in J.M. Ridge (ed.), *Mobility in Britain Reconsidered,* Oxford Studies in Social Mobility Working Papers: 2, Oxford: Clarendon Press, 1974.

Shibutani, T., and K.M. Kwan, *Ethnic Stratification: A Comparative Approach,* New York: The Macmillan Company, 1965.

Chapter 13

Another Look At Ethnicity, Stratification and Social Mobility in Canada*

A. Gordon Darroch

Introduction

Discussions of Canadian stratification and mobility have had as a central theme the relationship between class and ethnicity. Clearly, this is partly so because of the unique bicultural nature of Canada. But the dominant thesis of Canadian stratification studies does not have as its central focus the deprivation of any one group, rather it focuses on a more general relationship between ethnic pluralism and socio-economic stratification. The focus is succinctly expressed in the title of Porter's pioneering work, *The Vertical Mosaic* (1965). Specifically, it has become a first premise in the analysis of Canadian stratification that ethnicity has been a principal component, and indeed a principal cause, of the class structure. "Immigration and ethnic affiliation (or membership in a cultural group) have been important factors in the formation of social classes in Canada" (Porter, 1965:73).

In this paper I reassess the main assumptions of the thesis and re-examine the kind of evidence which has generally been cited in its support. A reanalysis of the main cross-sectional evidence in support of the conventional interpretation suggests that it may seriously exaggerate both the generality and

*Reprinted from *The Canadian Journal of Sociology* 4:1 (1979), by permission of the author and the publisher.

the strength of the relationship between ethnic status and socio-economic status. Further, a review of currently available but limited social mobility data for Canada reinforces the argument that there is no sound evidence to sustain the quite common assumption that ethnic affiliations operate as a significant block to educational and occupational mobility in Canada.

Why the Mosaic is Vertical

Perhaps the most commonly reiterated view of stratification in Canada has as its main datum the apparently significant and persistent relationship between ethnic affiliations and occupational status. These data have often been interpreted in terms of the postulate that the persistence of ethnic identity directly restricts social mobility. Porter's pioneering work clearly set the terms of reference for what has become the dominant view. In fact, in addition to the analysis of census data which he provided, only Bernard Blishen's subsequent series of researches on immigration and occupational status has systematically attempted to assess empirical implications of the thesis of *The Vertical Mosaic* (Blishen, 1958; 1967; 1970). Moreover, as to the precise nature of the empirical relationship to be found between ethnicity (or immigrant status) and class, Porter's original text is actually rather tentative. There were at least three ways in which the relationship was thought to hold. First, there was the implication of ethnic affiliations for entrance into positions of power and command. On this, Porter's evidence, like that of the impressive recent work of Clement, is unequivocal. Almost no elite positions are held by members of minority ethnic groups (Clement 1974:335). I will not consider this relationship further here.

Porter argued in a more general way that over time a reciprocal relationship between ethnicity and class may develop, beginning with the initial "entrance status" of immigrant groups. On the one hand, he suggested that there may be important ideological elements contributing to restricted mobility. "Speculatively, it might be said that the idea of an ethnic mosaic, as opposed to the idea of a melting pot, impedes the processes of social mobility. This difference in ideas is one of the principal distinguishing features of the United States and Canadian society at the level of social psychology as well as that of social structure" (1965:70). Whatever the merits of the original speculation, I suggest that it has not been the ideological implications of the mosaic idea which writing on stratification and mobility in Canada has taken most seriously, but the social structural implications. The latter may consist of a variety of processes which block the mobility opportunities of members of minority ethnic groups varying from the prejudice of "charter group" members to supposed low achievement aspirations of the minority group members (Blishen, 1970). In any case, the assumption that "ethnically blocked mobility" is especially characteristic of Canada, has served as one of the central propositions regarding the form of the Canadian class structure.

The argument that ethnic affiliations limit social mobility was given an explicit historical interpretation by Porter. In this perspective it is the lack of cultural assimilation which perpetuates initial "entrance status" differentials in the economic positions of immigrant groups. Recently, he has expressed the view in the following terms: "Over time this marked differentiation at the period of entry can either harden into a permanent class system, or can change in the direction of absorption, assimilation, integration, and acculturation as a result of which the relationship between ethnicity and class disappears" (1974:6). The interpretation is persuasive partly because of the tautological element in the synonym between the broad notion of assimilation or integration employed and the disappearance of the relationship between ethnicity and class. By definition, the disappearance of this relationship is integration. However, we cannot take for granted what the relationship between ethnicity and socio-economic status actually is, or whether it is, in any important sense, a resultant of continued ethnic identities themselves.

Clearly, the conventional view implies first, that there is a demonstrably general and quite strong relationship between ethnicity and class. Secondly, the view implies that a reduction of the salience of ethnicity would directly increase social mobility and, in so doing, materially reduce levels of economic and political inequality in Canada (Porter, 1974:13). It should be recalled that these are not the same processes, since it is entirely possible for mobility rates to alter over time without affecting the structure of inequality, depending on the source of the mobility.

Before reconsidering the nature of the known association between ethnicity and socio-economic status, the broader argument warrants some specification. It seems that the emphasis has been placed on two basic ways in which the salience of ethnicity is thought to prevent full and equal access to the opportunities for upward mobility which are presumed to exist in an industrial society such as Canada. On the one hand there is the relative deprivation in educational and occupational mobility opportunities which may result from heavy dependence on the selective recruitment of labor force skills through immigration policy (Porter, 1965:66). Some ethnic groups, the British and northern European groups especially, have attained relatively privileged positions in the class structure more or less immediately upon arrival. Other groups have been recruited to fill the less skilled, less well paid and less privileged positions in an expanding economy, although immigration policies have become less explicit in this respect in recent years (Richmond, 1967; Avery, 1975). But this is not the only, or the primary, means by which social mobility is thought to be restricted by ethnic identities. A surprisingly common theme in the literature reiterates an argument that the very persistence of subordinate ethnic communities and the loyalties they engender may deflect status aspirations and restrict achievement motivations which would otherwise lead directly to competing on the larger, societal labor market. This failure of aspirations, it is thought, limits the acquisition of individual qualifications, especially education, which most count toward ensuring occupational mobility (Vallee and Shulman, 1969:95; Porter, 1974:12; Breton and Rosenborough, 1968:4; Blishen, 1970:120). In other words, some forms of "ethnic mobility traps" (Wiley, 1967) presumably loom large in the structure of class in Canada.

Distinguishing between the effects of "cultural influences" — limited mobility aspirations, for example — and the effects of sheer discrimination is a difficult research task. The foregoing description represents my assessment that there has been a detectable tendency to emphasize the former in the ethnic stratification literature, but discrimination as a source of blocked mobility has not been entirely ignored. Although this balance of descriptive emphasis is important, in the reanalysis which follows I am concerned with the *gross* effects of ethnicity and immigrant status in stratification and mobility as they have been measured and interpreted in the past. Gross effects include, of course, both cultural or attitudinal influences and discrimination, as well as their quite probable interaction effects, as barriers to change in the status and class positions of ethnic groups.

Recently, there have been a number of thoughtful reconsiderations of the nature and importance of linguistic, ethnic and immigrant group inequalities in this country. For example, Lanphier and Morris (1974) carefully reassessed and specified the sources and trends of income inequality between francophones and anglophones in 1961 and 1968, indicating that the inequality was substantially less in the latter year, although the gains were largely restricted to the middle class and skilled workers among francophones. Income discrepancies between the linguistic groups actually seemed to have widened at lower skill levels. From a historical perspective, Avery (1975) has documented the significance of the overtly discriminatory practices of the Anglo-Canadian business community toward immigrants in the years 1896-1919. And I have been reminded that both Tepperman (1975:chapter 6) and Reitz (1977) have, in different ways, explicitly raised the question of the relative significance of inequalities among different immigrant and linguistic groups and in comparison with other group inequalities, such as that between men and women in the labor force. Perhaps most relevant to this study is Tepperman's pointed conclusion that the extreme version of the vertical mosaic thesis is "patently false," that is, the version in which ethnicity and social class are taken to be largely interchangeable and low status groups are characterized as passively accepting their inferior status (1975:156).

Ethnicity and Class in Canada: the Conventional Evidence

With a few exceptions, the evidence which is presented in support of the broad, ethnically blocked mobility thesis consists of cross-tabulations of socio-economic status indexes, usually occupation, by ethnic origin or immigrant group. It is noted at the outset that these data have generally been presented without controls for the effects of potentially confounding variables such as ethnic differences in age or sex composition, regional and rural-urban differentials, language fluency or variations in socio-economic background.[1]

Pineo has recently provided the first reconsideration of the data which Porter originally presented in examining the relationship between ethnicity and occupational position (1976). He uses census tabulations for 1951, 1961, and 1971 for ethnicity and occupational groups. A form of "status score" is assigned to each ethnic group and the product moment correlations between these scores and Blishen occupational status codes are computed for each of the three years. The status scores assigned to the ethnic groups are derived from two sources, first from the results of a previous national survey and second, from the mean occupational status of the ethnic group. Pineo acknowledges that the latter "loads" the evidence in favor of finding a relationship between ethnicity and occupational standing. In fact, the results are strikingly at odds with the common assumption of a relationship. Of the six correlations (two forms of ranking ethnic groups in three census years) the highest coefficient is .19 found for the association in 1961 between occupation and the "loaded" measure of ethnic status (Table 3:119).

Pineo also computes correlations for the grouped data to find the association between ethnic group "social standing" and mean occupational status. In 1931 and 1951, years for which the data are available, there are strong correlations of .81 and .77. For 1961 data the correlation is only .26.

In a very brief discussion Pineo concludes that the results are not consistent with the conventional image of a "vertical mosaic," but he indicates in reference to the group correlations, "It was apparently this reality to which Porter (1965) was reacting" (1976:120). Moreover, he suggests that in fact Porter's thesis was largely commenting on the relative status of ethnic groups and not on the life chances of individuals.

There is merit to separating the issues of group stratification from the analysis of individual class or status positions and mobility processes. Still, they have generally *not* been separated in the Canadian literature on the salience of ethnicity for stratification. Moreover, I think it fair to say that Porter's original discussion certainly intimated that there was direct significance of the hardening of entrance statuses into subordinate ethnic group statuses for individual mobility and for the openness of Canadian society in that sense. Porter was himself more guarded perhaps than most of us have been in interpreting his work. It seems clear that a relatively strong association between ethnic status and occupational position has been taken as demonstrably significant for individual life chances. Pineo's results are quite surprising exactly for this reason. They invite further consideration.

One obvious source of difference between Porter's original analysis of census data and that of Pineo is the form of the analysis itself. Pineo presents correlations, while Porter examined differences in the distributions of different ethnic groups in comparison with expected distributions based on

TABLE I

ETHNIC ORIGIN AND OCCUPATIONAL CLASSES, MALE LABOR FORCE, CANADA, 1931, 1951, AND 1961, PERCENTAGE OF OVER REPRESENTATION IN OCCUPATION BY ETHNIC GROUP (FROM PORTER, 1965: TABLE I)

	British total	British			French	German	Italian	Jewish
		English	Irish	Scottish				
1931								
Professional and financial	+1.6	+1.6	+1.0	+2.2	-.8	-2.2	-3.3	+2.2
Clerical	+1.5	+1.8	+1.0	+1.4	-.8	-2.2	-2.5	+.1
Personal service	-.3	0.0	-.5	-.7	-.3	-1.2	+2.1	-1.2
Primary and unskilled	-4.6	-4.4	-4.9	-4.8	+3.3	-5.3	+26.1	-14.5
Agriculture	-3.0	-6.1	+2.7	-1.5	+.1	+21.1	-27.6	-32.4
All others	+4.8	+7.1	+.7	+3.4	-1.5	-10.2	+5.2	+45.8
	0.0	0.0	0.0	0.0	0.0	0.0	0.0	0.0
1951								
Professional and financial	+1.6	+1.6	+.9	+2.5	-1.5	-2.2	-3.1	+4.2
Clerical	+1.6	+1.8	+1.3	+1.4	-.8	-2.5	-1.7	0.0
Peronal service	-.3	-.2	-.4	-.5	-.2	-1.2	+2.0	-1.4
Primary and unskilled	-2.2	-1.7	-2.2	-3.2	+3.0	-3.7	+9.6	-11.5
Agriculture	-3.2	-5.5	+.5	-1.6	-.3	+19.1	-14.7	-18.7
All others	+2.5	+4.0	-.1	+1.4	-.2	-9.5	+7.9	+27.4
	0.0	0.0	0.0	0.0	0.0	0.0	0.0	0.0
1961								
Professional and financial	+2.0	—	—	—	-1.9	-1.8	-5.2	+7.4
Clerical	+1.3	—	—	—	-.2	-1.8	-3.2	-.1
Personal service	-.9	—	—	—	-.2	-.7	+2.9	-2.4
Primary and unskilled	-2.3	—	—	—	+2.8	-2.1	+11.5	-8.9
Agriculture	-1.5	—	—	—	-1.4	+8.8	-9.5	-11.7
All others	+1.4	—	—	—	+.9	-2.4	+3.5	+15.7
	0.0				0.0	0.0	0.0	0.0

	Dutch	Scandinavian	East European	Other European	Asian	Indian and Eskimo	Total male labor force
1931							
Professional and financial	-1.1	-2.9	-3.9	-4.4	-4.3	-4.5	4.8
Clerical	-1.9	-2.7	-3.4	-3.5	-3.2	-3.7	3.8
Personal Service	-1.5	-1.5	-1.1	-1.7	+27.8	-3.1	3.5
Primary and unskilled	+1.4	+1.4	+12.4	+35.8	+10.2	+45.3	17.7
Agriculture	+18.5	+19.8	+14.5	-5.8	-20.9	-4.9	34.0
All others	-9.2	-14.1	-18.5	-20.4	-9.6	-29.1	36.2
	0.0	0.0	0.0	0.0	0.0	0.0	100.0
1951							
Professional and financial	-1.7	-2.1	-2.9	-2.4	-2.8	-5.2	5.9
Clerical	-2.4	-2.8	-2.8	-2.5	-2.9	-5.2	5.9
Personal service	-1.2	-1.0	+.6	+2.0	+23.9	-.6	3.4
Primary and unskilled	-1.7	+.5	+2.3	+5.7	-1.9	+47.0	13.3
Agriculture	+17.3	+14.7	+11.2	+3.4	-8.7	-7.8	19.4
All others	-10.3	-9.3	-8.4	-6.2	-7.6	-28.2	52.1
	0.0	0.0	0.0	0.0	0.0	0.0	100.0
1961							
Professional and financial	-.9	-1.9	-1.2	-1.1	+1.7	-7.5	8.6
Clerical	-1.7	-2.4	-1.7	-2.0	-1.5	-5.9	6.9
Personal service	-.5	-1.1	+.9	+5.1	+19.1	+1.3	4.3
Primary and unskilled	-2.0	-.2	0.0	+1.8	-3.6	+34.7	10.0
Agriculture	+10.3	+10.6	+6.9	+.6	-6.5	+6.9	12.2
All others	-5.2	-5.0	-4.9	-4.4	-9.1	-29.5	58.0
	0.0	0.0	0.0	0.0	0.0	0.0	100.0

the total labor force. In examining the relevance of the vertical mosaic thesis for immigrant groups, Blishen has followed the same strategy. Whereas correlations are sensitive to differences about means, Porter and Blishen's analyses were intended to assess differences in distributions per se.[2] I will preserve the original strategy of comparison in my reanalysis.

Table 1 reproduces the basic tabular data which Porter presented in examining the main thesis of The Vertical Mosaic. The data include tabulations for three points over a thirty-year period. They give the relationship between broadly defined occupational groups and ethnic origin groups in terms of the over and underrepresentation of each ethnic group in comparison with the distribution of the total male labor force. The data are by now very familiar to students of stratification in this country.

These data have been cited as indicating that there is a substantial and persistent relationship between social status and ethnicity in Canada. There is, no doubt, a pattern of overrepresentation clearly favoring the British and Jewish origin groups and showing the disadvantage of the French, Italian and native Indian and Eskimo populations. But consider the data in the form given in Table 2.

Table 2 presents, for each year of Porter's data, indexes of dissimilarity for each ethnic group between its occupational distribution and that of total labor force. The unweighted mean of the indexes is given at the bottom.

The index of dissimilarity has become a conventional, simple way of summarizing these kinds of data (Lieberson, 1963; Darroch and Marston, 1971). It has the appealing property of providing a direct, substantive interpretation which indicates the proportion of one population which would have to become redistributed in order to match the occupational distribution of the comparison population.[3] The index can be computed directly from Porter's data as the sum of either the positive or negative percentage differences between an ethnic occupational distribution and the total labor force distribution (the total "overrepresentation" or total "underrepresentation" over all occupational categories).

Porter was most impressed by the existence of a pattern of over and underrepresentation which was clearly to the advantage of those of British and northern European origin. He commented specifically on the seeming persistence of a general rank order of ethnic groups by occupation (1965:90). Yet there are two related features of the same data, apparent in Table 2, which are at least as noteworthy for the usual interpretation of ethnic stratification in Canada. In 1951 and 1961 the dissimilarities from the total labor force in occupational distributions for a number of ethnic groups are either low or moderate by a reasonable substantive interpretation of the indexes (say 10 to 15 percent). By 1961, in fact, seven of eleven ethnic groups have a dissimilarity index of 10 percent or less. The second related feature of the data is the distinct and progressive reduction in average dissimilarity between 1931 and 1961. This reduction seems at least as significant for our interpretation of the place of ethnicity in stratification as stable rank order of occupational advantage and disadvantage. The reduction is very substantial, from an average of just less than 30 percent to just less than 15, with the greatest portion of the change coming between 1931 and 1951 as far as these data reveal.[4]

Clearly, it is a matter of judgement to emphasize a stable rank order of ethnic group superordination and subordination or the reduced strength of the relationship, that is, the diminished average dissimilarity in occupational distributions of ethnic groups from a common standard. But the two features are distinct and must not be confounded in generalizing to the persisting importance of ethnicity in the class and status structures of Canadian society as I think they have tended to be. The dissimilarity indexes reveal the variation among ethnic groups in all years, and the importance of *specific* differences, such as the extraordinary persistence of distorted occupational distributions of the native populations in comparison to the substantial reductions for East European and other European groups. The indexes also strongly suggest that if ethnicity once was a central feature of the system of stratification in Canada, by 1961 it would likely be a significant factor in the occupational careers of only those with quite specific origins; the Jews and Asian origin groups, the Italians and, as noted, the native populations.

TABLE 2

OCCUPATIONAL DISSIMILARITY OF ETHNIC GROUPS FROM TOTAL MALE LABOR FORCE FOR 1931, 1951 AND 1961 (FROM PORTER, 1965: TABLE 1)

Ethnic group	Dissimilarity indexes		
	1931	*1951*	*1961*
Total British	7.9	5.7	4.7
French	3.4	3.0	3.7
German	21.0	19.1	8.8
Italian	33.4	19.5	17.9
Jew	48.1	31.6	23.1
Dutch	18.5	17.3	10.3
Scandinavian	21.2	14.7	10.6
East European	26.9	14.1	7.8
Other European	35.8	11.1	6.9
Asian	38.0	23.9	20.8
Indian and Eskimo	45.3	47.0	42.9
Mean (X̄)	27.23	18.82	14.32
Mean excluding Asian and Native groups (comparable to Lieberson's groups for American cities)	24.02	16.64	10.01

Of course, the computation of dissimilarity indexes is by no means an adequate test of the importance of ethnic affiliations for mobility opportunities. The striking moderation in occupational differences does have a very important implication for individual mobility, however, akin to what I think is the main implication of Pineo's low correlations. The generally low level of association between ethnicity and occupational position simply means that ethnicity will not be found to be a significant factor in competition with other variables in an adequate model of the processes of status acquisition in Canada in recent years. But the examination of occupational dissimilarity does preserve information on the variation in occupational distributions among ethnic groups which has been surprisingly persistent (the standard deviations of the dissimilarity indexes change little over the thirty years, from 14.4 in 1931, when the average dissimilarity is very high, to 11.5 in 1961, when the average is halved).

In any case, one major conclusion which a reconsideration of the original data makes imperative is that ethnic occupational differentiation has systematically and in many cases substantially reduced in the thirty years. Certainly, this adds weight to the growing reluctance to accept the idea that Canada has experienced a hardening of initial levels of ethnic entrance statuses into a permanent class system (Porter, 1974:6). Perhaps it suggests that we should be more concerned with the processes of occupational integration, despite continued immigration, over the period (Kalback, 1970: chapter 5). On the other hand, the variation among ethnic groups also suggests that we should focus on the bases of the continued salience of ethnicity for *specific* ethnic populations in the context of the broader tendencies toward integration. What are the processes of selective ethnic group exclusion and group closure?

Comparisons between simple indexes of dissimilarity not based on identical categories can be misleading. This is especially true when the populations being compared are quite variable and when rather specific differences are being examined. However, Porter's data has been taken as initial evidence of the exceptional significance of ethnic stratification in Canada. Porter had suggested at least that it distinguishes the United States from Canada in terms of ideology and, perhaps, in fact.

The 1951 data for Canada may be set beside Lieberson's data for the United States in 1950 (1963). Lieberson's data include more refined occupational categories, but unfortunately refer only to first or second generation immigrants and to selected *urban* populations for ten major cities. Yet if examined with caution, a comparison of average levels of occupational dissimilarity may help to put the Canadian data into some perspective.

For ten ethnic groups and for between three and nine cities, depending on available data, Lieberson reports an average occupational dissimilarity of 18.7 between the male labor force and first generation immigrants (foreign-born whites).[5] For second generation immigrant groups, the average index is lower at 13.5 (1963, Table 55:169). Despite the differences in the data, there is not much reason to think that levels of ethnic occupational differentiation in Canada distinguished this country strikingly from the United States. Even the most deprived populations in each country bear some similarity. In 1950, the average indexes of occupational dissimilarity for blacks in American cities, compared to the first generation immigrant population, was forty-three. The dissimilarity of native groups in Canada from the total labor force was forty-seven in 1951, as given in Table 2.

TABLE 3

OCCUPATIONAL DISSIMILARITY OF ETHNIC GROUPS FROM TOTAL LABOR FORCE, 1971 (FROM FORCESE, 1975: TABLE 2-3)

Ethnic Group	*Dissimilarity index*
British Isles	5.9
French	5.5
German	8.8
Hungarian	12.9
Italian	26.4
Jewish	29.8
Netherlands	10.9
Polish	9.6
Russian	8.2
Scandinavian	9.8
Ukrainian	8.0
Asiatic	16.3
Native Indian	29.0
Other	13.0
Mean (X)	13.9

I have dwelt on the reconsideration of Porter's original data because they gave impetus to one important aspect of the vertical mosaic thesis which has deeply influenced subsequent interpretations, perhaps much more than Porter intended. To consider a more recent contribution, I give a summary of detailed 1971 data presented by Forcese in Table 3 (1975). Again, where the author presented standard census cross-tabulations of ethnicity by occupation, I have simply computed dissimilarity indexes for each ethnic group from the *total labor force* distribution. There were twenty-two occupational categories in the original data.

In reviewing themes in Canadian stratification, Forcese examines the *Mosaic* thesis briefly using the data summarized in Table 3 and reference to a number of case studies. The discussion suggests again that ethnic stratification is an especially salient feature of the Canadian class structure.

The author suggests that the ethnic stratification is stable, or perhaps even deepening with the impact of current immigration (1975:41-49). The data do reveal a continuation of the general ranking of the groups in a broad occupational status *order*. Further, the dissimilarity indexes of Table 3 show that there was in 1971 very largely the same general pattern of occupational differentiation of ethnic groups as in 1961, with the Jewish, native Indian and Italian populations most dissimilar followed by the Asian origin group. But again the average index was not great, at 13.9, very slightly lower than in 1961 for Porter's data. Moreover, the apparently marginal average reduction very likely is indicative of continuing declines in ethnic occupational differences in general since, other things equal, dissimilarity indexes based on a larger number and more refined categories such as those in the 1971 data *tend to be greater* than indexes based on more gross categories (Lieberson, 1963:33-38).

A reviewer has suggested that the assessment of levels of ethnic occupational dissimilarity would be enhanced by comparisons with other social groups. It is not entirely clear which social groups, if any, are conceptually significant in such comparisons. No one has offered an interpretation of ethnic stratification, for example, that attempts to specify how much more or less salient ethnic inequalities are expected to be than other forms of inequality or whether they should be the most sharply drawn differentials in a society which is primarily characterized as "ethnically stratified." Still, such comparisons may provide useful contextual information in the absence of more conventional tests of significance.

It is possible to make two kinds of potentially relevant comparisons for exactly the same census occupational categories which Forcese used to report the occupation by ethnicity data for 1971, and on which I based the computation of the dissimilarity indexes of Table 3 (Kubat and Thornton, 1974: Table J3; 163-167). The first is to compare ethnic occupational dissimilarities to regional and provincial dissimilarities and the second is to consider the ethnic differentials in terms of the dissimilarity between men and women in the labor force in 1971. Again, for comparison with the previous analyses, I compute the index of dissimilarity between the occupational distribution of the population in question and the occupational distribution of the total labor force for Canada. For the Maritime provinces, the unweighted average index of dissimilarity is 15. Prince Edward Island has an index of 20, Newfoundland, an index of 17 and Nova Scotia and New Brunswick have indexes of 12. Quebec has an occupational dissimilarity measured at 8 and Ontario, measured at 5, which is the lowest index for all the provinces. Ontario, of course, has the largest proportion of the total labor force of any of the areas. The western provinces have an average dissimilarity of 12, varying from the national high of 22 for Saskatchewan, and 10 for Alberta to 8 for Manitoba and British Columbia. The Yukon and North West Territories combined have an index of 18. The mean of all eleven areas is 12.7. Thus, average regional occupational dissimilarity in Canada is only marginally less than overall ethnic occupational dissimilarity in 1971 (13.9). For the fourteen ethnic populations considered by Forcese the range of the index is between 30 for the Jewish and 6 for the French ethnic groups, somewhat greater than the range for the eleven provinces and territories, that is, between 22 for Saskatchewan and 5 for Ontario. On this evidence one would probably not want to make a strong case that ethnic occupational stratification was much more striking or salient for Canada as a whole than regional occupational differentials, though the two have quite different implications for structured inequality.

Considering the comparison between ethnic occupational differences and the differences between men and women in the labor force provides a context in which the former appear even less salient. Using the same occupational categories, and computing the dissimilarity between the distribution of women in the labor force and the total labor force distribution, gives an index of 28. This compares with the very highest indexes of ethnic dissimilarity: 30, for the Jews, 29 for Natives and 26 for the Italians, as given in Table 3. Perhaps more meaningful in this case would be the dissimilarity between employed men and women; the index is 43 for the 1971 data. That is, fully 43 percent of the women in the labor force would have had to alter occupational status in order to equalize the distributions. The latter computation will not surprise anyone who has examined labor force data on women. Women are proportionally overrepresented in only 6 of the 22 occupational categories given, but grossly so in clerical and related positions, positions in which 31.8 percent of all employed women worked in comparison to 7.7 percent of men. Women are also considerably overrepresented in medicine and health related occupations, in service, and in teaching and related positions (also see Tepperman, 1975:156-174).

These comparisons may provide additional perspective on the magnitude of ethnic occupational stratification in the early seventies. To reiterate, only the few, most extreme ethnic groups match the occupational imbalance which working women experience and simple regional dissimilarities in occupational distributions are very nearly as great as ethnic dissimilarities. The data reinforce the earlier conclusion that the question of the salience of ethnicity for stratification requires a good deal more specification than is implied by the broad notion of a country in which ethnic pluralism is a primary aspect of class and status structures.

Blishen has presented the most thorough analysis of the main dimensions of ethnic stratification yet conducted in Canada (1958; 1967; 1970). The analyses have largely focused on the relationships between immigrant groups and occupational ranks, rather than considering ethnic affiliation more generally. The particular strength of this work in the present context is that Blishen specified the implications of the vertical mosaic idea for interpreting the relationship between immigrant status and occupational mobility. He concluded that his analyses strengthen the main tenets of the ethnically blocked mobility thesis. "Thus, certain combinations of immigrant and ethnic statuses are associated with the restriction of opportunity. These status combinations impart a degree of rigidity to class lines and strengthen individual group culture, thereby deepening social cleavages" (1970:124). As above, a second look at the data is in order to see how it leads to this apparent support for the centrality of ethnicity as a determinant of the Canadian class structure.

Blishen's most recently published work reports very detailed tabulations of male labor force distributions in 1961 in terms of his six occupational ranks (1970). The tabulations are given for the Canadian-born population and for eleven immigrant groups (country of birth), by period of immigration (pre- and post-WW II) and by region (Ontario, Quebec, the West and Atlantic provinces). The extensive cross-tabulations which are reported are difficult to interpret at a glance. I have recomputed portions of the data which are directly relevant to the ethnic blockage thesis in a form which provides a direct, single summary measure of the differences in occupational *rank* between the immigrant populations. The statistic employed is that recently described by Lieberson as the Index of Net Difference (ND) (1976). ND is related to the dissimilarity index, but specifically takes account of the direction of the relationship between the *entire* distributions of two ordered, categoric variables such as occupational ranks. The index summarizes the net difference between the two opposite probabilities of inequality between groups on the ranked variable. The index varies from +1 to –1. The extreme values indicate that there is no overlap at all in the distributions, and the sign indicates the direction of relationship. The index is zero when the two probabilities of inequality are equal. As employed here, ND is a straight-forward, descriptive statistic which is particularly appropriate for Blishen's unique data comparing Canadian-born and immigrant groups by measured occupational status rank. Table 4 presents ND for several comparisons of the occupational ranks of immigrant and Canadian-born populations, by region.

TABLE 4
NET DIFFERENCES IN OCCUPATIONAL STATUS BETWEEN SELECTED IMMIGRANT GROUPS AND THE NATIVE-BORN POPULATIONS FOR FOUR REGIONS, 1961 (FROM BLISHEN, 1970)

Immigrant and Native-born populations compared	Net difference (ND) by region			
	Atlantic	Quebec	Ontario	West
British versus Canadian-born	.360	.400	.068	.121
American versus Canadian-born	.194	.245	.202	.099
Total European-born versus Canadian-born	–.160	–.007	–.253	–.218

The indexes assess the net advantage which three major immigrant populations, the British-born, the American-born, and the total European-born, have over the Canadian-born as a whole, in each of the four regions. As Blishen had concluded, the assessment of the *direction* of the advantage is congruent with the broad, conventional hypothesis that the Canadian-born generally suffer occupational mobility deprivation as a result of Canada's persistent dependence on the recruitment of the foreign-born to staff its industrial labor force and from the related deprivation in educational facilities and opportunities. That is, most of the Net Differences in the table are positive, indicating the tendency toward a net advantage of immigrant groups over the Canadian-born.

But again there are other features of the data which need to be considered. Of the twelve relevant comparisons given in the table, two reach a Net Difference of .30 or greater, a value which I take as indicating decisive occupational status advantage. The two cases are the advantage which the British immigrants have over Canadian-born in the Atlantic provinces and in Quebec. The latter is the largest ND (.400) in the table, reflecting, no doubt, the deprivation of the French-Canadian population in Quebec itself. But with respect to what I take to be more general implications of the blocked mobility thesis, the results are much more ambiguous. Using Blishen's "total European" category in these computations necessarily masks a number of specific differences. However, even in these data the most striking feature of the relationship between immigrant status and occupational status in Canada is not uniformity of inequality, but, on the contrary, the wide variation of the strength and the direction of the relationship by immigrant group and by region.

The table shows that in these data the status advantage of the British immigrants over the Canadian-born could not be considered very significant in Ontario (.068), and evidently the advantage is rather moderate in the western provinces, measured as a difference in the probabilities of occupational inequality of .121. The occupational benefits enjoyed by the American immigrants are more consistent across the regions, but insofar as they can be measured in this 1961 data, they are moderate in substantive terms. The greatest advantage is in Quebec, where the Net Difference for the American-born over the Canadian-born is .245. There is no advantage to speak of in the West (ND = .099).

Only in the Atlantic provinces can we detect an overall status advantage in occupational rank for the total European-born population in comparison to the Canadian-born. In Quebec, there is no advantage, and in Ontario and in the West *it is the Canadian-born* who have a net occupational advantage over the foreign-born. To take account of these clear variations would entail a much more detailed specification than we have had of the implications of the vertical mosaic thesis for the relationship between immigrant status, occupational mobility and regional economies.

I have not reconsidered all possible comparisons in occupational ranks between different immigrant groups and the native-born population. Blishen's original tables show that there are patterns of occupational advantage in some regions, for some immigrant groups. The second look presented here indicates it would be an error to emphasize either the generality of the patterns for Canada as a whole or the magnitude of the occupational inequality. In fact, a close review of Blishen's detailed tables for 1961 will show a tendency to overemphasize the advantage of immigrant groups over the Canadian-born populations.[6] With important exceptions, in particular for Quebec, the measured differences in occupational ranks between immigrant and native-born populations might just as well be described as not especially marked.

Blishen's data can be employed in another way which is relevant to a reconsideration of the ethnically blocked mobility thesis. As noted above, a central argument has been that over time the entrance status of immigrant groups may "harden" into a permanent class structure (Porter, 1965; 1974). On the other hand Kalback (1970) has presented considerable evidence based on census tabulations which supports an assimilationist view, as he calls it. That is, he finds systematic reductions over time in the dissimilarity between immigrant and non-immigrant populations in most aspects of economic and family life.

TABLE 5
INDEXES OF OCCUPATIONAL DISSIMILARITY BETWEEN CANADIAN-BORN POPULATION AND THE TOTAL PREWAR AND TOTAL POSTWAR IMMIGRANT POPULATIONS, BY REGIONS, 1961, (COMPUTED FROM BLISHEN, 1970)

Immigrant and Native-born populations compared	Dissimilarity index by region			
	Atlantic	Quebec	Ontario	West
Canadian-born versus total prewar immigrants	15.91	16.13	3.40	4.32
Canadian-born versus total postwar immigrants	29.55	7.03	13.41	9.58

Blishen's data on the differences between prewar immigrants and the Canadian-born may be suggestive with respect to the degree to which they reveal a deepening or hardening of occupational differentiation with time in Canada. Table 5 simply gives indexes of occupational dissimilarity between the Canadian-born population and both the prewar and the postwar immigrants for four regions.

In the first place the results reinforce the previous conclusions that there is really relatively little occupational differentiation between large populations such as these. Only in *one case* would much more than 15 percent of either population compared have to alter occupational ranks in the Blishen six category schema in order to match the other population's distribution. The exception is the nearly 30 percent dissimilarity between the Canadian-born and the postwar immigrants in the Atlantic provinces. More to the point, these data indicate that the prewar immigrants have noticeably lower dissimilarity from the Canadian-born than do postwar immigrants in three of the four regions. In Quebec, however, those immigrants who arrived earlier have sustained a moderate occupational differential which is twice as great as that of postwar immigrants. Perhaps these are not data which can do more than touch on the possible implications of the hardening of entrance status hypothesis. But whatever the relevant data may be, those at hand clearly do not give grounds for confidence in its general applicability.

Almost everyone admits to the inadequacy of the kinds of data we have routinely had available for examining the nature of ethnic stratification in Canada. In fact, despite shortcomings, the available data are not irrelevant to the main hypotheses. As the backward glances presented above suggest, they should lead us to be skeptical of the idea that ethnic affiliations are a basic factor in generally limiting mobility opportunities in Canada. Finally, we must be reminded that the conventional data do not bear directly on the central question of what role ethnicity plays in the actual processes of social mobility or how ethnic affiliations otherwise affect processes which reproduce or alter the class structure.

Mobility Studies and Ethnicity

As noted earlier, one conventional account of the effects of immigrant and ethnic statuses on stratification is couched in terms of limitations on individual social mobility. However, to date we have very few studies of mobility *per se* in Canada and even fewer relate ethnicity to occupational status changes. I review here some of the main findings of studies which attempt to measure the impact of ethnicity on mobility, including two which are unpublished.

Richmond (1964) compared the occupational mobility of postwar immigrants in a national study. He found the clear pattern of advantage of British immigrants over other immigrants which we have come to expect. He also reported that the initial advantage diminished over time and that differences in both career and intergenerational mobility were, in fact, comparatively slight between Great Britain and other European immigrant groups. Certainly the differences were not so great as to lend much support to a notion that language and national identity alone should be counted as crucial bottlenecks to mobility for European immigrant groups.[7]

On the other hand, focusing on French-English differences and not immigrant status, Rocher and de Jocas' study (1957) of intergenerational mobility in Quebec showed that in the 1950s French Canadians suffered more severe handicaps to social mobility than did English-speaking Canadians in the province. Dofney and Garon-Audy (1964) matched the procedures of the previous study and argued that the occupational status gains made by French Canadians between the mid-1950s and the mid-1960s were largely a result of the structural changes in labor force distributions, rather than a result of equalization of opportunity or of increased "exchange" mobility (but see Turrittin, 1974:173-74). To these have been added two recent and more detailed studies of occupational mobility of French and English Canadians. Cuneo and Curtis (1975) examined the differences between Anglophones and Francophones in relatively small samples of the population aged 25-34, living in Toronto and Montreal. They applied the basic Blau-Duncan model of status attainment processes and an extension of it, incorporating additional background variables. They compare the models for four subsamples, Francophone men and women and Anglophone men and women. They emphasize, in general, that their data as well as the American data actually give greater credence to a view that ascriptive factors, especially family background, play a very significant role in status attainment, in contrast to the more commonplace emphasis on the dominance of achievement, through education especially. More important here is the fact that they report measurable differences *between* Francophones and Anglophones especially with respect to the greater effect of family size on education among Anglophones and the greater effect of educational attainment on current occupation for Francophones than for Anglophones.

By far the most detailed and important study of the differences between Anglophones and Francophones in mobility and status attainment processes has recently been reported by McRoberts, Porter, Boyd and their colleagues, as part of a larger national study (1976). They compare the Francophone experience in Quebec with the Anglophone experience in Canada as a whole on the persuasive grounds that these are the principal respective occupational realms of the two populations. They carefully explore the sources of the differences between Anglophones and Francophones in intergenerational occupational achievement and they decompose the processes of status attainment through the application of the basic Blau-Duncan model. Like the previous studies they find that there are measurable differences between Anglophone and Francophone experiences. Applying loglinear analysis to control for differences in the marginals of mobility tables, they conclusively extend the analysis of Dofney and Garon-Audy. The differences in mobility are primarily the result of differential changes in labor force distributions affecting the two populations and the differences between the two groups have diminished in all respects. Moreover, their cohort analysis provides strong evidence of convergence in mobility patterns between the two groups especially for the youngest members of the labor force. With respect to processes of status attainment, the striking features are the similarities in form for the two linguistic groups (the relative size of the coefficients in the models are identical for each) at the same time that there are significant differences in the relative impact of specific variables, such as family size and father's education and they are such as to disadvantage Francophones in comparison to Anglophones (1976:75). In sum, the authors find what they consider to be surprising evidence of convergence in the experiences of Anglophones and Francophones and thus, evidence of the diminishing salience of linguistic stratification (1976:78).

A review of studies serves to provide some perspective on the evolution of our knowledge regarding ethnic-linguistic differences in social mobility. In the light of these most recent specifications of the mobility process, it is well to recall that conventional interpretations of Canadian stratification have broadly implied: (1) more obvious differentials in mobility experiences between French- and English-speaking populations than those reported, (2) perhaps more persistent differentials and, (3) differentials which were thought to hinge at least as much on differences in aspirations and values as on differences in opportunity structures. It is again of contextual interest that in the subsample comparisons which Cuneo and Curtis undertook, the gender differences in status attainment models were often as striking, and occasionally more striking, than the differences between Anglophones and Francophones. For example, the direct effects of education on first and current jobs were much stronger for men than for women in both linguistic groups (1975:21, also see Figures 2 and 3), although the authors are sensitive to the difficulties of drawing strict comparisons of this sort from their data (1975:fn 8:10-11).

Finally, the complexities of mobility processes revealed in recent work should remind us that the differences between Francophone and Anglophone experiences cannot be generalized to the way ethnic affiliations or immigrant status enter the mobility process. At the time of writing only two studies are known to me which assess the direct and indirect effects of ethnic origins and immigrant status on occupational attainment and income in competition with other variables, such as social origins and education. They are instructive, although both refer only to selective Ontario populations and neither are published. Unfortunately, the authors have indicated that publication of their studies is not forthcoming in the foreseeable future. I take advantage of the opportunity to report some important results here, though I take no credit for the research.[8]

Goldlust and Richmond (1973) provide mobility data on "ethno-linguistic" groups of immigrants for metropolitan Toronto. They show that there are, as expected, substantial differences among the immigrant groups in their average occupational statuses in their *former* countries, among their statuses after arrival and at two subsequent points in their occupational histories. But the pattern of occupational differences is also found to be a *direct* reflection of the occupational differences of their fathers' statuses, i.e., of their differences in socio-economic origins. For six of the eight "ethno-linguistic" groups there was a difference of *less than* three points on the Blishen occupational scale between the mean of the fathers' scores and the mean of the respondents' current occupational scores. Ethnic group differences correspond closely with the average differences in social class origins of the group members which were a result of selective immigration processes.

Taking the analysis a step toward the separation of effects, Goldlust and Richmond computed the contributions of several variables to *income,* including the effects of ethnicity which entered a regression analysis as a set of dummy variables. At the most, when the ethnic variables enter the regression first, they accounted for 7 percent of the variance in incomes among all respondents; the total variance in income explained was 35 percent, with education, current occupational status and father's occupational status accounting for almost all of the remainder. From the table given by the authors it appears that, when ethnicity is made to compete with the other variables in the regression, education, current occupation and father's occupation explain respectively 18 percent, 10 percent and 5 percent of the total variance, while the impact of ethnicity is entirely indirect, acting through these variables. In statistical terms, ethnicity appears to have *no* unique effects.[9]

A second unpublished work is a very extensive study by Ornstein (1974) based on a reanalysis of Porter and Blishen's data for Ontario high school students and their parents. One part of the study is a detailed analysis of the impact of ethnicity on occupational mobility undertaken by means of regression and analysis of variance techniques. Employing nine ethnic groups in the analysis, Ornstein first shows that ethnicity can account for a maximum of only 3.3 percent of the difference in occupational ranks (Blishen scores) of first jobs of this sample of the Ontario population and can account for 5.2 percent of the respondents' current job status differences. Ethnicity did account for slightly over 10 percent of the variation in educational attainment of the sample.

The author notes that the *pattern* of benefits in occupational ranks accruing to ethnic group affiliation is much as we expect — the Scots and English benefit most, the West Europeans and East Europeans follow in order and the recently immigrated Italian population is at the bottom. But again, I emphasize, a distinct pattern of advantage must not be confused with the significance of the effect of ethnicity on the actual occupational attainment of individuals.[10] Ornstein shows that the average differences among the ethnic groups in occupational attainment are not, in fact, very great. Moreover, the differences *within* the ethnic groups in occupational status are very much greater than the differences between them. The implications of this important finding have never been seriously considered in the Canadian context and warrant further comment.

If variations within ethnic groups in individual mobility experiences are generally large, and there are good *prima facie* reasons to think they might be, then it is quite conceivable that for some members of a given ethnic population there exist serious "mobility traps," while for other members ethnic identity may be of no consequence to mobility whatsoever. Still others may be able to translate their heritage into distinct occupational opportunities. Moreover, variations *within* ethnic groups in status achievement require explanations in terms of non-ethnic variables, that is, in terms of any number of factors which cannot themselves be broadly subsumed under the label ethnic identity or affiliation.

Consistent with my earlier discussion it should be noted that Ornstein is able to show that the results from his sample of Ontario residents are strikingly similar to the results found in examining the impact of ethnicity on mobility in an American national sample (Duncan and Duncan, 1968). It may also be added that in a longitudinal study of large metropolitan areas in the United States, for the decade 1957-1967, Featherman (1971) found only indirect effects of differences in "religio-ethnic" background (that is, acting through other variables) on occupational achievements. There was some significant, though not large, direct effect of the religio-ethnic variables on educational attainment, a finding also duplicated by Ornstein for Ontario. The impact of the ethnic mosaic again does not appear as unique to Canada as we have often thought it to be.

Despite the fact that these studies refer to limited segments of the Canadian population, the evidence they provide regarding the influence of ethnicity in the process of individual occupational mobility reinforces the conclusions derived from the re-examination of conventional cross-sectional data given earlier. Both kinds of evidence provide sufficient cause to be very skeptical of a thesis which argues that sustained attachments to ethnic communities forces some sort of trade-off, in which opportunities for upward mobility must be foregone as a price of maintaining "primordial" sentiments (Porter, 1974), or for that matter, as a consequence of restricted occupational aspirations or achievement motives.[11]

The Mosaic Revisited

One basic emphasis regarding the effects of ethnicity on the Canadian class structure has centred on the notion that a release from ethnic identities (assimilation) will result in enhanced mobility opportunities and subsequently, in relative status achievements. The thesis may be seen as a version of the theory of "modernization" which assumes that men and resources are increasingly freed from ascriptive ties in order to compete for achievement in the marketplaces of industrial or post-industrial society. In this respect, it is a functional theory of stratification.

With respect to ethnic community affiliations, at least, the argument no longer seems very convincing (but on ascriptive characteristics in general, see Cuneo and Curtis, 1975). Diminishing ethnic group attachments would have to affect one or more of the three conditions determining mobility rates, that is, to alter the opportunity structure, especially the occupational structure, or to affect differential rates of fertility between upper and lower status positions or to alter the rates of pure or exchange mobility between upper and lower strata. I have argued that recurrent emphasis has been given to a blocked mobility thesis in which ethnic assimilation is expected to increase exchange mobility, with some of those who occupy more privileged positions being replaced, or having their sons and daughters replaced, by those whose ethnic affiliations previously hampered their achievements. In any case, any argument about the effects of ethnic pluralism on stratification and mobility now requires this degree of specification.

It is generally known that the pure exchange portion of measured mobility rates for standard inflow-outflow tables is relatively limited in comparison to the mobility accounted for by structural changes in occupational distributions (see Turrittin, 1974: Table II for relevant Canadian data). Moreover, revisions of our view of the possible implications of ethnic affiliations for social mobility are necessitated by the most recent analyses of mobility opportunities in Canada and the United States. In attempting to overcome acknowledged limitations of standard mobility analyses by applying multivariate, contingency table analysis, Hauser and his associates have concluded forcefully that systematic variations in the relative intergenerational mobility chances of American men with different social origins are *entirely* accounted for by changes in occupational structure over time (1975a; 1975b). As the authors state, "Despite the many social changes in the United States in the last two decades, it is a more favorable occupational structure, *and only that*, which has sustained or improved the mobility opportunities of American men" (Hauser et al., 1975b:597: emphasis added).

McRoberts, Porter, Boyd et al adopted the same methodology in their analysis of the differences in mobility between Francophones in Quebec and Anglophones in Canada as a whole. They conclude, no less forcefully, "La comparaison des matrices croisant le statut socio-économique du père avec le statut actuel du fils en contrôlant les marginales n'a révélé aucune différence significative dans l'association père-fils entre les deux groupes. Ce fut également le cas lorsque nous avons étudié les différence entre les deux groupes, tant dans le cas de ceux qui étaient mobiles que dans celui des non-mobiles (qui se trouvent sur la diagonale principale)"(1976:77).

Thus, structural changes in Canada will surely be found to be the key to alterations in the relative mobility opportunities of members of various ethnic and immigrant populations. Further, given the review of evidence above showing that measures of the simple association between ethnic affiliation and socio-economic status are generally quite moderate, we may expect to find that in analyses of the process of status attainment, ethnic affiliations will play the role of one ascriptive factor among many variables and one which has only a slight effect on occupational achievement and income in Canada.

Conclusion

The vertical mosaic thesis has served as a provocative hypothesis. However, I have argued that in Canada as a whole it is an exaggeration of any data available to date to suggest that ethnic affiliations can be counted as a primary factor sustaining structures of class or status. Recent studies separately have tended to moderate an earlier, stronger emphasis on the centrality of ethnicity in this respect. What is clear is that there has been a quite stable pattern of occupational status positions among large ethnic and immigrant populations, although there is strong evidence that occupational differences have systematically declined with time. The pattern has been revealed in several, detailed examinations of the occupational distributions of ethnic and immigrant groups (Porter, 1965; Blishen, 1958; 1967; 1970) and less often, but no less convincingly, in terms of income and educational distributions (Royal Commission on Bilingualism and Biculturalism, 1969; vol. IV, 40-41; Kalbach and McVey, 1971:209). It is clearly important to recognize the implications of these patterns, for example, in terms of the ethnic bias in the recruitment and structure of elites in this country or, perhaps, in terms of ideology (Porter, 1965; Clement, 1974). But the tendency to conflate the existence of these patterns with an assessment of the degree to which ethnicity is a fundamental source of national structures of inequality has been unwarranted.

It bears noting that one of the most important results of the tendency to overestimate the magnitude of ethnic group differences and to focus on the putative central role of ethnicity in social mobility has been to divert attention from other, more consequential sources of the maintenance of the class structure in Canada. Drawing on a broad familiarity with Canadian social history, S. D. Clark made the argument clearly.

> If one were to quarrel with the Porter analysis of society as it was, it would be only on the score that by seeking to relate ethnic affiliation to the hierarchical structure he tended to obscure the underlying forces producing this hierarchical structure. Members of the British charter group were admittedly very much on top, but they were on the very bottom as well, occupying marginal farm lands in eastern Nova Scotia, northeastern New Brunswick, and eastern and central Ontario, or engaged in subsistence fishing industry in Newfoundland. The division of the country into French and English has led to viewing Canadian society too much from an ethnic standpoint. (1975:28)

The reassessment of evidence presented in this paper, I hope, adds weight to the conclusion for the present as for the past.

NOTES

[1]For a study which does employ all available census data in examining simultaneous effects, see Kalbach, 1965, especially chapters 4 and 5. For the use of survey data including socio-economic background to examine the social mobility of immigrants, see Richmond, 1964.

²I thank John Fox for drawing this point to my attention.

³There has recently been a rekindled discussion of the relative merits of dissimilarity measures, but for the straightforward purposes at hand their utility is not in question (Cortese et al., 1976; Taeuber and Taeuber, 1976). The indexes provided here compare each ethnic group's occupational distribution to a total distribution which includes the former. This way of re-examining the data simply adheres to the sort of comparisons made originally with the same data. As one reviewer pointed out, a single, summary measure of differences between distributions does not direct attention to numerically small differences between specific groups which may have particular importance, such as economic elites or other professional groups. This is true, of course, of any form of summary measure of expression, including simple declarative statements about the general features of distributional differences.

⁴Porter's Table III (1965:94) gives the same occupational distributions for the French and British origin groups *within* the province of Quebec. The indexes of dissimilarity computed from these data reflect the considerable differences which separate the two "charter" groups in that province, although, as Porter concluded, they suggest some lessening of the overall discrepancy in the thirty-year period. The indexes for 1931, 1951 and 1961 are respectively, 23.2, 17.0 and 14.5.

⁵England and Wales, Ireland, Norway, Sweden, Germany, Poland, Czechoslovakia, Austria, Russia and Italy.

⁶There is also some value for very detailed data in employing simple descriptive indexes. I note that ND for Ontario does not support Blishen's conclusion from his detailed tables to the effect that, as in Quebec, in Ontario "*most* immigrant groups have an advantage over the Canadian-born in terms of their degree of overrepresentation in classes I to III" (1970:117). In fact, this is not strictly true. Moreover, considering the *entire* occupational distributions, Table 4 shows for Ontario that *only* the American-born enjoy an advantage in occupational status, for the British-born there is a barely detectable difference and it is *reversed* for the total European population. Even for Quebec, although it is strictly true that "most" immigrant groups in Blishen's data had a net occupational advantage over the Canadian-born in the top three ranks, only for the American and British-born was the advantage moderately strong considering differences in the *entire* occupational distributions. The advantage disappears when the total European-born group is compared to the Canadian-born in that province.

⁷Most specifically, Richmond employed samples *matched* in terms of social class, background, education, length of residence and marital status to compare career mobility of British immigrants and other European immigrants. He concluded that British immigrants in Canada did have some advantage over non-British immigrants, when other things were equal, but that this advantage was a comparatively small one.

⁸I thank the authors of these studies for generously permitting me to report some of their findings in the absence of full publication of their work. Goldlust and Richmond have briefly referred to their findings in one recent paper (1974:209).

⁹The authors do not assess direct and indirect effects in the analysis, but they do report a separate analysis of interaction effects (AID) in which father's occupation is not entered as an independent variable. In this analysis ethnicity accounts again for a maximum of 7 percent of the total variance of income.

¹⁰Ornstein summarizes his separate analyses in a regression with many variables, including ethnicity. Computing the variance explained in occupational status so as

to *maximize* the effects of ethnicity and social class background, he finds that the 5.2 percent contributed by ethnicity is only greater than the predictive power of the respondents' first job (3.8 percent). By comparison educational achievement contributed 32.9 percent and father's occupation, 11.2 percent, accounting for a total of 53.1 percent of the variance in occupational status. In an analysis of the determinants of household income, including first and subsequent occupations as independent variables, ethnicity and father's occupation were found to have *no* significant predictive power — a conclusion similar to that of Goldlust and Richmond cited above.

[11]Providing one conceivable reason for the differences in occupational status among immigrant groups, Blishen (1970) suggests that the differences in occupational status of the groups on entering Canada may be translated into persistent differentials because, "aspirations are relative to distance of a given position from the one presently occupied" (p. 121). He is here citing Breton and Roseborough's study (1968) in which the employees of one large corporation were surveyed to consider the validity of a reference group hypothesis for explaining differential mobility aspirations and, ultimately, achievements. The authors provide evidence that French Canadian employees were *satisfied* with lower level achievements. Their data do not in fact show that differences in actual positions attained were a result of differential aspirations. Rather, they show that differences in *expressed satisfaction* between French- and English-speaking employees were related to the differences in reference group. I find the authors somewhat ambiguous on this point. They note, however, that their data do not allow them, in the end, to choose between an interpretation of ethnic differences in terms of differential opportunities or in terms of the postulated reference group effects on aspirations. In fact, the French Canadian employees may have tailored their sense of satisfaction — or their expressions of it — to felt circumstances of limited occupational mobility.

REFERENCES

Avery, Donald, "Continental European Immigrant Workers in Canada 1896-1919: from 'Stalwart Peasants' to Radical Proletariat." *Canadian Review of Sociology and Anthropology*, 12, 1975:53-64.

Blishen, Bernard R., "The Construction and Use of an Occupational Class Scale." *Canadian Journal of Economics and Political Science*, 24, 1958:519-531.
————, "A Socio-Economic Index of Occupations in Canada." *Canadian Review of Sociology and Anthropology*, 4, 1967:41-53.
————, "Social Class and Opportunity in Canada." *The Canadian Review of Sociology and Anthropology*, 7, 1970:110-127.

Breton, Raymond and Howard E. Roseborough, "Ethnic Differences in Status." In *Canadian Society*, edited by B.R. Blishen et al., pp. 683-701. Toronto: Macmillan, 1968.

Clark, S.D., "The Post Second World War Canadian Society." *Canadian Review of Sociology and Anthropology*, 12, 1975:25-32.

Clement, Wallace, *The Canadian Corporate Elite: An Analysis of Economic Power*. Ottawa: McClelland & Stewart, 1974.

Cortese, Charles F., R. Frank Falk and Jack Cohen, "Further Considerations of the Methodological Analysis of Segregation Indices." *American Sociological Review*, 4, 1976: 630-637.
————, "Reply to Taeuber and Taeuber." *American Sociological Review* 41:889-893.

Cuneo, Carl J. and James E. Curtis, "Social Ascription in the Educational and Occupational Status Attainment of Urban Canadians." *Canadian Review of Sociology and Anthropology,* 12, 1975:6-24.

Darroch, A. G. and W. G. Marston, "The Social Class Basis of Ethnic Residential Segregation: the Canadian case." *American Journal of Sociology,* 77, 1971: 491-510.

De Jocas, Ives and Guy Rocher, "Inter-Generational Occupational Mobility in the Province of Quebec." *Canadian Journal of Economics and Political Science,* 23, 1957:58-66.

Dofney, Jacques and Muriel Garon-Audy, "Mobilités professionnelles au Quebec." "Sociologie et Sociétés, 1, 1969:277-301.

Duncan B. and O. D. Duncan, "Minorities and the Process of Stratification." *American Sociological Review,* 33, 1968:356-364.

Featherman, David L. "The Socio-Economic Achievement of White Religio-Ethnic Subgroups: Social and Psychological Explanations." *American Sociological Review,* 36, 1971:207-222.

Forcese, Dennis, *The Canadian Class Structure.* Toronto: McGraw-Hill Ryerson, 1975.

Goldlust, John and Anthony H. Richmond, *A Multivariate Analysis of the Economic Adaptation of Immigrants in Toronto.* Unpublished ms., 1973.

Hauser, Robert M., John N. Koffel, Harry P. Travis and Peter J. Dickinson, "Temporal Change in Occupational Mobility: Evidence for Men in the United States." *American Sociological Review,* 40, 1975a:279-297.
_____"Structural Changes in Occupational Mobility Among Men in the United States." *American Sociological Review,* 40, 1975b:585-598.

Kalbach, Warren E., *The Impact of Immigration on Canada's Population.* Ottawa: Dominion Bureau of Statistics, 1970.

Kubat, Daniel and David Thornton, *A Statistical Profile of Canadian Society.* Toronto: McGraw-Hill Ryerson, 1974.

Lanphier, C. Michael and Raymond N. Morris, "Structural Aspects of Differences in Income Between Anglophones and Francophones." *Canadian Review of Sociology and Anthropology,* 11, 1974:53-66.

Lieberson, Stanley, *Ethnic Patterns in American Cities.* New York: Free Press, 1963.
_____, "Rank Sum Comparisons Between Groups." In *Sociological Methodology,* edited by D. R. Heise, pp. 276-291. San Francisco: Jossey-Bass, 1976.

McRoberts, Hugh A., John Porter, Monica Boyd, John Goyder, Frank E. Jones, and Peter C. Pineo, "Différences dans la mobilité professionnelle des francophones et des anglophones." *Sociologie et Sociétés,* 8, 1976:61-79.

McVey, Wayne W., and Warren E. Kalbach, *The Demographic Basis of Canadian Society,* Toronto: McGraw-Hill, 1971.

Ornstein, Michael D., *Occupational Mobility in Ontario.* Unpublished ms., 1974.

Pineo, Peter, "Social Mobility in Canada: the Current Picture." *Sociological Focus,* 9, 1976:109-123.

Porter, John, *The Vertical Mosaic.* Toronto: University of Toronto Press, 1965.

_____, "Canada: Dilemmas and Contradictions of a Multi-Ethnic Society." In *Sociology Canada: Readings,* edited by C. Beattie and S. Crysdale, pp. 3-15. Toronto: Butterworth, 1974.

Raynauld A., G. Marion, and R. Beland, *La répartition des revenus selon les groupes ethniques au Canada, Rapport Final.* Ottawa. Unpublished ms., 1967.

Reitz, Jeffrey, "Analysis of Changing Group Inequalities in a Changing Occupational Structure." In *Mathematical Models in Sociology,* Sociological Review Monograph, no. 24, edited by P. Krishnan, pp. 167-191. Keele, Staffordshire: University of Keele, 1977.

Richmond, Anthony H., "The Social Mobility of Immigrants in Canada." *Population Studies,* 18, 1964:53-69.

_____, *Post-War Immigrants in Canada.* Toronto: University of Toronto Press, 1967.

Royal Commission on Bilingualism and Biculturalism, *The Cultural Contribution of the Other Ethnic Groups: Book IV.* Ottawa: Queen's Printer, 1967.

Taeuber, Karl E. and Alma F. Taeuber, "A Practitioner's Perspective on the Index of Dissimilarity (comment on Cortese, Falk and Cohen)." *American Sociological Review,* 41, 1976:884-889.

Tepperman, Lorne, *Social Mobility in Canada.* Toronto: University of Toronto Press, 1975.

Turrittin, Anton H., "Social Mobility in Canada: a Comparison of Three Provincial Studies and Some Methodological Questions." *Canadian Review of Sociology and Anthropology,* 11, 1974:163-186.

Vallee, F. G. and Norman Shulman, "The Viability of French Groupings Outside Quebec." In *Regionalism in the Canadian Community: 1867-1967,* edited by Mason Wade, pp. 83-99. Toronto: University of Toronto Press, 1969.

Wiley, Norbert F., "Ethnic Mobility Trap and Stratification Theory." *Social Problems,* 15, 1967:147-159.

IV.

Ethnic Attitudes

Chapter 14

Ethnic Stereotypes and Prejudice:
Alberta Indians, Hutterites and Ukrainians*

Marlene Mackie

Cartoons, television, and casual conversation present us with frequent reminders of the proclivity for stereotypical expression. Bald men are virile. Spectacle-wearers are bookworms. Athletes are dullards. Women are prone to emotional display. Cadillac owners are gauche 'nouveaux riches' who smell like freshly killed money. Psychiatrists are mad as hatters; their kids, along with the preachers', are the neighborhood delinquents. Such thoughtways strike us as a bit silly but harmless enough, until they are applied to ethnic groups, especially downtrodden ones. Ukrainian-Polish-Newfie jokes are mildly offensive. Categorical depiction of Indians, Jews or blacks, however, moves beyond mere bad taste to inhumanity.

Since 1922, when Walter Lippmann introduced the concept into the social science literature, stereotypes have been an important consideration to students of ethnic group relations. The social psychology of ethnic relations attends to intergroup cognition, sentiment, and behaviour. However, because stereotypes were studied from the beginning in the context of prejudice, the concept assumed pejorative connotations. Hence, the relationship between the first two of the three pivotal variables (stereotypes, prejudice, behaviour) was not determined empirically.

*Reprinted from *Canadian Ethnic Studies* 6:1-2 (1974), by permission of the author and the publisher.

The following logic appears to have prevailed:[1] stereotypes represent the rhetoric of bigots; bigotry is immoral; immorality and right-thinking are mutually exclusive; therefore, stereotypes are false. In short, both professional literature and textbooks *assumed* one dimension of stereotyping to be error. For example, Harding et al. in the distinguished *Handbook of Social Psychology* (1969:4, emphasis in original) wrote that "a belief that is simple, inadequately grounded, at least partially inaccurate, and held with considerable assurance by many people is called a *stereotype*." This stance was taken in the absence of empirical evidence beyond the truism that all generalizations fail to reflect the complexity of "reality."

Emotionally satisfying though it may be, the proposition requires critical examination. One could argue that ethnic groups constitute an integral part of the social milieu of many Canadians. Therefore, it is reasonable to hypothesize that acceptance or rejection of those groups does not totally subvert outsiders' perception. Moreover, stereotypes contain neutral (descriptive) and flattering traits as well as the derogatory imagery which may serve to rationalize hostility. And, particularly in the case of initial encounters, reliance upon the knowledge of an ethnic group contained in one's culture, rather than individual conjecture, might result in an actual gain in perceptual accuracy (Fishman, 1956:33). In other words, a person's wisest course of action may be to judge a particular member of a group in terms of his information about the group as a whole. The advantage is one of statistical probability and he may be quite wrong. Unfortunately, thorough analysis of this important question exceeds the scope of this paper. The point is discussed in Sue and Kitano (1973:93). More general discussions of stereotypes are to be found in Brigham (1971), Campbell (1967), and Mackie (1973).

This paper presents a brief overview of a study fully reported in Mackie (1971).[2] Research conducted in Edmonton, Alberta between 1968-1970 incorporated two interrelated objectives: (1) to examine the accuracy of the stereotypes of the Indians, Hutterites, and Ukrainians entertained by an Alberta sample, and (2) to test the relationship between such ethnic imagery and prejudice.

Method

Stereotypes[3] of Indians, Hutterites, and Ukrainians were measured by two instruments, a semantic differential and an open-ended questionnaire. Each respondent completed only one type of questionnaire. Two techniques were used in order to counterbalance the inherent strengths and weaknesses of each method. In order to provide a stable frame of reference for the description of the ethnic groups, both instruments used this wording: "In comparison with Albertans generally, most *North American Indians/ Hutterites/ Ukrainians* tend to be . . ."

The semantic differential consisted of a set of seven-point bi-polar adjectival scales. Afterwards, the positive pole of each scale was labelled "1", the negative pole "7", and the neutral point "4" (e.g. "1" rich, "7" poor, "4" neither rich nor poor). In this context, "negative" means either the less preferable adjective or departure from normative patterns. A stereotype was operationally defined as those attributes for which consensuality existed in extreme (non-neutral) scale positions (Gardner, Wonnacott & Taylor, 1968). More specifically, stereotype traits were defined as those characteristics whose means fell between 1.0 and 2.5 and between 5.5 to 7.0, with an average deviation less than 1.5 scale units.

The open-ended questionnaire required respondents to describe the ethnic groups in their own words. These free verbal descriptions were later subjected to a content analysis by two coders working independently. If 20% or more of the respondents applied a given trait to a group, that trait was defined as part of its stereotype. The limit chosen represents a quite arbitrary compromise between the demands of the data and the definition of stereotypes. Although stereotypes have been conceptualized as frequently attributed group traits since Katz and Braly's 1933 study, the literature provides little guidance on the precise amount of agreement which constitutes consensus. Frequencies as low as 3% have been used. On the other hand, had consensus been taken literally (51% agreement), there would have been no traits to validate.

Prejudice (feelings about ethnic groups, as opposed to cognition of them) was measured by Bogardus (1925) social distance scales which assess

TABLE 1
DESCRIPTION OF THE SAMPLE

Demographic Variable	Number	Percent
SEX		
Males	222	37.6%
Females	368	62.4%
AGE		
15-24 years	269	45.7%
25-49 years	254	43.1%
50+ years	66	11.2%
EDUCATION		
2 years HS or less	177	30.2%
3-5 years HS	279	47.5%
1 or more years univ.	131	22.3%
SOCIOECONOMIC STATUS*		
Working class	151	27.1%
Lower-middle class	212	38.1%
Upper-middle class	117	21.0%
Farmers	77	13.8%

*SES was measured with Blishen's (1967) index.

respondents' willingness to admit groups to varying degrees of social intimacy.

Data were gathered by group-administered questionnaires from 590 members of 25 Edmonton, Alberta organizations. The groups were chosen to obtain coverage of sex, age, education, and socioeconomic status variables.[4] The organizations included community leagues, lodges, service clubs, a labour union, and nursing students. The sample is described in Table 1. Totals less than 590 occur when respondents did not provide demographic information.

Following LaPiere's (1936) validation design, the accuracy of stereotypes was assessed against data provided by available public records (census data, vital statistics, royal commission reports, etc.) and existing studies of the three ethnic groups. The purpose was to search out and present an accumulation of evidence of different types concerning the impressions others hold of a group.[5] Care was taken to avoid a pitfall pointed out by Lippmann (1922:78) in another connection: "When a system of stereotypes is well fixed, our attention is called to those facts which support it, and diverted from those which contradict it."

Stereotype Description and Validation

Table 2 summarizes the stereotypes of the Indians, Hutterites, and Ukrainians elicited by both instruments. Although the level of consensus for inclusion of open-ended traits in the stereotypes is defined at 20%, traits which exceed the 10% level are listed in the table for general information.

INDIANS

The perception of the Indians which emerged from the semantic differential is an overwhelmingly negative image of an ostracized group that neither shares the work or success values of the surrounding society nor receives its material rewards. The open-ended descriptions also emphasized their lack of commitment to striving, their poverty, low level of education, and rejection by outsiders.

Several characteristics which received a high level of endorsement on the structured instrument were not salient for respondents to the open-ended questionnaire. For example, when the idea was presented to them, 83% agreed that the Indians were very likely to have large families. However, less than 1% volunteered this observation. On the other hand, open-ended respondents were more willing to make reference to the Indians' low hygenic standards and problems with alcohol. The explanation lies perhaps in the instruments. While the respondents to the semantic differential scale were unwilling to acquiesce to the stark adjectival scales "drunken" and "dirty", the open-ended sample members did volunteer the same descriptive core surrounded with qualification and speculation concerning its origins. Only 2% of the open-ended sample made reference to any physical characteristics which differentiate Indians from the rest of the population.

After the stereotypes had been collected, the next step was to examine empirically the assumption that ethnic images are fallacious. The Indian traits were juxtaposed against a series of indices derived from public records and existing studies of the group to determine whether differences in these traits do exist between native people and the general population. Particular reliance was placed on the Hawthorn-Tremblay (1966-1967) report (*A Survey of the Contemporary Indians of Canada, Volumes I and II*) and ethnographies from the Community Opportunity Assessment studies (Hobart, 1967; Newman, 1967) undertaken for the Alberta Human Resources Research Council.

Government data showed the Indians to be correctly described as differentially poor, rural, prolific, and uneducated. Fisher (1966) recorded their devaluation of higher education. The Canadian Corrections Association (1967) and McGrath (1968) documented their trouble with legal authorities, and Sharplin (1964) and the Canadian Corrections Association (1967) their problems with alcohol. The descriptions, disliked and oppressed by others, are corroborated by Hawthorn-Tremblay (1966-1967) and statistics provided by the Human Rights section of the Department of Labour. The Hawthorn-Tremblay report spoke at length of their lack of commitment to the life patterns and values of the modern urban-industrial world (old-fashioned). The evidence bearing upon divergent work habits (Cameron and Storm, 1965) and hygenic standards (Hawthorn-Tremblay, 1967) is supportive but inconclusive. According to Hawthorn-Tremblay, non-materialism is an inaccurate ascription. In general, the evidence refutes the assumption that stereotypes are false.

HUTTERITES

The semantic differential stereotype of the Hutterites[6] contains a large number of traits, presumably because this group is distinctly different in many respects from the containing population. The image is a positive one of a clean-living fundamentalist people who manage to practice generally approved values. The lack of congruence between the images produced by the two instruments appears to be an instance of respondents recognizing the appropriateness of the scales provided but unable to volunteer detailed information about the group. This interpretation is reinforced by the fact that 14% of the respondents to the open-ended questionnaire left the Hutterite section completely blank.

Because few government documents relevant to the Hutterite stereotype could be located for validation purposes, reliance was placed upon social science field studies. Professional opinion (*inter alia,* Bennett, 1967; Eaton and Weil, 1955; Hostetler, 1965; Mange, 1964; Peters, 1965; Sanders, 1964) supported lay perception of the following Hutterite traits: religious, rural, large families, exclusiveness, devaluation of higher education, self-sufficient, hardworking, thrifty, pacifistic, law-abiding, sober, marital stability, sexually moral, not neglectful of children's needs, disliked, old-fashioned. Although

the Hutterite reputation for good physical and mental health was upheld in
the 1950's, insufficient data precluded judgement of the present validity of
these traits.

TABLE 2
INDIAN, HUTTERITE, AND UKRAINIAN STEREOTYPES

Group	Stereotype Trait	Sem. Diff. Mean	Open-Ended (%)
INDIANS			
	Not materialistic	2.4	—
	Poor	6.3	28.7
	Large families	6.2	—
	Uneducated	6.1	29.3
	Believe univ. unimport.	5.8	—
	Disliked by other groups	5.8	14.0*
	Rural	5.7	—
	Oppressed by others	5.7	20.0
	Unambitious	5.6	15.0*
	Old-fashioned	5.6	—
	Often in trouble w/law	5.5	—
	Lazy	—	30.3
	Dirty	—	28.0
	Drink excessively	—	21.0
	Shy, quiet	—	13.0*
	Incompetent work habits	—	12.7*
	Sad	—	11.4*
HUTTERITES			
	Religious	1.3	23.7
	Self-sufficient	1.5	—
	Hardworking	1.7	20.7
	Sober	1.7	—
	Thrifty	1.8	—
	Seldom in trouble w/law	1.8	—
	Stable marriages	1.8	—
	Seldom fight	2.0	—
	Healthy	2.0	—
	Sexually moral	2.1	—
	Mentally healthy	2.3	—
	Not neglectful of child.	2.4	—
	Rural	6.6	13.3*
	Old-fashioned	6.5	22.3
	Large families	6.3	—
	Cliquish	6.3	42.3
	Believe univ. unimport.	6.0	—
	Disliked by other groups	5.6	—
	Communal social organization	—	18.7*
	Shy, quiet	—	16.7*
	Peculiar dress	—	13.3*
	Different culture	—	12.7*
	Competent work habits	—	10.7*
	Exclusive concern personal problems	—	9.7*

UKRAINIANS

Religious	2.3	—
Not neglectful of child.	2.3	—
Hardworking	2.4	29.0
Ambitious	2.4	9.7*
Self-sufficient	2.4	—
Large families	5.5	—
Retention of culture	—	29.3
Cliquish	—	18.7*
Uncouth	—	18.0*
Warm toward others	—	15.7*
Old-fashioned	—	15.3*
Happy	—	14.0*
Thrifty	—	12.7*
Strong family ties	—	12.0*

*Not part of Stereotype

UKRAINIANS

In general, a flattering image of the Ukrainians emerged from both instruments. They were depicted as a contented people, clinging to some remnants of their European culture, and endeavoring to succeed in their adopted country. There are overtones of the peasant imagery (uncouth, old-fashioned) which presumably made the Ukrainians an object of ridicule through the ethnic "humor" which circulated in the province several years ago. However, neither this nor any other ethnic group was consensually described as stupid, the common denominator of the "Ukrainian jokes". Moreover, respondents apparently had difficulty in differentiating this relatively assimilated group from the general population. (Many of the semantic differential scale means are close to the neutral point; only two open-ended traits exceeded the 20% criterion level.)

Primary sources of validation data were a sample survey of Alberta Ukrainians (Hobart et al., 1967) and various reports of the Commission on Bilingualism and Biculturalism. Only one Ukrainian trait, determined retention of cultural heritage, was valid (Commission on Bilingualism and Biculturalism, 1969). The Ukrainians do not differ from the majority society in family size, ambition, or religious fervor (Hobart et al., 1967). Insufficient resources prevented validation of the remaining three Ukrainian traits.

DISCUSSION

To summarize, 39 traits were assigned to the Indians, Hutterites, and Ukrainians. According to the validation procedure, 27 of these traits are accurate, four are inaccurate, and eight remain unverified. (Although insufficient validation data precluded judgement of eight traits, existing data supported five of them.) These results must be viewed with caution. Attitudinal findings are always a partial function of the techniques chosen to measure them (Ehrlich and Rinehart, 1965). It is the thrust of the evidence rather than its detail which is significant.

The investigation does establish that error is not the critical aspect of stereotyping. While stereotypes may not "tell the truth, the whole truth, and nothing but the truth", neither are they divorced from reality. At least some of the cultural differences caught up in folk perceptions are objectively there. Moreover, accurately perceived differences are more substantial than the "kernel of truth" suggested by some scholars (Klineberg, 1950). The study provides no justification for the inclusion of inaccuracy in the definition of stereotypes. On the contrary, accuracy is a variable and further inquiry is required into the conditions under which stereotypes are correct or incorrect.

Because of the assumption of inaccuracy and the methodological problems involved in determining degree of stereotype accuracy, the literature contains few hypotheses concerning the conditions under which stereotypes are valid or invalid. However, Triandis and Vassiliou (1967) argue that first-hand experience with an ethnic group is predictive of accuracy. Campbell (1967:821) suggested that

> The greater the real differences between groups on any particular custom, detail of physical appearance, or item of material culture, the more likely it is that that feature will appear in the stereotyped imagery each group has of the other (emphasis in original deleted).

Schuman (1966:440) hypothesized that stereotypes "are more likely to be accurate when they concern a group that has changed relatively little over a long period of time" and further that "stereotypes should tend to be more descriptive of prior than of current phases of ethnic history" (p. 441). Schuman also felt that positive traits would be more accurate than negative ones, since a suspicious outgroup would require less evidence before it was willing to believe an unflattering description. Conflict theorists, on the other hand, view the "true" behaviour of the outgroup as the cause of ethnocentrism (in the sense that groups have incompatible goals and compete for scarce resources) and negative traits as relatively accurate evaluations of outgroup behaviour (Campbell and LeVine, 1965:31).

This study's findings offer some support for Campbell's position and for Schuman's first two hypotheses. The fact that the Hutterite and Indian stereotypes are more accurate than the Ukrainian stereotype suggests that degree of assimilation affects both elaboration and accuracy of stereotyping. Both the Indians and the Hutterites are quite different from the general population. Their distinctive characteristics seem to have attracted the attention of outsiders, who have incorporated the differences into their images of these groups.

Since respondents' personal contact with ethnic groups was not ascertained, this investigation sheds no light on Triandis and Vassiliou's hypothesis.

How do the present findings bear upon the controversy regarding accuracy of positive versus negative traits? In general, the results indicate that regardless of directionality, the hypothesis inadequately conceptualizes the conditions of stereotype validity. Although the inaccurate traits tend to be favourable attributions, this offers little support for Schuman's hypothesis. The Indian stereotype contains mostly unfavourable traits and the Hutterite stereotype mostly favourable traits. Yet both groups are "underdog" groups and both sets of characteristics are generally accurate. The initial hypotheses are faulty because they assume an equivalency between prejudice and stereotyping. People who subscribe to stereotypes range from friendly, to indifferent, to hostile towards the object groups. Their imagery contains favourable, neutral, and unfavourable traits. Clearly, stereotypes represent more than the cognitive dimension of prejudice. The following section discusses the relationship between stereotyping and prejudice in greater detail.

Prejudice and Stereotypy

SOCIAL DISTANCE QUOTIENTS

In order to examine the relationship between ethnic imagery and prejudice, the latter was measured by social distance scales. Respondents were asked to which of the following types of social contact they would admit the average member of each of 24 ethnic groups:

1. to close kinship by marriage
2. to my club as personal friends
3. to my street as neighbors
4. to employment in my occupation
5. to citizenship in my country
6. as visitors only to my country
7. would exclude from any country

The social distance quotient (SDQ) for a given group was determined by computing the arithmetic mean of the number beside the most intimate relationship permitted by a respondent. Small means denote low social distance.

Table 3 shows the order of acceptance of the 24 groups. As in most other social distance studies conducted elsewhere, respondents' own nationality, Canadian in this case, received the top ranking. With the exception of the Ukrainians and Poles, the first 11 positions were accorded to Western European groups. Groups of non-Caucasian racial origin occupy the bottom one-third of the positions. Less social distance was expressed toward blacks than toward orientals or Canadian Indians. The Hutterites occupy the last rank. However, the social distance expressed towards the Hutterites undoubtedly partially reflects respondents' compliance with the Hutterites' desire to remain apart from the rest of society.

These results were compared with those of Hirabayashi (1963) who conducted a study in Edmonton using the same method. A rank order correlation of .94 indicates remarkable stability in the *rank* accorded these 24 groups. The *numerical scores*, however, showed substantial reduction which indicates that between 1963 and 1969 only the Hutterites failed to gain in acceptability.

TABLE 3
SOCIAL DISTANCE QUOTIENTS

Ethnic Group	Semantic Differential S.D.Q.	Open-Ended S.D.Q.
Canadians	1.10 (1)	1.07 (1)
British	1.30 (2)	1.33 (2)
Americans	1.39 (3)	1.43 (5)
Dutch	1.41 (4)	1.46 (6)
Norwegians	1.42 (5)	1.37 (4)
Swedes	1.43 (6)	1.34 (3)
Germans	1.59 (7)	1.72 (10)
French Canadians	1.67 (8)	1.76 (11)
Ukrainians	1.67 (9)	1.67 (7)
Poles	1.71 (10)	1.72 (9)
French	1.74 (11)	1.71 (8)
Hungarians	1.84 (12)	1.89 (12)
Italians	2.07 (13)	2.18 (15)
Negroes	2.21 (14)	2.17 (14)
Jews	2.22 (15)	2.08 (13)
Russians	2.28 (16)	2.28 (17)
Chinese	2.32 (17)	2.34 (18)
Japanese	2.34 (18)	2.37 (19)
West Indians	2.34 (19)	2.27 (16)
Eskimos	2.40 (20)	2.40 (20)
Indians (India)	2.46 (21)	2.47 (21)
N.A. Indians	2.50 (22)	2.52 (23)
Metis	2.63 (23)	2.48 (22)
Hutterites	3.68 (24)	3.69 (24)

RELATIONSHIP BETWEEN SOCIAL DISTANCE AND STEREOTYPING

The following hypothesis derived from the literature's assumption of covariance between stereotyping and prejudice: as the social distance position of an ethnic group increases the amount and degree of stereotyping of that group increases. Amount and degree of stereotyping refer to quantity of traits and extremity of trait ascription, respectively.

Stereotypes had been obtained in the study for the Indians, Ukrainians, Hutterites, and Jews. Although the Jewish stereotype was excluded from the validation portion of the study, all four stereotypes were used in the test of this hypothesis. Only the conclusions are discussed here; the reader is referred to Mackie (1971) for the details of this analysis.

In order to test this hypothesis, the total sample of respondents was divided into subsamples which expressed low social distance and subsamples which expressed high social distance in relation to the four ethnic groups. Their stereotyping behaviour was then compared. Prejudiced respondents did not assign a greater number of traits. Contrary to what one would expect if the above hypothesis were true, disposition to admit an ethnic group to close association was found to be related to richer cognitive imagery concerning that group. Further, antipathy towards ethnic groups was not directly associated with degree of stereotypy (extreme semantic differential means which deviate from the neutral "4" position).

However, the above findings do not exclude the possibility that prejudiced people assign a limited number of derogatory traits. Therefore, the relationship between high social distance and assignment of unflattering traits was explored. The results indicated that greater social distance is not associated with either more frequent or more extreme attribution of negative traits. Nonetheless, a few exceptions to this pattern did reflect the possibly universal affinity for calling enemies by "bad" names. Perhaps the confusion of sterotypy with prejudice emanated from preoccupation with epithets (e.g. dirty, stupid) which express both aversion and behaviorial description. It must therefore be emphasized that most stereotypes encompass a far greater proportion of favorable and neutral traits.

DISCUSSION

With regard to the relationship between stereotypy and prejudice, the data support the conclusion that other factors besides affection or antipathy for a group influence impressions of that group. In view of this study's results, the proposition that hatred is *only* built out of false impressions becomes questionable. Stereotypes are also the product of a need to cognitively "map" the ethnic group environment.

CONCLUSION

The results suggest that contemporary Albertans are fairly accurate observers of the ethnic scene. Had a similar study been conducted 25 years ago the conclusion might have been quite different (Palmer, 1974).

The dispute of minority group sympathizers should not be with outsiders who recognize differences but rather with those who confuse difference with inequality. Canadian society cannot be understood apart from the activities of ethnic groups striving to preserve their unique identities. If there are distinctive cultures and if a culture's distinctive values and consequent character are worth defending, then there must be some differences perceptible to others. However, the history of the three Alberta groups under purview demonstrates that cultural differences may be met with disdain rather than respect. Hostile imagery has indeed had deleterious consequences for certain stigmatized groups. For example, in the United States, the allegedly lower intellectual potential of blacks has been used to justify school segregation. "Undesirable" Jewish traits provided the Nazis with rationalization for their "final solution". Nevertheless, the fact that stereotypes have played a role in the victimization of minority groups does not answer the theoretical questions addressed by this study.

The study has established that stereotypes are not fallacious by definition. Accuracy is a *variable* and further inquiry is required into the conditions under which stereotypes are correct or incorrect. Moreover, stereotypes and prejudice are not invariably co-existent phenomena. Equating the terms leads to the absurd conclusion that the images of people who are friendly or indifferent toward ethnic groups cannot be labelled stereotypes. Stereotyping is normal behaviour which is not confined to pathological personalities.

NOTES

[1]Exceptions do, of course, exist. Scholars who have taken a more critical position include Campbell (1967), Fishman (1956), and Schuman (1966).

[2]The interested reader is referred to the original work for the methodological details, literature citations, and supporting evidence which had to be omitted from this abridgement. The assistance of Gwynn Nettler with the parent study is gratefully acknowledged.

[3]Stereotypes are defined as consensual folk beliefs about the characteristics of social categories. In other words, a sample of laymen agree in their assignment of a collection of traits to a given ethnic or non-ethnic group. The idea that the traits differentiate the group from the majority society is implicit. Although this definition omits reference to stereotype inaccuracy, the variable under purview, it otherwise conforms to decades of academic usage (Vinacke, 1957).

[4]Existing groups were used in order to expand the scope of the sample beyond the usual university student samples. Although the aim was not representativeness, the comparison of sample characteristics with the 1961 Edmonton census distributions makes explicit possible limitations to the generalizability of this study's findings. As compared with census distributions, the study sample overrepresents young people and those from higher education and socioeconomic status levels. With the exception of the 15-24 age category where females are overrepresented, sex ratios are reasonably congruent with those for the Edmonton area. Preliminary analysis assured that the stereotypes assessed for accuracy represented the views of the sample as a whole and not those of only a few demographic subsamples.

[5]The original paper required 170 pages to discuss the validation material. Only a summary presentation is possible here.

[6]The Hutterite stereotype is discussed at length in Mackie (1975).

REFERENCES

Bennett, John W., *Hutterian Brethren: The Agricultural Economy and Social Organization of a Communal People*. Stanford: Stanford University Press, 1967.

Blishen, Bernard R., "A Socio-Economic Index for Occupations in Canada." *The Canadian Review of Sociology and Anthropology*, 4, 1967 (February):41-53.

Bogardus, Emory S., "Measuring Social Distances." *Journal of Applied Sociology,* 9, 1925:299-308.

Brigham, John C., "Ethnic Stereotypes." *Psychological Bulletin,* 76, 1971 (July):15-38.

Cameron, Ann and Thomas Storm, "Achievement Motivation in Canadian Indian, Middle- and Working-Class Children." *Psychological Reports,* 16, 1965:459-463.

Campbell, Donald T., "Stereotypes and the Perception of Group Differences." *American Psychologist,* 22, 1967:817-829.

Campbell, Donald T. and R. A. LeVine, *Propositions about Ethnocentrism from Social Science Theories.* Mimeographed paper, Northwestern University, 1965.

Canadian Corrections Association, *Indians and the Law.* Ottawa: Queen's Printer, 1967.

Commission on Bilingualism and Biculturalism, *The Cultural Contribution of the Other Ethnic Groups.* Ottawa: Queen's Printer, 1969.

Eaton, Joseph W. and Robert J. Weil, *Culture and Mental Disorders: A Comparative Study of the Hutterites and Other Populations.* Glencoe: Free Press, 1955.

Ehrlich, Howard J. and James W. Rinehart, "A Brief Report on the Methodology of Stereotype Research." *Social Forces,* 43, 1965:564-575.

Fisher, A. D. "Education and Social Progress." *Alberta Journal of Educational Research,* 12, 1966 (December): 257-68.

Fishman, Joshua A., (1956) "An Examination of the Process and Function of Social Stereotyping." *Journal of Social Psychology,* 43, 1956 (February): 27-64.

Gardner, R. C., E. Joy Wonnacott, and D. M. Taylor, "Ethnic Stereotypes: A Factor Analytic Investigation." *Canadian Journal of Psychology,* 22, 1968: 35-44.

Harding, J., H. Proshansky, B. Kutner, and I. Chein, "Prejudice and Ethnic Relations." Pp. 1-76 in Gardner Lindzey and Elliot Aronson (eds.), *The Handbook of Social Psychology,* Volume 5. Reading: Addison-Wesley, 1969.

Hawthorn, Harry B. and M. A. Tremblay, *A Survey of the Contemporary Indians of Canada, Volume I.* Ottawa: Indian Affairs Branch, 1966.

—————, *A Survey of the Contemporary Indians of Canada, Volume II.* Ottawa: Indian Affairs Branch, 1967.

Hirabayashi, G. K., "Social Distance and the Modernizing Metis." Pp. 355-374 in B. Y. Card, G. K. Hirabayashi, and C. L. French, *The Metis in Alberta Society.* Edmonton: University of Alberta, 1963.

Hobart, Charles W., *Community Opportunity Assessment, General Report.* Edmonton: Human Resources and Research and Development, Executive Council, 1967.

Hobart, C. W., W. E. Kalbach, J. T. Borhek, and A. P. Jacoby, (1967) *Persistence and Change: A Study of Ukrainians in Alberta.* Edmonton: Ukrainian Canadian Research Foundation, Inc., 1967.

Hostetler, John A., *Education and Marginality in the Communal Society of the Hutterites.* Washington: Department of Health, Education and Welfare, 1965.

Katz, Daniel and Kenneth W. Braly, "Racial Stereotypes of 100 College Students." *Journal of Abnormal and Social Psychology,* 28, 1933:280-290.

Klineberg, Otto, *Tension Affecting International Understanding.* New York: Social Science Research Council, 1950.

LaPiere, Richard T., "Type-Rationalizations of Group Antipathy." *Social Forces,* 15, 1930:232-37.

Lippmann, Walter, *Public Opinion.* New York: Harcourt, Brace, 1922.

Mackie, Marlene, "The Accuracy of Folk Knowledge Concerning Alberta Indians, Hutterites, and Ukrainians." Unpublished doctoral dissertation, The University of Alberta, 1971.

_____, "Arriving at 'truth' by Definition: The Case of Stereotype Inaccuracy." *Social Problems,* 20, 1973 (Spring): 431-447.

_____, "Outsiders' Perception of the Hutterites." (1975) *Mennonite Quarterly Review* (Forthcoming).

Mange, Arthur P., "Growth and Inbreeding of a Human Isolate." *Human Biology,* 36, 1964 (May): 104-33.

McGrath, W. T., *Report of the Alberta Penology Study.* Edmonton: Queen's Printer, 1968.

Newman, Morton, *Community Opportunity Assessment, Appendix F. Indians of the Saddle Lake Reserve.* Edmonton: Human Resources Research and Development, Executive Council, 1967.

Palmer, Howard, "Nativism in Alberta: 1925-1930." Paper presented at the Meeting of Canadian Historical Association, Toronto, 1974.

Peters, Victor, *All Things Common: The Hutterian Way of Life.* Minneapolis: University of Minnesota Press, 1965.

Sanders, Douglas E., "The Hutterites: A Case Study in Minority Rights." *The Canadian Bar Review,* 42, 1964 (May): 225-42.

Schuman, Harold, "Social Change and the Validity of Regional Stereotypes in East Pakistan." *Sociometry,* 29, 1966 (December): 428-440.

Sharplin, C. D., *The Indian Alcoholic: His Social Characteristics.* Mimeographed paper, Edmonton: Alcoholism Foundation of Alberta, 1964.

Sue, Stanley and Harry H. L. Kitano, "Stereotypes as a Measure of Success." *Journal of Social Issues,* 29, 1973:83-98.

Triandis, Harry C. and Vasso Vassiliou, "Frequency of Contact and Stereotyping." *Journal of Personality and Social Psychology,* 7, 1967:316-328.

Vinacke, W. Edgar, "Stereotypes as Social Concepts." *Journal of Social Psychology,* 46, 1957 (November): 229-243.

Chapter 15

Reciprocal Exploitation in an Indian-White Community*[1]

Niels W. Braroe

In this chapter I shall examine the manner in which conceptions of self and others held by Indians and whites contribute stability to a community structure of roles and values which is riddled with apparent inconsistency and contradiction. As a point of departure, I shall focus on a recurrent type of behavior: the practice by Indians and whites alike of "victimizing" one another, of misrepresenting the self and self-motivations in social and economic transactions. The insight gleaned from consideration of these performances will be offered in support of the hypothesis that these misrepresentations allow both Indians and whites to resolve value and role contradictions which might otherwise engender social conflict or personal disorganization.

I

The perspective adopted in this chapter draws on the work of Rose, Goffman, Berreman and others relating to the nature of the self and human interaction. Human beings are categorized according to the major roles they

*Reprinted from the *Southwestern Journal of Anthropology* 21:2 (1965), by permission of the author and the publisher.

enact in society, roles being a "cluster of related meanings and values that guide and direct an individual's behavior in a given social setting . . ."[2]. Roles and the self are seen as growing out of continuous social symbolic interaction in which individuals present and express themselves in ways intended to influence a shared definition of the situation. A large portion of this interaction is concerned with crediting or discrediting the selves thus presented: "this imputation — this self — is a *product* of the scene that comes off . . .".[3]

Two aspects of this perspective are prominent in the following pages. The first deals with the tendency of the participants in a community or a social setting to arrive at a working consensus, an agreement about how they will behave toward one another and upon the symbols and meanings which will guide this action. Secondly, people generally work to support consensus and devise means of avoiding its disintegration and the associated failure of self-validations.

> A person is an individual who becomes involved in a value of some kind . . . and then makes a public claim that he is to be defined and treated as someone who possesses the value or property in question. The limits to his claims, and hence the limits to his self, are primarily determined by the objective facts of his social life and secondarily determined by the degree to which a sympathetic interpretation of these facts can bend them in his favor. Any event which demonstrates that someone has made a false claim, defining himself as something which he is not, tends to destroy him.[4]

This paper explores self and other images of white and Indian persons vis-à-vis one another. Attention is directed to the ways in which each credits or validates the roles and self of the other in the context of a community "working consensus" that provides the framework of day-to-day interaction. One question is central to this discussion: how do Indians adapt to circumstances of economic and social deprivation? How do they adapt to membership in the lowest category of a rigidly hierarchical status system?

II

Jasper is town of about 2400 persons on the western prairie of Saskatchewan.[5] Small-scale cattle ranching and mixed farming are the predominant economic activities of whites in this region; they come to Jasper for goods and services, and often move there after retirement. In Jasper there are two general stores, a movie theatre, two small hotels, a pub, three Chinese-owned restaurants, several auto and farm equipment stores and so on. The town, however, is no longer the isolated focus of patterns of leisure and consumption, as area residents now make frequent trips to a shopping center in a small city about sixty miles away.

Twenty miles from town is a small non-treaty Indian reserve which is the home of about a hundred and ten Plains Cree. The Indians make their living by the sale of poplar posts to ranchers and to the lumber yard in town, and by seasonal agricultural labor. All receive government relief, their most stable source of income. Jasper Indians do not identify with whites to the extent that white cultural goals and values are outwardly accepted and Indian ones entirely rejected. They revere generosity and sharing, for example, and ridicule white ideas about the dignity of work, the accumulation of material goods, punctuality and the like. The fact that so few of them are acculturated — that is, display their selves as white — is not difficult to understand given the nature of their relations with the dominant society; these relations impede the communication of white culture and limit the participation of Indians in white institutional activities. Until six years ago there was no school for Indian children; even now their school is segregated on the reserve. Since most parents do not value education, class attendance is poor. Children do not learn to speak English until they are six or seven years old. Jasper Indians uniformly profess belief in "Indian" religion and emphatically call attention to their participation in it. None of the Indians are even nominally Christian, and there is no record of any effort in the past generation to convert them. No one among them has ever served in the military.

While Indians go to town frequently, even in the worst weather, the reserve itself is isolated. Whites seldom visit it and never live there. A policeman said, "We don't really know what goes on up there, don't really care as long as they don't make trouble in town." Lacking electricity, reserve Indians have no radios or television sets, and hence are further isolated by minimal exposure to mass media.[6] Occupational opportunities in town do not exist. None of the merchants or businessmen questioned said that they were willing to hire Indians, even for the most menial tasks.

Similarly, the legal status of Indians and their dependence on paternalistic government relief are important factors in their marginal involvement in the local economy. They do not have the capital resources to increase the income from communally-owned reserve holdings. They have not learned skills that would bring them regular employment in the Jasper community or allow them to emigrate to a more favorable urban location.[7]

Attitudes of whites toward Indians are obstacles to Indian assimilation. The common denominator of nearly all of these attitudes is that Indians are childish and irresponsible. For some, such as the man to whom Indians bring their dilapidated cars for repair, this is mixed with pity. He knows that his work will likely go unpaid, but he says, "They can't help it, they're just kids with money. They got nothing, and whenever they do get a little money they can't wait to spend it." At the other extreme there are people who share this appraisal of Indian character as child-like, but who express a spare-the-rod-spoil-the-child opinion. They insist that Indians should be compelled to behave responsibly and that they ought to be given no social privileges or aid until they do so. Others, including many ranchers, think that Indians should be allowed to rot. "I can make a living off this land," they say, "why can't they? It's because we help them so much that they're so lazy."

Jasper whites not only consider Indians to be irresponsible, but speak of them as worthless. Some see them circumstantially so, others consider Indians worthless as human beings. For the latter, Indians are innately without value, and no amount of "help" by white society will ever make Indians self-sufficient. They are regarded as parasites, a liability inherited from the past. Few whites, however, display active hostility toward Indians, not excluding those who consider them little more than superfluous appendages to white society. The absence of malice on the part of whites is one of the most remarkable aspects of Indian-white relations. Even those white men who have been involved in brawls with Indians do not bear animosity toward them. In fact, both Indians and whites describe these events with the greatest amusement.

The conception which whites have of Indians differs dramatically from whites' image of themselves. They extol responsibility, independence and self-sufficiency. The residents of Jasper and its surroundings feel themselves close to the western frontier era — indeed this part of North America was the scene of the closing days of the "Old West." A sentiment commonly expressed by Jasper whites is one of confidence in the face of adversity, of dauntlessness in the confrontation of nature. Town-dwelling men speak with pride of the ability to "take care of myself." Only Indians go on relief. The image of the strong, silent cowboy is taken seriously in Jasper. With it go the attributes of unwavering integrity, fairness and helpfulness. Jasper is a particularistic community, where people applaud the man who is willing to help others without demanding repayment; but they believe that a man must not accept a hand unless he intends to reciprocate someday. These values pervade the complex, reticulate cooperative work groups among ranchers.

III

The whites' emphasis upon the values of integrity and charity are often not discernible in their day-to-day behavior toward Indians. Indians who have cut and cured poplar posts near the reserve, and who do not have trucks, persuade whites to haul the posts to town. For his small investment of time, the white charges as much as 25 percent of the load's value; customarily he goes into the lumber yard office to collect his money from the manager while the Indian unloads the posts in the yard. Whites say that one has to pocket one's money before the Indian "gets his hands on it," or risk never being paid. Again, whites frequently take advantage of the restrictions placed upon Indians in disposing of reserve resources. The law forbids Indians to sell cattle or hay without permission from the Indian agent, and the money from such sales is supposed to go to a common reserve fund rather than to individual Indians.[8] To circumvent this, Indians sell these things to whites, but for only a fraction of their value. Similarly, a few ranchers take advantage of the Indians' desire for spending money, by arranging to place cattle on reserve pasture for much less than it would cost if legal channels were used. In this way a small "grazing fee" is collected by an Indian who needs money for a trip to a Sun Dance on another reserve, and the white is enabled to feed his cattle for a pittance. Indians are overcharged for merchandise and services in town, and they are paid less for their labor than a white man would be. Indian women are not infrequently objects of white sexual gratification.

White belief in the irresponsibility of Indians is demonstrated continuously. For example, at the suggestion of some Jasper residents, the Indian department no longer gives relief money directly to the Indians. Instead, a local general store receives these funds, which are credited to Indian families to whom supplies of food and clothing are doled out on a weekly basis.

While not all whites engage in these practices, those who do are neither publicly nor privately censured by those who do not have such dealings with Indians. Neither do white members of the Jasper community comment upon the less direct deprivation of Indians. The legal and political status of Indians is, of course, a matter of national governmental policy. But whites make no effort to bring about policy changes which might lead to Indian self-sufficiency, nor do they take action at the local community level to provide Indians with occupational skills or agricultural training which would improve Indian standards of living.

In a particularistic community where standards of honesty and humaneness are prized, the exploitation and deprivation of a segment of that community stands out as a manifest anomaly. It is not out of place to ask how the conceptions of self which incorporate these values also incorporate behavior and attitudes which contradict them. One way to minimize this conflict is to insist upon maintaining social distance between whites and Indians. This amounts to ignoring that a conflict exists. To a certain extent, the white members of the Jasper community take this solution. For instance, an examination of back issues of the weekly Jasper newspaper for its sixty year history revealed that, apart from mentions of Indians in the "Police Court" column, there has been no recognition that an Indian reserve exists near Jasper. Not even editorial notice has been taken of the Indian members of the community.

It is impossible, nonetheless, for Jasper whites always to ignore the presence and condition of Indians. There are other features of white deportment toward Indians which lend understanding of how apparent value contradictions are resolved. To identify these, it is useful to consider some of the ways that Indians, in turn, "con" white men.

Jasper Indians find one source of income in the poplar posts which they cut from reserve lands and (illegally) from the nearby forest preserve. Ordinarily, these are soaked in a "bluestone" preservative for about a day. Sometimes an impatient Indian will paint the posts with laundry blueing instead and then sell them to an unsuspecting white man. Another quick way of getting money is to sell a quantity of posts sight unseen, telling the buyer that they are stacked at some spot on the reserve. When the white man returns later, having found no posts, the Indian innocently conjectures that "somebody musta stole 'em." Again, Indians are able to stack posts for white buyers in such a way that there appear to be more than there actually are.

The "con game" played by Indians against whites is often carried out in the context of enduring relationships. For example, one Indian, John Sweet Grass, receives a monthly disability check from the government for about seventy dollars. Each month, he takes part of it to the owner of an appliance store in Jasper to "hold" for him, with the understanding that he may request small amounts of it at any time. By the end of every month John has overdrawn his allowance, and the financial state of affairs betwen him and his "banker" is hopelessly confused, as it has been for years. In effect, John has a reliable, permanent source of spending money. The storekeeper laments, "I really don't know anymore *how* much he owes me, I probably never will. What can I do? If I don't take care of him, he'll probably starve."

At every turn, Indians act the part of con artists in their dealings with whites. An Indian will call at the home of an absent white man and tell his wife that her husband instructed him to get from her several dollars due him for some work done. When the husband returns, his wife discovers that the payment was for an imaginary task — *he* hasn't seen the Indian in weeks.

Incidents of Indians duping whites occur with persistent, almost monotonous regularity: an Indian persuades a white to transport him and his family home from town in sub-zero weather for some agreed-upon price. When they arrive at the reserve, the Indian proclaims that he "hasn't got the money now, but I'll pay you later," which means never. A common way for Indians to borrow money is to offer some useless, worthless item as security — a piece of clothing or household utensil — and then never return to claim it, nor to pay the debt.

One of the most celebrated recent coups concerned the illegal sale of a water pump and windmill by several Indians to a neighbouring rancher. This man paid for the machinery and steel tower on which it was mounted without a permit from the Indian agent, whose office is more than a hundred miles from Jasper. The rancher and his son dissassembled the purchase and took it home. That night, the same Indians collected the tower and pump, hauled it into town, and resold it the next day to a junk dealer. In these transactions, whites do not hold Indians guilty for their behavior. They do not complain to the police when they suffer losses, even in cases where there is proof that Indians are the malefactors. A rancher from whom Indians regularly poach chickens, says, "They know that all they have to do is ask me for 'em if they were really hungry, but they'd rather steal 'em."

Why, one may ask, does a white man, whom we should expect to know better, buy a pig-in-a-poke? Why, in their relations with Indians, do whites keep coming back for more? Why is an Indian lent money when all past experience must teach that it probably will never be returned? One outcome of the usual sequence of events in a con is that the "mark" learns his lesson; he is presumably a poorer but a more cautious man. We must look elsewhere for the source of white gullibility than in some sort of "mass stupidity" or failure to learn from experience. In fact, Jasper whites *expect* to be conned by Indians; storekeepers extend credit to Indians knowing that the accounts will never be settled.[9] It may be suggested that whites allow Indians to con them in order that Indian irresponsibility and childishness may be demonstrated and confirmed. A rancher pays an Indian in advance for his labor in stacking bales of hay. When the Indian does not show up to fulfill his part of the bargain, the rancher's image of the Indian as irresponsible is validated. His tolerance of the social deprivation of Indians can then be justified: "They *are* children and irresponsible. They are not really men, so they cannot be expected to participate in the adult world." Similarly, those whites who directly exploit Indians are provided a means of preserving a defensible image of self: "Sure, he takes advantage of me, but then, that is to be expected of children. I graze my cattle on the reserve, but then I'm the one who takes care of him, who gives him money, and sees that he does not starve." Not a few whites are persuaded that Indians have no desire to adopt white roles. A veterinarian claimed, "The last thing they want is to live like white men — they're no more than unemployed buffalo hunters, and happy just like they are."

IV

Looking at these transactions from an Indian point of view, an arresting feature is disclosed. Most Indians do not accept white judgments of their role, their self or their personal worth. Still, they seldom openly dispute white conceptions of Indian character — in fact, as we have seen, they behave in such a way to validate the white image of themselves.

Indians do not regard themselves as foolish children; on the contrary they consider themselves rather artful and successful exploiters of white men. What they do is to represent themselves to white audiences as the sort of persons whites take them to be, and represent themselves to other Indians as something different. In their performances before whites, Indians acknowledge irresponsibility, but they perform for a dual audience; to other Indians they are seen as turning to account (mistaken) white imputations of themselves.

Backstage, in Goffman's terminology, Indians "drop the front." In this region, "the impression fostered by the performance is knowingly contradicted as a matter of course"[10]. Jokes are made about the stupidity of whites and the ease with which they are taken in. Fine points of strategy are discussed. "The way to get off easy," according to one informant, "is to act like a dumb Indian in front of the magistrate." This way, the punishment for being drunk and disorderly will be lighter than a white man would receive, and "credit" can even be arranged — the magistrate will give the guilty Indian months to pay his fine.

Much of this backstage activity resembles that reported by Berreman for the Aleut. Aleuts, though they identify with whites as a *valuation group*, respond to the denial of entrance into white institutional activities by valuation group alienation. They have come to look more appreciatively at white society, but, deprived of acceptance by whites, they orient themselves negatively towards those people toward whose cultural values and goals they are drawn. "Role segregation" and "role-distance" are two of the means Aleuts employ to cope with their ambivalence.[11]

Earlier, we observed that Jasper Indians are excluded from playing white roles, and that structural barriers prevent Indians participation in the larger society. It was noted that, to a greater or lesser extent, most Jasper Indians do not perform in the presence of a white audience in a fashion which suggests that they embrace white cultural goals. The impression of them was that they are relatively "unacculturated." Nevertheless, it is evident that Jasper Indians too have begun to identify positively with white culture. In spite of the barriers to acculturation, they show signs of having recognized the taking of white roles as desirable. Perhaps one of the facilitating circumstances of this process has been the similarity between some of the principal values of traditional Plains Indian culture and those of the Anglo-American Jasper community. Standards of masculinity, competitiveness, a dual standard of sex behavior, qualities of leadership and the like are features of value orientations among Jasper whites which are remarkably like value orientations of the formerly more autonomous Plains Cree. We may expect that a group of one cultural heritage will identify with a group of another with greater ease when their conceptions of the male role contain analogous properties.

Many aspects of the structural relations between whites and Indians have worked toward acceptance by Indians of white cultural goals and meanings. For one, the extermination of the buffalo and the demise of the traditional pattern of Plains subsistence forced Indians to search elsewhere for means of livelihood. Formerly, Indians were spatially less isolated from whites than today; in the last ten years all of the white families but one which lived in the hills near the reserve have moved away because of the cold, lonely winters. Today also, with modern mechanized agriculture, the demand for Indian labor has declined. In the early reserve period, after the turn of the century, it was common for Indian families to live for long periods on the property of ranchers for whom they worked. Some Jasper adults, in fact, were born on ranches where their parents lived permanently, in familiar interaction with their white employers.

Indians have other opportunities for exposure to white culture. All Indian women now go to the hospital in Jasper to have their children; Indian men mix with whites in the pub; Indian children now have a white schoolteacher: Jasper Indians maintain close relations with members of other reserves who are more acculturated than they.

Continuous face to face interaction over generations leads to some consensual definition of the situation, and it is reasonable to expect that the subordinate Indians should have incorporated into their conceptions of self some of the content of white roles. One piece of evidence indicating that Indians have come to regard whites as a positive reference group is that they frequently judge their own behavior by white standards. It is not uncommon for Indians to show remorse about excessive drinking, for example. Most Indians express a desire to be self-supporting, and to own land and cattle the same as their white neighbors. An excerpt from the author's field diary is illustrative:

> Saturday nite: Charlie Running Calf, his wife and I strolled around town this evening. Charlie, who had been hauling bales on Newcomb's ranch for the past two days, had just come from the pub and was a little tight. We passed Roger McDougal. Charlie said, "Hiya Roger, how you been," in an expansive tone. Charlie's wife said, "*Charlie,* you can't talk to those people like that." He replied, "Whatdya mean, I'm a *workin'* man, ain't I?"

However much Indians embrace white culture, they are refused the privilege of playing white roles. They cannot go into business for themselves, as has been indicated, because their legal status prohibits the accumulation of the capital necessary to engage in full-scale farming or ranching. Nor have they skills which would allow wage employment off the reserve. Consequently, Jasper Indians are alienated from their valuation group just as Berreman's Aleuts were. If they cannot be white, however, it is necessary for them to define the self ". . . along defensible lines". This must futhermore be done in a way that permits validation of this self by whites. To the Indian, then, his "irresponsible" performances declare: "Because I can trick white men so easily, they are not as smart as they think they are. *I'm* the one who's taking advantage of them. I can make a living by my wits.

V

We have looked at some of the ways whites and Indians in a small community portray the self in the ordinary course of daily life. We have seen also how the actions of each group validate the claims of the other. Indians and whites successfully predict one another's behavior, in a manner which mutually credits images of Indian and white selves. Among the consequences of this exchange, two are selected here for discussion.

In his article, "On Cooling the Mark Out," Erving Goffman[12] addresses himself to the problem of adaptations which people make to failure, to the ways that individuals deal with repudiations of the self which are implied by the unsuccessful fulfillment of some role. It often becomes necessary that a person whose self has suffered failure be "consoled" by some other person. He is helped to adjust to his loss, his is "cooled out." This is particularly important when a person is deeply engaged in this self, and where its loss reflects upon him negatively. It sometimes occurs, Goffman adds, that the various participants in a network of interaction take measures to avoid altogether the troublesome procedure of cooling out; they attempt to cover up the fact that a person has failed or that his value as an individual is negligible.

Such processes may be recognized in transactions between Jasper whites and Indians. Indians do not have the liberty of playing white roles, but at the same time they increasingly identify with these roles and with white cultural values. They are accordingly in the plight of people whose worth is denied. Indians cannot salvage much of their value in the estimation of whites, but they do have means of saving face in the eyes of other Indians. This is accomplished, we have noted, when the Indian sub-community observes one of its members making a fool of a white man, bringing off some deception with impunity. In effect, the validation of this transaction by white serves to "cool out" Indians. Now, few Jasper Indians show evidence of serious personal disorganization, a consequence, it is proposed, of whites and Indians having found a way of avoiding a confrontation. Whites, at the same time, are spared the malaise of recognising moral inconsistency in their own behavior.

Routines of self-presentation and identification in Jasper have consequences for stability at the structural as well as at the personal level.[13] The successful cooling out of a failure means that he will be less likely to protest or to threaten the established system of social relationships. The position of Indians in Jasper is one of subordination and deprivation. The social-psychological dynamics of role-playing and identification take place in a manner which contributes to the perpetuation of a caste-like status system. Indians are provided an "out," entailing adjustment to a place in their social environment which would otherwise be intolerable. The alternative to acquiescence, of course, would be for Indians to try to alter their environment, to challenge white superordination. Support for this assertion can be found in historical data, and in the examination of instances where the customary validations of Indian and white images of self fail.

Nearly a hundred years ago, not far from Jasper, a group of white traders "massacred" a small band of Indian horse-thieves. The expedition was organized by a white man whose horse had been stolen by an Indian, sold back to him, and then stolen again by the same Indian; the whites attacked a camp where they believed the culprit was hiding. The significant aspect of white ideas about Indians at that time was that they were held responsible for their behavior and punishable for their deceptions. In this and numerous other instances, whites were not indulgently disposed to treat Indians as irresponsible, and the outcome was frequently violent.

Today, when representations of Indian and white selves fail, persons are embarassed, insulted or provoked. An Indian, for example, inopportunely asked a white man in town for several dollars. He was refused, and told that he was a worthless beggar, incapable of properly supporting his wife and children. The Indian was affronted, enraged, and the two men exchanged blows in the street. It was not so much the refusal that brought violence, as the white's rejection of the self presented by the Indian. The normal course of interaction was disrupted when the white man withheld agreement to a definition of the situation including an image of the Indian as uncommitted to white values and unobligated by white standards of responsibility.

In this chapter I have decribed something of the tenor of Indian-white interaction, employing the social-psychological perspective which stresses role-taking, performances and the self. It was suggested that a social structure including the superordination of whites over Indians is supported through a consensual definition of the situation embodying images of self which Indians and whites present to one another. The analysis was not exclusively concerned with the *results* of acculturation, or the extent to which Indians overtly embrace white values, but considered as well the kinds of involvement of these values in selves identified with whites and Indians vis-à-vis one another. In other words, the emphasis has been on the *mechanisms* of acculturative processes rather than upon the conditions of culture contact or the larger, more abstract, results of contact. As much space has been devoted to the "how" of persistence of Indian segregation — the complimentary presentation of diverse self images — as to the "why."

A final comment is in order. Looking at the results of acculturation rather than at the daily interplay between whites and Indians, one might conclude that differences in cultural values expressed in the different presentations of self represent points of tension or potential conflict between whites and Indians. The evidence presented above suggests that such a view is not entirely accurate. The different sets of values embodied in Indian and white roles constitute an accommodation or a *solution* to certain conflicts and not merely a source of them. It is, in fact, because of the contrasting images of Indian and white man that interaction proceeds with as little conflict as actually occurs.

NOTES

[1] The research upon which this paper is based was done in the summer of 1963.

[2] A.M. Rose, "A Systematic Summary of Symbolic Interaction Theory," *Human Behavior and Social Processes* (ed. by A.M. Rose) (Boston, 1962), p. 10.

[3] E. Goffman, *The Presentation of Self in Everyday Life* (New York, 1959), p. 252.

[4] E. Goffman, "On Cooling the Mark Out," *Human Behavior and Social Processes* (ed. by A.M. Rose) (Boston, 1962), p. 500.

[5] The name "Jasper," and the names of all informants mentioned in this paper, are pseudonyms.

[6] Several families have quite recently acquired small transistor radios.

[7] One family of Jasper Indians does travel to Alberta each summer to work on the beet farms there. They return at the end of each season to spend the winter on the reserve.

[8] Six years ago, the Indian Affairs Branch supplied reserve families with a total of about seventy cows: today there are only about twenty-five. They have been sold (illegally), eaten and allowed to starve or freeze to death.

[9] White residents of Jasper, especially those who have fewest contacts with Indians, and who are the most literate members of the community, point to a novel as an accurate portrayal of Indian character. *Stay Away, Joe,* by Dan Cushman, describes the slapstick adventures of a young Indian in his con game with white society. "If you want to know what Indians are *really* like," they advise, "read that book, it's a scream."

[10] Goffman, 1959, *op. cit.* (note 3, *supra*), p. 117.

[11] G.D. Berreman, "Aleut Reference Group Alienation, Mobility, and Acculturation," *American Anthropologist,* vol. 66 (1964), p. 235.

[12]Note 4, *supra*.

[13]Both Indians and whites are, of course, largely unaware of the social and personal consequences of their behavior. It is likely that this ignorance is requisite to the achievement of these results.

Chapter 16

Multiculturalism and Ethnic Attitudes in Canada*

John W. Berry, Rudolf Kalin, and Donald M. Taylor

The present study was designed to investigate the attitudes of Canadians toward multiculturalism. For the purposes of this research, multiculturalism refers to the existence of ethnic groups in Canada which derive from cultural traditions other than French or British, some members at least of whom wish to maintain their identity. The term also refers to the current policy of the Federal Government which seeks to promote the retention of these heritages and the sharing of them among all Canadians. The historical roots of the research lie in Book IV of the Report of the Royal Commission on Bilingualism and Biculturalism concernced with "the contribution made by the other ethnic groups to the cultural enrichment of Canada, and the measures that should be taken to safeguard that contribution" (Book IV, p. 1). In 1971 a "policy of multiculturalism within a bilingual framework" was announced by the Prime Minister in response to the recommendations contained in Book IV. It sought to promote the retention of characteristic cultural features by those groups which desired to do so, and to encourage the sharing of these cultural features with other members of the larger

*Reprinted from *Multiculturalism and Ethnic Attitudes in Canada,* Ottawa: Supply and Services Canada, 1977, by permission of the authors and the Minister of Supply and Services Canada.

Canadian society. The policy was based upon the assumption that if an individual is to be open in his or her ethnic attitudes, and have respect for other groups, he or she must have confidence in his or her own cultural foundations. Given this assumption, the policy is also designed to help break down discriminatory attitudes and cultural jealousies.

The Research Question

A number of questions for research are implied in the policy. Two of the more obvious are whether Canadians view cultural diversity as a valuable resource, and whether confidence in one's own identity is a prerequisite for accepting others. These two questions constitute the core of the present study.

More specifically, the research reported here consisted of an examination of four attitude domains. The first dealt with the attitudes held by Canadians toward a variety of ethnic groups in the country; in this study these are referred to as "ethnic attitudes." The second domain involved general beliefs regarding cultural diversity, and more specific attitudes concerning various aspects of the multiculturalism policy; these are referred to as "multicultural attitudes." Third, as the Report of the Royal Commission (Book IV, p. 5) indicates, immigration from a variety of national origins creates the possibility for multiculturalism; clearly, attitudes toward immigration form an essential part of the study of attitudes toward multiculturalism. And finally, sections of this study were directed toward an area of concern implied in the Prime Minister's statement, namely, the psychological phenomena of ethnic prejudice and discrimination.

The Survey Instrument

A survey instrument was developed to gather information in all four attitude domains, and to assess demographic characteristics of respondents. The instrument not only employed "opinion" questions, but also made extensive use of psychological scales and sorting procedures in an attempt to improve reliability and validity of the data. For most opinion questions, respondents were provided with 7-point rating scales. These scales were used to express respondents' degrees of agreement/disagreement, their behavioural intentions, and the degrees to which specific ethnic groups possessed given characteristics.

The Sample

The sample of respondents was selected from a national sampling frame, covering approximately 95% of the population of Canada. Excluded were persons located in the extreme northern parts of the country, and those living on reservations and in institutions.

The sample design was complex and included stratification as well as clustering. The principles guiding the stratification procedures were region and population density. All census metropolitan areas were included in the sample. Stratification further ensured that in the rest of Canada, in each region and within regions each level of population density was adequately represented. Clustering was a way of making the sampling procedure economically feasible. It involved limiting the geographic areas from which sampling units were to be obtained. The sample selection process involved three stages. In the first, 374 census enumeration areas were chosen; in the second, 2844 households were selected; in the final stage 2628 eligible persons were obtained. To be eligible for inclusion in the sample, a person had to be at least 16 years of age and able to speak English or French. Interviews were completed with 1849 respondents; that is, the completion rate was 70%.

Each respondent was interviewed in person. On the average an interview took about one hour to complete. Interviews were conducted during June and July 1974, in either French or English. The interviewers were members of the field staff of the Survey Research Centre at York University and the Centre de Sondage at the Université de Montréal.

An examination of the sample's basic demographic (region of residence, age, sex), ethnic (ancestral country of origin, mother tongue) and socio-economic status (occupation, income and education) characteristics indicates that it closely approximates the characteristics of the Canadian population as revealed in the 1971 Census.

Variations in attitudes according to a number of background variables were examined. Among these were region of residence, ethnicity and socioeconomic status of respondent. In addition, analyses were carried out to examine variations in attitudes according to degree of urbanization, religion, political party preference, age and sex.

Demographic Variables

Geographic region. Respondents were categorized according to region of residence (Atlantic provinces (N = 176), Quebec (N = 488), Ontario (N = 695), Prairies (N = 291), British Columbia (N = 199). Additional analyses were carried out on the five largest metropolitan areas (Montreal, Toronto, Winnipeg, Calgary-Edmonton, Vancouver). Degree of urbanization was also considered within each region (rural, towns, small cities, and where possible metropolitan areas).

Ethnicity. A complex code was used to group respondents into four categories. This code took into account: (1) father's origin, (2) mother's birthplace, (3) ethnic self identity, (4) mother tongue, and (5) language of interview. In simplified terms, an Angloceltic Canadian was defined as a respondent whose father's ancestry was British or Irish. A French Canadian was a person who derived his ancestry from France. An anglophone "other ethnic" was a respondent whose father's ancestry was other than Angloceltic or French and who gave the interview in English. A francophone "other ethnic" was a person of non-British/non-French origin who gave the interview in French.

Generational status was another aspect of ethnicity that was examined. Respondents were categorized as immigrants, second, or third and higher generation Canadians. Since relatively few francophones in Canada are immigrants or second generation, generational status is strongly related to ethnicity. In order to control for ethnicity francophone respondents were excluded from this analysis and it was carried out separately for Angloceltic and "other ethnic" respondents.

A further analysis of ethnicity categorized respondents of "other ethnic" origin into the most numerous national descent groups (Dutch, German, Italian, Polish, Russian, Scandinavian, Ukrainian).

Socioeconomic status. Three indices of this demographic variable were employed: (1) head of household's occupational status (Blishen index), (2) head of household's income, and (3) respondent's educational level.

Political party preference. Respondents were grouped according to which of the four major federal political parties they supported. Since party support is related to ethnicity (French Canadians tend to be primarily Liberal), separate analyses were carried out within anglophone and francophone subsamples. Respondents who expressed a preference for something other than the four major parties were excluded from this analysis.

Age and sex. These were the final variables that were used in the analysis of attitudes.

Inter-relationships among demographic variables. Many of these demographic variables were related to each other. Of particular interest are those variables within the socioeconomic cluster, and their relationships to ethnicity and region. First, the three socioeconomic indices were substantially interrelated, with occupational status and education exhibiting the strongest relationship, and education and income the least. However, they were far from identical as measures of status, and so the three indices were employed separately in all analyses.

Among regions Ontario was high on all three socioeconomic variables; whereas, the Atlantic provinces and Quebec were lower, particularly on income and education. There was also a strong relationship between region and ethnicity, with the largest proportion of French-Canadian respondents residing in Quebec. And finally, there was a clear relationship between ethnicity and all three socioeconomic variables. French-Canadian respondents tended to occupy lower educational and occupational status categories, while Angloceltic respondents were notably higher on all three status indices.

Psychological Values

In addition to collecting demographic information on respondents, some of their psychological characteristics were assessed. The survey instrument included measures of authoritarianism, ethnocentrism and personal values, all of which have previously been related to ethnic prejudice. Since these measures have been extensively used in other societies, primarily the United States, it was possible to provide a tentative comparison of American and Canadian residents. The scales for authoritarianism and ethnocentrism were shown to measure coherent belief systems which correlated substantially with each other. While precise comparisons are difficult, Canadians appeared to be more authoritarian than Americans, but were not shown to be different from Americans in ethnocentrism. Canadians, like Americans, valued a world at peace and family security most highly and a world of beauty and social recognition the least. The value equality, which is predictive of ethnic tolerance, appeared in the middle of the value hierarchy in the present Canadian as well as in United States' sample. Analyses of differences within the present sample showed that French-Canadian respondents occupied a unique position in terms of the psychological characteristics under consideration. They, as compared with anglophone Canadians, were more authoritarian and ethnocentric, and they placed a relatively higher value on salvation and social recognition and a lower value on freedom and true friendship. Francophone "other ethnic" Canadians were like French Canadians in some respects and like anglophone Canadians in others. Angloceltic and anglophone "other ethnic" Canadians were not different from each other in terms of these psychological characteristics. A geographic analysis showed remarkable similarity among residents from Ontario to British Columbia. Quebec, being populated primarily by French Canadians, showed a profile essentially similar to that of French Canadians. Respondents from the Atlantic provinces were more authoritarian and ethnocentric than residents from other anglophone regions. Socioeconomic status differences were in line with previous research. Educational level, the index of socioeconomic status chosen here, showed a strong linear and inverse relationship with authoritarianism and ethnocentrism. With regard to values, it was found that the highly educated, as compared with the less educated, placed a lower priority on a comfortable life and on salvation, and a greater priority on freedom and self-respect.

Attitudes toward Immigration

Attitudes toward immigration were assessed in the present survey because of their relevance to multicultural ideology. Three attitude areas were tapped: (1) perceived consequences of immigration, (2) the acceptability of various types of immigrants, and (3) behavioural intentions toward immigrants and discrimination against them.

To assess perceived consequences of immigration, respondents were asked for their opinions regarding possible consequences of further immigration. They had to indicate their degree of agreement/disagreement with ten potential outcomes, such as "more unemployment," "this country would be better off" and "the purity of the Canadian race would be affected."

Analyses of responses showed that the ten items reflected a general attitude toward immigration consequences. The responses to the ten items were averaged to obtain an overall attitude score. Subsequent analyses were performed on this score as well as on the specific items dealing with "unemployment" and the "purity of the Canadian race."

The assessment of acceptability of immigrants was accomplished by asking respondents whether the government should accept or reject various types of immigrants, such as immigrants "who are coloured," "who have relatives in Canada," "who are highly educated," and "who are from communist countries." While some of these categories may be ambiguous (e.g., are immigrants from communist countries "pro-" or "anti-" communist?) it would have been difficult to be completely specific within the context of a national survey. After establishing that responses to the ten separate items reflected a general attitude, items were averaged to yield a total acceptability score. Subsequent analyses emphasized the total score but also dealt with the specific items concerning "coloured immigrants" and those from "communist countries."

Behavioural intentions toward immigrants were assessed by asking respondents a series of questions dealing with their willingness to interact with immigrants and members of the majority groups, of high or low status, in business or personal relationships. A discrimination score was constructed to reflect respondents' preference for English Canadians (in the case of anglophone respondents), or French Canadians (in the case of francophone respondents) over immigrants.

The attitude scales just described correlated significantly with each other. However, the correlations were far from perfect, indicating that while the scales reflect a general attitude toward immigration, each scale also measures something unique.

Attitudes toward immigration in the total sample. Perceived consequences of immigration were slightly positive, but there was considerable difference of opinion. Of greatest concern to respondents was the possibility that "there would be more unemployment" with continued immigration. There was, however, reasonably strong consensus that the identity of English and French Canadians, and the relations between these two groups, would not be affected.

Most types of immigrants were rated to be quite acceptable. Considered as most acceptable were "immigrants who could be useful to this country," "immigrants with a skilled trade," and "immigrants who are highly educated." The only types of immigrants that received negative ratings were "immigrants from communist countries" and "anyone who wants to immigrate."

In view of the abundant public debate on the issue, it is notable that "immigrants who are coloured" were found to be acceptable.

Regarding their behavioural intentions, respondents showed a considerable willingness to interact with immigrants. However, they also expressed a slight but consistent preference for members of the majority groups. These results suggest that there is still discrimination against them, with other things being equal. Discrimination was greatest against high status immigrants in a business relationship, and was least against low status immigrants in a business relationship. The combination of these results with those reported earlier suggests the following paradox. While highly educated and skilled immigrants are considered highly desirable for admission to Canada, there is some reluctance to use their services, especially if they are of high status.

Geographic differences. Quebec residents were least positive in their perceived consequences of immigration; they found "immigrants from communist countries" less acceptable than residents of other regions, and they were most prone to show discrimination against immigrants. The Atlantic provinces followed Quebec in these attitudes. The more negative attitudes in Quebec and the Atlantic provinces were primarily obtained from rural respondents. Residents from Ontario, the Prairies and British Columbia were very similar in terms of these attitudes, except that Ontario residents were least concerned about unemployment. There were virtually no differences in the views of respondents from the five largest metropolitan areas, except that Montrealers showed a greater tendency to discriminate against immigrants than respondents from other cities.

Ethnicity differences. The pattern of results from the geographic analysis suggests that ethnicity may be the basis of geographic differences. Such was in fact the case. French-Canadian respondents were least positive in their perceptions of the consequences of immigration. They were also most concerned about "unemployment" and the "purity of the Canadian race." French Canadians also found immigrants of all types, and particularly "immigrants from communist countries" less acceptable than members of the other ethnic categories, and they were most prone to show discrimination against immigrants. Detailed analyses showed that French-Canadian attitudes cannot be explained as a Quebec regional response, or as a result of the Catholic religion. French Canadians outside Quebec were very similar in their attitudes to French Canadians from Quebec. Anglophone Catholics were indistinguishable in their attitudes from anglophones of other religions.

There was a remarkable similarity between the attitudes of Anglocelts and members of "other ethnic" groups as a whole. Recency of immigration was virtually unrelated to the attitudes under consideration, after controlling for ethnicity of respondents. The classification of respondents from "other ethnic" origin showed that those of Russian and Ukrainian descent were somewhat less positive in their perception of immigration consequences, more concerned about unemployment, and found immigrants of all kinds less acceptable than members of other non-English/non-French descent groups.

Socioeconomic status differences. Three indices of socioeconomic status showed very similar relationships with immigration attitudes. The higher the socioeconomic status of respondents the more positive they were in their attitudes. Education was most strongly related, followed by income and occupational status.

Political party preference differences. Attitude differences between the supporters of various political parties were more pronounced among francophones than among anglophones. Among francophones, Liberal and New Democratic Party supporters had more positive attitudes toward immigration than supporters of the Progressive Conservative and Creditiste parties. In the case of anglophone respondents, differences among supporters of the four political parties were small or nonexistent, except that supporters of the Social Credit Party showed the least acceptance of immigrants, especially "coloured" and those from "communist countries."

Age differences. The relationship between age and immigration attitudes depended on the specific attitude variable involved. Respondents in their thirties and forties were most positive concerning perceived consequences of immigration. Younger and older respondents were less positive. Concerning the other attitudes, the older the respondents, the less acceptable they found all types of immigrants and the more they tended to discriminate.

Sex differences in attitudes toward immigration were very small or nonexistent.

The relative importance of predictors of immigration attitudes. A more complex strategy, was employed: (1) to isolate the most important variables predictive of immigration attitudes, (2) to assess their relative importance, and (3) to compare the predictive power of psychological versus demographic variables. Results of this analysis showed that of the demographic variables ethnicity and educational level were the most important independent predictors of immigration attitudes. Ethnicity was more important than educational level. Other demographic variables were related to some specific attitude variables, but these relationships did not attain the strength of the two major predictors. When psychological variables were included in the analysis, ethnocentrism consistently became the most important predictor of immigration attitudes.

Attitudes Toward Ethnic Groups

Respondents' attitudes toward various ethnic groups in Canada were assessed in three ways. First, respondents were asked to indicate which groups they were aware of in the Canadian population. Secondly, they were provided with a set of cards, with names of ethnic groups on each, and were asked to sort the cards on the basis of their perceived similarity. And last, respondents were asked to rate a number of ethnic groups on ten attitude dimensions.

Awareness of Ethnic Groups

Respondents were asked which groups, who originally came from various parts of the world, they were aware of now in Canada. The purpose of this question was to discover the relative visibility of various groups in an open-ended manner.

The groups mentioned most often (around 50% of the time) by respondents were Italians, British, French and Germans. Other groups such as the Ukrainians, Chinese and Poles were the next most frequently mentioned groups; however, these groups were only named by a quarter or less of the respondents. In general, the most numerous groups were also the most visible. Yet, the Italians who are less numerous than the Germans but who have more recently immigrated to Canada, were more visible than the Germans. Such a finding suggests that both group size and recency of immigration are important determinants of visibility.

A second finding is that while Anglocelts and French Canadians tend to be aware of the same groups, and in much the same order, there were a few notable differences. For example, Angloceltic respondents were more aware of Ukrainians, Scots and Dutch, while French-Canadian respondents were more aware of Greeks, Jews and Belgians.

Perception of Ethnic Groups

The second step in the analysis of ethnic attitudes was to find out how respondents organized their perceptions of ethnic groups. The method used to examine this issue was to provide each respondent with 27 cards, with the name of a different ethnic group on each card. On a twenty-eighth card was printed "Myself." The respondent was asked to sort the cards into piles according to which ethnic groups were thought to be similar to each other. The respondent was free to create as many piles, and to put as many ethnic group cards in a pile as he or she wished. By assessing the frequency with which any two ethnic group cards were placed in the same pile, we were able to perform an analysis of how respondents perceived or categorized the ethnic group. Using multi-dimensional scaling, separate analyses were carried out for Angloceltic and French-Canadian respondents.

The ethnic group which Angloceltic respondents considered closest to "Myself" was "English-Canadian" (about 75% of the time) while "Myself" and "English-Canadian" were placed with "French-Canadian" about half of the time. Angloceltic respondents appeared to focus on two major features of the "other ethnic" groups when making their categorizations. The first was the length of time a particular group was established in Canada in considerable numbers. The second dimension appeared to be based upon visible group differences.

French-Canadian respondents also made a charter groups — "other ethnic" group distinction in their classification of groups. "Myself" was most often placed with "Québecois" (90%), "French-Canadians" (84.0%) and "English-Canadians" (56%) while the frequencies for "other ethnic" groups was much lower. French-Canadian respondents frequently placed the

"English-Canadian" and "French-Canadian" group cards together (69%). The results of the analysis for French-Canadian respondents mirrored those of the Angloceltic respondents. French-Canadian respondents appeared to categorize the various ethnic groups along two dimensions, again an established Canadian-new Canadian and a visible difference dimension, although the dichotomies were not as clear as for the Angloceltic respondents.

Attitudes Toward Selected Ethnic Groups

In the study of attitudes it was necessary, for purposes of comparison, to pre-select a number of ethnic groups to serve as the focus for study. The pre-selection of groups was guided by statistics on ethnic concentration in the 1971 Census, the result of informal pilot research, and the literature on ethnic group relations. On this basis nine groups were chosen: English-Canadians, French-Canadians, Immigrants in general, Canadian-Indians, German-Canadians, Chinese-Canadians, Ukrainian-Canadians, Jewish-Canadians and Italian-Canadians. In addition, for each respondent two groups which had been nominated earlier were added making a total of eleven. Respondents were asked to provide ratings for each of the eleven groups on ten adjective dimensions: hard-working, important, Canadian, clean, similar to me, likeable, stick together as a group, wealthy, interesting and well known to me.

Attitudes in the total sample. In general respondents appeared to be at least tolerant of "other ethnic" groups, and there was no evidence of extreme ethnic prejudice; however, respondents did have clear preferences. They reacted very positively to the two charter groups in comparison to "other ethnic" groups. Of the non-charter groups, North European groups were evaluated relatively favourably (e.g., Germans, Belgians, Dutch, Scandinavians) compared to the South and East European groups (e.g., Greeks, Italians, Poles, Yugoslavs), who were in turn rated more favourably than several other groups (e.g., East Indians, Negroes, Spaniards, Portuguese).

Geographic differences. Respondents in Quebec were generally the least positive in their evaluation of non-charter groups. In addition, certain groups such as the Germans, Ukrainians and Chinese were rated relatively more favourably in the Prairies and British Columbia than in other regions, and Canadian Indians were rated relatively less favourably in those two regions.

Ethnicity differences. The most important determinant of ethnic attitudes to emerge from numerous analyses was the ethnicity of the respondent. Firstly, both Angloceltic and French-Canadian respondents evaluated each other relatively highly. However, own group evaluation by French-Canadian respondents was higher than own group evaluation by Angloceltic respondents. Angloceltic respondents' evaluation of French-Canadians, while relatively favourable, was not as positive as French-

Canadian respondents' evaluation of English-Canadians. Each charter group, then, serves as a positive reference group for the other.

In contrast, both Angloceltic and French-Canadian respondents held less favourable attitudes toward all other groups. These less favourable attitudes were relatively more negative among French-Canadian than among Angloceltic respondents.

Socioeconomic status differences. Generally respondents lower in socioeconomic status (particularly in education) held more favourable attitudes toward their own group, and relatively less favourable attitudes toward "other ethnic" groups. Although a fairly consistent trend, the finding is not as strong as that found for ethnicity.

Attitudes Toward Multiculturalism

This attitude domain is concerned with the ideology and policy of multiculturalism. "Ideology" refers to the general beliefs associated with the existence of cultural diversity in Canada. "Policy" refers to the present multiculturalism policy of the federal government. Specifically we were interested in respondents' knowledge of the policy and their attitudes toward it. In all, six series of questions in the survey were directed at these issues.

The multicultural ideology of respondents was assessed through the use of a nine-item scale. Two examples illustrate the nature of the items: "Canada would be a better place if members of ethnic groups would keep their own way of life alive" and "The unity of this country is weakened by ethnic groups sticking to their old ways." In the first example a positive and in the second, a negative statement is made about the existence of cultural diversity in Canada. By averaging responses to all nine items (taking into account the positive or negative direction of each item), an overall indication may be obtained about the acceptance of a multicultural ideology.

The perception of one aspect of multicultural policy was assessed by presenting respondents with three options describing how a country might deal with immigrants. One option involved "assimilation" (people are encouraged to give up ways of life), another "permissive integration" (people are allowed to maintain old ways of life), and a third "supportive integration" (people are encouraged to maintain old ways of life). Respondents were asked which option they thought was current policy in Canada.

Knowledge about the policy was assessed by asking respondents whether they knew about the federal government's policy of multiculturalism, and if not, if they had heard about it.

Perceived consequences of multicultural policy were assessed by obtaining respondents' reactions to five statements, such as "our Canadian way of life will be destroyed" and "Canada will be richer in culture." An average score across the five items was calculated.

Attitudes toward multicultural programmes were measured by presenting respondents with six present or potential multicultural programmes, such as "community centres where people from various cultural backgrounds can meet each other and share their heritage." Respondents' reactions were summed to yield an average programme attitude score.

Behavioural intentions to multiculturalism were measured by asking respondents' intentions concerning three possible political actions: "vote for a political candidate who supported such a programme," "try to convince other people that the programme was a good one" and "be willing to pay taxes to support such a programme." Responses were averaged to yield a general behavioural intentions score.

The approach taken to multicultural attitude assessment was to begin with a broad and somewhat abstract enquiry into ideology, and from there to proceed to more concrete attitudes concerning policy consequences and programmes, and then to very concrete examples of behaviour which might be exhibited in response to the policy. All four attitude domains were significantly related among themselves; for example, respondents with a positive multicultural ideology score tended also to have positive attitudes on the other three scales. Furthermore, the four attitude scales and the two knowledge questions were also consistently related. For example, those who perceived the policy as being one of assimilation tended to have lower multicultural ideology scores and also less favourable attitudes on the other three scales. That is, we have obtained evidence of a cluster of attitudes which appear to be stable and internally consistent. This finding implies some degree of reliability for the results as a whole.

Attitudes toward multiculturalism in the total sample. Knowledge of the multiculturalism policy was not widespread (only one fifth knew about the policy), and most people perceived the government's current policy to favour "permissive" rather than "supportive" integration. Despite this low level of knowledge and the inaccurate perception of the policy, multicultural attitudes were generally positive. With respect to multicultural ideology, respondents were on the whole slightly in favour of cultural diversity in Canada. The perceived consequences of multiculturalism were also slightly positive. Although programme attitudes were greeted with general acceptance, there was evidence of greater acceptance for some programmes (e.g., "community centres" and "folk festivals") than for others (e.g., "radio and television shows in languages other than English or French" and "teaching, in regular school programmes, of the languages of the major cultural groups who have settled in Canada"); indeed, respondents showed slight rejection of the last two programmes. Finally, behavioural intentions were less favourable than attitudes. This contrast in support between the ideology and the behavioural intentions may be understood in terms of the abstract through to concrete dimension which was noted above. It may well be that Canadians think that the idea of multiculturalism is good, that some of the programmes are enjoyable, but that they do not want to get involved. Overall, however, the climate for multiculturalism is fairly positive; the ideological base is supportive, and there are some specific programmes which appear to be generally highly acceptable. Detracting from this conclusion is the existence of some programmes which if promoted may be rejected, and the notable lack of acceptance when personal commitment is involved.

Geographic differences. Respondents from Quebec were less positive in their attitudes regarding multiculturalism than those from other regions. This regional analysis is supported by the pattern of attitudes across the five metropolitan areas; the response in Montreal was consistently less favourable than in the other major cities. With respect to degree of urbanization, there was a tendency, especially in the Atlantic region, for increased urbanization to be associated with more positive attitudes.

Ethnicity differences. A likely interpretation of these regional differences is in terms of ethnicity. This interpretation was confirmed; French-Canadian respondents were consistently least positive in their multicultural attitudes. Furthermore, the less positive attitudes were not limited to French Canadians living in Quebec, but extended to those outside of Quebec. Angloceltic respondents, whether from Quebec or elsewhere, had consistently more positive attitudes. Religion did not account for these attitude differences; anglophone Catholics were generally more positive than francophone Catholics, and were indistinguishable from anglophones of other religions.

Multicultural attitudes were highly similar among angloceltic, anglophone and francophone "other ethnic" respondents, all standing in contrast to the attitudes of French-Canadian respondents. Recency of immigration in terms of generation was not related to these attitudes. There was evidence that among some groups of "other ethnic" origin (notably Ukrainian and Russian) perceived consequences and behavioural intentions were somewhat less positive than among others. These differences did not extend to multicultural ideology and programme attitudes.

Socioeconomic status differences. The three measures of socioeconomic status were very similar in their relationship to multicultural attitudes; the higher the socioeconomic status the more positive the attitudes. And of the three variables, it was consistently education which was related most strongly.

Political party preference differences. For most multicultural attitudes, the political party preference of the respondent was a significant factor. Generally, among both anglophone and francophone respondents, Social Credit supporters were least positive, while Liberal supporters were most positive. Among anglophone respondents, New Democratic Party and Progressive Conservative Supporters were generally favourable and similar to Liberal supporters; however, among francophone respondents, Progressive Conservatives were similar to Creditiste supporters in having less favourable attitudes.

Age differences. On three of the four multicultural attitudes, as age increased, attitudes became progressively less positive. However, on the fourth (perceived consequences) and the question regarding knowledge and perception of policy, no age trend was apparent.

Virtually no sex differences appeared in any of the multicultural attitudes. When differences did appear, they were for single items only, and suggested that females were somewhat more positive than males.

The relative importance of predictors of multicultural attitudes. Multiple regression analyses showed that among the demographic variables, ethnicity and education were consistently the most important independent predictors of multicultural attitudes, with age contributing as well on all but the perceived consequences. When the psychological variables were included in the analyses, ethnocentrism emerged (in three cases) as the most powerful predictor, surpassing but not eliminating the demographic variables; on behavioural intentions, the ethnicity of the respondent remained the single most important predictor.

Structure of the Attitudes

Many questions arise when examining such a large number of attitudes. These questions involve such fundamental issues as their coherence, their relationship to ethnocentrism and to the major independent variables, and their validity.

Coherence of attitudes. To assess the relationship among the attitudes, an overall correlation matrix was generated, and then it was factor analysed. In the matrix, all attitudes correlated in the expected direction; for example, ethnocentrism and multicultural ideology were negatively related, while ethnocentrism and discrimination showed a positive relationship. Furthermore, most of the attitudes were significantly related, suggesting a fair degree of coherence. In the factor analysis, this was confirmed, with two factors emerging as the most appropriate solution. The first was one of general prejudice and all attitude scales loaded on this factor. The second was an ethnic groups factor and all groups except "Italians" loaded on it. One variable (discrimination) loaded on both factors. This factor structure means that while all of the attitudes tend to correlate with each other, general prejudice and attitudes toward immigration and multiculturalism tend to cohere in one cluster. Attitudes toward specific ethnic groups tend to cohere in another cluster.

The ethnocentrism hypothesis. Further relationships among these attitudes were studied in order to assess the hypothesis that ingroup and outgroup attitudes would be negatively related. When attitudes toward one's own group (English or French Canadian) were correlated with attitudes toward all "other ethnic" groups, a clear pattern emerged: all correlations were negative, and all (except for attitudes toward Canadian Indians) were significant. In sharp contrast attitudes toward the other charter group were both positive and significant. This same pattern emerged in there further analyses, in which attitudes toward all "other ethnic" groups were correlated with the ethnocentrism scale, the discrimination and the multicultural ideology scale scores. On the basis of the earlier similarity judgements, it may be asserted that the two charter groups serve as positive reference groups for each other. Given this classification, and this pattern of correlations, it is clear that there is an ethnocentric structure to the ethnic attitudes of Angloceltic and French-Canadian respondents.

Correlates of attitudes. Throughout the earlier descriptions of how attitudes were related to various background factors, there was consistent evidence that both ethnicity (French Canadian vs. Angloceltic) and socioeconomic status (particularly education) were contributing. Since they are known to be mutually related, a question arises concerning their independent contributions to the attitudes. Two-way analyses of variance were carried out. For all attitudes (except evaluation of English Canadians) both ethnicity and education significantly and independently affected the level of attitudes. Thus it is clear that in any interpretation of the distribution of these attitudes both background factors must be taken into account.

Cultural and economic security. During earlier discussions of these attitudes, it became apparent that the cultural and economic security felt by various groups (particularly ethnic and socioeconomic groupings) may also be factors in the distribution of attitudes. To assess this possibility, two new variables were constructed. Correlational analyses indicated that, for both the Angloceltic and French-Canadian samples, feelings of cultural and economic security were significantly related to most attitudes. Among both groups, feelings of security were positively associated with such attitudes as acceptability of immigrants, multicultural ideology and multicultural behavioural intentions. On the other hand, feelings of security were negatively related to the ethnocentrism score, discrimination against immigrants, and the evaluation of one's own group. Thus the notion of security appears to be of some value in understanding the distribution of most of these attitudes.

Validity of attitude measurement. In all surveys and other studies of attitudes, questions of validity arise. In particular, there are problems concerning the prediction of behaviour from attitudinal data, and the distortion of responses to attitude scales due to acquiesence response set or to social desirability. A number of checks and internal controls suggest that this study has attained a reasonable degree of validity. These controls include the occasional use of behavioural intention scales and of balanced item content within scales.

A further issue concerns the validity of the observed differences between Angloceltic and French-Canadian respondents. While recognizing that cross-cultural studies are fraught with problems of this nature, there are some controls available to ensure comparability of data. These include adequate translation checks, and the analyses of the structure of the data. In the present study the structure of attitudes of Angloceltic and French-Canadian respondents was similar, they bore similar relationships to independent variables, and there was consistency in the difference between the groups, no matter which specific attitude was being measured. All these point to a valid finding of differences in attitudes between the two majority groups.

Some Emerging Themes

Up to this point in the study all data have been analysed and presented rather systematically. However, some findings may be drawn together thematically, around a number of issues which either emerge from the data or which are important in studies of Canadian attitudes.

Public and private attitudes. Often survey results are greeted with the reaction that such things have been known all along. In some cases public statements have previously indicated the likelihood of a particular result, or in other cases the finding appears to be just good common sense. However detailed studies of attitudes, such as this one, can be defended against both views. In the first case, there is no necessary relationship between public pronouncements and attitudes held by the population. Sometimes officials and opinion leaders reflect public sentiment and sometimes they do not. In the second case, there are usually many obvious or common sense views of an issue, and they often do not coincide. In both cases, studies of attitudes are needed in order to assess the validity of the public and common sense knowledge.

The issue of race. Racism is a topic of major concern to many people, and the question naturally arises whether there is evidence for racism in our study. A number of points need to be made in response to such a question. First, there was a rejection of "explicit" racism in the sample; that is, there was little evidence of overt bigotry. Second, though, there was evidence that race (in the sense of physical differences) was employed as an important dimension in the perception of groups, and in the judgement of similarity to respondents. And, even more importantly, many groups which are racially-different were at the lower end of the evaluative ranking of groups in Canada. Thus there is some evidence that race is an issue, and is being employed by Canadians in their acceptance or rejection of groups of people. Moreover, it should be noted that a survey technique is not the most suitable way to study "pockets" of racist belief or activity; field studies are necessary to pick up such troubled areas.

Attitudes in anglophone Canada. It is reasonable to expect that attitudes might differ across the regions and peoples of anglophone Canada, given the varied history of settlement, contact with ethnic diversity, and ethnic background. However, except for the Atlantic provinces, these attitudes were remarkably constant from Ontario on westward; the "rift" between East and West did not appear. In the Atlantic region, attitudes were generally less accepting of diversity and more ethnocentric when compared with the balance of the anglophone sample.

Attitudes of Angloceltic and "other ethnic" Canadians. It is also reasonable to expect that those of "other ethnic" backgrounds might have more positive attitudes toward cultural diversity than those of Angloceltic background. However, in general there were few differences, both being generally positive. It is difficult to know whether to interpret this lack of difference as a lower-than-expected response from "other ethnic" respondents, or as a greater-than-expected response from Angloceltic respondents.

Generational status. Despite an indication in the literature that attitudes would be related to generational status, there was generally no relationship found. One possible interpretation of this finding is that the concern here was for a broad range of attitudes toward both one's own and other groups. In contrast, much of the other literature has been concerned only with one's own group and its linguistic and cultural position.

Political party preference. In keeping with a general view of their respective ideologies, and with other literature on the topic, there were fairly clear but small differences in attitudes according to respondents' preferred federal political party. Among both anglophone and francophone samples, Liberal and New Democratic Party supporters held the more positive attitudes, while Progressive Conservative and Social Credit/Creditiste supporters held less positive attitudes.

Socioeconomic status. Consistently in the patterning of attitudes, the roles of socioeconomic status variables were indicated; in all cases, higher status respondents held more positive attitudes than those of lower socioeconomic status. These differences were particularly evident for educational level, but the same pattern was generally exhibited for the occupational status and income measures as well. A number of interpretations are possible, all of which receive some support in our data and in the literature. One of these is that more positive attitudes are simply the norm of higher socioeconomic status groups, and that the expression of less positive attitudes is not acceptable. Another is that immigration and multiculturalism may affect more directly the position of lower socioeconomic groups; hence more negative attitudes accompany their vulnerability. However, no single interpretation is likely for such a fundamental patterning of results.

Native peoples. As a group unlike either the two charter groups or those of "other ethnic" background, attitudes toward native peoples are an important element in understanding a multicultural society. First, native peoples were viewed as relatively similar to themselves by most respondents, but second, they were placed at the bottom of the evaluation scale. And in the structural analysis of attitudes, Canadian Indians seemed to occupy a position which was supporting neither the ethnocentrism hypothesis nor the multicultural assumption. The evidence suggested that native peoples occupy a special position in the attitudes of Canadians; this position may be best characterized by the term "marginal." That is, there appears to be some recognition of their special status as indigenous people, but this is insufficient to create a set of positive attitudes toward them.

Attitudes of Ukrainian and Russian Canadians. On a number of attitudes, respondents of Ukrainian and Russian "other ethnic" background exhibited a lower acceptance than those of many other backgrounds. However, not all attitudes showed this reduced level of acceptance. An

analysis of the pattern revealed that on some attitudes, such as certain multicultural programmes, their attitudes were very positive, but on many (such as
perceived consequences of immigration, acceptability of immigrants, perceived consequences of multiculturalism and the ethnocentrism scale) they
were among the least positive. This lower level of acceptance stands in
contrast to other findings in the area; but this contrast may be understood
in terms of the above pattern. This pattern indicates that Ukrainian and
Russian Canadians favour multiculturalism when it means own group
cultural maintenance, but are less in favour when multiculturalism refers to
the development of other groups. One possible interpretation is that since the
cultural survival of these two peoples is being threatened in their homelands,
their distinctiveness as a people depends in part on their position in a
multicultural Canada. Thus a set of protective attitudes can be viewed as a
response to such a situation. Another possible interpretation is that the notion
of multiculturalism was too closely identified with immigration in the survey
context. Since further immigration from their homelands is unlikely, a lower
level of support was exhibited by them than by the balance of the "other
ethnic" respondents.

Mutual attitudes of Angloceltic and French Canadians. In a number of
ways, data from this study indicated that there exists a set of fairly positive
attitudes between the two charter groups. These data suggest that each group
acts as a positive reference group for one another. One interpretation of this
finding (which is surprising in the light of the conventional wisdom on the
subject) is that when Angloceltic and French Canadians view each other
within the context of multiculturalism a relative similarity and mutual
acceptance will emerge; but when they are asked about their attitudes in
the context of biculturalism, a relative dissimilarity and mutual rejection
become manifest. That is, the comparative context of intergroup relations
(and of studies of these relations) may be a crucial factor in determining how
Angloceltic and French Canadians will relate to each other. If this is the case,
the multicultural context may actually promote bicultural acceptance;
however it may do so at the risk of rejecting the "other ethnic" groups.
Although multiculturalism appears to foster mutual attitudinal acceptance,
it may or may not be beneficial to actual intergroup relations. On the one
hand it may blind Canadians to the conflicts that actually do exist between
the two groups, and on the other hand the shift away from bilingualism and
biculturalism toward multiculturalism may increase the feelings of insecurity
of French Canadians, and thereby reduce the level of these positive attitudes.

French-Canadian attitudes. Two features of French-Canadian attitudes
stood out in this study. While evaluating their own group very positively,
they tended to hold the most negative attitudes toward "other ethnic" groups.
Such a pattern of attitudes has been termed one of ethnocentrism. Our data
indicate that this pattern cannot be explained on the basis of the linguistic,
regional or religious features of French-Canadian life. Rather it appears to
be related to the socioeconomic, demographic and cultural features of life

in French Canada, one which has been termed a "siege culture." That is, this pattern of protective attitudes makes sense as a response to the cultural and linguistic threat experienced in an English continent, and to the precarious demographic position of both the declining French-Canadian birth-rate and the tendency for immigrants to integrate into anglophone Canada. Psychologically, self and group protection has involved the development of ethnocentric attitudes.

Implications for Multiculturalism

The present study was designed to answer two major questions. One was whether Canadians view cultural diversity as a valuable resource, and the other whether confidence in one's own identity is prerequisite for accepting others, as the Prime Minister stated in the announcement of the multiculturalism policy (the multicultural assumption).

The climate for multiculturalism. Respondents in our survey showed a reasonably high level of overt tolerance for ethnic diversity and a general acceptance for multiculturalism as a social fact. However a certain level of covert concern and reluctance to accept ethnic diversity was also uncovered. Although overt racism was low, race was shown to be an important dimension for categorizing people, and racially different groups appeared at the bottom of the perceived ethnic group hierarchy. The present study also revealed a considerable lack of knowledge concerning multiculturalism as government policy. Degree of support for multicultural programmes depended on the specific programmes involved. Community centres and folk festivals were positively received, while respondents had reservations about third language teaching and broadcasting.

Analysis of the multicultural assumption. Although the present study did not contain a direct measure of "confidence in one's own identity," it was possible to test the multicultural assumption by making certain assumptions concerning indirect measures. Taking own group evaluation as a measure of confidence, the assumption was clearly not supported. On the contrary, an ethnocentric pattern of attitudes emerged, with the most positive ingroup attitudes being associated with negative outgroup attitudes. By taking measures of economic and cultural security as indices of confidence, the multicultural assumption was supported. Those who were most secure were also tolerant toward "other ethnic" groups. Such apparently contradictory results suggest conceptual ambiguities in the multicultural assumption. Clearly, "confidence in one's own identity" cannot be equated with positive own group evaluation. Results from the present study and from earlier investigations of the authoritarian personality suggest that positive evaluations of one's own group is associated with other group tolerance only when self evaluation is objective and not defensive.

Conditions for intergroup tolerance. The results of our study point to three interrelated conditions for intergroup tolerance: group definition, objective own group evaluation, and group security. Individuals should feel that they belong to a group that is well defined both in objective and subjective terms. Individuals should have a positive, but objective appraisal of their own group, which is free of defensiveness and exaggeration. And finally, individuals should be secure in their cultural and economic context. All three conditions are viewed as necessary for intergroup tolerance to flourish. The absence of any one may turn the others into promoters of intergroup conflict instead.

V.

ETHNIC CONFLICTS

Chapter 17

Indian Land Claims and Rights*

Lloyd I. Barber

Indian grievances have been with us in this country since the early stages of European penetration of the North American continent. Until very recently, they have received minimal public attention. During the 1960's the federal government made attempts to form an Indian Claims Commission which would act as an adjudicatory body and would have the authority to settle claims brought before it. As I understand it, the legislation, which was never passed, would have created a Claims Commission in Canada not unlike the Indian Claims Commission in the United States. In the late 1960's, the government apparently decided that not enough was known about the nature and extent of Indian claims to launch into an adjudicatory process. Accordingly, the government found it preferable to arrange for extensive preliminary study and consultation before establishing special processes for claims settlement.

Special funds were provided to Indian organizations so that they could carry out research on grievances and rights and subsequently articulate their claims. At the same time, the government undertook to appoint someone

*Reprinted from *The Patterns of "Amerindian" Identity,* edited by Marc-Adélard Tremblay; Quebec: Les Presses de l'Université Laval, 1976, by permission of the author and the publisher.

outside the Indian community and outside government, to enquire into the issues, in consultation with Indians, and provide an independent "outside" source of advice. As a result, I was appointed Indian Claims Commissioner in December of 1969. Essentially, my job is to make recommendations on machinery or processes for settlement. I have no authority to settle claims though I can and do attempt to evaluate specific claims which come to my attention for the purpose of making recommendations on how to go about settling the issues involved.

The colonial policy of Great Britain with respect to Indians in Canada was set out in a Royal Proclamation in 1763 shortly after the Treaty of Paris. The history of native lands prior to that time is very interesting and is relevant to current issues in the St. Lawrence Valley and in the Maritimes. In the early 1600's, with the establishment of Champlain's colonies in the St. Lawrence Valley, the settlers were involved with the Indian people of the area in the fur trade, the economic life blood of the colony. Thus the Indians were essential partners with the colonists from the very early days.

Efforts to convert the Indian people to Christianity and to European ways were undertaken by missionary societies. Some Indian colonies were established under the auspices of the missionaries but the favored method was for missionaries to go out among the tribes in their homelands and work with them. While the fur trade grew and expanded, the population of New France during the French regime was not large, being fewer than 100,000, and such agriculture as we carried on around settlements did not seriously encroach upon Indian lands. France, as a colonizing nation, did not form an explicit theory of aboriginal title and did not treat with the indigenous people for surrender of their rights in the land. This, as we shall see later, poses special problems for Indian claims in those areas of the country originally colonized by France.

After the transfer of New France to Britain, various British precedents and practices with respect to Indian lands began to be applied. These were confirmed by the Royal Proclamation of 1763 which followed immediately upon the cessation. The Proclamation provided for the protection of Indian lands from settlers and others until such time as the Indian rights to the land had been surrendered to the Crown. In effect, it precluded anyone other than the Crown from dealing with Indians for land and laid the basis for the treaty-making process in Canada. This process, which in certain respects is still underway, resulted in the surrender of Indian rights over vast territories, the creation of Indian reserve lands, and the establishment of a variety of promises in exchange for native land rights.

The first of these treaties in Canada was carried out in Southern Ontario and was very simple in format. The Indians involved simply surrendered their rights for cash payments, some reserve land, and the right to hunt and fish on unoccupied Crown land. However, as settlement moved westward, there evolved a somewhat better deal in the light of adjustment faced by Indian people as settlement came upon them. The treaties gradually evolved to a format where the government agreed to additional provisions for health, education and economic development.

The major treaties cover Indian people in Ontario, the Prairie Provinces, the Northwest Territories and parts of British Columbia. For Indians in most of British Columbia, in the Yukon, in Quebec and the Maritimes, and for the Inuit, there have been no treaties or minor treaties only. Under the *B.N.A. Act,* responsibility for Indians and Indian lands was vested in the federal government (by contrast Australian responsibility for Aborigines was vested in the states). In 1867, the Inuit were not thought of and no mention was made of them. However, a Supreme Court decision of 1939 defined Eskimos as Indians for purposes of the *B.N.A. Act.* As a result of this history and other details which I have not sufficient time to explore here, about half of Canada's registered Indian people and the Inuit have not had treaty settlements with the Canadian government. The position of Canada's non-status native peoples is an entire story in itself.

From these circumstances flow two broad classes of Indian claims and grievances in Canada. The Indians covered by treaty claim in general that treaty provisions have not been fulfilled; that promises made at treaty time were not recorded in the treaties and have not been lived up to; and that lands set aside for Indians were surrendered under dubious circumstances, thus depriving many Indian people the opportunity for economic self sufficiency in a new way of life; and that, in general, the spirit of the treaties has not been lived up to by the various governments in Canada. While there are a variety of specific claims falling into this category of misfeasance, malfeasance and nonfeasance, one concrete example will serve to elucidate some of the issues and some of the complications in dealing with even the simplest of these claims.

Treaty seven, which covers Southern Alberta, has a provision which requires the payment to the five bands of Indians involved of $2,000 worth of ammunition each year unless ammunition becomes comparatively unnecessary, at which time, the $2,000 will be spent otherwise for the benefit of the Indians with their consent. The Indians claimed that they received ammunition intermittently if at all and that their consent was never received for other expenditures. On this basis, they asked for 90 years back payments with interest — a sum of some $650,000. Following the production of inconclusive records by the federal government, negotiations began with the Indians sticking by their $650,000 figure and the government countering with $160,000, or 80 years of ammunition payment without interest. An agreement was reached for $250,000 plus $25,000 expenses.

I would like to say that this matter has been settled. Unfortunately, not all of the stipulations have been agreed upon. One of these was that the Indian bands would decide how the money was to be split amongst them. This they have not decided. Two of the bands are large in size and understandably interested in a per capita distribution. Three of the bands are small in number and understandably desire a five-way split of the $250,000. This by way of example of the great complexity involved in settling this kind of claim.

The other broad category of claim stems from the lack of any original settlement of the native right in the land. While the circumstances vary somewhat from area to area in Canada, the basis for the aboriginal claim in British Columbia, the Yukon, the Northwest Territories, Quebec and the Maritimes has its roots in the Royal Proclamation as outlined previously.

When the present boundaries of Quebec were established in 1912, the *Quebec Boundaries Extension Act* obliged Quebec to recognize the native interest in the added territory and to compensate for it. As the act states:

> "... the Province of Quebec will recognize the rights of the Indian inhabitants in the territory above described to the same extent, and will obtain surrenders of such rights in the same manner, as the Government of Canada has heretofore recognized such rights and has obtained surrender thereof, and the said province shall bear and satisfy all charges and expenditure in connection with or arising out of such surrenders."

You are all aware, from the press coverage of the events, of the efforts of the Natives affected to stop work on the James Bay hydro project pending the settlement of the Indian rights in the land in Northern Quebec. Negotiations between the government of Quebec and the native peoples of the North are in an advanced state of progress. We can expect to hear more in the near future on this important extension of the historic process of recognizing rights in the land possessed by pre-European inhabitants.

In the Yukon, negotiations are underway between the federal government, territorial government and the status and non-status Indians of the Territory. These negotiations arose following the presentation of the paper *Together Today for our Children Tomorrow* by the Yukon Native Brotherhood to the Prime Minister and some of his colleagues. While negotiations are slow and difficult, progress is being made in working toward a concrete recognition of the rights of the native population land neither surrendered by treaty nor seized in combat.

The Northwest Territories is a case different from all others. In the first place, the vast bulk of the Territories, a million square miles or so, is Eskimo country. The Inuit, you will recall, have no treaty. They are now engaged in putting together their position on land claims and in conjunction with this effort are undertaking, with the support of the Department of Indian and Northern Affairs, a land use study to determine the traditional patterns of movement over and use of that vast country. Preliminary discussions to outline the issues are now underway and progress is being made.

The Mackenzie River area, including Great Slave and Great Bear Lakes, has traditionally been Indian country. This area, some 450,000 square miles, is covered by two treaties. Treaty 8 was done in 1899 and covers the region south of Great Slave Lake and includes most of the north half of Alberta, part of northeastern British Columbia, and some of the northwestern Saskatchewan. Treaty 11, done in 1921, covers the remainder of the Mackenzie River area.

Both treaties 8 and 11 provide for reserve lands of 640 acres per family of five. These reserves were never established in the Northwest Territories and so the treaty provisions remain unfulfilled. From time to time, there have been attempts to settle these treaties. In 1959, a Commission under Mr. Justice Nelson of Prince Albert examined this situation and made recommendations. No action was taken.

The Indians of the Northwest Territories claim that treaties 8 and 11 did not have the effect of removing their native title in the land but were merely treaties of peace and friendship. Mr. Justice William Morrow in his judgment in the celebrated caveat case added weight to this view by indicating that he thought the Indians had a sufficient interest in the land to be allowed to file a caveat against the land. Since the judgment came down in the fall of 1973, the Indians of the Northwest Territories have further developed their thinking in relation to their interest in the land. In a recent speech in Saskatoon, Mr. James Wah-shee, President of the Northwest Territories Indian Brotherhood, summed up the thinking of territorial status and non-status Indians this way:

> "The Indian and Metis people of the Northwest Territories at a historic, week long meeting at Fort Good Hope in June, 1974, declared their continuing ownership of 450,000 square miles of traditional land and rejected land surrender in return for compensation as a land settlement model. In so doing, they embraced an approach to settlement of native claims which is a radical departure from the tradition of dealing with the land rights of Indian people. They have rejected the notion that land settlement necessarily means the extinguishment rather than the preservation of rights."

For its part, the government is reluctant to become involved in any process which might appear to be a renegotiation of a treaty. However, there is recognition of the fact that the treaties in the North which were virtually carbon copies of treaties made much earlier in the South and are based upon assumptions that agriculture would substitute for buffalo hunting, are not satisfactory for northern conditions. In many areas of the North, 640 acres won't keep one moose alive let alone a family of five. Because the land provisions of treaties 8 and 11 are unfulfilled, the government is prepared to engage in discussions leading to a comprehensive settlement in the Northwest Territories. Very preliminary discussions have been undertaken with the main topic of interest being the form and structure for further discussion and negotiation.

In the Maritimes, the Indians claim that title to their land was not extinguished by the few treaties done in the area. As one proof of this, they point to the lack of any compensation as is inherent in other treaties, both pre- and post-Confederation.

While the Maritime region was under French control, the resident Micmac and Malecite Indians were allies of the French. When Acadia was ceded to the British in 1713, the British claimed that the resident Indians thereby became their subjects and that title to their lands fell to the British Crown. Both the French and the Indians denied these assertions. The French maintained that the Indians had been allies, not subjects, of the King of

France. The French could not, according to that reasoning, have transferred to Britain a sovereignty and land title which they did not hold themselves.

To date, the issue of aboriginal claim in the Maritimes has neither been fully acknowledged nor repudiated. The Union of Nova Scotia Indians has advanced a strong position asserting their right to be included within the aboriginal rights negotiation process. The federal government policy on these issues, enunciated in August, 1973, is:

> "In all these cases where the traditional interest in land has not been formally dealt with, the Government affirms its willingness to do so and accepts in principle that the loss and relinquishment of that interest ought to be compensated.
> "There are other areas of the country where no treaties of surrender were entered into, such as Southern Quebec and the Atlantic provinces. The Government's view is that land claims in these areas are of a different character from those referred to earlier in this statement."

The situation in British Columbia is moving along, but slowly. A couple of years ago the Union of British Columbia Chiefs submitted its claims for redress based on the loss of traditional use and occupancy of land in British Columbia. Since that presentation, the claim of the Nishga Indians which related to their traditional homeland in the Nass Valley was fought to a draw in the Supreme Court of Canada. However, the government of Canada has entered into negotiations with the Nishga and into discussions concerning the larger issues in British Columbia. Unfortunately, so far, the British Columbia government has not acknowledged any responsibility for the aboriginal rights of its native inhabitants. As in other areas of the country, failure by the provinces to participate fully in the process of redress can render the possibilities for satisfactory resolution of the issues very difficult, if not impossible.

In this brief overview, I have tried to provide a summary of the background and current situation regarding two main categories of Indian claims in Canada. In doing so, I may have concentrated unduly on the comprehensive or aboriginal rights areas to the detriment of the more specific land loss and band fund type claims. However, even a brief run through of a few representative cases would take far more time than is available. Let me simply state that it is quite likely that all 550 or more bands in the country will have one or more of the specific type claims regardless whether they are located in the treaty areas or the non-treaty areas of the country.

All this, of course, points to a need for machinery to deal with the various kinds of grievances that the Indians will bring forward. In this regard, it is useful to look to the experience of the United States where there have been two basic approaches to settlement of Indian claims. The first of these is the Indian Claims Commission, a special tribunal which was established nearly 30 years ago and which has now completed something over half of its work. This body has carried out its work by relying on an adversary process whereby the Indians and the Justice Department argue the issues before the Commission which, after hearing the cases, issues a verdict. This approach has not been satisfactory. It is slow, costly, and does not seem to get at the sense of grievance, giving rise to the claims, but rather relies upon money compensation to settle the issues. Canadian Indians have not favored this kind of an approach.

The second approach, used in Alaska, draws from the experience of the Commission, but relies on negotiation, and attempts to relate settlement to current and future needs of the people. The *Settlement Act*, passed in December, 1971, calls for a cash payment of roughly half a billion dollars over a period of years, together with royalty payments of roughly half a billion dollars more and a land allotment of approximately 40 millions acres, which is in the order of 15% of the State. These assets are to be administered through native corporations and the general idea is that they will be used for social and economic development.

In contrast to this experience, we in Canada have just begun to recognize the need to settle Indian grievances fairly and honorably. Appropriate mechanisms are slow to evolve because of the complexity of the issues and the reluctance of Indian people to get locked into any process which has the capability of providing solutions which to them would be unsatisfactory. The Indians have been engaged in a period of researching their claims. Many are now coming forward in a well prepared manner. However, the process of research and articulation of claims is far from over. It would be inappropriate, in my view, and counterproductive to lock in to any given settlement mechanism until such time as processes now underway are given much greater opportunity to work through to fruition.

In the meantime, ad hoc negotiation on specific issues is taking place. As I have pointed out, a great deal of negotiation or discussion leading to negotiation is underway at present and while there have been few settlements so far, the process is working in a healthy direction, despite its inherent "messiness." This is not to say that arbitration machinery will not be necessary, but simply to point out that the experience in courts in Canada, and in the Claims Commission in the United States, has caused Indian people in this country to shy away from any process which has finality inherent in it.

I hope that this outline gives you some appreciation of the current state of Indian claims in Canada. I would like to close with some observations on the implications of all of this for Indians and for other Canadians.

In simple terms, we are faced with a backlog of grievances which go back 100 or 200 or even 300 years in history. Normally, our governments do not attempt to go back this far in examining and correcting injustices and it is easy to see why this is so as a general rule. The case for Indian grievances, however, is unique and exceptional. The original people of this country have never been in a position to make their case and insist on their unique rights. Until very recently, their grievances have not been fully brought to light because of serious weaknesses in communications and the very one-sided nature of the relationship between Indians and others in this country. Indian grievances are not new to Indians nor are they new to the Department of Indian Affairs The rest of us, however, have not known much about them and the Indians have never been in a position to put their claims forward in a clear and forceful way which would make them fully understandable to us. For this reason alone, it is valid that these very old grievances be dealt with now, in spite of all of the difficulties.

There is an additional and overriding reason why the grievances must be dealt with in a just and equitable manner. Over the years, the relationships between Indians and the government have been such that strong feelings of distrust have developed. This distrust goes far beyond distrust of government to the entire society which has tried, since day one, to assimilate Indian people. Indian people, who once dwelt proud and sovereign in all of Canada, have resisted with stubborn tenacity all efforts to make them just like everybody else. It seems to me that it is from these roots that all of the grievances stem. Indians have constantly insisted, and will continue to insist, that they are a special people who have an inherent right to a special status as a nation within a nation.

Indians are concerned with their future as Indians within a large and powerful society and culture. They are now demanding in an educated, articulate and forceful way, that past transgressions against their special status and special rights be cleared up as a pre-condition to their self-determination about how they will take their position proud and independent, side by side with us in shaping a new future. They have given up much in this country, and they feel that the assistance they receive from government must be seen as a right in recognition of this loss and not merely as a handout because they are destitute. In short, the grievances are real, the claims arising from them are genuine, and redress must be provided if our native peoples are to find their rightful place in this country.

The implications of all of this for Canadians are significant. Extensive settlements in the North and elsewhere will give Natives a strong position, economically and politically. It will no longer be necessary to indulge in token involvement because in many areas they will have the power to plan an increasingly important part in the developments taking place. This presence will, in many ways, make things difficult for white developers and governments who want to hurry on with frontier development but it seems to me that this will be much healthier than the consequences of development which does not include native people in a direct and influential way.

Recent experiences in Kenora, Cache Creek and Ottawa must have made even the most indifferent Canadian aware that native frustration is building up and that we cannot expect that native people will much longer confine their misery to their own communities as they have in the past.

Finally, it seems to me that we Canadians, rich and successful beyond the fondest dreams of our ancestors, have an unique opportunity to demonstrate to our native brethren and to the world that we can deal with a difficult internal problem in an enlightened way and to show that people can resolve their differences, complicated and historic though they be, can live harmoniously through democratic processes.

Chapter 18

The Idea of a Homeland*

André Bernard

Material well-being is not everything. It is far from being all that Quebec French Canadians yearn for. Indeed, Quebec French Canadians who favor an increase in their collective well-being do not want to give up any of their cultural or social particularities as a price for such an increase. One thing is clear: most French Canadians living in Quebec and in the bordering regions want, at the same time, to keep using French *and* to increase their collective well-being. Material well-being is the dominant objective for many; national survival is the dominant objective for others; but most French Canadians agree on the crucial importance of both these objectives.

Moreover, a great many of them want to reach a third objective which has little to do with material well-being, but has extreme emotional value. They would like the territory they inhabit to be their homeland, a territory where they can live with total dignity, permanently free from the frustration now imposed on them by what they see as economic inequalities drawn along language lines, free from the frustration now imposed on them by a political system dominated by "others". By and large, Quebec's French Canadians are ready to support changes which would let them feel more at home in Quebec.

Unlike the other two collective objectives pursued by a large proportion

*Reprinted by permission from *What Does Quebec Want?* by André Bernard, James Lorimer & Co., Publishers, Toronto, 1978.

of the French-speaking population of Quebec and neighboring regions, the idea of a national homeland challenges the present Canadian constitutional framework. The language problem could be largely solved by a measure of territorial unilingualism, or by improvements in the bilingual solution that has been tried since 1968. Settling the economic problem does not necessarily require a constitutional reorganization. But the idea of a national homeland necessarily challenges the current Canadian constitutional framework. In this sense, Pierre Trudeau, Prime Minister of Canada, was perfectly aware of the realities of the situation when he said, after the Quebec election of November 15, 1976, that the real question was, "Can francophones of Quebec consider Canada as their country, or must they feel at home only in Quebec?"

Surprisingly, the idea of a national homeland for French-speaking Quebecers does not seem to worry the English-speaking experts who comment on Quebec. The language problems and the economic problems seem more pressing, and they make the headlines and are described in detail. But nationalist feelings, which are really the root of the matter, are neglected altogether. People will say: "What Quebec really wants is more control over all things cultural; what Quebec wants is a series of specific concessions; what Quebec really wants is this, or that." No one mentions the fundamental desire: a homeland for a nation. In my view, as a conclusion drawn from years of reading and interviewing, it is on this idea of a "true" homeland for French-speaking Quebecers that Parti Québécois leaders will try to unite Quebec. The other objectives, language and economics, coincide with this third objective, but this one alone necessarily leads to the demand for sovereignty.

Territorial Symbols

Those who hold the view that French Canadians can feel at home only in Quebec have succeeded in changing the label by which Quebec French Canadians identify themselves. Fifteen years ago, nobody in Quebec would have used the term "Québécois" to designate an inhabitant of the Province of Quebec: this label was applied only to the inhabitants of Quebec City. The French-speaking inhabitants of the province of Quebec were called French Canadians, just like "Francophones" in the other provinces of Canada. Only the French-speaking inhabitants of the maritime provinces, who were descendants of the French settlers who came to "Acadia" (now New Brunswick and Nova Scotia) in the seventeenth and early eighteenth centuries, had a separate name: Acadians. In the St. Lawrence Valley, the French settlers of the same period had taken the name of "Canadiens", because their territory, New France, was locally known as Canada. Indeed, for more than 150 years after the British conquest of New France in 1759-1760, the French-speaking inhabitants of Canada described themselves as "les Canadiens" and labelled the English-speaking newcomers "les Anglais". After Confederation, the expression "French Canadian" progressively displaced the former appellation. And now, in the 1970s, a large proportion of

French-speaking Quebecers call themselves "les Québécois" (and they include under this term any inhabitant of the province of Quebec who considers Quebec his homeland).

During the 1960s, several surveys included questions about the ethnic loyalties of French-speaking Canadians, but normally these surveys made no reference to the term "Québécois," because that term was not yet in general use in Quebec. In these surveys of the 1960s, respondents were asked whether they considered themselves French Canadians or simply Canadians. These surveys showed that 20 to 25 per cent identified themselves as "French Canadians only", and 40 to 60 per cent as "French Canadians first", with the remainder (between 20 and 35 per cent, depending on the survey) saying they were "Canadians first". The first known survey of the whole Quebec population to use the word "Québécois" was conducted in 1970, a few years after the new name had begun to become popular. This survey, conducted by sociologist Maurice Pinard, revealed that, of a sample of 4,889 French-speaking Quebec adults, 21 per cent considered themselves "Québécois, 44 per cent "French Canadians", 34 per cent "Canadians", and one per cent something else. According to Parti Québécois sources, private surveys completed between 1973 and 1976 indicate that a majority of French-speaking Quebecers now call themselves "Québécois".

This increasing popularity of the term "Québécois" shows how important the territorial symbol of Quebec is in the social thinking of contemporary French-speaking Quebecers. In a way, those who label themselves "Québécois" express their political loyalty to the society bounded by Quebec frontiers, Quebec values and Quebec institutions. But a political loyalty is rarely exclusive. People who express a loyalty to their country generally feel related to both larger and smaller territorial symbols as well: North America, the Western World, a province, a region, a city. However, one of these loyalties is generally dominant. A "true" Canadian is a Canadian first, then a Manitoban, Albertan or whatever. In Quebec, currently, fewer than one third of French-speaking adults consider themselves "Canadians first". When asked which government they favor, Ottawa or Quebec, four French-speaking Quebecers out of ten say Quebec, one says Ottawa, two say both, two say neither, and one starts to argue. Outside Quebec, six English-speaking Canadians out of ten favor Ottawa, and only one favors his provincial government (two others say both, and one neither), or roughly so[1]. According to the survey data used on the CBC radio program *Sunday Morning* on April 3, 1977, when asked which government they think of when asked "which government is yours", 50.7 per cent of the Quebec respondents of both languages said Quebec and 32.7 per cent said Ottawa.

In Quebec, contrary to the norm in the rest of Canada, the dominant loyalty of the largest number is addressed to the symbols of the province, and not to those of Canada. This loyalty, however, is restrained by conflicting views related to other rallying symbols. Thus, according to a small survey conducted in 1968 by political scientist H. D. Forbes among Quebec youth, 77 per cent of the 699 young people who answered the question said that they considered the whole of Canada as their country and only 20 per cent said that their country was restricted to Quebec alone. The survey also showed that individuals were ready to accept several designations in order to identify themselves: 80 per cent of this sample of Quebec youth accepted the term "Québécois" as fitting them (a percentage which far exceeds anything that has been obtained for a sample of the whole population). But, at the same time, 78 per cent of these respondents accepted the term "Canadien français", 65 per cent accepted the term "Canadien", 30 per cent the expression "Américain du Nord", and 15 per cent the word "Français". The loyalty to Quebec exists, but it is (or was) a loyalty tempered by other loyalties. It is clear that many Quebecers see Quebec as their homeland, just as many Canadians see Canada as their homeland. But the idea of Canada, as a territorial symbol, conflicts with the idea many Quebecers have of their homeland. The territory of Canada includes Quebec.

If a break-up of the Canadian federation were to occur, the territorial symbols would undoubtedly lead to fierce arguing about boundaries, because many Quebecers, notably the leading publicists of the independence movement, consider that their part of Canadian territory should be roughly proportional to the percentage traditionally constituted by Quebec in the Canadian population, that is 30 per cent.[2] At present, Quebec territory covers 523,860 square miles, or 15.4 per cent of Canada's 3,560,238 square miles of land. The part of the Quebec continental peninsula known as Labrador, which is now Newfoundland territory, covers 101,881 square miles (3.0 per cent of the total (Canadian surface). The islands located east of the 79° 30′ longitude, north of the Quebec peninsula, account for another 4.6 per cent of Canada. Parti Québécois members who talk about Quebec territory usually consider that in the event of a break-up of Canada, a sovereign Quebec should cover the territory of the province, plus the federal territory east of the 79° 30′ longitude, and the islands in the St. Lawrence, plus possibly Labrador. Labrador was awarded to the then Dominion of Newfoundland in 1927 by the British Privy Council, in settlement of claims made at the time by Newfoundland and the then separate Dominion of Canada (Newfoundland joined the Canadian federation in 1949). Quebec was the part of Canada which was "truncated" as a consequence of the British Privy Council decision, and the population of Quebec, by and large, has maintained the view that Labrador is "rightly" part of Quebec. In any case, if the Canadian federation were to break up, the territorial vision of Quebec which prevails among "les Québécois" would lead to a lot of aggressive arguing. If the Parti Québécois gains the support of a majority of the Quebec electorate (which constitutes 28 per cent of the Canadian population) in favor of a sovereign state, it will probably insist on at least 20 to 22 per cent of Canadian territory for that state.

It is clear that territorial symbols play a large part in the definition of a "homeland". They even play a part in the expression of loyalties in the daily behavior of many citizens of Canada. Hence the standing joke in Canada of telling people who go into or out of Quebec not to forget their passports. When a Quebecer says he is "a Canadian first", there can be no doubt that he considers the whole territory of Canada *his* country. This is a psychological response, for he has been told that this part of the world belongs to Canadians, that a Canadian is at home everywhere within the borders of this vast area. He loves the picture of beautiful Lake Louise in the Canadian Rockies, or of charming Nova Scotian coves, and even if he has never been out of Quebec, he cherishes such scenes as his private property — just as English-speaking Canadians hold to the landscape of the Gaspé coast or picturesque Quebec City. Territorial symbols carry deep significance for many people. The idea that a territory can be a "property" dominates the whole world: indeed the whole world has been divided into pieces, and it is a life objective for millions of individuals to acquire a small piece of land that would be "private property". Naturally, territorial symbols, and eagerness to own land, lead to conflicts over the most desirable resource on earth: a place in the sun.

Quebecers who want to bring about Quebec's accession to sovereignty thus want to establish their "shared property claims" over the territory which they consider the homeland of the Québécois. These Quebecers do not identify themselves with English-speaking Canadians living outside Quebec, but they feel themselves to be members of a "new and developing" Quebec society. They consider Lake Louise and Peggy's Cove foreign beauty spots, just as Switzerland, Rome or Washington, D.C. are nice places to be in, but places which do not "belong" to Quebecers: what belongs to Quebecers is Quebec.

Area and Power

Property rights over a piece of land imply a definite control by the owner over his territory. The whole idea of private ownership of land is to endow individuals with unquestioned authority over an area: the principle of private ownership, on which most people agree, enables individuals to "reign" supreme over an area of known dimensions, without having to resort to force or violence in order to establish their sovereignty.

Many Quebecers feel that they are "outsiders" when they go out of Quebec to other Canadian provinces. At the same time, they feel that "outsiders" (that is, Canadians from other provinces) have a lot of say about what goes on in Quebec. Many Quebecers, moreover, have the feeling that they have no say in Canadian affairs, and can influence no government other than that of Quebec.[3] According to a survey conducted in 1968 by political scientist John Meisel, 58 per cent of the 632 French-speaking respondents of the Quebec sample felt that they had no say in Canadian politics; only 34 per cent of the 927 Ontario respondents had such a feeling. Statistics on the relative interest shown in federal and provincial elections illustrate similar attitudes. Voter turnout in the last few Quebec provincial elections has hovered between 80 and 85 per cent, while it stands in the 60-to-75-percent range in provincial elections held in other parts of Canada. Conversely, while voting turnout in federal elections reaches 80 per cent in English-speaking Canada, it stays around 70 per cent in French-speaking Quebec. For many Quebec voters, the government of Quebec is theirs, while the federal government of Canada is the government of English-speaking Canadians.

Quebecers who feel that way naturally wish for more powers over their own area for the government which they consider their own. Such attitudes reflect the sense of belonging to that particular society defined by the French language, the territorial symbols of Quebec, and Quebec-based institutions. However, these attitudes are not held with the same degree of intensity by all Quebecers: loyalties are divided, and a majority of Quebec voters are confused or ambiguous on the question of identifying *their* government, *their* territory, and *their* reference group.

In spite of this ambiguity, when asked to express their position on the debate between the Parti Québécois and the federal government, a majority of French-speaking Quebecers say they favor the concession of more powers to the Quebec government. In a 1973 survey conducted by a McGill University research team led by Richard Hamilton and Maurice Pinard, among 861 French-speaking respondents 13 per cent said they were in favor of Quebec independence, and another 39 per cent said they wished that more powers would be transferred from Ottawa to Quebec; only three per cent of this sample wished that Quebec could transfer powers to Ottawa, while 21 per cent were in favor of maintaining the existing division of powers between the two governments (23 per cent had no opinion). The CBC *Sunday Morning* survey (April 3, 1977) revealed that 35.5 per cent of the people interviewed in a representative sample of French and English Quebecers were in favor of maintaining the existing division of powers. On the other hand 38.6 per cent favored an extension of Quebec's powers, 12.4 per cent favored an extension of Ottawa's powers, and 13.5 per cent abstained.

It is safe to hypothesize that the fundamental motivation behind Quebecers' opinions in favor of Quebec independence or increased autonomy is related to the sense of identity felt in relation to the French-speaking society of Quebec. Indeed, another survey conducted by Maurice Pinard in 1970 revealed that, among 795 respondents who said that they favored Quebec's secession from Canada, 52 per cent said that they were motivated by "nationalistic" economic reasons; these economic reasons were of the following type: "*We* would become stronger; *our* savings would stay home; *we* would administer *our* resources *ourselves; our* taxes would be reduced. . . ." The other respondents favoring Quebec secession did not mention a motivation related to economics, but were motivated by sentiments such as cultural independence, improved collective status, reduction of ethnic tensions and so on.

Conversely, the fear of possible Quebec secession depends little on nationalist attitudes but rather almost entirely on economic insecurity. Both before and after independence, a secessionist country usually finds some of its outside markets cut off for various reasons. During the transition period leading to secession, clashes between extremist groups for and against separation cause chaos and violence and lead to economic stagnation. In the case of Quebec, leading entrepreneurs and managers could exile themselves and leave Quebec without economic leadership, the prey of leftists. Economic fears are held by the leading opponents of the Parti Québécois, and the fight against independence is essentially based on the fear of economic losses,[4]

Surprisingly, however, few people ever argue for or against Quebec independence from an institutional viewpoint. Institutional arguments and references to particular aspects of the federal set-up or to questions related to federal-provincial relations rarely show up in the answers obtained to open questions about Quebec independence asked by sociologists or political scientists who conduct surveys in Quebec or Canada as a whole.

Quebec and Canadian Federalism

The average Canadian does not seem to understand that the immediate issue involved in Quebec independence is the federal government's own presence in Quebec. The average Canadian does not even know the correct answers to questions related to the division of powers between the federal and the provincial governments. A Canada-wide survey conducted in 1968 by the Institute for Behavioural Research of Toronto revealed, for instance, that 52 per cent of the respondents did not know that unemployment insurance was a federal responsibility, 38 per cent did not know that foreign affairs were a federal responsibility, and 40 per cent were not aware of the fact that education was a provincial responsibility. Governmental institutions and division of powers are matters which, in the view of a majority of Canadians, do not warrant much attention and do not need to be known with any degree of precision. Indeed, a survey conducted for the Montreal French daily *La Presse* after the 1974 federal election showed that a majority of the voters in the Montreal area went to the polling booths without knowing the name of any local candidate except the Liberal, and with a very scant idea of the problems which had been discussed during the campaign.[5]

The general ignorance of the workings of governmental institutions probably explains the fact that, for a majority of the people, Quebec independence is not naturally related to what it is meant to achieve: a reorganization of governmental institutions operating in Quebec. What the Parti Québécois is for is a peaceful reorganization of the federal system, in terms of the federal presence in Quebec and federal power over Quebec. What is at stake is the federal presence in Quebec.

Although this does not show up in surveys, the federal government is the institution most immediately and directly concerned by the secessionist option of many Quebecers. Indeed, if a break-up of the Canadian federation were to occur, its most perceptible effect would be a reorganization of federal departments, offices and crown corporations. It has been estimated that between 15 and 20 per cent of federal employees would stop working under the

authority of the federal government and start working under the authority of
the Quebec government. Most of the federal employees likely to be involved
are already residents of Quebec and work in offices located either in Quebec or
in the federal capital. It has been estimated that about two thirds of the
personnel involved would not even need to move to another office building;
among the rest, however, there are several thousand who would have to move
from Ottawa to Montreal or Quebec City. The moving of several thousand
households subsequent to a governmental reorganization is the *minimum* to
be expected as a consequence of Quebec's accession to sovereignty.

This governmental reorganization, in the view of Parti Québécois
leaders, is the only means available to French-speaking Quebecers who want
to apply in Quebec policies which differ from those which are applied in the
rest of Canada. On many questions which are now the responsibility of the
federal government, French-speaking Quebecers hold views which differ from
those of English-speaking Canadians: this is the case in matters of language,
culture, scientific development, communications, agriculture, trade, and so
on. French Canadians are poorly represented in the associations which lobby
in Ottawa, and they are a minority in every federal committee or council.
When the demands from Quebec differ from those of Ontario, the latter are
likely to prevail, and the French-Canadian representatives cannot easily
obtain "special treatment" for Quebec.

With a declining proportion of the total Canadian population, French-
speaking Quebecers (now between 20 and 23 per cent of Canada) cannot hope
to dominate the government side of the Canadian House of Commons any
more.* However, French-speaking members of Parliament have constituted
between 40 and 55 per cent of the government benches since 1896, except for
the periods of Conservative rule: 1911-1921, 1930-1935 and 1957-1963, or 21
of the last 81 years. Such a feat was achieved because Quebec sent a solid bloc
of Liberal representatives to the House of Commons, while English-speaking
Canadians were more or less evenly divided between Liberals and
Conservatives. In federal elections, Quebec helped the Liberal party and kept
it in power. But, even with its overrepresentation on the government side of
Parliament, Quebec never obtained more than one third of the Cabinet posts,
and the Quebec ministers in Ottawa were not able to introduce even such timid
measures as French words on the federal cheques issued to Quebec residents
until the 1960s, when bombs began to explode in Quebec and showed how
exasperated some Quebecers had become.

In spite of the leadership of Prime Minister Trudeau after 1968, a number

---

*The 1971 census found 3,668,000 inhabitants of Quebec who stated that they spoke
French only; 713,000 others had French as their mother tongue but were able to speak
both French and English; and 522,000 more, who spoke both French and English, did
not have French as their mother tongue. Out of 21,568,000 inhabitants of Canada
(1971), unilingual French-speaking Quebecers account for 17 per cent of the
population of the country. Quebecers who speak French, whatever their mother
tongue, account for 23 per cent of the total Canadian population.

of Quebec interests have been frustrated by federal policies. The priority of the Trudeau Cabinet has been "Canadian unity" and measures which would have upheld Quebec's autonomist positions have generally been brushed aside. The Quebec government position on a constitutional amendment formula for Canada has been perhaps the most significant case; another case has been the Quebec government position on social affairs; a third one, the Quebec government position concerning communications. Among less publicized questions which have raised problems in the area of "national unity", one can mention the negotiations on the James Bay hydro project, the debate on container terminals, production quotas and subsidies in agriculture, tariff negotiations, immigration, Quebec's international relations, the Quebec Pension Plan, Quebec housing policies, and many others.

When the Quebec government states a position which runs against the federal position, it usually does so for reasons related to Quebec's particular circumstances: its demographic structure, its industrial structure, its foreign markets and types of exports, its language, and other distinctive characteristics.

Although they could not detail what powers should be held by Quebec, a majority of French-speaking Quebecers are aware of the situation in which French-speaking Quebecers find themselves when dealing with the federal government. A large part of the news related to the Canadian government in the Quebec media consists of conflicting statements uttered by Quebec and Ottawa ministers on some aspect or other of their continuing quarrel. And it is not surprising that a majority of French-speaking Quebecers consider the division of powers a source of waste which could be eliminated by giving one single government complete authority over the areas where conflicting interests lead Ottawa and Quebec to confront each other.

Quebec's Case Against the Federal Government

The Quebec provincial government has been the upholder of the interests of French Canadians since 1867. And in the view of Quebec nationalists these interests have regularly been at odds with those of the rest of the Canadian population. The federal government has, for instance, undertaken the building of railways and canals which have served the interests of the English-speaking population of the country and of Montreal, but it has neglected the areas of Quebec inhabited by French Canadians. The federal government, between 1914 and 1918 and between 1939 and 1945, greatly developed the industrial capacity of Canada, but did so to the benefit primarily of southern Ontario and, to a lesser extent, of English-speaking Montreal. By and large, the federal government of Canada, since 1867, has been the government of English-speaking Canadians and the government of Quebec has been the government of French Canadians.

The Quebec case against the federal government is not a case against federalism; it is a case against a system prejudicial to French Canadians.

Federalism is based on the idea that the areas of governmental action where conflicts are likely to develop along territorial lines should fall under the authority of territorial governments, while the areas of governmental action where various territories can find a common interest should be administered by a common, central, federal government. The Canadian federation developed a division of powers between the provincial governments, on one side, and the central government, on the other side, which was an application of the federal principle to the particular circumstances of the British North American colonies in 1867. Matters of local interest, which could not fit into any single Canadian standard, were left to the provinces. These provincial concerns included education, a particularly delicate question in a country where two language groups and various religious denominations coexisted. Provincial powers also included the administration of natural resources and agriculture (the latter falling also under federal jurisdiction in its more general aspects). In addition, the provincial jurisdiction covered local government as well as public services and regulations established for local purposes or private objectives.

The authority of the provincial governments was delineated in a restrictive manner in four sections of the constitutional statute which created the Dominion of Canada in 1867 (sections 92, 93, 94 and 95 of the British North America Act, 1867). The authority of the central government, on the other hand, was stated in very broad terms in one section of the statute (section 91) and reiterated in the sections relating to the provinces so as to restrict the extension of provincial powers. Paragraph 10 of section 92 stated that the Canadian Parliament had control over interprovincial communications and over public works which it considered of general Canadian interest. Section 93 gave the Canadian government the authority to interfere in educational matters if the rights of denominational schools established before 1867 were being threatened by provincial legislation. Section 95 stated that both the federal Parliament and the provincial legislatures could make laws relating to agriculture and immigration but that the federal laws would have precedence.

In its division of legislative powers, the British North America Act of 1867 put the central government in a dominant position. The new Canadian government had authority over practically every area of governmental action except those which related to municipalities, education and local matters. In the area of tax revenue, the central government found itself with 60 per cent of all taxation receipts in Canada, the provinces and municipalities being left with the greatly unpopular direct taxation (which, in any case, the central government could also use). Moreover, the federal government was given the power to disallow provincial legislation which ran counter to federal interests (this federal power over provincial legislation was described in sections 55, 56, 57 and 90 of the Act).

Administrative powers in the provinces were to be held by a federal nominee, the Lieutenant-Governor (sections 58 and 59 of the Act). In 1878 and again in 1891, the Lieutenant-Governor of Quebec used his authority and tried to curb provincial initiatives, in spite of constitutional practice which had already restricted the powers of the Lieutenant-Governor in other provinces. This federal control over Quebec, through the Lieutenant-Governor, led to two serious crises, one in 1878, the other in 1891-1892. Canadian Senators are also nominated by the federal government and they are in no way representatives of "provincial interests".

In view of the Fathers of Confederation, the areas of governmental action which were left to the provincial governments were indeed very limited. But the history of the Canadian federation has proved that the Fathers of Confederation underestimated the conflicts which could arise in the areas of responsibility awarded to the federal government. Federal policies in several areas benefited some provinces at the expense of others, and as early as 1870 provincial governments began to fight to protect aggrieved regional interests. Nova Scotia felt so underprivileged during the first 30 years of Confederation that its provincial government came to take serious autonomist stands. So did Quebec, especially after 1886. Later, it would be Alberta and British Columbia. The pressure put on the federal government to let the provincial governments take initiatives gradually led to a reassessment of the division of powers in the Canadian federation. New areas of government action were opened and left to the provinces (roads for automobiles, electricity, natural resource development, etc.), while others were taken by the central government (radio, foreign affairs, unemployment insurance, family allowances, pensions, etc.).

While Canadian federalism was evolving according to the circumstances, reflecting the interplay of political forces and regional interests, Quebec became more and more dissatisfied and its government took autonomist positions more and more frequently. It introduced new taxes in 1882 (corporation taxes) and in 1892 (succession duties), and was among the first to resort to corporate income taxes (1932), personal income taxes (1939) and sales taxes (1940). It showed its opposition to federal involvement in such matters as prohibition (notably on the occasion of a 1898 plebiscite on the subject), agriculture (notably between 1911 and 1920), welfare payments, including pensions and unemployment insurance (notably during the 1930s).[6] Quebec rejected federal proposals related to taxation from 1945 to 1957 and obtained the establishment of a federal program of equalization payments. In the 1960s, an opting-out formula to be applied to federal grants to provincial governments was established at Quebec's insistence, and the Quebec government was the only one to take advantage of the formula: instead of benefiting from federal grants, Quebec gained access to tax rebates.

For more than 40 years now the Quebec government has generally provided the main institutional opposition to governmental centralization or policy standardization in Canada. It was often the only government to oppose federal initiatives. It is the only provincial government that maintains services in many areas in which the federal government has the monopoly of action outside Quebec. In Quebec, there is a fullfledged Department of Revenue, which reaches into the pocket of every individual and corporate taxpayer in Quebec. No other province has such an organization. The Quebec government has a disguised department of foreign affairs, with delegations in a dozen foreign cities, intergovernmental agreements in several areas, regular exchange programs, and so on. No other province in Canada has anything approaching this, not even Ontario. The Quebec government has a Department of Immigration, as does Ontario: Quebec has a Department of Communications, with a provincial radio and television corporation (Radio-Quebec). In the field of agriculture, Quebec maintains the most extensive provincial services in Canada. In the field of labor, Quebec maintains manpower centres, the only provincial manpower centres in Canada. Quebec also maintains a provincial police, a provincial pension plan, a provincial housing corporation, a provincial film board, and dozens of other provincial offices, commissions and services which one rarely finds in other provinces.

There are very few areas of governmental activity in which the Quebec government has not established its own services which compete, on Quebec territory, with federal services in the same areas. This competition is visible not only to Quebec civil servants but to thousands of Quebecers and is resented as sheer insanity, not only because it wastes millions of dollars but also because the provincial programs are generally considered better suited to Quebec needs, while lacking the budgets necessary in order to be effective.

Parti Québécois activists object to the federal government's moves toward centralization, because they believe that decisions taken in Ottawa are taken either by English-speaking senior bureaucrats or by committees where English-speaking civil servants or ministers are a majority. In the view of Quebec nationalists, Ottawa decisions made by French Canadians are extremely rare, and decisions which favor Quebec or Quebec interests generally reflect the impact of crises such as the Quebec terrorism of the 1960s or the growth of Parti Québécois support in the 1970s. When a decision is taken in Ottawa, it is generally the result of pressures put on the decision-makers by interest groups in which French Canadians are a silent minority. English-speaking civil servants are linked to all kinds of interests and they usually try to defend those interests, just as French-speaking civil servants do — but, at the decision-making levels, for every French-speaking civil servant one finds four or five English-speaking civil servants. When Ottawa launches a new program, such as the 1971 Opportunities for Youth project or the 1972 Local Initiatives Program, applications for jobs, subsidies and information coming from English-speaking Canadians flow in for several weeks before such applications start to come in from French-speaking Quebecers in any number. This is probably explained by the "grapevine effect": more English-speaking applicants hear about the program first.

Among examples of federal decisions considered detrimental to French Canadians, those which come up most often are immigration, certain welfare programs, federal actions in the cultural sector, and the auto pact. But other examples abound: the Borden line for oil imports, freight rates, and so on. Nationalists like to quote immigration statistics*: between 1901 and 1964, out of 8,089,823 immigrants to Canada, only 112,740 were French, that is 1.5 per cent of the total. Among the immigrants of other than British or French origin who opted to live in Quebec, three out of four chose English as their "official" language.**

When European governments started their welfare programs in the 1920s, pressure mounted in Toronto and other large cities of Canada for old-age pensions and similar transfer payments. At the time, older citizens accounted for eight per cent of Ontario's population but they accounted for less than four per cent of Quebec's French-speaking population. By having Ottawa pay for old-age pensions, the English-speaking pressure groups angered Quebec civil servants who saw no need for such pensions in Quebec and considered that their province had more pressing needs than old-age pensions, even though they were seen as a generous idea. The federal law was enacted in 1927, and Quebec, in 1936, was the last province to sign the agreement.

In the 1950s, English-speaking Canadians became aware of the cultural impact on Canada of the United States, and pressure groups started a campaign for federal action on the cultural sector. French-speaking Quebecers, at the time, felt no threat from the United States culture industry; on the contrary, they were of the opinion that "culture" was the main reason for the existence of a provincial government and were in favor of provincial action in this sector. Quebec fought against the federal decision to finance cultural programs. Quebec lost. Millions of dollars were spent by the federal government in various programs which primarily benefited English-speaking individuals and their institutions. Between 1960 and 1975, according to available statistics, French-speaking Quebecers and their institutions got less than 15 per cent of the hundreds of millions of dollars which were spent in federal scientific and cultural grants, subsidies and research contracts.

In the 1960s, Ontario and the federal government became concerned about the huge deficits registered in the Canadian trade in automobiles, trucks and auto parts. An agreement was negotiated with the United States and with the leading American car-makers. The Quebec government at the same time was trying to attract European and Japanese car-makers in order to start a

---

*See Rosaire Morin, *L'immigration au Canada* (Montreal: Les Editions de l'Action nationale, 1966). Morin quotes Pierre Laporte (page 144) who, as a minister of the Quebec government, declared on February 10, 1965, "It is clear that immigration as organized by the government of Canada has not been organized in the cultural interests of French Canada." (*Journal des Débats,* 1965, p. 464, translation).

**In 1961, according to census data, in the Montreal metropolitan area, 97 per cent of the 1,353,480 people of French origin had French as their mother tongue; 5.6 per cent of the 377.625 people of British origin had French as their mother tongue (93.92 per cent had English) and 23.72 per cent of the 135,731 people of other origins had chosen French as their "official" language, while 76.32 per cent had chosen English.

small-car industry in Quebec. Quebec's interests were at odds with those of Ontario. According to Quebec spokesmen, the European car-makers received no help from the federal government. The Canada-United States auto pact led to a substantial increase in industrial activity in Ontario, which had an inflationary effect that was not compensated for by counter-measures in regions suffering from economic stagnation. Quebec was unable to develop an auto industry of any size and it suffered from Ontario-induced inflation; Quebec's economic structure came out of the adventure still more underprivileged.

Immigration policies, welfare programs, cultural and scientific development programs, and the Canada-United States auto pact are only four of a dozen examples Quebec nationalist leaders cite to show how the federal government protects interests which run counter to those of French-speaking Quebecers.* Even though many federal decisions taken since the mid-1960s have had a pro-Quebec bias, the history of Canadian federalism confirms the general feeling held by a majority of French-speaking Quebecers that they would be better served if the Quebec government had a larger share of tax revenues and a monopoly over the numerous areas of government action where French-speaking Quebecers have interests which conflict with those of English-speaking Canadians.

Theoretical Advantages of Federalism

The belief that the federal government serves the interests of English-speaking Canadians and has a detrimental effect on French-speaking Quebecers has a great impact in Quebec. Moreover, many French-speaking Quebecers fail to see the relevance for the Quebec population of the theoretical advantages of federalism.

The most important theoretical advantage of federalism is the equilibrium that it maintains between two different sets of political institutions, federal and provincial. The institutional balance created by federalism limits the tendency of governments to centralize, to control and to standardize everything. The persistence of regional or provincial governments is a guarantee of some limits to standardization and a minimum degree of territorial dispersion of public expenditures. In a federation, the central government has to face contending power structures which impede its dominating tendencies. In a federation, citizens can turn to another government when they fight against a bureaucracy. In a federation, decisions which serve the interests of the whole country are easily made and obeyed because there is one central authority empowered to reach them; at the same time, territorial governments can safeguard local interests and regional particularisms. This great theoretical advantage of federalism is often quoted by those who take issue with the Parti Québécois.[7] However most nationalists

---

*A periodical such as *L'Action nationale* provides a good survey of these examples.

have a fundamental objection to the argument. They approve of the idea of an institutional balance in a federation, but in their view there can be no effective balance if the regional communities are different in size and in culture.

Nevertheless, the idea of making several cultural communities coexist within a large territory and under one set of economic regulations is seen as another great advantage of federalism. Federalism enables different cultural communities to benefit from a common market and from economic structures which permit a better use of productive resources and lead to higher standards of living. Industries which could not develop in any of the individual communities if they were not federated can become profitable and prosper. Such economic benefits can sustain each of the cultural communities and its particular culture. Those who uphold the federal principle in Quebec usually say that Canada, Yugoslavia, Switzerland and India are good examples of coexistence between different and sometimes antagonistic linguistic communities.[8] These four federations, and other federations which have similar features, show the world an example.

From this viewpoint, Canadian federalism can be seen as a great success. Canadians rank among the wealthiest peoples on earth, and the French-speaking minority has succeeded in maintaining its culture and its identity, while benefiting from the general economic prosperity of Canada. The French- and English-speaking communities of Canada have worked together through the federal institutions in relative peace for more than a hundred years. The presence of a French community in Quebec has offered other Canadians the opportunity to know, close to them, a different, great, world-wide culture. However, French-speaking Quebecers who feel threatened by the attractive power of English-speaking North America, notably the leaders of the Parti Québécois, generally believe that the culture safeguards offered by Canadian federalism are insufficient. They would feel more secure if they could control all the governmental institutions which operate in their territory, while maintaining the economic co-operation that exists among the various regions of Canada.

In some sense, while they may be badly informed on the workings of federal institutions, French-speaking Quebecers often seem very pragmatic when they talk about federalism. They are not impressed by its theoretical advantages. They want to protect the cultural identity of their society and assure it a secure and promising future. They wish that English-speaking Canadians could understand this objective of leaving the Quebec government free to expand its services so as to better safeguard the interests of French-speaking Quebecers (the interests of English-speaking Quebecers being considered as already safeguarded by Quebec's location in North America).

Many politically active French-speaking Quebecers, including Liberals, Conservatives and Péquistes, take great pains to explain that Quebec's French-speaking majority is not anti-English; this majority is only concerned with the survival of the French-speaking "nation" and the economic prosperity of Quebec. These Quebecers believe that nobody but themselves

304   *Part V Ethnic Conflicts*

can realize these goals and, as a consequence, only the government controlled by French-speaking Canadians should exert power in Quebec.* But they are aware of the economic constraints on the ideal of maximum political autonomy for Quebec. In a word, these Quebecers want Quebec to have the greatest amount of political autonomy consistent with the maintenance of beneficial economic relations with the rest of Canada.

Federalism is infinitely varied in its practice. If the European Economic Community is federalism, the "sovereignty-association" scheme put forward by Parti Québécois leaders is also federalism. Federalism in the Canada of the 1970s is very different from the federalism of the 1870s. Canadian federalism differs from West German federalism, which in turn differs from Australian federalism, and so on. Federalism is evolving and adaptable. The flexibility of federalism offers Canadian political leaders the possibility of compromises between English Canada and French Quebec which could satisfy a majority of those who hold to a territorial perception of what their country should be, and who have only a rudimentary knowledge of governmental institutions.

What Quebec Wants

Those French-speaking Quebecers who say that they are "Québécois" and that their homeland is Quebec usually call for a maximization of the Quebec government's power over Quebec territory. These pro-Quebec French Canadians are clearly a majority in Quebec. A majority of French-speaking Quebecers has already supported the Parti Québécois in the November 1976 provincial election. Surveys have shown that between 60 and 75 per cent of French-speaking Quebecers favor an extension of the Quebec government's powers. Approximately 70 per cent of them identify themselves as "Québécois" or as "French Canadians first". The strength of this pro-Quebec feeling, although relatively recent, has been steadily growing for the last two decades.

Surveys of the 1950s and early 1960s conducted by the Canadian Institute of Public Opinion and by Montreal's Groupe de Recherche Sociale showed that, at that time, concern for Quebec provincial autonomy was highly correlated with educational levels. In other words, only the elite was aware of the possibilities of government action in cultural matters. By the mid-1960s, this elite concern with government action and provincial autonomy had gained ground in the French-speaking urban population. In the 1970s, as we have seen, surveys revealed that the trend was being maintained: concern for the future of the French language and the French-speaking population of Quebec seems to be shared by quite a large proportion of Quebec's population. If this interpretation of available survey data corresponds to reality, there are reasons to believe that nationalist feelings could eventually

---

*The Parti Québécois ministers, now, and the Union Nationale premier, Daniel Johnson, in 1966, have been the best-known exponents of such views.

overcome the economic fears which stand in the way of the Parti Québécois quest for Quebec political independence.

Recent survey data show that a majority of French-speaking Quebecers now agree on a series of fundamental objectives, the first of which relates to the status of the French language in Quebec. According to a study by l'Institut Québécois d'Opinion Publique, published in three Quebec dailies on May 24, 1974, 67 per cent of the French-speaking people surveyed were in favor of making French the only official language of Quebec (19 per cent) or, at least, the priority language (48 per cent). According to the same report, 59 per cent of the French-speaking Quebecers interviewed favored a law making it compulsory for immigrants and immigrants' children to enrol in the French school system. Most English-speaking Quebecers (between 65 and 80 per cent of those who were interviewed, percentages varying according to ethnic origin) favored official bilingualism in Quebec and English schools for Quebec immigrants. The viewpoints of the English-speaking minority of Quebec were (and still are) sharply contrasted with the French Quebec perspective in the matter of language. In spite of the objections raised by the English-speaking minority of Quebec, in spite of the tendency of two French-speaking Quebecers out of ten to agree with these objections, and in spite of some disapproval of the 1977 Charter of the French Language,* it is clear that the majority in Quebec is united behind the objective of preserving and extending the use of the French language in Quebec. This objective is related, in the view of French-speaking political leaders, to the paramount objective of national survival.

Another objective pursued by French-speaking Quebecers relates to regional economic development. The inhabitants of Quebec are particularly dissatisfied with the state of their economy. They perceive themselves as being exploited by English-speaking managers, and they see the federal government as ignoring Quebec's economic interests. Although linguistic discrimination cannot explain much of Quebec's economic lag behind New York State or Ontario, French-speaking Quebecers tend to put a great deal of emphasis on this factor. On the whole, French-speaking Quebecers would like to see the Quebec government foster the industrial development of Quebec, especially outside Montreal, to the benefit of French-speaking entrepreneurs, managers and workers.

A third objective on which one finds a large degree of agreement concerns the control that French-speaking Quebecers should exert over the political institutions which operate in Quebec. Many Quebecers tend to consider Quebec their homeland and they feel a loyalty to the Quebec government and to the territorial symbols of Quebec. This loyalty outweighs the loyalty felt toward the federal government and the territorial symbols of Canada. In spite

---

*As revealed by the Goldfarb survey published September 26, 1977, in the Southam dailies. See *The Gazette,* Montreal, September 26, 1977, page 1. The data published by the Southam papers were somewhat contradicted by a survey commissioned by the *Reader's Digest,* October 1977.

of their dual loyalties and all the ambiguities such divided loyalties can nourish, most French-speaking Quebecers favor an extension of the powers of the Quebec government — in other words, some kind of "devolution" from the federal government to the government of Quebec.

Survey data published in April 1977 showed that 33 per cent of the French-speaking Quebecers were already willing to go along with the Parti Québécois as far as "souveraineté-association". Another survey, published by the *Reader's Digest* in October 1977, showed that the proportion of those who support "souveraineté-association" has grown substantially, reaching the 38 per cent mark in the whole of Quebec and 44 per cent as far as Francophones alone are concerned.*

In sum, these objectives, which would result in increased autonomy, perhaps going as far as "souveraineté-association", are what a majority of Quebec voters want. Quebec is trying to become as French as the rest of Canada is English, in order to safeguard the French-speaking community, in order to insure the survival of French. Quebec is trying to give its government all the powers required to develop Quebec industry and foster economic progress for the French-speaking population. There is indeed a majority united behind these objectives, but this majority is not consolidated under a single political leadership. Most of it supports the Parti Québécois, while parts of it are scattered among the other parties.

NOTES

[1] These figures are shown by the surveys in the following texts: Mildren A. Schwartz, *Politics and Territory — The Sociology of Regional Persistence in Canada* (Montreal: McGill-Queen's University Press, 1971), pages 104, 125; Vincent Lemieux, Marcel Gilbert and André Blais, *Une élection de réalignement — L'élection générale du 29 avril 1970 au Québec* (Montreal; Editions du Jour, 1970), pages 90-93; Jane Jenson and Peter Regenstreif, "Some Dimensions of Partisan Choice in Quebec, 1969," *Canadian Journal of Political Science/ Revue canadienne de science politique,* vol. III, no. 2 (June 1970), pages 308-317.

[2] For example, see Raymond Barbeau, *J'ai choisi l'indépendance* (Montreal: Les éditions de l'homme, 1961), pages 34, 35.

[3] This has been documented in David J. Elkins and Richard Simeon, "Regional Political Culture in Canada," *Canadian Journal of Political Science/ Revue canadienne de science politique,* vol. VII, no. 3 (September 1974), page 406.

[4] A good example of this is *Québec, le goût de l'indépendance,* a study by the Chamber of Commerce of the Province of Quebec (Montreal: Editions du Jour, 1969).

[5] *La Presse,* July 13, 1974, page A-5.

---

*The answers to the question relating to "souveraineté-association" were, for the whole of Quebec, 38 per cent for, 44 per cent against, 18 per cent undecided; and, for Francophones alone, 44 per cent for, 37 per cent against, 19 per cent undecided. The *Reader's Digest* based its survey on a 823-person sample. This study is recommended reading. See *Reader's Digest*, October 1977, pages 55ff.

⁶A chronology of the autonomist idea in Quebec is available in Robert Rumilly, *L'autonomie provinciale* (Montreal: Editions de l'arbre, 1948).

⁷One particularly articulate description of the advantages of federalism can be found in Gilles Lalande, *Pourquoi le fédéralisme?: Contribution d'un Québécois a l'intelligence du fédéralisme canadien* (Montreal: Hurtubise/HMH, 1972).

⁸Ibid., pages 21, 27, 169.

Chapter 19

Race Relations in Canada*

D. H. Clairmont and F. C. Wien

On a numerical basis, racial minorities have not been a significant portion of the Canadian population since the early years of European settlement. It is not surprising, therefore, that Canadian writings and public concern on the subject of race and ethnic relations have been dominated by attention to what we would call ethnic relations (i.e., relations among cultural sub-groups within a common racial category) — particularly French-English relations and European immigration patterns. The Canadian mosaic image has largely been constructed out of this reality; in much of the literature, racial groups are included in the picture primarily to illustrate the vertical nature of the mosaic.

In the United States, the reverse appears to be the case. A large oppressed racial minority has dominated public and academic attention and from time to time there are protests by or on behalf of the forgotten ethnics (Novak, 1972). Given this situation and the pervasive influence of American events in Canada, it is understandable that the way in which race relations is perceived in Canada and, to some extent, actual behaviour, are significantly affected by American patterns.

*Reprinted from Sociological Focus 9:2 (1976) by permission of the authors and the publishers.

It is worthwhile for a number of reasons to look specifically at race relations in Canada. Because of demographic and other changes, the subject is of increasing importance in the country while at the same time the significance of some ethnic differences appears to be declining. In addition, racial minorities have long roots in Canada. Their relation with the larger society has been marked by subordination, control and in some instances by sustained efforts at assimilation. Their history, therefore, presents a different side to the popular image of the mosaic. There are also sufficient differences with the American experiences that an attempt to sort out the unique features of the Canadian situation is warranted.

American Influences

Social science theorizing about race relations in Canada has been heavily influenced by American models. Racial minorities such as Blacks and Native peoples have also been significantly affected by the attitudes, styles of behaviour and social movements of their counterparts in the United States. On the whole, Canadians in their definition of situations, in their role models and their social policies, have drawn considerably from the American experience.

There appear to be at least three distinct American sociological approaches to race relations, each of which has been applied in Canada and merits brief consideration here: evolutionary universalism, internal colonialism and descriptive pluralism. The perspective identified as evolutionary universalism essentially posits that American society is proceeding by an evolutionary route to resolve its racial antagonisms in that citizenship is being expanded and ascription and particularism are giving way to achievement and universalism as variables patterning the bulk of social relationships (Parsons, 1971). From this vantage point, cultural and structural supports for racial antagonism and communal boundaries, while perhaps subject to some erratic shifts, will progressively diminish. This perspective is the chief basis for the celebration of the "melting pot" ideology of American society and also provides the underprinting for the liberal social problems approach that is so common in American (and Canadian) writings on race relations. The central thrust of this literature has been on the gap between standards and actuality in socio-economic status, and on individual prejudice and discrimination as explanatory variables. Emphasizing consensus and desiring integration, these social scientists have tended to see racial groups as aggregations rather than as organic entities; they have underestimated the staying-power of racial categorization as a basis for organization and mobilization, and have exhibited little awareness of alternative directions which diverse racial groups might pursue. The particular theoretical perspective with which evolutionary universalism is most closely associated is structure-functionalism.

In Canada, this approach has been particularly common in studies of the small, scattered Black population (Potter, 1961; Henry, 1975). Although the associated melting pot ideology has not been dominant in Canada, for reasons to be discussed below, it has nevertheless been quite pervasive in White attitudes towards certain racial minorities and in policies of assimilation and relocation directed at the native Indian, Inuit and Black populations (Clairmont and Magill, 1974; Chamberlin, 1975).

The internal colonialism approach to race relations has deep historical roots in American thinking but in the twentieth century it has become widespread only in the past decade. Emphasizing the economic system and racial antagonism, it sees race relations as complicating the inevitable class struggle of capitalism, with Blacks and Indians bearing a disproportionate share of the exploitative burden that keeps the system going. In this perspective race relations assume considerable importance since the oppressed Non-Whites, concentrated in the urban ghetto and patrolled by an occupying army of police, are often identified as the core of the vanguard who will force widespread qualitative societal change (Blauner, 1972). There is also the premise that capitalism is the principal barrier to racial harmony and equality. Marxist and neo-marxist theory is most often associated with the internal colonialism perspective. In the Canadian context, the expansion of white European settlers across North America at the expense of the aboriginal population, plus the establishment of reserves and the rigid control of the native population through the Indian Act by the federal government has made the internal colonialism perspective the dominant one in describing Indian-White relations in Canada (Carstens, 1971; Patterson, 1972; Frideres, 1975). Some native spokesmen have, however, resisted complete identification with the internal colonialism model, by articulating the differences between the Third World and the aboriginal or Fourth World (Manuel and Posluns, 1974). The metropolitan-hinterland variation of the internal colonialism model is also frequently seen in Canadian writings (Cohen, 1970; Davis, 1971).

Recently a third general perspective, descriptive pluralism, has emerged among American students of race relations. It has developed largely in response to the resurgence of sub-group loyalties and identification and the advocacy, especially by native Indians and Blacks, of collective rights and group autonomy. Numerous social scientists have written to challenge the melting-pot model in terms of both empirical support and social policy and have stressed the importance of intermediate, ascriptive groupings between the level of the family and mass society (Fein, 1970; Novak, 1972; Greeley, 1973).

Although there is no particular theoretical system which unifies the descriptive studies, the theoretical and comparative work of scholars such as van den Berghe (1967) and Schermerhorn (1970) is compatible with this approach. The descriptive pluralism framework is the most congruent with past and present Canadian social science studies of race relations. In fact, until the recent popularity of this approach in the United States, it was a distinguishing characteristic of Canadian studies which usually featured descriptions of the settlement patterns and communal organization of racial minorities (Clark, 1974).

If we turn to interaction between racial minorities across the border, the close ties of Native peoples and Blacks are particularly striking. Until the significant West Indian immigration of the past fifteen years, virtually all Blacks in Canada had come here from the United States. Loyalist Blacks, some free, some slave, came to Nova Scotia during the American revolution. Refugee Blacks, all free, settled in Nova Scotia as a consequence of the War of 1812 while many others, escaping the oppression of slavery via the "underground railroad," settled in Southern Ontario and the West during the pre-Emancipation nineteenth century. The bulk of the latter returned to the U.S. after the Civil War, however, and many Nova Scotia Blacks, like white Maritimers, emigrated to the New England states in the last half of the nineteenth century and first years of the twentieth (Winks, 1971). The small Canadian Black community has drawn heavily upon the larger American Black population for its heroes (e.g., Martin Luther King), policies (e.g., affirmative action), organizational models (e.g., Nova Scotia Association for the Advancement of Coloured People) and even its leaders (e.g., recruitment of Baptist pastors in the United States) (Clairmont and Magill, 1970).

With respect to the aboriginal population, the border between Canada and the United States was, of course, established only in recent times and in some instances through the middle of Indian cultural groupings. Consequently the border has much less meaning for native people, both symbolically and also legally through the provisions of the Jay Treaty, and in fact there is extensive mobility among Indians between the two countries. Organizations such as the American Indian Movement have chapters in Canada, and at a recent conference in Canada the World Council of Indigenous Peoples was established.[1]

It is fair to say that the Canadian population generally has been fascinated with and well informed about American developments in race relations. The initial response of young Canadians to the U.S. civil rights movement of the early 1960's was to volunteer for projects in the U.S. South, and some support organizations such as SNCC chapters were established at Canadian universities for fund-raising purposes. It was not until several years later that public attention turned to the Canadian situation. The Ku Klux Klan has also moved across the border in certain periods, becoming established in Ontario and Alberta, and American immigrants to Canada ranging from Loyalists with their slaves to war resisters and liberal professors have brought their perspectives on race relations to this country. Canadians have often copied U.S. policy initiatives, sometimes profiting from the trial run experienced in the U.S. but also adopting policies at the point when, with good reason, they were falling out of favour south of the border, as in the case of the residential boarding school concept for "educating" native people and the disastrous U.S. Indian termination policy of the 1950's.

The above is not to suggest that America is responsible for the bigotry and racial discrimination that occurs in Canada — in some respects the American record in race relations has been much better than the Canadian. It does suggest, however, that the race situation in the United States is an important contextual variable for what happens in Canada and how we interpret these events, and it will continue to be so. At the same time, however, there have historically been significant differences in the nature of race relations between the two countries and in the dominant ideology that characterizes them. There has also been a substantial increase in non-white immigration to Canada via the Commonwealth connection over the last fifteen years, for which American precedents are not entirely appropriate. We turn now to these considerations.

The Canadian Way

In contrast to the United States, Canada has often been characterized as being a mosaic rather than a melting-pot in terms of race and ethnic relations. The implication is that Canada is composed of a multiplicity of collectivities or sub-groups, each with its own cultural, racial or historical identity, who co-exist in an atmosphere of mutual toleration within a liberal democratic form of political economy. Such a system, sometimes labelled organic liberalism, stands in contrast to the conception of a new cultural and biological blend being created in America "in which the stocks and folkways of Europe, figuratively speaking, were indiscriminately mixed in the political pot of the emerging nation and fused by the fires of American influence and interaction into a distinctly new type," (Gordon, 1961).

Much scholarly effort has been expended concerning both the empirical and normative supports of the so-called Canadian Way. It is obviously an ideal construct which has been of some value in the attempt to grasp the uniqueness of Canadian reality and it remains an important consideration in a Canada still being shaped by immigration. In examining the roots of Canadian pluralism, most scholars point to the basic conception and constitutionally enshrined principle of Canada having been founded by the English and the French. The historic duality is congruent with an organic liberalism model and has been seen as the context within which other ethnic and even racial groups can establish claims and maintain some autonomy. While native people ironically have not been included among the charter groups, their special status has been recognized in treaties, the British North America Act and subsequent legislation.

Patterns of immigration and settlement have also contributed to the mosaic. European immigrants, for example, came in much larger numbers in relation to the domestic population in certain decades such as in the early 1900's than was the case in the U.S. and settled in self-contained communities. Non-white minorities have also either chosen or been restricted to their own communities — rural and isolated in the case of Blacks and Indians, urban and ghettoized in the case of the Chinese.

Another set of factors often presumed to be at the root of Canada's essential difference regarding race and ethnic relations is the conservative philosophy of the Loyalists fleeing the American revolution and the particular brand of liberalism brought to Canada from Europe after the mid-nineteenth century by the immigrants. Some writers also point to the threat of American expansion into Canadian territory as the West was being settled by Europeans, leading to a development pattern that was more orderly and controlled by the central government than was the case on the American frontier, and consequently less destructive of native and immigrant communities (Clark, 1968; Chamberlin, 1975). In comparison with the American treatment of the Indian population, for example, there is evidence that in Canada reserves were set up close to traditional hunting grounds rather than relocating native communities further west; the boundaries of reserves have not been redefined or violated as much, and both treaties and Indian policy via the Indian Act have had a more stable, more legally enshrined character than was the case in the United States (Lurie, 1968).

In a structural sense, then, of racial minorities living in identifiable communities and sharing a distinctive culture or life-style, it can be argued that the racial minorities contribute to the image of a mosaic in Canada. In other respects, particularly in their relationship with the larger society, the experience of the racial minorities parts company with that of the ethnic groups. Porter (1965) and Hughes and Kallen (1974) among others have documented the vertical nature of the mosaic, with white Anglo-Saxons at the top of the socio-economic pecking order, and the non-white groups at the bottom. The relationship with the larger society is better characterized by terms such as dependence, control, and domination-subordination than it is by the rhetoric associated with equal participation in the mosaic. Segregated Black schools, the relocation of the West-coast Japanese during W. W. II, the detailed controls spelled out in the Indian Act including, in the past, limitations on the right to vote, to organize and to carry out traditional cultural ceremonies, the racial limitations included in a series of Immigration Acts of which the Chinese Immigration Act of 1923 is but one example[2] — these are instances of the kind of relation that has existed between the racial minorities and the dominant white society. Sustained attempts at cultural assimilation have in particular been directed at the Indian and Inuit population, through the efforts of missionaries to "civilize" the natives and by secular educational authorities in more recent times (Cardinal, 1969; Hobart and Brant, 1969; Manuel and Posluns, 1974).

Pierre van den Berghe (1967) has used the term "Herrenvolk Democracies" to describe the situation in the United States and South Africa where liberal democracy has existed only for the white population. Similarly in Canada, while the institutionalization of race relations is significantly less, non-whites have more often been the unwilling subjects, of policies formulated and administered by the white population than active participants in shaping their own future (Hughes and Kallan, 1974; Thomson, 1974). Moreover, the Canadian Way, while legitimizing ethnic differences and emphasizing liberal democratic means of interest resolution, also has a practical corollary: a high degree of sensitivity among Canadians to the size and concentration of ascriptive groupings and the association with these variables of expectations of differential advantage. In other words, it was not left to the mosaic ideology alone to effectively guarantee collective rights, as exemplified by English manipulation of immigration policy to limit French immigrants in the hundred years after the conquest, and by the French Canadian "strategy" of "la revanche des berceaux." Immigration policy and the size of the ascriptive groupings have always been contentious issues in Canada. This fact, when reinforced by racist attitudes and ideologies, has caused Canadians to be especially sensitive to non-white demographics and to take appropriate action to keep their numbers small and ensure that they pose no threat (e.g., by blocking Chinese immigration and discouraging Blacks from settling in the West). Despite an apparent decline of racist stereotypes and ideologies, it is not surprising that fear and distrust would begin to grow as this immigrant-dependent society began to find that in recent years non-whites have made up an increasing proportion of total immigration and many more are eager to come.

Recent Trends in Race Relations

Since the Second World War and particularly in the 1960's substantial changes in the significance and nature of race relations have taken place in Canada. In particular race relations have become much more important than they have traditionally been in the society, due to the receding importance of ethnic differences among the English-speaking white population, changes in the number, distribution and composition of the racial minorities, increasing organization and the extension of citizenship rights among the latter, and other factors.

While the English-French duality and attendant problems in ethnic relations remain very important, there is considerable evidence that ethnic differences among the English-speaking European population are becoming less significant, multiculturalism policy notwithstanding. Reitz (1974) has shown, for example, the high rates of language loss among Germans, Poles, Ukrainians and Italians in urban areas across Canada, and it is expected that cultural and structural assimilation will continue among groups such as these, particularly when sources of renewal are diminished by the changing composition of immigrants to Canada (Breton, 1968). Noting this trend, some social scientists argue that the celebration of multiculturalism serves only to enhance the status of "ethnic" leaders and keeps the English-speaking Canadian population from mobilizing itself adequately to deal with the important problems of American domination and social justice (Horowitz, 1972).

Demographic changes have also elevated the relative importance of race relations. Prior to the immigration of the post-World War II period, Blacks constituted about 0.3% of the Canadian population and were concentrated chiefly in Nova Scotia, Montreal and South-Western Ontario. The Inuit, strung out along the Arctic coast, accounted for approximately 0.1% while estimates of the native Indian population (excluding non-status and Métis) are slightly higher than 1%. The Asian population, chiefly Chinese and Japanese, were concentrated in the urban areas of Vancouver, Toronto and Montreal and contributed about 0.5%. In total, the non-white population prior to the war was about 2% of the Canadian population. The Asian group was declining — virtually all were the products of immigration between 1870 and the early 1920's and with the government-imposed immigration restrictions of the 1920's, the disproportionately male population was not reproducing itself (Kalbach and McVey, 1971). The Black population was growing but not significantly since the small trickle of immigrants from the United States and the West Indies was offset by a probably larger movement to the United States. The native Indian and Inuit population has been increasing dramatically. Almost faced with extinction as a result of the European invasion, they had recovered their pre-European population by the end of World War II, and they have been the fastest growing group in Canada in the last two decades (Kalbach and McVey, 1971). In 1968, the rate of natural increase of Indians peaked at 3.4%, declining in 1970 to 2.9%, to be compared with a 1.5% rate of increase in the Canadian population (Frideres, 1974).

Post-World War II immigration has boosted the percentage of Non-Whites in Canada, although their numbers are still small.[3] About 160,000 Blacks, overwhelmingly from the West Indies, have immigrated to Canada since 1946 according to government statistics. This figure is probably a significant understatement; newspaper accounts indicate that in recent years there has been a flourishing business in "illegals" who are exploited in low-wage industries. It appears that in 1976 there may be about a quarter of a million Blacks in Canada, or about 1% of the total population. Asian immigration during the same period has been about 290,000 and the Asian sub-group now accounts for approximately 2% in Canada. Of these, 120,000 immigrants have been from China making them the largest Asian sub-group in Canada. Japanese immigration totalled about 10,000 while those identified with the Indian sub-continent have been counted at 125,000 persons. As a result of the post-World War II immigration and the large natural increase among Native peoples, the proportion of Non-Whites has more than doubled and is now approximately 5% of the Canadian population. The addition of the Métis and non-status Indian population would further increase that proportion by one or more percentage points, depending on the criteria and population estimates used.

The significant non-white immigration in recent decades reflects a significant liberalization of Canadian immigration policy, with the major change occuring in 1962.[4] While the degree of opening up is controversial — it is one thing to have a non-discriminatory policy and quite another to facilitate, in an equitable manner, immigration among all foreigners — there is no doubt that it has led to sharp increases in the number of non-white immigrants arriving in Canada from Commonwealth countries. The estimated proportion of Black and Asian to total immigration has gone from 2% in 1946-61 to approximately 37% in 1973 and 1974 (Richmond, 1975). Overall, the non-white proportion of total post-war immigration has been slightly better than 15%. Most of these new immigrants have settled in the major metropolitan areas, with Blacks settling chiefly in the Toronto area and Asians in Vancouver and Toronto. The urbanization of the long-standing racial minorities has also proceeded apace; for example, in 1961, 87% of Canadian Indians lived in rural areas whereas in 1971 the figure had dropped to 69.3% (Statistics Canada, 1974). Again the larger urban areas have drawn the bulk of the urban migrants.

The greater visibility of non-whites and tensions in race relations are also related to the changing composition of post-war immigrants, as well as their numbers. In contrast with previous immigrants, they are much more urbanized, more highly educated, better placed occupationally and more actively involved in the host society. This trend was evident even before the 1962 Immigration Act which based selection on a points system emphasizing educational and occupational qualifications. For example, among foreign-born Asiatics, 14.3% of the post-war immigrants had "some university or degree" compared with only 2.2% of the pre-war Asiatic immigrants (Kalbach and McVey, 1971). In sharp contrast to the 1931 data, by 1961 almost 50% of the Asians in the labour force were classified as managerial, professional and technical, and craftsmen and production workers (Vallee, 1975). A study in 1974-75 in Toronto dealing with an indicative though not representative sample of Black adults (largely immigrant) revealed that 60% had achieved at least "grade 13 or community college" and that about one-third were in the occupational categories professional, managerial and technical, and another 15% in skilled crafts. Only 2% were in unskilled labour and 11% in service-recreation (Head, 1975). Another study reveals that the total family income of immigrants from the West Indies in 1972 surpassed that of immigrants from Greece and Italy, although it is still well below the figures for the British, French, Americans and other groups (Manpower and Immigration, 1974).

While these and other figures reveal the improved educational and occupational levels of post-war immigrants, the social costs and disadvantages of being non-white still persist. There is evidence of economic exploitation of immigrants, especially the illegals, and non-white immigrants still suffer significantly from employment and other forms of discrimination (Head, 1975). In relation to their position back home, many non-white immigrants have probably experienced a drop in occupational status as a result of their immigration.

Social and economic disadvantage is particularly acute for the long-standing racial minorities in Canada, however, particularly Blacks and Native people (Institute of Public Affairs, 1969; Adams et al, 1971). The most promising developments in recent years have been that the legal rights and citizenship privileges of non-whites have been institutionalized and new organizations have developed among non-whites to protect and enhance their interests and to effect greater correspondence between their official citizenship and their everyday treatment by the majority. Beginning in the mid-1940's, human rights legislation and commissions have been established in most Canadian provinces and at the federal level. Canadian Indians have organizations in each of the provinces, and at the national level the National Indian Brotherhood and the Native Council of Canada represent status and non-status/Métis concerns respectively. The Inuit Tapirisat was established in 1971. Among Nova Scotia Blacks, the N.S.A.A.C.P. was formed in 1945 and the Black United Front in 1969; Blacks throughout Canada have formed a National Black Coalition. Such organizations along with government departments have spawned a host of social and cultural programmes. There have also been developments linking various non-white groupings. This is particularly the case among Native Indians and Inuit who have come together in organizations such as the Committee for Original Peoples' Entitlement and the Federation of Natives North of Sixty. Non-whites also often find themselves grouped together with respect to governmental institutions (e.g., human rights commissions) and policy issues (e.g., multiculturalism, immigration). Not much is known about their attitudes and behaviours vis-à-vis one another. The sparse data suggest that a positive empathy exists (Clairmont, 1963; Head, 1975). These organizational developments also reflect the "shrinkage" of society due to mass media, urbanization, transportation developments, the expansion of government and the thirst for resources to exploit. Native-born Blacks living on the outskirts of cities have increasingly found their land and homes threatened by urban developments. Native people, whether in the Arctic, northern Manitoba or James Bay, find their life-styles and land rights threatened by hydro-electric, oil and gas explorations.

It is evident that part of the white reaction of these organizational and demographic changes outlined above has been one of fear and hostility. Native people have experienced substantial racial antipathy in communities such as Kenora (Stymeist, 1975), Regina, Inuvik and Frobisher Bay, and the pressing of aboriginal title and land claims promises to lead to more conflict in the future in most areas of the country. In the case of non-white immigrants who have migrated heavily to urban areas such as Toronto and Vancouver, numerous racial incidents have occurred. In Vancouver, for example, members of the Indo-Pakistani community talk of establishing vigilante groups to prevent harassment. They are the subject of vicious "paky jokes" circulating in Canada; also they are most likely to be singled out by Canadians as non-desirable immigrants (Richmond, 1975). In Toronto the blatantly white racist Western Guard movement promotes its anti-immigrant, save Western civilization campaign (Head, 1975). Frideres (1975) compares survey data collected in Calgary in 1965 and 1975, and finds a lesser degree of acceptance of non-white immigrants by white respondents. Race relations have, in short, become a significant issue in Canadian society.

Implications for Policy and Theory

Since World War II and particularly since the early 1960's some progress has been made in making the racial minorities more active and, in some respects, more equal participants in the Canadian mosaic. There is also reason to believe that they find the mosaic concept quite attractive insofar as they desire to retain the integrity of their cultures and communities. A recent study of the Chinese has revealed that the majority of Chinese post-war immigrants live in the traditionally Chinese areas and that over 90% wish to retain their language and thus maintain cultural heritage (Lai, 1971). Black immigrants are seeking to define their place in the Canadian mosaic and those with longer roots in the society are attempting to revitalize their culture. Similar attempts at cultural revitalization are evident among native people along with the continuing struggle to preserve and develop the reserve communities. It is not only a matter of self protection and enhancement of interest groups but also a question of pride in their own heritage and confidence that Canada will be richer if the diverse groups are allowed to maintain and develop their own identity.

This raises the question then whether a harmonious multi-racial society can be created in a country that has both a tradition of racism and an ideology potentially congruent with racial and cultural diversity. Are there some strategies that might be employed to achieve such a goal? This is not idle speculation; Canada has a falling birth rate, as do most of the countries from which it has historically drawn immigrants. Recently the Economic Council of Canada has noted that if Canada is to attain in the near future the kind of economic growth characteristic of the post-war era, it will have to maintain if not increase current immigration levels and that, under the present universalistic immigration policy, would imply more non-whites.

The government's response to these challenges has not been clearly articulated. With respect to immigration, it appears that at least the level, if not the composition, of immigration will be cut back in response, in part at least, to the tensions we have noted above. At the same time the priorities of the multiculturalism policy are being changed to give greater attention to the socio-economic problems of the "visible minorities." This rearrangement suggests that the race question does not quite fit into the mosaic concept as it has been traditionally understood and that the ethnic mosaic as perceived by the politicians may be passé, less significant to respond to than the French-English duality and the white/non-white bifurcation. On another front, the Department of Indian Affairs in 1969 proclaimed a new Indian policy that in many respects resembles the American termination policy of the 1950's. It recommended that other government departments and the provincial governments take increasing responsibility for Indian affairs as part of a gradual process of eliminating the special status and protected lands of Indian people. In the face of vociferous protest by native organizations, the Government publicly withdrew its policy, but there is considerable evidence that in practice it is being implemented, perhaps over a longer time period than originally envisaged. An economic development plan is to facilitate the transition. Although theoretically the extensive control exercised by the Department of Indian Affairs will be eliminated, native spokesmen fear that the reserve communities will be lost, as they were for some tribes in the U.S., and that the historical obligations incurred by the Europeans will be unilaterally dismissed. They argue for the recognition of and compensation for aboriginal title and land claims which will provide the basis for economic development based around the reserve communities.

The trend of government policy, then, appears to be in the direction of continuing efforts to reduce the vertical nature of the mosaic for non-whites, but in doing so it also appears to be moving away from the realization of a multiracial and multicultural organic liberalism. Cynics might well contend that the government is responding to white fears and distrust concerning the growing number of non-whites while simultaneously attempting to salvage its official morality by treating more equitably the small proportion of non-whites in the country. It could also be argued that current policy proposals might produce greater acceptance of non-whites by the majority and thus lay the basis for their more harmonious immigration in the future.

The intellectual community has also not fully come to grips with the potential inherent in the situation. There does not appear to be a profound appreciation for the cultural contribution of non-white groups, for example, nor a willingness to see them develop their own institutions to any significant degree (Wien et al, 1976). Nor have Canadian social scientists developed adequate theoretical models to interpret race relations in modern societies such as Canada. None of the three theoretical approaches referred to earlier are rich enough in concepts and propositions to enable us to account for and attempt to predict race relations in Canada. Evolutionary universalism has merit at the individual level but it does not get at the extra-individual reality — the continuing significance of collectivities based on ascriptive criteria and the fact that people remain extremely sensitive regarding developments at that level while behaving more universalistically at the individual level. The internal colonialism approach applies less as the races approximate each other more in terms of income and occupation and as their interaction becomes more diversified. Descriptive pluralism is useful insofar as it suggests the importance of intermediate groupings between the individual family and the state and the insufficiency of other bases of social identification, such as occupation. The theoretical elaboration of these insights, connecting them with the structural aspects of society and their historical development, has not been achieved, however.

The continuing significance of communal boundaries based on race, under conditions of increasing modernization and in the face of (hopefully) receding racist ideology and stereotyping poses a theoretical enigma to students of race relations. To some extent the Canadian Way model described earlier provides some insights. Insofar as its organic liberalism component is concerned, it has stressed the political and social significance of corporate affiliation beyond the family and apart from the state. This resonates well with some current conceptions of modern North American society which see society structured such that one's relative advantage is tied to one's corporate attachments (e.g., companies, unions, etc.). Corporate attachments provide that "extra edge" which is so important to relative advantage in a society where there is an increasingly high level of education, expanding bureaucracy, a high degree of organization and an apparent inability to provide all with satisfactory employment. Affiliation with racial groups may be seen in this context of competitive advantage, providing a basis for mobilization and advancement on the one hand or denigration and limitation on the other. Racial ascription is clearly a relevant variable, given the relative ease with which one can assign or be assigned to racial collectivities and the empirical evidence of racial strife and inequality throughout the world.

If the above is indicative then a theory of race relations in modern western societies such as Canada must be *holistic,* connecting structural aspects of society with the way interest groups are organized bureaucratically and symbolically (Cohen, 1974), *comparative,* examining societies with different racial mixes and with different ideologies, and *contextual,* taking into account the shrinking world and the fact that individuals and groups are sensitive to occurrences and race relations elsewhere. Current racial tension in Canada has as much to do with anticipated numerical growth of non-whites as with the present numbers, and is rooted as much in white fear and guilt concerning their privileged position as it is with racial bigotry in the conventional sense.

NOTES

[1]Inuit in the MacKenzie Delta Region have always had close ties with their Alaskan counterparts and have been significantly influenced by them with respect to nativistic pentecostalism and land claims (Clairmont, 1963).

[2]The 1923 act almost completely closed the door to Chinese immigrants; only forty-four were allowed to enter between 1923 and 1947 (Lai, 1971).

[3]The numbers are also very difficult to estimate and the figures given should be treated with caution. Our estimate of the Black population is slightly higher than usually reported but it appears to be consistent with Richmond (1975).

[4]The liberalization of immigration policy has its roots in the World War II experinece; the Canadian government relaxed its restrictions on Chinese immigration at that time since China was an ally.

REFERENCES

Adams, Ian, William Cameron, Brian Hill and Peter Penz. 1971 The Real Poverty Report. Edmonton: Hurtig.

Blauner, Robert. 1972 Racial Oppression in America. New York: Harper and Row.

Breton, Raymond. 1968 "Institutional Completeness of Ethnic Communities and the Personal Relations of Immigrants." pp. 77-94 in Bernard R. Blishen et al (eds.), Canadian Society: Sociological Perspectives. Toronto: Macmillan (3rd·edition).

Cardinal, Harold. 1969 The Unjust Society. Edmonton: Hurtig.

Carstens, Peter. 1971 "Coercion and Change." pp. 126-145 in R. J. Ossenberg (ed.), Canadian Society: Pluralism, Change and Conflict. Scarborough: Prentice-Hall.

Chamberlin, J. E. 1975 The Harrowing of Eden: White Attitudes Toward North American Natives. Toronto: Fitzhenry and Whiteside.

Clairmont, D. H. 1963 Deviance Among Indians and Eskimos in Aklavik, N.W.T. Ottawa: Northern Coordination and Research Centre, Canada Department of Northern Affairs and National Resources.

Clairmont, D. H. and Dennis W. Magill. 1970 Nova Scotia Blacks: An Historical and Structural Overview. Halifax: The Institute of Public Affairs.

1974 Africville: The Life and Death of a Canadian Black Community. Toronto: McClelland and Stewart.

Clark, S. D. 1968 The Developing Canadian Community. Toronto: University of Toronto Press (2nd edition).

1974 "Sociology in Canada: An Historical Overview." Paper presented at a joint session of the International Sociological Association and the Canadian Association of Sociology and Anthropology. Toronto. August.

Cohen, Abner. 1974 Two Dimensional Man: An Essay on the Anthropology of Power and Symbolism in Complex Society. Berkeley: University of California Press.

Cohen, Roland. 1970 "Modernism and the Hinterland: The Canadian Example." pp. 4-27 in W. E. Mann (ed.), Social and Cultural Change in Canada, Vol. I. Toronto: Copp-Clark.

Davis, Arthur K. 1971 "Canadian Society and History as Hinterland Versus Metropolis." pp. 6-23 in R. J. Ossenberg (ed.), Canadian Society: Pluralism, Change and Conflict. Scarborough: Prentice-Hall.

Fein, Lawrence. 1970 "The Limits of Liberalism." Saturday Review of Books. June: 83-96.

Frideres, James S. 1974 Canada's Indians: Contemporary Conflicts. Scarborough: Prentice-Hall.

1975 "Prejudice and Discrimination in Western Canada: First and Third World Immigrants." Paper prepared for Conference on Multiculturalism and Third World Immigrants in Canada. The University of Alberta. September.

Gordon, Milton M. 1961 "Assimilation in America: Theory and Reality.." Daedalus. 90:263-85.

Greeley, Andrew M. 1973 "Making It in America: Ethnic Groups and Social Status." Social Policy. 4:21-29.

Head, Wilson A. 1975 The Black Presence in the Canadian Mosaic. A Study of Perception and the Practice of Discrimination Against Blacks in Metropolitan Toronto. Toronto: Ontario Human Rights Commission.

Henry, Frances. 1973 Forgotten Canadians: The Blacks of Nova Scotia. Don Mills: Longman.

Hobart, C. W. and C. S. Brant. 1969 "Eskimo Education, Danish and Canadian: A Comparison." pp. 68-87 in Anand Malik (ed.), Social Foundations of Canadian Education. Scarborough: Prentice-Hall.

Horowitz, Gad. 1972 "Mosaic and Identity." pp. 465-73 in Bryan Finnigan and Cy Gonick (eds.), Making It: The Canadian Dream. Toronto: McClelland and Stewart.

Hughes, David R. and Evelyn Kallen. 1974 The Anatomy of Racism: Canadian Dimensions. Montreal: Harvest House.

Institute of Public Affairs. 1969 Poverty in Nova Scotia. Halifax: Dalhousie University.

Kalbach, Warren and Wayne W. McVey. 1971 The Demographic Bases of Canadian Society. Toronto: McGraw-Hill.

Lai, Vivien. 1971 "The New Chinese Immigrants in Toronto." pp. 120-140 in Jean Leonard Elliott (ed.), Minority Canadians: Immigrant Groups. Scarborough: Prentice-Hall.

Lurie, Nancy O. 1968 "Historical Background." pp. 49-81 in Stuart Levine and Nancy O. Lurie (eds.), The American Indian Today. Baltimore: Penguin.

Manpower and Immigration. 1974 Three years in Canada. Ottawa, Department of Manpower and Immigration.

Manuel, George and Michael Posluns. 1974 The Fourth World: An Indian Reality Don Mills: Collier-Macmillan.

Novak, M. 1972 The Rise of the Unmeltable Ethnics. New York: Macmillan.

Parsons, Talcott. 1971 The System of Modern Societies. Englewood Cliffs: Prentice Hall.

Patterson, E. Palmer. 1972 The Canadian Indian: A History Since 1500. Don Mills: Collier-Macmillan.

Porter, John. 1965 *The Vertical Mosaic.* Toronto: University of Toronto Press.

Potter, Harold H. 1961 "Negroes in Canada." Race 3: 39-56.

Reitz, Jeffrey G. 1974 "Language and Ethnic Community Survival." Canadian Review of Sociology and Anthropology, Special Edition on the occasion of the 8th World Congress of Sociology, Toronto: 104-122.

Richmond, Anthony H. 1975 "Black and Asian Immigrants in Britain and Canada: Experiences of Prejudice and Discrimination." Paper presented at Conference on Multiculturalism and Third World Immigrants in Canada. Edmonton: University of Alberta. September.

Schermerhorn, R.A. 1970 Comparative Ethnic Relations: A Framework for Theory and Research. New York: Random House.

Statistics Canada. 1974 Perspective Canada: A Compendium of Social Statistics. Ottawa: Information Canada.

Stymeist, David H. 1975 Ethnics and Indians: Social Relations in a Northwestern Ontario Town. Toronto: Peter Martin Associates.

Thomson, Colin A. 1974 "The Ultimate Canadian and the Blacks: 1860-1920." A paper presented to the Canadian Association of African Studies Conference. Halifax. February-March.

Vallee, Frank G. 1975 "Multi-Ethnic Societies: The Issues of Identity and Inequality." pp. 162-202 in Dennis Forcese and Stephen Richer (eds.), Issues in Canadian Society: An Introduction to Sociology. Scarborough: Prentice-Hall.

van den Berghe, Pierre L. 1967 Race and Racism. New York: John Wiley.

Wien, F., P. Buckley, H. Desmond and K. Marshall. 1976 Opinions from the Centre: The Position of Racial Minorities in the University. Halifax: The Institute of Public Affairs. Forthcoming.

Winks, Robin W. 1971 The Blacks in Canada: A History. Montreal: McGill-Queen's University Press.

Chapter 20

Canada: Dilemmas and Contradictions of a Multi-Ethnic Society*

John Porter

The decade of the 1950s was notable for a naive belief in the affluent society; that of the 1960s for its concern with poverty. It would appear that the 1970s is to be the decade of organized minorities. Although all minorities take on the appearance of reality once they are organized, some are more real than others. Indians and other non-whites are something more than a statistical group because they live mainly in cohesive communities and have distinctive physical characteristics. On the other hand the pseudo-minorities who make their appeals with the rhetoric of liberation from oppression — youth, women and homosexuals, to take some examples — are, at least at their present stage of organization, statistical categories that lack sociological coherence. Though they may act like real minorities with a degree of readiness for confrontation, these pseudo and statistical minorities are more like interest or pressure groups which invoke the right of association to influence those in power.

Policy responses of governments and other power groups to organized minorities have produced a new terminology: positive discrimination, preferential hiring, or benign quotas. These policy responses are quite

*Reprinted from *Transactions of the Royal Society of Canada,* Series IV, Volume X (1972) by permission of the author and the publisher.

different from human rights legislation, fair employment practices legislation, and the like, which provide individuals — not groups or collectivities — with rights, enforceable in the courts, against discrimination. Perhaps it is a measure of the failure of these instruments, fashioned as they were for the individual, that people have had to organize as minorities to redress grievances when it becomes apparent that deprivation is concentrated within particular statistical groups in the social structure. But the new instruments, focused as they are on groups, and providing what might be called group rights — say to proportional representation within all institutional hierarchies — constitute a radical departure from a society organized on the principle of individual achievement and universalistic judgements, towards one organized on group claims to representation on the basis of particular rather than universal qualities.

The new ideas are pervasive, and can even be found in the *Eighth Annual Review* of the Economic Council of Canada, where there is a discussion of social indicators.[1] Among these indicators there would be one to deal with the distributive aspects of economic outputs, but with groups as well as individuals considered as recipients — age, sex, and ethnic groups, for example.

No liberal social scientist would argue against social reform, or the elimination of poverty, or the provision of opportunity. He might be concerned, however, with what is an important shift of emphasis in the decade of the organized minority where claims are made not as individuals but as members of minority groups. When discrimination and deprivation are measured in terms of group membership, as ultimately they are, then the reduction of these conditions seems most easily achieved through positive discrimination in which institutions, corporations, and universities, for example, are required to maintain quotas throughout their hierarchical structures to make them representative with respect to minorities. Here is the first dilemma, for such policies will raise problems for the individual since in order to make his claims he will have to determine the minorities to which he belongs, and one can visualize a somewhat complex passbook arrangement indicating the answers. One's memberships could cross-cut in several ways, making it necessary to calculate the maximum advantage. Thus, in a preferential employment and career program one's prospects for advancement would be greatly enhanced by being say non-white, of non-English mother tongue, female, under 30 (or perhaps over 50), and lesbian.[2]

The possibilities are endless since societies can be viewed as intersecting sets of minorities and majorities defined by an infinite number of criteria, all of different relevance at different times.

If the epoch of the individual comes to an end the rise of the meritocracy which Michael Young so feared[3] will be prevented by positive discrimination, which does not use merit as the principal criterion of selection. It might be difficult to make judgments about which of the two would lead, if not to the good, at least to the better society. With the individualized achievement of the meritocracy — as all who have studied the problem know — the educational and opportunity structures have been class-biased and even the criteria of merit have been class-tinged. (In the age of organized minorities the criteria of selection are seen to be tinged by race, sex, age, and heterosexuality.)

It is important to be aware of the kinds of problems which are likely to emerge when we deal with inequality on the basis of group rather than individual claims. I want now to deal with some problems in the context in which we are accustomed to talking about minorities, that is, ethnic minorities.

In discussions of the relations between ethnic minorities and majorities, the dominant theme seems to be that of equality: equality of legal, political, and social rights, equality of opportunity, and equality of economic well-being. The unequal distribution of things which are valued in the society is also the dominant theme in the analysis of social class. It would seem that ethnic differentiation and social class differentiation, or social stratification, are often the same thing in societies which are made up of various ethnic groups. The political quest of modern democracies has been to overcome inequalities, although there is a good deal of dispute about definitions and means.

To understand the interplay between ethnic inequalities and class inequalities it is important to look at how ethnic differentiation within a society develops. In most historical instances it has been through conquest or migration. In the case of conquest the victors enslave their victims in varying degrees or relegate them to inferior statuses and forms of work. This can be seen in the successive conquests over centuries, which hardened into the classical caste system in India. It can also be seen in the quasi-caste systems of Central and South America, and in North America where the descendants of the indigenous groups in both the United States and Canada represent one of the most visible underclasses to be found anywhere. In the developing nations of the third world, ethnic pluralism has resulted from the transporting of indentured labour groups from their original habitats to another for specific kinds of economic activities, or it has resulted from European powers bringing into administrative units, convenient for their own purposes, tribal groups of very differing cultures.

For new nations developed in formerly unpopulated regions, such as the United States and Canada, ethnic differentiation has arisen through immigration, which was determined by the host or charter group who got there first, or who conquered and determined the conditions under which other groups might enter. These conditions ranged from unfree slave immigration to free selective immigration under which the host society made invidious judgments about the appropriateness of various groups for particular jobs. Migration is an economic process by which one factor of production, labour, moves with the other factor, capital. The entire process is selective; people get sorted out according to their believed-in equalities or aptitudes for different economic activities. We can see in our time the building up of stratification systems through ethnic migrations. In the United States it is the Puerto Rican and the Black moving into urban areas. In England it is the migration of the coloured newcomer from Commonwealth countries. Throughout western Europe, it is the migration of Italian, Spanish, and Portugese labour, 80 per cent of it unskilled, and sometimes with a minimum of social and legal rights.

Economic forces have created the inequalities of ethnic stratification. There are jobs, for example, which the host or conquering groups do not want to do or consider demeaning, servicing jobs. Or stratification is necessary for the building up of a labour force of a particular type of economy — the plantation economy where labour force needs have been met most frequently through slavery or indentured labour. Or, as with the building up of the Canadian west, a region can be developed with a more or less freely moving migration. Over time this marked differentation at the period of entry can either harden into a permanent class system, or change in the direction of absorption, assimilation, integration, and acculturation as a result of which the relationship between ethnicity and class disappears. The stratification order that exists, hardened or modified, has a subjective counterpart in the evaluations which are made about the standing or place of various ethnic groups in the population and the degrees of social distance — that is, the degree of intimacy which they are prepared to engage in with members of other groups — that prevail between people of different groups. These subjective counterparts can be determined with considerable precision. It would seem then that the promotion of flourishing ethnic communities is directly opposed to absorption, assimilation, integration, and acculturation and could lead to a permanent ethnic stratification and thus is likely to interfere with the political goal of individual equality. Such a contradiction is present in the hypothesis of Frank Vallee, in his study of French-Canadian communities outside Quebec, communities that are like immigrant ethnic groups anywhere else in Canada in that they are spatially dispersed and without territory. His hypothesis is as follows:

> . . . the more a minority group turns in upon itself and concentrates on making its position strong, the more it costs its members in terms of their chances to make their way as individuals in the larger system. . . .
>
> Among ethnic minority groups which strive to maintain language and other distinctions, motivation to aspire to high-ranking social and economic positions in the larger system will be weak, unless, of course, it is characteristic of the ethnic groups to put a special stress on educational and vocational achievement.[4]

Vallee argues that any collectivity has limited resources and energy and cannot spend them on maintaining ethnic-specific institutions and at the same time prepare its members for achievement in the larger society of which it is a part.

Both Canada and the United States have been experiencing a revival of ethnicity. Although the causes are no doubt multiple, one important force in

Canada has been the assertion of Quebec nationalism, and in the United States the demands of non-white power groups, particularly at the community level.

In Canada when the Royal Commission on Bilingualism and Biculturalism was established in response to the strength of French nationalism in Quebec, the government felt compelled to include in the Commission's terms of reference" . . . the contribution made by the other ethnic groups to the cultural enrichment of Canada and the measures that should be taken to safeguard that contribution."[5] An entire volume was to be devoted to the matter of the other ethnic groups.[6] Since that time there have been numerous conferences on the subject as well as a great deal of promotion of the idea of multi-culturalism.

Now, there is a federal government policy on multiculturalism and some provincial governments are following along. There is much political rhetoric on the subject by leaders of all parties. Here is a recent example by Mr. Yaremko, the Ontario Provincial Secretary and Minister of Citizenship, in announcing the multi-cultural conference "Heritage Ontario":

> No other part of the globe, no other country, can claim a more culturally diversified society than we have here in this province. . . . But does everyone really grasp that Ontario has more Canadians of German origin than Bonn, more of Italian origin than Florence, that Toronto has more Canadians of Greek origin than Sparta. That we have in our midst, fifty-four ethno-cultural groups, speaking a total of seventy-two languages. . . . Just a hundred years ago the Canadian identity was moulded in the crucible of nationalism; it is now being tempered by the dynamics of multiculturalism.[1]

Mr. Yaremko also touched upon another cause of the current revival of ethnicity and that is the large non-British component of post-war immigration. He then went on to make the common mistake of seeing this component, made up of people from such a variety of countries, as being in some way homogeneous:

> There are generally speaking four demographic groups among us — Indians, Anglo- and Franco-Ontarian, and members of the third element. . . . One effect of the postwar boom in third element immigration has been to bolster ethno-cultural groups, some of which have been here through four generations. The government has welcomed and encouraged this immigration. We have recognized and helped foster all our constituent cultural communities. Is it then any wonder that these communities have heightened expectations in many areas?[8]

In the bolstering of ethno-cultural groups, as Mr. Yaremko puts it, the postwar immigrants have played an important leadership role because of their long association with nationalist political struggles in their European homelands. They have continued their activities, often ideological as well as national, aimed at keeping alive in Canada the culture they believe is being obliterated abroad. This leadership has managed in some cases to shift the focus of activity of their national organizations from the problem of integration within Canadian society to the problem of cultural survival either in Europe or in Canada as a locus for cultures in exile.[9]

There is much confusion in the current discussion of multi-ethnicity and multiculturalism. This confusion does not attach to bilingualism or multilingualism. Recently Canadians have appeared more willing to accept bilingualism as an acknowledgement of their history. The main difference between a bilingual and a multilingual society is that the latter would be more costly or difficult to administer. While bilingualism is possible and multilingualism is difficult, I am not able fully to understand how biculturalism and multiculturalism have any meaning in the post-industrial world into which we are moving. Those who read government pronouncements and royal commission documents on the subject might agree that attempts to deal with these concepts and the related one of ethnicity in recent years have generated some complex sophistry. Most of it is aimed at avoiding the conclusion that ethnic groups are descent groups — when they are not also statistical artifacts, as I shall try to argue shortly.

It seems to me that making descent groups of such importance because they are the carriers of culture borders on racism with all the confused and emotional reactions that that term brings. If races have been evaluated as inferior and superior, cultures may also be so evaluated. In fact, the laudable objective of making all ethnic groups and their cultures of equal importance and making all groups proud of their heritage is to overcome invidious judgments about culture which in their social effects at least can be as far reaching as invidious judgments about race. Racism and culturism stem from the fact that both are linked to the maintenance of descent group solidarity and endogamy.

Because of history and territorial distribution and claims, Canada can certainly be called a biethnic, bicultural, and bilingual society. As social and cultural change takes place and Quebec enters the post-industrial world we may end up being no more than bilingual. It is difficult to see how multiculturalism can survive without locality under the levelling forces of urban environment and a post-industrial culture of science and technology. It is pointless to obscure these facts with the webs of pseudo-anthropology that characterize government reports and political speeches on the subject. In the confused rationalization of multiculturalism in Canada it is possible to distinguish two major themes: culture as history and culture as a way of living. The former involves the continuation of historical cultures (say of Canadian immigrant groups) in the face of social change or their suppression in their countries of origin. The latter involves the desirability of multiculturalism in the face of the homogenizing trend of technology and bureaucracy. As well, the development of pride in ancestry is thought to be an important compensation for deprived status. I want to examine these alleged values of the multiethnic society.

Among the purposes of a multiethnic, multicultural Canadian society, it is said, are the transmitting and safeguarding of the various cultures from which Canada's immigrant groups have come. No academic would seriously dispute the desirability and responsibility of preserving culture, particularly in its expressive forms, but also, in the behavioural sense of culture, because we want to know how people lived at different times and places.

There seem to be two ways in which this responsibility for preserving culture can be met. One is through the cultural association and the other through the ethnic group. Presumably, if some people were interested in keeping alive some knowledge of past ways of doing things they could band together to form an association to do so. Some people find the culture of ancient Egypt fascinating and rewarding to study. But if the culture of ancient Egypt is of value the various groups that promote it — archaeologists who acquire money to investigate it and amateur Egyptologists who make it a hobby — must recruit new members to carry on their interests. One way — assuming they had managed to maintain the necessary age and sex distribution — would be to require as a condition of membership that members marry within the Egyptology group, and, given the traditional right of parents to use their children as objects of cultural aggression thus ensure the survival of the culture of ancient Egypt through the generations. Alternatively, they can do as they always have done and that is to recruit members by persuading them that studying and keeping alive this particular culture is a good thing. Governments or philanthropists might well be persuaded to subsidize such activities. All nations can be multicultural if they encourage such associational transmission of culture. A society of multicultured individuals is one in which people can be exposed to a wide variety of human expression, and so become liberated from whatever narrow cultural confines into which they might have been born.

The transmission and safeguarding of culture through ethnic groups may appear a more efficient mechanism, because ethnic groups are biological descent groups. Recruits are always available if the groups have succeeded in imposing rules of endogamy on their members. If they do not they will lose the primordial link with tribe or nation and the exclusive ethnic claims on culture will be eroded. Endogamy is a process of exclusion. There was a time when lowering rates of endogamy could be taken as an index of lessening prejudice. In the current return to ethnicity the opposite judgment seems to be being made. It is better to exclude than to include. The metal of endogamy is more attractive because it is unmeltable.

It would appear, however, because of urbanization and high levels of industrialization the prospects for rates of endogamy sufficiently high for survival are not good. The alternative is for groups to develop new associational forms of cultural survival. The prospects for this method of transmission are not good either because the ethnic bases of existing associations tend to exclude the outsider. As one observer of ethnic group activity in Toronto has noted:

> Even those organizations which are not by policy "closed" to outsiders do not usually make special efforts to attract outsiders and make them welcome. Most ethnic groups provide an active cultural life for their members. . . . However, each of these sets of activities is separated from the others by an opaque curtain

partially but not wholly caused by language problems. Certainly very few outsiders are aware of this great variety of activity going on constantly in the metropolitan area.[10]

Such exclusiveness does not make much of a contribution to a multicultural Canada.

The survival of historical cultures in only one of the expressed purposes of multiethnicity. The second major theme in the discussions of multiculturalism involves cultures as different ways of living in the contemporary world. A society with a number of different cultures in which the members of relatively exclusive groups behave alike is said to be heterogeneous or diverse rather than homogeneous and uniform. (Since all are observing their own cultural norms it would seem that such diversity is more enjoyed by the beholder — from whatever Olympus he might be viewing it — than by any of the actors within their enclaves.) Be that as it may, a strong case can be made for ethnic group affiliation for its role in solving problems of personal identity in the impersonal and shifting world of modern bureaucracy and technology. There are two social contexts within which this psychic shelter function of ethnic affiliation merits discussion. One is that of recently arrived immigrants, and the other is the continued ethnic identifications for the Canadians born of second and subsequent generations (and that really means all of us) — two distinct groups which are counted together in much of the current discussion of ethnic origin. For the immigrant the transition to a new social environment can be fraught with psychic hazards, particularly if he comes from the Azores or the Abruzzi to metropolitan Toronto. The question from the point of view of general social goals is whether the useful staging camp role of the ethnic community becomes permanent, or whether some dispersion into the wider community of various immigrant groups is more desirable. A suggestion that such dispersion is desirable now brings the cry of "liberal assimilationist".

It really seems questionable that we seek our psychic shelters through ethnic identification. There is no doubt that ethnic groupings can play this role, but at the cost of perpetuating ethnic stratification. Identities and psychic shelters can be found in other forms of association and interest groups, which are not based on descent, for it is this aspect of the ethnic group which is the source of irrational, invidious comparison.

One of the most compelling arguments for the maintenance of strong ethnic affiliations is to enhance the self-concept of members of low status groups. When compensation for low status can be derived from taking pride in one's culture or one's origin, programs can be devised to ensure that all cultures are treated as "worthy" despite the varying degrees of inequality which their members experience, and so there is less need for programs aimed at eliminating the inequality which is associated with ethnic differentiation.

There is some evidence that pride in one's own group does enhance one's view of oneself and this improved self-image is likely to make a firm base from which to achieve. But there are contradictions here. Many cultures do not emphasize individual achievement, nor do they provide the appropriate skills for it. From the point of view of the Indians and Metis, does the promoting of their own culture help them toward equality in the post-industrial society? The same question may be asked of some immigrant cultures. The answer lies to some extent in language rather than culture. Identification with and the use of their own language, particularly in education, may be an important facilitator of mobility for very low status groups.

For example, the use of an immigrant language, say Italian or Portugese, combined with English in school may help a child in overcoming learning impediments that arise from one language at school and another at home. He acquires some self-confidence because his language is not despised. But such use of language is quite different from the goal of ethnic communities as permanent and "worthy" to compensate for low status, or as psychic shelters in the urban-industrial world. We would hope for a society in which the compensatory role of the ethnic community is not necessary, and, as I have suggested, the development of ethnic communities as psychic shelters can perpetuate ethnic stratification.

Earlier, I suggested that in Canada ethnicity may be a statistical artifact arising from census definitions and procedures. The Canadian census insists on classifying one's ethnic origin by one's ancestor who first arrived in North America traced through the male line only (there is something for women's lib). That procedure excludes both American and Canadian as acceptable ethnic origins. Even after four generations one cannot have a Canadian ethnicity — despite the fact that one might have lost the threads of one's male ancestry. And this is not because large numbers of the 84 per cent of the Canadian-born population in 1961 did not see themselves as being Canadian in origin; otherwise the officials would not have had to instruct enumerators what to do with that sizeable number of people who could be expected to so respond. However, if people insisted on reporting Canadian as origin after these attempts to dissuade them, the enumerators might accept it. Since none of the census tabulations tells us anything about these people it must be assumed they are included under "other" or "not stated".[11]

There was some considerable public discussion of the ethnic question before the 1961 census, but the matter never seems to have been raised publicly with respect to the 1971 census. This is an indication of the new saliency that ethnicity had acquired in Canadian society, and of the political sensitivity produced by the increasing immigration from European countries, other than Britain, by the new ethnic leadership to which Mr. Yaremko referred, and by the publication of the bilingualism and biculturalism reports. Among the census takers themselves, however, there seems to have been some considerable disagreement, as they report in a working document on the preparation for the 1971 census.[12]

Arguments for and against the inclusion of each question were made. On the ethnic question the document reports: "this question has given rise in the past to emotional feelings on the part of respondents but while its inclusion is sometimes criticized *there is a heavier demand for data on ethnicity than on most other items.*"[13] The statement reflects a significant contradiction in Canadian society. Some are obviously repelled that anything should be made of one's biological descent group, but on the other hand more information is demanded about these groups than about others. This contradiction is further reflected in the reasons given for including the question, for example, "Great use is made of census data on ethnicity by national and cultural organizations who are anxious to retain their identity." A supporting reason is given: "A cross-classification of ethnic groups with mother tongue or language now spoken provides a good measure of the degree of assimilation of different groups." For data which can serve the needs of measuring both assimilation and ethnic identity, one would have expected that the census takers would have given consideration to improving their recording instrument, for among the reasons against including the question is : "there is a relatively high degree of reporting error since respondents may not know their ethnic background." One awaits with interest the 1971 census data on ethnicity. They are based on self-enumeration.

The hesitancy of census officials on the ethnic question no doubt reflects a lack of consensus on the part of the Canadian public. For some, probably a minority, the problem of Canadian nationalism is more important than that of European or other nationalisms. But some of the resistance to the ethnic question is because many people remember that making much of one's descent group, or trying to discover and make something of another's, was thought to be morally improper because of the racialism of the inter-war years. Similarly, it is thought by some today to be improper to raise the question of origin of faculty in Canadian universities. In the preface to his extensive 1961 census monograph on immigration and ethnicity, Kalbach refers to his distinguished predecessor at this task, W. Burton Hurd, whose monograph on the 1941 Census, *Ethnic Origin and Nativity of the Canadian People,* was published for limited circulation in 1965. Kalbach says:

> Circumstances surrounding the delayed publication of Professor Hurd's last work attest, in part, to the sensitivity of the ethnic origin issue during the immediate postwar period. The debate concerning the propriety of asking questions about ethnic or racial background and the struggle to eliminate ethnic and racial distinctions from official records of vital events and decennial censuses continues.[14]

The dilemma of the liberal social scientist on this matter is clear enough. On the one hand he might want to see the end of this preoccupation with biological descent groups for its atavistic, genetic, and racial overtones and the uses to which ethnic and racial categories can be put. He would prefer to see individuals as humans. On the other hand he finds such data an important indicator of prejudice and discrimination.

The census, however, is not an appropriate instrument for the analysis of such phenomena compared to, say, carefully designed sample surveys. In my view we would be well served if the question were abandoned and the artifactual character of ethnicity removed.

Ethnicity quite obviously has a saliency apart from the census. Official documents refer to ethnic organizations as evidence of a group's "collective will to exist". Even the terminology is reminiscent of what Ernest Cassirer called mythical thinking.[15]

By an ironic twist, ethnicity has become a good thing. Now all are encouraged to have an ethnicity — other than Canadian — and ethnic communities should flourish, and all should identify with their descent groups.

The old liberal position is now pejoratively referred to as "liberal assimilationist". It is said to be overly rational, secular, and universalistic or ". . . an over-hasty and naive apostasy of a naively held scientific faith".[16] The liberal assimilationist ignores the primordial attachment of human beings and so he has ". . . betrayed a profound misunderstanding of the human condition."[17] These are views expressed by Andrew Greeley, an American sociologist, who is a very active supporter of Irish nationalism in particular and ethnic diversity in general. He is widely read and praised by the multiculturalists in Canada.

Considering as alternatives the ethnic stratification that results from ethnic diversity and the greater possibilities for equality that result from the reduction of ethnicity as a salient feature of a modern society I have chosen an assimilationist position, and between the stavistic responses that can arise from descent group identification and the more liberal view that descent group membership is irrelevant to human interaction I have chosen the latter.

NOTES

[1]Economic Council of Canada, *Eighth Annual Review,* Ottawa, 1971, 70ff.

[2]In the context of minority representation in a professional organization see Pierre L. van den Berghe, "The Benign Quota: Panacea or Pandora's Box", *The American Sociologist* (June, 1971).

[3]Michael Young, *The Rise of Meritocracy* (London, Thames and Hudson, 1958).

[4]Frank G. Vallee and Norman Shulman, "The Viability of French Groupings Outside Quebec", in Mason Wade, ed., *Regionalism in the Canadian Community,* 1867-1967 (Toronto: University of Toronto Press, 1969), 95.

[5]Royal Commission on Bilingualism and Biculturalism, *Report,* Book I, XXVI.

[6]*Ibid.,* Book IV.

[7]Press release of address at the Canadian Club, Toronto, March 20, 1972.

[8]*Ibid.*

[9]Elizabeth Wangenheim, "The Ukrainians: A Case Study of the 'Third Force'" in B.R. Blishen *et. al.,* eds., *Canadian Society: Sociological Perspectives* (Toronto: Macmillan, 1968), 658.
See also Judith A. Nagata, "Adaptation and Integration of Greek Working Class Immigrants in the City of Toronto, Canada: A Situational Approach", and Clifford J.

Jansen, "Leadership in the Toronto Italian Ethnic Group", in *The International Migration Review,* Vol. 4, No. 1, (1969), 25-69.

[10]*Ibid.,* 660.

[11]See Joel Smith, "Melting Pot-Mosaic: Considerations for a Prognosis", *Minorities North and South,* Proceedings of the Third Annual Inter-Collegiate Conference on Canadian and American Relations, Michigan State University, 1968, for an interesting comparison with the United States.

[12]Dominion Bureau of Statistics, Ottawa, 1969, "The 1971 Census of Population and Housing: Development of Subject Matter Content", 13.

[13]*Ibid.*

[14]Warren E. Kalbach, *The Impact of Immigration on Canada's Population,* Dominion Bureau of Statistics, Ottawa, 1970, V.

[15]Ernest Cassirer, *The Myth of the State* (New York: Doubleday, 1955).

[16]Andrew Greeley, "The Rediscovery of Diversity", *The Antioch Review* (Fall, 1971), 349.

[17]*Ibid.* See also Andrew Greeley, "The New Ethnicity and Blue Collars", *Dissent* (Winter, 1972).